INTO ALL
THE WORLD

INTO ALL
THE WORLD

A Century of Church of God Missions

CENTENNIAL CELEBRATION

1909–2009

GLOBAL MISSIONS

LESTER A. CROSE
CHERYL JOHNSON BARTON
DONALD D. JOHNSON

Warner Press
ANDERSON, INDIANA

Coordinator of Publishing & Creative Services
Church of God Ministries, Inc.
PO Box 2420
Anderson, IN 46018-2420
800-848-2464
www.chog.org

To purchase additional copies of this book, to inquire about distribution, and for all other sales-related matters, please contact:

Warner Press, Inc.
PO Box 2499
Anderson, IN 46018-2499
800-741-7721
www.warnerpress.org

Cover and text design by Mary Jaracz.
Edited by Stephen R. Lewis.

ISBN-13: 978-1-59317-371-5

Printed in the United States of America.

09 10 11 12 13 14 15 /VP/ 10 9 8 7 6 5 4 3 2 1

TABLE OF CONTENTS

FOREWORD

Into All the World: A Century of Church of God Missions is an exceedingly important book for all with a passion for world evangelization and a desire to see how the Church of God (Anderson, Indiana) fits into the Great Commission branded onto the heart of every Christian. When talks about the celebration of the 2009 centennial of Global Missions began, the first suggestion was to update *Passport for a Reformation* by Lester Crose. It has been in constant use, especially as a reference book, since its 1981 publication. But it only carries the reader from the beginnings of the Church of God in 1880 until its centennial in 1980. Much has happened since.

Cheryl Johnson Barton and Donald D. Johnson were chosen to update *Passport for a Reformation* in this new volume. Cheryl has been a career missionary in Japan since 1982. She is well acquainted with the Asia–Pacific region and has traveled in many parts of the world. She is an excellent writer and editor, which gives this book great readability. Some of her best contributions to the North American Church of God are the series of international testimony books that she has compiled and edited and the missions curricula for children that she has written.

Donald Johnson has dedicated his life to Church of God missions. He served as a missionary in the Caribbean (1955–61), as an associate to Lester Crose (1968–75), and as executive secretary-treasurer of the Missionary Board (1975–85). He also taught missions courses at Anderson University School of Theology. In retirement, he continues to be a counselor and friend of the global church. Don is perhaps the primary missiologist in the Church of God today. And Don also happens to be Cheryl's father.

Looking backward helps us better understand how to move forward. We do not wish to glorify the past but to learn from it. Our review of history will help us chart a course into the future as we walk hand in hand with Christ, following the leading of the Holy Spirit.

Robert E. Edwards
Coordinator, Global Missions
Church of God Ministries

FOREWORD TO
PASSPORT FOR A REFORMATION

This book was written in response to the need for an overall history of the worldwide missionary work of the Church of God reformation movement. Its publication date is announced during the 1980–81 year of centennial celebration now in progress in all of our churches in many countries around the world.

The purpose of this book is to present an authentic and well-documented account of the beginnings and development of our missionary outreach in area after area and country after country.

Through the years many small books and booklets have appeared giving brief accounts of the history and expansion of our missionary outreach in a number of areas of the world. Those publications, along with reports and extended articles in our church periodicals, have kept the church in America and abroad both informed and challenged.

The author, Dr. Lester A. Crose, gives us an up-to-date and authentic account covering a period of ninety years since our first missionary crossed the boundary into another country to share the message of salvation through Jesus Christ.

For that task, and task it was, he was well prepared, having served as missionary in several fields, and having been chosen to carry the heavy responsibility of executive secretary of the Missionary Board for twenty-one years. During those years in office he periodically visited all of our mission fields for consultation with both missionaries and church leaders on continuing outreach and development. On such visits he kept careful notes and obtained statistical information that have been a most valuable source for the preparation of this volume.

The church is indebted to this dedicated missionary and Board executive for the careful and painstaking research he did in preparing this latest piece of literature dealing with the history and development of the Church of God reformation movement. It will be a source of information for years to come.

Adam W. Miller
Dean Emeritus, Anderson School of Theology

PREFACE

What a privilege it has been to collaborate with my father in updating *Passport for a Reformation*, the premiere history of the Church of God worldwide mission effort through North American eyes. Although we added only thirty years to Lester Crose's masterpiece, in addition to several appendices, this has been a significant undertaking for us. Since Dr. Crose's book is incorporated as the first seven chapters of *Into All the World: A Century of Church of God Missions*, it is important to note three differences between those chapters and the last three.

First, because Dr. Crose personally experienced much of what he wrote as the son of early Church of God missionaries, as a missionary himself, and as a mission executive, he could write knowledgeably in the first person. I too am a Church of God MK (missionary kid) who grew up to be a missionary, and my father was a mission executive. But we have primarily reported other people's experiences and, therefore, have used the third person.

Second, for the most part, Dr. Crose wrote in chronological order. We chose to write topically rather than in precise chronology, although most subjects appear in the general order they occurred within the decades. Our effort is a narrative of people and events rather than a strict history book of facts and figures. With the index, which was not included originally, we trust it will still be easy to access historical information.

Third, to my knowledge, Dr. Crose did not write with a specified page limit; we did. As such, we had to choose very carefully both what to include and what to let go. Some may argue that we should have written more about one subject and less about another, but in the end we had to make the call and we tried to do so fairly. Undoubtedly, much was left out. We hope it will be written about elsewhere before history is lost. Print media, correspondence, and hard copies of minutes of even very important meetings are increasingly thought of as outdated relics of the past—rather a frightening reality if one considers the saying, "Those who forget history are doomed to repeat it."

While we have done our best to present an accurate history, we offer apologies for any mistakes, particularly in the listings of missionaries, to whom we owe a great debt of gratitude and for whom we are grateful to God.

We chose to highlight twenty-one individuals in an appendix titled "Ministry Partner Biographies." They represent each of the six regions of the world where the Church of God has ministered during these past 130 years. They were chosen after consultation with many people and therefore present a good cross section of mission activity around the world. These individuals may not have served the longest among missionaries, nor were all sent out by the Church of God in North America. However, each biographical sketch is of someone who has made a significant regional contribution to the work of Church of God missions.

Having spent two years on this project, I am reminded that I have much for which to be thankful. I am grateful for my Church of God heritage and for the privilege of being a missionary for nearly thirty years. I appreciate the insights and suggestions of those who read this manuscript as it was in process: Norman Patton, James Albrecht, Maurice and Dondeena Caldwell, and John Johnson. While Dr. Crose wrote in retirement in Anderson, Indiana, I did the bulk of writing in Japan while actively engaged in my daily assignment there. Thus my father's contributions as principal researcher were indispensable, as were his informed perspectives.

I am also indebted to the quick responses to countless e-mails I sent to colleagues on the field and in Anderson, and to Joseph Allison and Stephen Lewis of the Publishing and Creative Services team of Church of God Ministries. Finally, I am grateful to three peers who reviewed the book after the writing was completed: Barry Callen, Robert Davis, Sr., and Steven Rennick. All of these individuals contributed in producing this important volume that celebrates one hundred years of organized missions of the Church of God in North America (1909–2009).

Cheryl Johnson Barton
Missionary, Tokyo, Japan

PREFACE TO
PASSPORT FOR A REFORMATION

The Missionary Board of the Church of God is the vehicle for thoughtful and concerned efforts in world mission on the part of Church of God Christians in the United States and Canada. This Board functions under the General Assembly of the Church and is founded and maintained under the assumption that all Christians are called to world mission and some are particularly gifted for special assignment in the mission task. Throughout the history of this reformation movement, the focus has often been on those who have been called in particular, but the real responsibility for mission has rested on the total church.

It is significant that this book is being published during the centennial year of the Church of God in the seventy-second year of the Missionary Board. The organized work of missions has been important to the life of the movement, and even before the Missionary Board was formulated in 1909, missionary activity was already being undertaken. Ninety out of our one hundred years have witnessed active involvement in world missions.

Response to human need has always motivated Church of God people, but I am impressed that efforts to respond to that need through the Missionary Board have always been based on a biblically sound theology of mission and on the best in mission philosophy. As you will see as you read *Passport for a Reformation,* method and practice have not always reflected intent and knowledge.

In an effort to chronicle this tremendous story, the Missionary Board approached a forty-four-year veteran of both field and administrative experience. Dr. Lester A. Crose was asked to "share out of his knowledge and experience" the missionary story of the reformation. We are all indebted to Lester for this remarkable effort.

I suppose one always reads a book about a subject in which one has had special interest to determine whether the author has been successful in noting one's own preconceived ideas on the subject. I fell victim to this temptation. What I found was encouraging to me as I know it will be to you. (1) Early in the movement, missionary motivation, zeal, and response to human need were strikingly evident. (2) There has always been a keen openness to what is best for the church abroad as opposed to the structure of programs suited to what the church may desire in North America. (3) National people were sought and recruited from the beginning, and they figured significantly in the development of many new works. (4) The Missionary Board, often through the leadership of the author of this book, has positioned itself in the vanguard of education for mission at home and structure for mission abroad. (5) The quality of missionary leadership and dedication has been superb.

If you are looking for missionary stories only, you may be disappointed. If you are hoping for a challenge, you will find it in the lives of hundreds of dedicated servants who carried the passports of several nations, but who also carried the passport for a reformation.

Donald D. Johnson
Executive Secretary-Treasurer (1975–85)
Missionary Board of the Church of God

INTRODUCTION

In the past thirty years, the Church of God reformation movement's worldwide efforts, first through the Missionary Board and now through Global Missions, have focused on partnership as the model for its missionary endeavor. The understanding of partnership has evolved during this time into a more mature relationship with our brothers and sisters overseas. With this growth, the partnership model is now moving towards one of mutual dependence. While this book chronicles one hundred years of organized missions effort from North America, a cadre of world partners has emerged and led the international Church of God in vigorous spiritual, organizational, and numerical growth concurrent with our (North America's) faithfulness in missions. In fact, the impetus for growth internationally has shifted from North America to our partners abroad. This relational change is cause for celebration.

This switch in initiative has yet to be fully recognized and understood in North America. For some who have seen the change emerging, it has been cause for concern. The move to interdependence has resulted in a paradigm shift that does not fit comfortably if one sees North America as the predominant partner whose ideas, money, and personnel control and set the pace for worldwide mission expansion. However, to recognize and foster both a shared burden and a mutual responsibility for mission is cause for celebration.

As the reader will see, the Church of God has been established in new countries as a part of strategic planning and effort by our world partners. The number of congregations overseas is now more than double the number in North America. And the number of constituents outside of North America is more than three times the number in North America. This phenomenal growth has taken place since 1985. This expansion is cause for celebration.

As the Church of God continues to move forward *Into All the World*, there is reason to believe that the greatest days for mission are in the future. The Church of God in North America is not relieved of its New Testament obligation as our partners exercise their New Testament responsibility.

On the contrary, as mutually dependent partners, we must live out "Together We Go to Make Disciples."[1] This is now no longer just a national challenge for North America but also an international one. It is in this sense that we can celebrate these hundred years as we continue to work together.

Donald D. Johnson
Executive Secretary-Treasurer (1975–85)
Missionary Board of the Church of God

Introduction to
Passport for a Reformation

The writing of this book has filled the need to present in narrative style a historical record of the cross-cultural missionary enterprise of the Church of God reformation movement. It is restricted to those missionary activities that have taken place outside the United States of America and Canada. To cover ninety years of effort on the part of scores of missionaries has required an arbitrary determination on my part as to what to include. Numerous outstanding events had to be omitted due to lack of space.

Therefore, I opted to write from my own perspective, that of a missionary kid, missionary, and mission administrator. In many respects the story represents the pilgrimage of my own relationship to the missionary movement of the reformation movement. I wish I could have written about the significant contribution of every missionary, but that could not be. I am leaving to others the opportunity to write in detail about what took place in each country where North American missionaries served.

Throughout the book I have used some vocabulary reflecting usage of words during certain periods of time. The word *saints* denoted believers who were saved from their sins and living a holy life. *The truth* meant that body of beliefs from the Word of God generally held by the reformation movement. *The Church of God reformation movement* or *the reformation movement* or *the movement* all indicate the group called out of denominationalism by Daniel Sidney Warner, beginning in 1881, which now has its general offices in Anderson. Indiana. In the first two chapters, I used the word *native* in its correct and highest meaning. Subsequently, *national* is employed due to the connotation later surrounding *native.* Instead of *United States of America* I have chosen to use the commonly accepted word *America.* There are other words that are strictly missionary lingo, but the context in which you discover them will no doubt reveal their meaning.

Thanks to the Missionary Board of the Church of God for granting me this opportunity to describe the development of concepts, methodologies, and approaches in world evangelization over the ninety years covered. The basic philosophy and theology of missions remained constant, as I have endeavored to show. Special thanks to Adam W. Miller and to

Donald D. Johnson for taking time to read the manuscript, making valuable suggestions. I have appreciated the extra work generously given by Patti Reed and Rosetta Means, and especially Shirley Dickinson, who did the typing. A number of my students at Anderson School of Theology deserve mention, as they elected to do research for me instead of writing semester papers. And Ruthe, my understanding wife, deserves my sincere thanks for her patience during the time of preparation and writing. So many times the normal routine of our home life was interrupted.

I stand in debt for having been a part of the modern missionary movement. A small payment has been made, as I have enjoyed making this contribution, a part of the total volume of material prepared for the observance of the centennial of the Church of God reformation movement.

CHAPTER 1
PIONEERS IN MISSION
(1880–1900)

Immediately following its inception in 1881, the Church of God reformation movement rode on the wave of *flying* ministry. Groups of itinerant evangelists crisscrossed the Midwest of America by horseback, buggy, and train. These pioneer evangelists stopped wherever opportunity made it possible, preaching, singing, and distributing literature. They called people out of the current confusion of denominationalism into the light of the New Testament church. They preached salvation from sin, calling people into the fellowship of the saints. Walking in the "evening light" (Zech 14:7—one of the graces of the coming kingdom of Christ), they put forth every effort to spread the truth about holiness and unity.

These youthful, energetic, and dedicated evangels went where the Holy Spirit led them. They ventured forth with faith that God would support them and the cause they represented. When in one place a few believers were established they would move on. There was little, if any, organization. Pastoral leadership rarely emerged for groups of believers. A New Testament pattern in proclaiming the good news was sought and followed. Being nonsectarian, these preachers of the gospel were against denominationalism, and they sought and practiced Christian unity. Going a step further, these men and women claimed belief in the universality of the church, and that the entire world was the field to harvest.

By 1882 the *Gospel Trumpet,* edited by D. S. Warner, a prominent early leader of the movement, was being read in Canada. By 1888 Warner and his evangelistic company were in Ontario, Canada, for a series of meetings. Within a year a group in Welland, Ontario, had left denominationalism, and a pastor was ordained for the flock.

During the first decade of the movement, the emphasis was mainly on reformation in North America, but early in 1890 a call went out in the *Gospel*

Trumpet to send literature even to overseas countries of the world. That call apparently created interest in "the old country"—Europe. In 1892 W. J. Henry and J. H. Rupert were working in England preaching the truth. Dr. G. R. Achor gave up his practice as a physician and sailed for England in 1893, taking with him over ten thousand tracts and books. A horse-drawn "gospel van" was built and used in evangelistic work throughout England, Ireland, Scotland, and Wales. Other evangelists such as J. W. Daugherty, W. W. Titley, and Lena Shoffner joined the group. In this same year, one of the pioneers wrote, "A new epoch has come in this last reformation." The good news was to go to every nation. Actually, in 1894 D. S. Warner was making plans to go on a preaching tour around the world, but his health was failing. He died in December of 1895, and E. E. Byrum became the editor of the *Gospel Trumpet.*

Many of the saints in the North Central states were of German background and knew the German language. By 1895 a printing press in Milwaukee, Wisconsin, was publishing a semimonthly paper called the *Evangeliums Posaune* (German *Gospel Trumpet)*. In 1894 J. H. Rupert had gone to Germany from England and was locating many persons who were friends and relatives of saints in America. J. H. Rupert and his wife worked in Hamburg, and soon other leaders such as George Vielguth and Karl Arbeiter were to go to Germany. Very quickly the reformation movement became established in Germany.

The work in Scandinavia had its beginning in 1895 through the efforts of the saints in America who had originally come from that part of Europe. Now they wanted to return to carry the good news of the gospel-the truth. Thomas Nelson and O. T. Ring were among the first to go, followed by S. O. Susag to Norway, Nels Renbeck to Denmark, and Carl J. Forsberg to Sweden. This expansion, as well as that in the British Isles, developed less rapidly than that which was started in Germany during the last decade of the nineteenth century. Furthermore, all these efforts in Europe were primarily extended evangelism out of America, a part of the flying ministry of the first decade of the reformation. Those efforts fell short of what is generally considered today as cross-cultural missionary endeavor.

Missionary Work Defined

First, who is a missionary? In simplest terms, a missionary is a person called by God and sent by God's Church to proclaim the gospel to people of another culture. A missionary is one who assists those who have accepted

Jesus Christ in other nations to fellowship with one another in congregations. To complete the cycle, those new congregations of believers will send out missionaries into other nations. This follows the example of the Apostle Paul in the early church.

Is every Christian a missionary? Yes and no. If we embrace the concept of the *lay apostolate,* we must accept the idea that every Christian should be a *flaming evangel,* a person who is sent to minister to those in need. But where the gifts of the Spirit are revealed in the New Testament, apostleship is one of those gifts. The words *apostle* and *missionary* have the same meaning, the first being of Greek derivation and the other of Latin derivation. So even though every Christian should be on some form of mission, there is a sense in which certain persons, as God wills, receive the spiritual gift to be cross-cultural missionaries. This means that missionaries are those who introduce the good news to persons having behavioral patterns and traditional ways of life different from their own.

And so, from this point on, this book is about the acts of Church of God apostles, or missionaries. In the beginning of the reformation movement, our pioneers apparently and understandably did not comprehend totally what missionary work really was. They simply followed the Lord as they felt impressed to serve him. But that indeed led quickly into cross-cultural experiences, as we shall now see.

Into Mexico

Even though as early as 1891, J. W. Byers, one of our earliest pioneers in California, began to study the Chinese language to work among Chinese in California, his real interest centered in learning Spanish in order to do work among the Mexicans during the grape harvest at Boston Rancho. During that same year, the Spirit impressed B. F. Elliot while he was preaching on a street in Santa Barbara, California, to carry the good news to the Spanish-speaking people. He decided to obey God, just as Paul did, and "go unto the Gentiles." Someone loaned Elliot a Spanish grammar book and a Spanish New Testament. With these he learned the Spanish language and was ready to go into Baja California, Mexico. In San Diego, where Elliot was to take the boat for Ensenada, D. S. Warner pressed two dollars into his hand. It was exactly the amount needed to make up the boat fare. With B. F. Elliot on his first trip was S. C. Shaw and Elliot's five-year-old son.

In Ensenada, the three rented an upstairs room for a dollar a week. The law prohibited street preaching, but Elliot and Shaw did door-to-door evangelism, talking with and praying for the people. Then they pushed southward. A good-natured Swiss man loaned them a donkey, which was a desirable means of transportation in those days. The donkey was loaded down with equipment and food, but there was room for the boy to ride and also for a good supply of Testaments and Gospels. This was indeed the first cross-cultural missionary endeavor of the reformation movement, and it was into an area occupied by people then known as Indians and Spaniards. God blessed Elliot with a degree of success. He developed a permanent mission in Ensenada and did evangelistic work as far south as La Paz and across the Gulf of California to Mazatlan and on into the interior. During the following eight years, Elliot made at least four trips into Mexico. He recounts his ventures of faith in a book published in La Paz in 1906 titled *Experiences in the Gospel Work in Lower California, Mexico.* By 1897 Elliot wanted to start a Spanish *Gospel Trumpet,* but E. E. Byrum discouraged him, saying there were too many problems to begin such a venture.

Confluent Forces in India

A young Indian man by the name of A. D. (Alla-ud-Din) Khan in East Bengal Province of India was reared a strict Muslim, but early in life he came under the influence of some Australian Baptist missionaries. In December 1893, while still in secondary school, he was converted to the Christian faith, and six months afterward he was baptized. That brought on several months of severe persecution by Khan's family and friends. First, they appealed to his feelings. Then some resorted to sorcery and witchcraft. Finally, his food was poisoned, but he survived, maintained his faith, and was finally given his liberty by the family.

In 1895, when A. D. Khan was seventeen years of age, he began studies in the London Mission College of Calcutta[1] in the big city. He observed churches of many denominations, and he was uncertain which one to attend. On his own he began a serious study of the New Testament. Following are some of his conclusions:

1. God has but one church.
2. God's church is named by God.

3. Christ is the head of the church.
4. The Holy Ghost is the administrator of the church.
5. God organized the church and appoints ministers.
6. There must be unity in the church in all matters of doctrine and practice pertaining unto life and godliness.
7. There are no sinners in the church of God.
8. A hireling ministry and program worship is foreign to the church of God.
9. The love of God is the only tie that binds believers together.
10. The Word of God is the only guide in all matters, doctrinal and spiritual.

About this time A. D. Khan read an advertisement by a man in Texas promising religious literature samples. The requested dime was sent and several religious papers received. Among them was the *Gospel Trumpet,* which immediately caught his attention. He agreed with the articles on sanctification, holiness, unity, and divine healing, so he wrote for several books and other literature. This began regular correspondence with E. E. Byrum. Clearer light on the truth flooded his soul. By 1896 Khan committed himself to the truths of the Church of God reformation movement, and he started Saturday night meetings in a Calcutta shop. He also began publishing in both English and Bengali a paper called the *Fire Brand, an anti-sectarian holiness monthly journal.*

Several young men, three of whom were destined to become leaders in the Church of God in India, joined A. D. Khan in his efforts. R. N. Mundal, a convert from Hinduism, was one of these. Khan married one of his daughters, and two other daughters, Sonat and Nalini, spent their entire lives as leaders at The Shelter in Cuttack, a home for unprotected minor girls that was started within a year or two. Mosir Moses, a convert from Islam, was to become the main leader in Calcutta for the duration of his life. And J. J. M. Roy from the state of Assam, also studying in a college in Calcutta, felt the call to full-time service before returning to his home in Shillong, where he devoted the rest of his life to the ministry.

Early in 1897 the Gospel Trumpet Company sent a half-ton shipment of books and tracts plus two small hand-operated presses to A. D. Khan. But something even more dramatic was happening, which aroused the compassion of the saints in America. What became known as the Great

Famine struck India, with more than twenty thousand deaths daily. An appeal was made through the *Gospel Trumpet,* and twenty-one hundred dollars was raised immediately. Gorham Tufts, Jr., of the Open Door Mission in Chicago was chosen to take the gift to India. He contacted Robert and Laura Jarvis, who had established the Faith Orphanage in Lahore. They had approximately two hundred children whose parents had died as a result of the famine. The Jarvises began reading the *Gospel Trumpet* and rejoiced in it. Within two years A. D. Khan had made contact with them and established relationships.

Gorham Tufts remained in India a little over a month. On his return to America, he stopped in Port Said, Egypt, to distribute literature. Port Said was the largest coaling station in the world, and ships from all over the world took on fuel at this port at the north end of the Suez Canal.

By 1898 A. D. Khan completed his work at the college in Calcutta and devoted his whole time to the Lord's work. He had read about missionary homes in America and had started one in Calcutta known as the Church of God Missionary Home, an Apostolic Bible Institute and Publishing House. Khan made an evangelistic tour into the southern state of Kerala. This was really the beginning of the work of the Church of God in South India. He also made a tour into the state of East Bengal, where his original home was located, but his efforts in the town of Bogra were not too successful.

Early in 1899 Mosir Moses made an attempt to enter Tibet, reaching only the boundary. He remained in a border town for one year, trying again and again to gain permission to enter Tibet, but failing. He studied the Tibetan language, distributed Gospels, and witnessed to many Tibetans on the Indian side of the border. This illustrates the missionary zeal of a young church. It should be noted here that the work of the Church of God in India was started by Indians and not by American missionaries.

By this time the brethren in India were requesting missionaries from America, and you will read about that in subsequent chapters. Two events gave motivation to our missionary outreach in India: A. D. Khan's experiences, including contacts with E. E. Byrum, and relief work among the starving people of India. The church in America responded with love and service. This became the second missionary outreach by the Church of God in America.

A Way Is Being Prepared

An interesting story surrounds the life of a young man named William J. Hunnex, a Britisher who lived in London in the year 1880. He attended a missionary rally in Albert Hall where he heard a young woman speak who had been serving in China as a missionary with the China Inland Mission. They fell in love, were married, and both went out to China with this same Board, which had been founded by James Hudson Taylor in 1866. They had two sons, William A. and Charles E., who grew up in China. In 1900 the Boxer Rebellion broke out against all foreigners. Many hundreds of missionaries were killed, but the Hunnexes were spared. In the next chapter you will learn what happened to these two sons, who were by that time young men.

A second development was taking place in East Africa. During the last decade of the nineteenth century, the British felt forced to annex certain areas. The slave trade of Africans being sold needed to be stopped. There was rivalry with the French for control of the Indian Ocean. Egypt was expanding deeper into Africa. Consequently, Britain invaded Egypt in 1882 to protect its vested interests in the recently completed Suez Canal. German expansionism had absorbed Tanganyika, now known as Tanzania. Missionaries and explorers entered Kenya, with missionary Krapf being among the first. Then those like David Livingston fired British interests. In 1895 Kenya became a British East Africa Protectorate, and in 1900 Kenya was formally annexed by Great Britain. To further aid in the development of the interior of Kenya, work began in 1896 on the Mombasa-Kisumu railroad. It required five years to complete. Gradually, Britain gained full control, using force when necessary. Tribal authority came to an end. Taxes were levied, and white settlers, or farmers, moved into the highlands of Kenya. Missionaries also pressed into the interior. The stage was set for the beginning of what is now the Church of God in Kenya.

We are ready to see how multiple spontaneous and independent missionary efforts on the part of Church of God persons brought about the formation of the Missionary Board of the Church of God. We enter two decades of emerging interest and involvement in world missions.

CHAPTER 2
TOWARD A UNITED OUTREACH
(1900–1918)

With the turn of the century, there materialized very rapidly within the movement a diversity of independent expressions of concern for those who had never heard about salvation through Jesus Christ. An explosion of Spirit-led events challenged individuals to dedicate themselves to go into foreign countries where Christ was almost unknown and to endure the hardships and uncertainties of living in unfamiliar cultures. Most of the time they struggled by faith with inadequate finances. In many countries, fatal diseases were prevalent. It required tremendous courage, especially for families, to answer the call to missionary service.

Expansion and growth of the work continued during the first decade of the new century in spite of a lack of coordination. From the beginning, the movement frowned on organization. In fact, there was teaching against organizing the work of the church, for it was believed that humanly inspired direction would hamper the leading of the Holy Spirit. Therefore, those who felt called to go went on their way with zealous commitment but with no official sanction or recognition by the church. They were inspired to reach "all the inhabited countries of the world." What a challenge for such a small group of people! To take the gospel into all the world was a command they well recognized from the Word of God. Therefore, these early missionaries were constrained to convert those of the non-Christian world. They proclaimed the good news that Jesus Christ is the Savior from sin and that through repentance and belief in Christ anyone from any nation could enter the kingdom of God. This was done primarily through evangelistic preaching. Literature was used extensively. Copies of the *Gospel Trumpet,* books, and tracts were distributed on trains and ships, along roads, in the cities, and at the doors of homes. By 1906 over thirty thousand dollars worth of literature had been sent into other countries of the world by the Gospel Trumpet Company.

It should be noted, however, that early in this reformation's world outreach, forms of ministry other than evangelism quickly developed. The evangelistic approach always remained paramount, however, even to the present day. But sometimes famine occurred where the missionary resided. Orphans were left homeless. Or thousands of refugees came flooding in. This required relief work on the part of the missionary. Compassion was expressed in yet other ways. Where there was mass illiteracy, even among children, education in one form or another appeared necessary. Where disease and unsanitary conditions prevailed, some form of medical assistance was required. Strong campaigns were launched against prostitution. At times agricultural and vocational projects were initiated. All these forms of service were employed at one time or another to meet the needs of persons in countries where our early missionaries went. As a result groups of converts to Christ began to appear in the islands of the West Indies, in Central America, in several countries of Europe, in Egypt and Syria (now known as Lebanon), in Kenya (later to be with the Church of God), in India, Japan, China, and Australia. Thus the Church of God reformation movement began around the world.

Those were the days when a passport could be secured for a fee of only one dollar. It was simply a large certificate from the secretary of state, folded neatly to pocketsize, giving a description of the bearer to aid in identification and requesting proper recognition and protection if necessary for the person or persons identified therein. A picture was also affixed. As a boy my first appearance on a United States passport was on one of those certificates.

As early as 1897, when Gorham Tufts was sent to India with relief funds, some organization took place, though probably not recognized as such. The *Gospel Trumpet* requested that money be sent to the editor for distribution. In 1905 a "Home and Foreign Missions Fund" was established under the care of the editor of the *Gospel Trumpet*. The editor, E. E. Byrum, decided when, where, and how funds were to be sent or used in the cause of missions. Also a "Missionary Box Fund" was created to assist in raising funds for the support of missionaries. This was to subsidize a missionary's income beyond what she or he had received directly from the saints. In reality, these simple forms of organization were very successful.

The first decade of this century was characterized by a type of unorganized, spasmodic, freelance missionary service. Some attempts were more successful than others. This is not to suggest that God was not at work through all of them, because sincere men and women of God did the best they could under varying circumstances. Some individuals who went were more able and gifted than others. Furthermore, during this decade these highly dedicated persons went forth with practically no briefing and no recourse to knowledgeable persons when they were faced with problems and difficulties on the field.

To the Islands of the West Indies

Several early attempts were made to evangelize the islands. Unfortunately, little follow-up materialized, so in most places it was several years later when the work actually began. In 1901 James S. McCreary went to Cuba. In Havana, he did evangelistic work among the soldiers and natives who knew English. Also in 1901, evangelism was carried on in St. Kitts by Fred A. Dunnell. Outdoor meetings were conducted by J. E. and Martha Wilson in 1909 on the Bahama Islands. And in 1905 Edward B. Grant felt called of God to go to Bermuda to start the work there.

It was in Jamaica where the movement's pioneer missionary efforts were very successful from the beginning. In January of 1907, a great earthquake practically destroyed the city of Kingston, the capital of Jamaica, taking over one thousand lives. In April a letter from Isaac DeLevante appeared in the *Gospel Trumpet* telling of the earthquake in Jamaica and appealing for missionaries to come. DeLevante was a Jamaican Christian who had read the *Gospel Trumpet* and felt constrained to write to the Church of God in Anderson for assistance. Earlier in 1906 George H. Pye had stopped in Kingston on his way to Trinidad and had written back home that he had discovered a group of people in that city who were willing to accept the pure gospel. In Anderson, a young couple, George and Nellie Olson, who were workers in the Gospel Trumpet Home, were feeling directed into missionary work. When this call came from Jamaica, they were convinced, after much prayer that they should accept and began immediately to make preparation to go to Jamaica where the needs were so great. That call was confirmed in June during the first camp meeting held in Anderson when a young Jamaican, A. S. McNeil, who had come under the influence of H. M. Riggle in Pennsylvania and was also attending the camp meeting, urged the Olsons to go.

E. E. Byrum gave the Olsons $150 from the Missionary Fund, and many of the saints attending the camp meeting pressed money into their hands and pockets. When they landed at Port Antonio on the north shore of Jamaica, they had only $87.25. They changed boats and the next morning landed at Kingston, where they found the city still in ruins. George Olson went in search of Isaac DeLevante while Nellie waited in a park with their baby boy. The first meeting was held in the open air the following day, and a woman was converted. Almost no funds came from America, but in a way that was good, for it placed the financial responsibility for the work on the shoulders of the Jamaican converts from the very beginning. The work grew so rapidly that the first Assembly was held the following year. In that same year, expansion into the country areas was started. Those were difficult days, however. The Olsons lived by faith, and God supplied their needs.

Early in 1906, George Pye and his wife felt called of God to sail for Trinidad. They rented a hall in Port of Spain and conducted evangelistic meetings. N. S. Duncan arrived that same year but remained only a short time. The work seemed to grow rapidly, but financial difficulties plagued the missionaries. By 1908 there was mention of a Trinidadian named Edward Cumberbatch, who was the first native minister of the Church of God on that island. I had the privilege of working with Cumberbatch in Trinidad and Tobago while serving as a missionary there during World War II. His son Carlton has been president of the West Indies Bible Institute (now West Indies Theological College) for many years.

C. E. Orr was in Trinidad for a brief evangelistic tour. But there was apparently no understanding about establishing congregations, thereby maintaining continuity. This was in contrast to the beginning of the work in Jamaica. Within two years, George Pye returned to America. This form of independent and short-term missionary service was not establishing a strong national church, and it required many years to rectify this error in missionary strategy.

On his way home from Trinidad, N. S. Duncan stopped in Barbados and reported opportunities there, but nothing was done on that island for several years.

Happenings in Europe

A continuation of independent activities persisted. William and Anna Cheatham in 1907 were working in England to secure five hundred subscriptions to the *Gospel Trumpet*. They were using a "tabernacle tent" in rural areas. That same year, the Cheathams and the Titleys went to Belfast, Ireland, where they conducted open-air meetings and rented a hall. By the following year, there was a small congregation in Belfast and the Cheathams were holding meetings in the "tabernacle tent" shipped from England. In 1904 Brother Robert Springer went to Switzerland and distributed literature. The following year George Vielguth made his first visit to Switzerland and in 1907 began holding regular meetings. By 1908 there were a few scattered saints being visited by Karl Arbeiter and George Vielguth. This appeared to be an extension of the work out of Germany. The year 1907 marks the beginning of the work in Budapest, Hungary, with contacts being made from Germany. As early as 1902, German workers established a work in Russia, with Ferdinand Schwieger going there in 1907. And in 1909 Rudolph Malzon and Otto and Gertrude Doebert experienced considerable success in evangelizing German villages in eastern Poland, the Ukraine, and the Caucasus—all parts of Russia. Finally, in 1909 Adam and Mary Allan, both natives of Scotland, and their daughter Naomi left Portland, Oregon, and sailed for Scotland, where they started a work in Aberdeen, mostly through the distribution of literature.

The most flourishing work of the Church of God in Europe was emerging in Germany. At the turn of the century, George Vielguth (from a German family in the Church of God in America) sailed for Hamburg and began a congregation. He went on to Essen. Through a second trip two years later, the congregation in Essen was established. Karl Arbeiter also came to Germany the next year. Vielguth made his third trip to Germany in 1906, taking the Doeberts with him. It was at this time that the first conference of the Church of God in Germany was conducted. The reformation movement was spreading in Germany, with the center being established in Essen. A weekly publication of a German *Gospel Trumpet* was started. A missionary home was built in Essen, with Otto Doebert and his wife as managers. It was said that gospel literature was being distributed throughout Russia. In the second Assembly held in 1909, there were saints from Russia, Poland, and all parts of Germany. It should be noted that, in order to encourage the work in Germany, E. A. Reardon visited the saints there on his way home from his one-year stay in Egypt.

Two Important Visits from India

Major focus again centered on India. At the turn of the century, another famine brought suffering and death to thousands. Again the saints in America responded and Gorham Tufts sailed the second time to India with seventeen hundred dollars. Not only were people starving to death, but the plague was killing more. Tufts also carried a large amount of literature with him, valued at more than one thousand dollars. It was on this trip that Gorham Tufts met A. D. Khan. Both of them were vitally interested in the support of the Faith Orphanage in Lahore operated by the Jarvises. In fact, Brother and Sister Jarvis had now taken their stand with the Church of God reformation movement, and they felt the need for more missionaries to assist them in caring for the orphans.

By this time J. J. M. Roy had completed a graduate degree in Calcutta[1] and returned to his home situated in the Khasi Hills in the state of Assam, in northeast India. His call from God was to spread the good news among the tribal people of that mountainous area. He began to write E. E. Byrum requesting that missionaries be sent to assist in that large undertaking. By 1901 the Jarvises needed a furlough, and so they spent a number of months in America visiting over one hundred congregations and traveling some thirty thousand miles. Returning to India after having generated considerable interest in the work of the orphanage, they took with them Andrew Shiffler from Denver, Colorado, and Mrs. Jarvis's sister Marie. All four missionaries devoted themselves steadfastly to caring for and training the orphans.

Progress was being made in Calcutta. The name of the paper published by A. D. Khan was changed from *Fire Brand* to *Victory*. Brothers Moses, Biswas, and Holdar were reaching out to Bogra, East Bengal state. A. D. Khan was visiting the work at the orphanage in Lahore. The first camp meeting of the Church of God was held in Calcutta. There was, however, one setback. E. E. Byrum began receiving letters from the brethren in Calcutta saying they could no longer have any connection with Gorham Tufts. The break finally came as he became superintendent of the Apostolic Bible School in Calcutta.

E. E. Byrum felt impressed in 1903 to invite A. D. Khan to America to have wider contact with the church. A favorable response was received, and A. D. Khan arrived in the United States in time to attend the camp meeting in Moundsville, West Virginia. Khan observed that this visit "brought East and West in closer touch with one another." He traveled extensively throughout the churches creating great enthusiasm for the missionary cause. While in America, he wrote a book entitled *India's Millions,* which influenced many of the saints to consider seriously some form of missionary service. This was really the first major promotion of missions in the movement. What soon happened in India was the harvest of Khan's seed planting while in America.

For some months E. E. Byrum had been giving serious thought to making a world tour. An increasing number of people in the movement were feeling led to foreign fields as missionaries, and they were writing the editor of the *Gospel Trumpet* for information and advice. Also, letters were coming in from other countries where the movement's literature had been received and read. Many of these readers were seeking spiritual advice and more information about the Church of God, so E. E. Byrum felt it would be good if he were more familiar with the world situation. To assist further in his editorial work he wanted to observe a number of original manuscripts of the Bible so that he could see certain passages of Scripture that the "higher critics" were saying were not in the original manuscripts. And finally, Byrum wanted very much to visit India, going with A. D. Khan as Khan returned so that he could see what was developing in the Church of God there.

In January 1904 they sailed from New York. With them were the first missionaries of the Church of God going to India: George and Mary Bailey, with their one-year-old boy, and Evalyn Nichols, all from the Northwest. They visited museums and libraries in Oxford, London, Paris, Venice, and Rome, and they observed the Muslim world in Tangiers, Morocco. In Port Said and Cairo, Egypt, the missionaries distributed literature. And they included in their trip a pilgrimage to the Holy Land. Their arrival in Calcutta was in time for the annual camp meeting. By then there were thirty saints in the missionary home in Calcutta, and the movement was progressing. E. E. Byrum visited Shillong, Bogra, and Lahore. Robert Jarvis had started the Faith Missionary Home in Lahore, as well as having carried on the orphanage. There is a note that says twenty dollars per year per child was required to keep orphans. Evalyn Nichols took an interest in the work in Assam and began immediately to learn the Khasi language. Upon completion of his visit in India, E. E. Byrum returned home by way of Japan and China. Later that year the Church of God Association of India was formed as a legal entity. Also, two more missionaries arrived from America: Josephine McCrie for Calcutta and Edith Ashenfelter for Lahore.

The following year George and Mary Bailey felt the climate of India too severe for the family, so they returned to the United States, saying they would encourage younger persons to volunteer for missionary service. A. D. Khan's wife died from cholera. Amos Abernathy arrived in Lahore from America to be in charge of gardening at the orphanage. It was not long until he was married to Edith Ashenfelter. A major move took place that had a significant effect on the work for many years. A. D. Khan felt impressed to move to Cuttack, the capital of the state of Orissa, several hundred miles south of Calcutta. The Calcutta Missionary Home and the publishing work found a new home, and this became the main center for the movement in India. Revival broke out among the people and a great spiritual awakening took place. Persecution was experienced. The first annual camp meeting was held, bringing people from many parts of India. Josephine McCrie moved to Cuttack from Calcutta. In the north, Brother Roy started a paper in the Khasi language called *Ka Jingshai Ka Gospel,* meaning "The Light of the Gospel." The group of saints in Calcutta continued meeting in homes under the leadership of Mosir Moses.

During the next few months, tragedy struck. In Lahore, the orphanage was destroyed by fire. Marie Jarvis died from a severe fever. In the Khasi Hills, Victor and Florence Maiden and their four children, along with Ira Zaugg, arrived to establish the Industrial Missionary Home about ten miles outside of Shillong. Soon afterward James Strawn joined the industrial project. The concept of an industrial farm was believed necessary to give employment to new converts who were being persecuted. But this location proved to be fatal to the project, for malignant malaria was prevalent. After only six months in Shillong, death came to Jesse Earl and Laura Grace, the two oldest Maiden children. In three days, three-year-old James Ray died. Within the next three weeks, Florence, Victor's wife, died, and after five days Glenn, the five-year-old, succumbed. James Strawn, who had arrived only three months before, also died. All these deaths were from what was commonly called "black water fever," or malignant malaria. What a blow this was to the group of believers in the Khasi Hills. Still today their tombstones are easily seen in a cemetery just outside Shillong. I have been there several times and have felt the sacredness of the spot where faithful missionaries are buried.

Grief-stricken, Victor Maiden gave up the Industrial Missionary Home and went to Lahore to assist at the orphanage. But a year later he too died from malaria. Two bright spots during this time were the marriage of A. D. Khan to Naline Lata Patia of Cuttack and the securing of a missionary home in Lahore. Thaddeus Neff and Alice Hale arrived from America to assist at the orphanage in Lahore and to do evangelistic work. Lottie Theobold came to Cuttack. Laura Jarvis died after seventeen years in India, and after two years Robert Jarvis married Lottie Theobold, who had come from Cuttack to Lahore to help in the work among the orphans. Andrew Shiffler left Lahore for Darjeeling, an important town in the foothills of the Himalaya Mountains, where he opened a colporteur supply depot to provide literature, including Bibles, for distribution among the tribal people of that area.

In 1908 the second important visit of A. D. Khan to the United States began. George P. Tasker and Hiram A. Brooks were chosen in America as a delegation to foreign lands in the interest of missions. On their way to India, they stopped in Egypt for a few days, and we shall see later the result of that visit. Tasker, Brooks, and Khan visited the saints in Shillong, Lahore, Calcutta, Cuttack, and in the newly opened field in Cannanore, South India, where J. M. Spadigum was in charge. Illness prevented Tasker and Brooks from going on to Japan and China. Instead they decided to return to America by way of Egypt, and A. D. Khan went with them. On this second trip, Khan was absent from India for almost two years. He traveled throughout America speaking to large crowds at camp meetings. He made a trip with E. E. Byrum to the British West Indies and Central America, meeting early missionaries there. As during the first visit, A. D. Khan generated significant interest in taking the gospel to all peoples of the world. And he played an important role in the formation of the Missionary Board when it was organized in 1909.

For the First Time in the Near East

When E. E. Byrum and company were on their way to India in 1904, they stopped for several days in Egypt, visiting both Alexandria and Cairo. They went on the streets distributing literature but had no particular results. But through reading his Bible, an Armenian medical doctor named G. K. Ouzounian, in Alexandria, received the light the following year calling him out of Babylon (denominations) into the unity of the people of God. Two years later, at the invitation of Hanna Arsanious, an Egyptian Christian who had read some Church of God literature and had written to America for someone to come to Egypt to help, George P. Tasker and Hiram A. Brooks stopped in Egypt for an extended visit on their way to India. This was a good opening. They were permitted to distribute literature and to conduct evangelistic services. Meetings were conducted primarily in Alexandria and Assiut in Upper Egypt. There appeared to be real potential, but both the visitors and the few Egyptians felt the need for a missionary to come immediately. E. A. Reardon left the missionary home in Chicago at once and arrived in Egypt before Tasker and Brooks went on to India. Reardon remained in Egypt for only seven months, living in Assiut, but he helped build a foundation for the work in Assiut under the leadership of Mossad Armanious and in Alexandria under G. K. Ouzounian. The seed had been planted and was beginning to bear fruit, but after Reardon returned to America no resident missionaries of the Church of God were sent to Egypt until 1923, even though a request for missionaries from the saints in Egypt was frequent. Contacts were maintained through correspondence and occasional visits by missionaries passing through Egypt.

A kind of historical accident occurred one day in 1907 on a street in downtown Cairo. Tasker, Brooks, and Reardon met Vartan Atchinak and his wife who, along with her sister Asma Trad, had started the Bible Lands Gospel Mission in Schweifat, a village on the Lebanese hillside just out of Beirut. The Atchinaks were on their way to America to find teachers for the school. They would prefer Church of God teachers. Even though the response was not immediate, Church of God missionary teachers did arrive later in Syria.

Into Japan and China

Crossing the bay between San Francisco and Oakland on a train ferry, A. U. Yajima, a young Japanese Presbyterian minister from Hawaii, picked up and read a copy of the *Gospel Trumpet*. His heart was touched with the truth contained therein. Later, in response to a letter he wrote to E. E. Byrum, Yajima was told to contact J. D. Hatch in Los Angeles. Hatch took Yajima to the Lodi Camp Meeting in central California, which was the main camp meeting in California at the time. During that meeting, Yajima was impressed to seek conversion, which he had never experienced, and to ask for more light on the truth of God's Word. My father, John D. Crose, then a young minister, gathered along with others around A. U. Yajima as he knelt at the altar.

After working briefly in the Gospel Trumpet office in Moundsville, West Virginia, Yajima felt called of God to return to his homeland, Japan, and take the good news to his own people. Arriving in Tokyo in 1908, he started a work of the Church of God by doing personal visitation, conducting meetings, and having a paper printed called *Pure Gospel.* He felt the need for assistance, and so he wrote to America for missionaries. The response was almost immediate. J. D. Hatch and W. G. and Josie Alexander, along with their daughter Grace, sailed for Japan in 1909. The Alexanders had been impressed by Yajima at the Lodi Camp Meeting and had felt the call to Japan at that time.

In chapter 1, mention was made that William J. Hunnex, his wife, and their two sons survived the Boxer Rebellion in China. During 1904 the parents sent William and Charles to America for higher education. Soon after their arrival, both came into contact with the movement, but in different places. By 1905 both young men were at Moundsville working in the Gospel Trumpet office, and they generated considerable enthusiasm regarding missionary work in China. Both of them wanted to be missionaries to China. Having grown up there, they knew the language and the culture. William A. Hunnex married Gloria Hale, sister-in-law of Mabel Hale, from Kansas, and they sailed for China in 1909 to begin a work in Chinkiang. Charles waited another year before he was ready to go.

A Second National Agency Is Born

The need for some form of organization to bring together and coordinate the missionary outreach of the Church of God reformation movement became evident by 1909. Twenty years of voluntary and independent expressions of missionary endeavor were now culminating in the formation of a Missionary Board. During the next fifty years, the church looked to the Board to lead in giving expression and direction to the church's missionary interests.

The Missionary Board became the second Church of God agency to organize on a national level. Harold Phillips writes in his book *Miracle of Survival,* "The Gospel Trumpet Company was the first organized institution of the Church of God movement—the first such organization to be incorporated, and thus the first to be governed by legally registered by-laws." That was in 1904.

Good as these early missionaries were who went out on their own under God, problems began to arise and multiply. This gave the church at home a growing concern for the well-being and future of its missionary expansion into new fields and the growth of work already existing. Many of these pioneer missionaries felt responsible to no one but to God. There-fore, each one did what he or she felt should be done, seeking always the guidance of the Holy Spirit. But strained situations began to develop where there were more than one or two missionaries. Living in a new culture, many were unable to cope with new and strange situations arising. This caused differences among missionaries and sometimes between missionar-ies and native workers. No one was available to give advice. A few began to write home to E. E. Byrum, but he was already overloaded with correspon-dence and therefore was unable to devote the time and energy necessary to care for these important matters.

Financial support also was creating some misunderstandings. Mis-sionaries went to the field on faith—faith that God would supply their needs. But some could tell the story of their work better than others, by letter or when they were home on furlough, and therefore, they got more support. Churches became aware of these developing inequities, and pas-tors were asking questions and suggesting there might be a better way. Also, new missionaries going out on their own were most of the time ill-equipped, not knowing how to care for themselves, how to live in another country so different from their own, or how to learn a language. Conse-quently, the inevitable happened.

Following is a quotation from George P. Tasker's diary dated June 12, 1909:

> On June 12, 1909, after an address on Government in the Church, H. M. Riggle, after presenting our plans for a missionary paper, to be called the *Missionary Herald*, recommended that, "certain breth-ren should be recognized amongst us, by common consent, as hav-ing and exercising in behalf of the Church, the responsibility and care of the foreign missionary work. They should be capable of ad-vising, instructing, encouraging and restraining." The names here presented, and that were acknowledged by the immediate rising to

their feet of the entire assembly of ministers, were D. O. Teasley, J. W. Byers, E. E. Byrum, E. A. Reardon, G. P. Tasker, H. A. Brooks and D. F. Oden. Brother Riggle then said, "it is intended that the entire ministry should cooperate with these brethren," to which all said, "Amen."

This was a bold step forward for a church that did not believe in organization. It was to provide purpose, meaning, and coordination to former independency. It was to make possible more systematic giving so that missionaries would receive more equitable remuneration for their services. It should be noted that all these brethren had been abroad except one. It was assumed that their observations and experiences would enable them to know better how to look after missionary funds and personnel.

The official minutes record, "The first formal meeting of the Missionary Board of the Church of God, chosen and appointed by common consent of the ministers present at the annual camp meeting held at Anderson, Indiana, June 1909, was held in Room E34 of the Gospel Trumpet Home, June 8, 1910." Decisions of great importance were made. Bylaws were adopted to govern the society. Following are the first officers elected who became the first board of directors: D. O. Teasley, chairman of the Board; E. E. Byrum, vice-chairman; and G. P. Tasker, secretary–treasurer. Teasley remained chairman until F. G. Smith was named president in 1912, and Tasker remained secretary-treasurer until he went to India the same year and was succeeded by J. W. Phelps. A letter was sent to the Gospel Trumpet Company describing the organization of the Missionary Board and giving authorization to turn over, on request, to the secretary-treasurer all funds collected for missionary work by the Gospel Trumpet Company. The letter also outlined the principle business of the seven men as follows: (1) to act as an advisory board in the matter of missionaries going to foreign fields; (2) to have charge of all collections and disbursements of missionary funds; and (3) to take a general interest in the dissemination of missionary information.

A "Home and Foreign Missionary Fund" was established. The treasurer was authorized to keep the funds of the Missionary Board with the Gospel Trumpet Company until further action was taken. Church people were already beginning to send in money on a regular basis to support missionaries. The idea of sending and supporting missionaries was in the process of being firmly established.

Three goals were set by the Board for itself:

1. More correspondence with the missionaries,
2. To develop a worldwide vision and to become acquainted with and interested in the worldwide field, and
3. To make a more systematic effort towards more systematic giving.

The Board also decided to encourage missionaries to "undertake only as much work as can be perpetuated by the means regularly supplied." Preparatory instructions were framed for "intending missionaries":

1. A thorough working knowledge of the Bible and its fundamental doctrines,
2. An acquaintance of history and principle doctrines of various non-Christian world religions,
3. An intelligent understanding with the evidences of Christianity and the origin of the Scriptures, and
4. A knowledge of religious geography and history of other countries, especially where he is to work, and the situation of Christianity in that country.

In that first annual meeting twenty-seven missionaries were recognized: British Isles, four; China, two, Japan, four; British West Indies, two; Germany, four; and India, eleven. There were actually only nineteen missionaries because eight of those listed were evangelists. The first missionaries appointed by the Board during that meeting were N. S. Duncan and his wife, who were to go to Barbados. Duncan had been in Trinidad before. In order to have the necessary funds to go, he was selling his property in the United States. The Board also approved Charles E. Hunnex for service in China. The missionary family grew rapidly, and eight new missionaries were sent out during the next year. Within two years sixty-five regular missionaries were on the field: India, twenty; British West Indies, eighteen; Denmark, two; Germany, six; Russia, five; Ireland, one; China, five; Japan, four; and Egypt, four. Actually, seventeen of those listed were evangelists or pastors, not missionaries in the strictest sense. Six new missionary homes were built and properties purchased.

Certain policies were being formulated for the benefit of the work. It was thought caution should be exercised "in the immediate establishing of orphanages." There was reason for this because so many wanted to start orphanages and the Board considered such an objective not to be the prime purpose of missions. Encouragement was given to those preparing for missionary service to take correspondence courses being offered by the Church of God Missionary Home in New York City. An early attempt was made to regularize the disposition of funds raised by missionaries home on furlough. The Board had to deal with the necessity of making a 50 percent cut in missionary allowances when the bottom dropped out from under missionary income early on. And it was thought best that "the native church should support its own native ministers in a native style." To be sure only true missionaries were sent to the field, a motion was adopted that only "apostles" should be sent.

In 1912 the Missionary Board moved all missionary correspondence from the general files of the Gospel Trumpet Company to missionary files in the Board's office. By 1914 the Missionary Board was in need of holding property and carrying on legal business. Therefore, it became incorporated under the laws of the State of Indiana, adopting a new constitution to conform to those laws related to the incorporation of a not-for-profit organization. It was necessary to add four members, making a membership of eleven. From then on the Missionary Board could register in other countries as an alien corporation in order to hold properties and do business.

From the very beginning, it was considered imperative to have a missionary publication. D. O. Teasley was selected as editor of the *Missionary Herald,* which was a paper for missionary activities only. It drew together and united all efforts. It kept the church informed. In the opinion of some, it helped to develop for the Church of God a modern missionary movement. Unfortunately, it existed for only three years, and in 1913 the *Gospel Trumpet* made an announcement that it would devote one issue per month to missionary emphasis.

Missionary Board Has Positive Effects

Following the formation of the Missionary Board, all signs pointed toward a more united outreach. Coordination, however, did not always come easily. Most missionaries gladly accepted the Missionary Board as a point of reference for helpful advice and positive direction. Churches at home appeared pleased with the decision of the ministers to appoint the Board and responded in such a manner as to prove they could do better together through the Missionary Board what would be impossible for them to accomplish individually.

This had an immediate effect on the mission field where growth and expansion took place, hindered only by the ominous clouds of World War I. Properties for churches were being purchased in Jamaica, and George Olson was making visits to the Cayman Islands, Panama, the Canal Zone, and the San Blas Islands to carry the truth there. After nine years of work in Jamaica, George Olson reported in 1916 that there were twenty-six congregations and the church properties were being held by local boards of trustees whose members must be confirmed by the American board. L. Y. Janes was in Jamaica to help for a while and hoped to go into Spanish-speaking work in Central America. When E. E. Byrum and A. D. Khan made their stop in Jamaica in 1910, Khan offered his pocket watch as a gift to George Olson. Olson accepted it graciously. Shortly afterward Nellie Olson was permitted to buy a horse so that she or her husband could visit members of their congregation in Kingston. A gift of dried fruit, a kind of trial shipment that the Olsons greatly appreciated, was received from J. W. Byers. Later a committee was appointed by the Missionary Board with Jennie Byers responsible for the collection and distribution of missionary fruit (dried peaches, apples, apricots, and prunes). This project was promoted all over America. Unfortunately, it died out during the war, primarily because the dried fruit would spoil before reaching the missionaries.

When N. S. Duncan and his family arrived in Trinidad, having been appointed by the Missionary Board to revive and establish the work, he did just that. E. N. Reedy and Archie Rather soon came, and then George Coplin and Frank Shaw, who went later to Barbados. Thaddeus and Katrina Neff followed and started a work in Princess Town among the East Indians. During World War I, Neff had some difficulty in persuading authorities that he was not a German spy. Early ministers in Trinidad, working with the missionaries, established groups of saints in a number of towns on the island.

When George Coplin and J. Frank Shaw sailed to Barbados from Trinidad, they found four persons professing to be saints, and so a congregation was started at Mile and a Quarter. Coplin built the large church

building in Bridgetown, and for a while he had the oversight of the work
in both Barbados and Trinidad. Shaw purchased The Grange, a missionary
residence in Bridgetown that had been the home of a former postmaster
general. My wife Ruthe and I lived in it during World War II, and that is
where our son John was born. Shaw helped build many of the small country churches. L. W. and Opal Brookover arrived during this period of time,
remaining for many years. In 1915 Coplin and Shaw visited British Guiana, now known as Guyana, and became acquainted with George L. Jeffrey. After embracing the truth, Jeffrey and his one congregation came with
the Church of God. In Panama and the Canal Zone, the efforts of George
Olson were effective in establishing small congregations among West Indians who had come from Trinidad and Jamaica to work on the digging of
the Panama Canal. Further north in Mexico, Dave (D. W.) and Mae Patterson were assisting B. F. Elliot.

In Germany, the saints were continuing to raise money to support
their missionaries as they went to German colonies in Russia. A new group
was started in Budapest, Hungary. William Hopwood became pastor of the
congregation in Birkenhead, England, where he remained until his death
in 1936. The work in Switzerland centered in Zurich, with Gottfried Zu-
ber as leader. Adam Allan moved from Scotland to Ireland, where he remained until his death years later. But the chief progress in Europe during
this period was in Denmark. A great revival broke out in 1912 and 1913.
Converts were found in several towns and cities. Evangelists came and
went. Congregations were established, and by 1915 there were thirteen.
During those early years, the congregations felt considerable opposition
from the state church. The big question always asked was, "Have you seen
the church?" And that's how the Church of God saints greeted each other.

During its annual meeting in 1912, the Missionary Board had conversation with Vartan Atchinak and Asma Trad from Syria, now known
as Lebanon, about the possibility of sending a missionary teacher to their
school in Schweifat. That summer Bessie Hittle (later Russell Byrum's
wife), Minnie Tasker (George's wife), and Josephine McCrie arrived in Beirut and went on to Schweifat, a village just outside Beirut. Later that year,
F. G. Smith and his wife, with Nellie Laughlin, a public school teacher
from Vermont, and George Tasker, arrived. George and Minnie Tasker and
Josephine McCrie went on to India, leaving Bessie Hittle, Nellie Laughlin, and the Smiths in Syria. House meetings were conducted. Bessie and

Nellie gave less time to the school and more time to evangelism. Converts, especially among young women, came from among the better families of the village. Feeling the need for a manual to teach new converts the truths of the Bible, F. G. Smith wrote *What the Bible Teaches,* and as he wrote it, it was translated into the Arabic language. As World War I began, Americans were advised to leave the eastern Mediterranean because it was ruled by Turkey, an ally of Germany. The Smiths left Syria, and shortly afterward Bessie Hittle also left, leaving behind a happy, earnest company of saints. Nellie Laughlin elected to remain, not knowing what the future would bring but feeling she could be of help to the people. All contact with her was cut by 1917. But she was able to find food to keep the small community of believers alive, and she spent her time indoctrinating these young converts in biblical truth. Nellie had become a full-time missionary and was the only missionary of the Church of God in that entire area. The few saints in Egypt had their own leadership and an occasional American visitor before the war.

Faith Orphanage in Lahore, India, was discontinued due to the general feeling that the need was no longer present. Those missionaries directly connected with the operation of the orphanage, such as Abernathy, Zaugg, Neff, and Hale, returned to America. In Shillong, Indian leader J. J. M. Roy married missionary Evalyn Nichols, and they took the family name of Nichols-Roy. Their productive labors together spread over six decades. Soon after A. D. Khan returned to India from his second visit to America, seven and a half acres of property was purchased in Cuttack. The deed for it was held in the name of "Church of God Association of India." This holding became known as Mount House, which consisted of a missionary home and ultimately a chapel. The congregation that emerged was self-supporting and self-propagating, and they conducted meetings in nearby villages. A. D. Khan managed the United Printing Works. George and Minnie Tasker arrived in India in 1912 and had been sent by the Missionary Board to be a "directing force" for the significant work emerging in that country. Tasker took up headquarters in Lahore, remaining there until the work at Lahore closed down in 1921. The Shelter was started in Cuttack in 1914 by A. D. Khan and was operated by E. Faith Stewart, a new missionary, plus Sonat and Nolini Mundal, Khan's sisters-in-law. The home was for the protection of minor children and was greatly needed. Three years later seven acres of land was purchased in Cuttack for The Shelter, and within two more years the main building, which is still being used, was erected. At that time, a child could be supported by a sponsor for five dollars a year. An elementary school for girls was soon started for these girls.

Some progress was being made in Japan, although it was considerably slower than in India. In 1911 W. G. Alexander purchased two acres of land in what was then a suburb of Tokyo called Musashi Sakai. He built there a missionary residence, quarters for Japanese leaders, and a chapel. A printing press was used for turning out six thousand copies each month of the *Pure Gospel* in the Japanese language as well as other pieces of Christian literature. J. D. Hatch remained in Tokyo, where he worked with Brother and Sister Maekawa. They held street meetings and distributed tracts, even on something new—"electric cars." Hymns were translated into Japanese. J. D. Hatch became seriously ill after a few years of service and returned to America in 1916, where he died soon after. Zuda Lee Chambers went to Japan the following year and began her work in Tokyo, first of all by studying the difficult language. Shortly after the close of World War I, an excellent piece of property was purchased in the Hongo district of Tokyo. This soon became the headquarters of the work of the Church of God in Japan.

Across the East China Sea from Japan, things were happening in China. William and Gloria Hunnex were already there starting a work in Chinkiang, some 150 miles up the Yangtze River from Shanghai. Individual saints in America had been giving to a "China Fund" sponsored by the *Gospel Trumpet*. A missionary home was erected on one acre of land purchased just outside Chinkiang. It provided living quarters for missionaries, a chapel, classrooms, and later a small orphanage. The main street in Chinkiang soon had a rented hall where services were conducted. Charles Hunnex was appointed by the Missionary Board in 1910 as a missionary to China but was advised by the Board to wait until some rioting calmed down before departing from America. Pina Winters was also sent to do general missionary work with the Hunnexes. Charles soon opened a new work in Yangchow from which emerged Chinese leadership. In 1912 a revolution changed the monarch into a republic, which gave hope for more freedom. Tracts and a paper in Chinese gave evidence of a strong literature emphasis. Because of a serious illness, Charles returned to America. While recuperating in the Church of God Missionary Home in Oakland, California, he met and married Annabel Lee from Nebraska. Before returning to China,

Charles brought to the attention of the Missionary Board a serious problem for the Chinese Christians. In America the saints greeted each other with a holy kiss, and they were not given to drinking tea or coffee. But in China, as Charles pointed out, tea was the common drink and the practice of the holy kiss did not seem to fit at all into the culture. The Board suggested that in China they make whatever adjustments were necessary on these matters. In 1916 Daisy Maiden and Belle M. Watson were appointed as missionaries to China, and they went out with William and Gloria Hunnex, who were returning to China following their first furlough. Daisy and Belle first of all took up the study of the Chinese language in the Nanking Language School, only fifty miles away from Chinkiang.

An Australian by the name of E. P. May came into contact with the Church of God in America as a young man. For several years he was a worker in the Gospel Trumpet Home in Anderson. In 1917 he went back to his homeland to establish the truth first of all in Sydney. He rented a hall and called it the Unity Mission. It could accommodate 150 persons. He started publishing the *Australian Gospel Trumpet* and carried on considerable correspondence with interested people. Unfortunately, after seven years he ran into financial difficulties and a fire destroyed the printing equipment and supplies. Also, differences arose between him and church leaders in America. Relationships broke off, and there was no more contact with E. P. May until 1963.

In Kenya, East Africa, there was further preparation for Church of God entry into that country. By 1901 the railroad from Mombasa and Nairobi had reached Kisumu on Lake Victoria. This opened up the Western Province. American Quakers from Richmond, Indiana, settled at Kaimosi in 1902 and the Church Missionary Society of the Church of England at Maseno in 1908. A. W. Baker, a Christian British attorney in Johannesburg, South Africa, and founder of the South African Compounds and Interior Mission, sent Robert Wilson north to Kenya to establish a mission in the interior among primitive African tribes. Following some exploration, Wilson decided on a large piece of land given by Chief Otieno in Bunyore, situated between Kaimosi and Maseno. In 1905 this new mission was started and named Kima, Wilson's nickname for his wife. In the local vernacular, *Kima* meant "anything with life having a healthy condition." How appropriate for what Kima was destined to become in terms of Christian life and witness.

The first few years were difficult. Wilson built a house and small church building. Even though the singing of Christian hymns by the missionaries, with Mrs. Wilson playing the small harmonium, attracted curious individuals, the Africans were shy and hesitant. In the beginning, the girls and women would "fly away." After two years, A. W. Baker sent an African Christian evangelist, Johana Bila, from the Zulu tribe to assist in the work. That was also the year of the Great Famine. Bila was successful in that a number of Africans were converted. Unfortunately, Bila's ministry lasted only three years, for he died from fever and was buried in Kima. About the time of his death, the first baptismal service was conducted and two Bunyore people were baptized. It took two more years before thirteen more were baptized.

At the beginning of World War I, H. C. Kramer and his wife Gertrude arrived to replace Harley and Bonnie Richardson (he died of malaria), who had replaced the Wilsons (he had suffered a sun stroke). A. W. Baker, accompanied by his daughter Mabel, came with the Kramers to inspect the mission. When her father returned to South Africa, Mabel elected to remain in Kenya to devote her entire life to missionary service there. Mrs. Kramer and Mabel Baker began the long and arduous task of learning the language, reducing the language to writing, and then translating portions of the Bible. That tremendous and difficult job extended over many years. First the Gospel of Mark and then John were translated. Then came a translation of the entire New Testament, which was published by the American Bible Society. During the war years, famine and smallpox, flu and the plague, were always present. But progress was made. A school for children was conducted in the afternoons with the use of wall charts and a few slates. Sewing classes were started for girls. The women were superstitious about eating chicken. Chairs were for men only. Gradually, Christian concepts changed some of these cultural patterns. Over in America, not knowing anything about what was developing in Kenya, Samuel Joiner and his wife, along with William J. Bailey and his wife Lilly, were becoming burdened for the lost in Africa. In 1917 the Missionary Board of the Church of God gave approval for these persons to go as missionaries to Africa when the way should open. That took place, as we shall see, within five years.

World War I spanned the years 1914–18. Missionary outreach was limited. No new areas were entered in so-called non-Christian lands. The work in Europe was greatly curtailed, and missionaries were forced to leave. The one exception was Denmark, where the war seemed to have little effect on the growth of the church. In Germany, Poland, Russia, and Latvia, the indigenous movement of the Church of God struggled on, even though separated from the church in America. There was considerable loss in church property, some displacement of individuals, and the occasional falling away from the truth. In America the constant shortage of funds hindered growth in the British West Indies. Any income increases were offset by inflation. There was little left over for new outreach. Syria was cut off from America by a blockade set up by the Allies in the Mediterranean to seal off Turkey, an ally of Germany and ruler of all the eastern Mediterranean. Half of the people of Lebanon, then a part of Syria, died of starvation during the war. By the time the Missionary Board met in mid-1917, however, they foresaw the overthrow of Turkey as opening fields to the Muslim world. Board members also saw the revolution in Russia as a hope for democracy in that country. Plans, they said, should be made in advance to take advantage of approaching opportunities. And the record of the Board meeting in 1918 just before the war ended states that, in spite of war in some parts of the world, other places were open and "white unto harvest." Opportunities in the West Indies, South America, Australia, Japan, China, and India were cited. The stage was set for something great to happen when missionaries would be free again to go into all the world, and the Missionary Board had behind it ten years of valuable experience.

CHAPTER 3
MOVING OUT BETWEEN THE WARS
(1918–1945)

The war to end all wars had been fought and won by the Western Allies. World War I came to an end on November 11, 1918, and the world was to be safe for democracy, assisted by a new world body called the League of Nations. A redistribution of colonies emerged, mainly in the Middle East and Africa. Germany and Turkey lost everything, and Great Britain, France, and Belgium profited greatly. With the exception of a few skirmishes here and there, peace had come again to the world and people once more could move about freely. All of this was immediately reflected in missionary movement out of America.

During its first meeting following the war, the Missionary Board felt the need to discover the exact nature of the situation around the world, especially in countries where missions of the Church of God existed. F. G. Smith, then president of the Missionary Board, and E. A. Reardon, valued Board member, were chosen to go on a "missionary inspection tour." This was because both had experienced brief missionary service in the eastern Mediterranean. They proceeded westward, visiting Japan, China, the Philippines, Australia, India, Egypt, Syria, Palestine, France, and the British Isles—a journey covering forty-six thousand miles and requiring eleven months. They observed various missionary methods being used not only by Church of God missionaries but by other Protestant agencies. They made note of the condition of the Church of God mission stations and missionaries and of the prospects for expansion following the war. Their report to the church in America is found in a booklet published by the Missionary Board in 1920 titled *Look on the Fields,* which also included reports and information on missions in Europe, the British West Indies Islands, the Canal Zone, and South America, which had not been included in the tour by Smith and Reardon. This booklet did much to enlighten the saints in America about what was going on in their mission and what needed to be done. A fresh wave of enthusiasm and a renewed dedication to the task ahead were generated.

Near the back of *Look on the Fields,* E. E. Byrum, then vice-president of the Missionary Board, wrote a few pages about "the urgency of missionary action." It was straightforward promotion asking for donations for the support of present missionaries, for making possible the sending of new missionaries where urgently needed, for partial support of native workers, and for badly needed church buildings. Byrum suggested making out a will and printed a sample document. He also asked for gifts from Sunday schools.

Smith's and Reardon's report to the Missionary Board was much more detailed. They endeavored to interpret the situation accurately on each field and the valid needs as they observed them. Smith and Reardon then hoped to establish priorities that the Board could consider. They presented new opportunities and felt this called for planned expansion. A suggestion was made to update some methods they felt required change. All of this only confirmed the following paragraph which is found in F. G. Smith's "Report of the President" to the Missionary Board on June 9, 1919:

> The one thing that towers above local interests, sectional interests and national interests—the work that knows no distinctions of race, color or speech; the work that can therefore legitimately command and merit universally the support of every child of God, is MISSIONS. Church institutional work of every kind and description is simply auxiliary; whereas the work of missions is not auxiliary to anything and cannot be subjected without destroying its life and character, for it is *church work itself.* It is not a mere business enterprise to be measured in terms of dollars and cents, but a direct soul-saving work. It does not differ in fundamental character from the church work in our own local congregations in this country.

Time was taken in the 1920 Missionary Board Annual Meeting to outline some "plans for organization and conduct of our missionary work." Some goals for expansion were considered. There was observed a "development of new internationalism." Individuals throughout the church were beginning to break through the barriers of isolationalism and to look on the fields, which were ripe and ready for harvest. To gain a broader perspective on what was happening in the world of missions, Missionary Board president F. G. Smith encouraged the Board to join the Foreign Missions Conference of North America, the interdenominational gathering of those bodies devoted to missionary work. Copies of the *International Missionary Cable Code Book* were ordered to be distributed to all our missionaries so that cables could be sent to and received from the Board by means of a few code words instead of several sentences. That saved a great deal of money as well as making possible more frequent and quicker communication between the Missionary Board and missionaries, and between missionaries located in different countries. That was important at this time of a fresh moving out because correspondence both ways was by boat mail, which sometimes required months before a missionary could receive a reply to a very important question.

That same year the Missionary Board opened its own account with Anderson Banking Company, no longer to carry on its financial business through the Gospel Trumpet Company. Discussion took place about the relationship of a mission to the native church that was developing. In retrospect, it is not too difficult for us today to know what position the Board should have taken on that subject, for that was an era of political colonialism, and the concept of colonialism easily rubbed off on missionaries and Board members. Financial matters were cared for on a more businesslike basis. Field budgets were developed and were submitted to the Missionary Board for consideration and adoption, usually after reducing the asking considerably. Furlough allowances were now granted to missionaries on furlough in America. Before, they had lived on the freewill offerings received from the churches visited. There was one decision, however, that was destined to cause many problems in relationship with the young churches developing in each of the countries where we had missionaries.

Following a method commonly practiced by most Protestant missions, the Missionary Board created the office of field secretary, which was held by a missionary at each mission. This person became the representative of the Board. This was initiated when Floyd W. Heinly and his family were sent to India as missionaries to assume control over our missionary endeavors there. The Board took considerable time and several pages in the minutes of the meeting to detail the responsibilities of the field secretary. For a time, the results were almost disastrous in India. In retrospect, we can say that this was a major error committed by the young Board relative to the work in India. Recall for a moment the high quality of able leadership in the Indian church. Strong letters of protest from these leaders were received by the Board. They objected to having a missionary appointed by the Missionary Board in America to manage the work of the Church of God in India. After all, the movement in India had its own missionary board, and the brethren felt they were capable under God to give guidance to the work in their own country. But this pattern of organization of a mission followed exactly the colonial system of control and administration. The common saying was, "He who pays the piper calls the tune." The American church by that time was supporting the missionaries and much of the work in India. And so the decision stood. The attitudes of colonialism prevailed. We cannot be overly critical of those on the Board at that time, for this was the manner in which most missionary endeavors around the world were organized. However, the decision did create serious problems during the following years in India, and it set back the clock of time that should have led rapidly to self-reliant churches. Instead, the young churches became mission oriented and ultimately developed a mission complex. They became known as mission churches without self-identity and the ability to stand alone as viable churches.

During the early to mid-twenties, other innovations materialized. The Missionary Board voted to buy a camera and an adding machine. In one meeting, considerable concern was expressed as to whether or not a self-starter should be purchased as special equipment for the automobile to be sent to Jamaica. There were more important items of business. Missionary salaries were reviewed to make certain that a degree of equality was maintained in what was being received by all missionaries. A Grant-in-Aid plan was worked out for the support of native workers, and it was tried as an experiment in Jamaica and Syria. Report blanks that were to be filled out daily were devised for missionaries and then for national workers by which monthly information would be received by the Missionary Board from each missionary and worker on how many sermons were preached, how many homes were visited, how many sick were prayed for, how many baptisms were done, how much time was spent in study and preparation, how many personal interviews were done, and on and on. Believe me, that system did not last very long! Systematized budget askings from the missions assisted the Board during its annual meetings to give intelligent consideration to each field and arrive at a responsible operating budget for the next year. At first some missionaries had difficulty with the process. Even such a person as H. M. Riggle, who was at the time a missionary in Syria, had some serious misunderstandings with the Board over this, and the minutes record a temporary "disaffection" on the part of Riggle. For the first time in its history, the Missionary Board began the practice at the beginning of each of its annual meetings to appoint a resolution committee to facilitate its work.

When the Missionary Board was first incorporated in 1914, there were eleven members elected to comply with the requirements of the State of Indiana. By 1921 a larger representation was felt necessary. Consequently, the Board revised its Articles of Incorporation to allow for fifteen members to be in lots of three for five-year terms. This allowed for continuity in the work of the Board. Members were selected through nomination by the Board and then accepted or rejected by the Ministerial Assembly meeting each June in Anderson, Indiana. Later on, nominees were presented by the Missionary Board in pairs for each of the three expiring terms each year and the General Ministerial Assembly would vote by ballot. Down through the years, there was no major change until Articles of Reorganization were adopted by the Board in 1970, and then in 1980 its membership was enlarged from fifteen to twenty persons. From the beginning of its existence, the Board had been charged with the responsibility of carrying on missionary work among minority groups in America.

After ten years it was felt impossible for the Board to be responsible for both home and foreign missionary work, so it requested that another Board be formed to assume the responsibility of home missionary endeavor. In 1921 such a Board was brought into being by the General Ministerial Assembly and named the Board of Church Extension and Home Missions. One final item should be mentioned related to the Missionary Board. In 1923 it produced the first Missionary Manual for missionaries, presenting relationships of the missionary as well as rules and regulations governing his or her activities. As would be expected, that manual reflected the thinking and attitudes of colonial days. How well I recall as an eleven-year-old boy my first compliance with the manual. When my parents and the two of us boys landed in Port Said, Egypt, on our way to Syria in 1923, the first thing we did was to proceed to a store and purchase white pith helmets for each of us, for that was what was recommended in the manual to prevent sun stroke. All four of us came out of the store wearing those white sun helmets, identifying us with the colonial world!

In 1923 a great earthquake rocked Japan, causing much destruction and suffering in Tokyo. Although our missionaries and the Japanese Christians of our fellowship were unharmed, the Christian community in America sent relief to Japan to help rebuild homes. Recovery was slow but was assisted greatly by these expressions of love and concern. Another tragedy had taken place in Turkey, where tens of thousands of Armenians were massacred. Refugees poured down from Turkey into Syria, settling for the most part in large camps in Aleppo, Damascus, and Beirut. My father became much involved in refugee work through the Near East Relief soon after arriving in Syria. As a boy scout, I helped in collecting blankets and empty five-gallon kerosene tins for use by the refugees. Throughout the history of our missionary movement, our missionaries have demonstrated Christian love and compassion when famine, earthquake, flood, war, or any other calamity resulted in human suffering. In 1926 the Missionary Board sent thirteen hundred dollars to the Near East Relief to be used for the Armenian refugees in the Beirut area. And for several years, the Church of God Mission in Syria conducted a medical clinic and held meetings and a Sunday school in that same refugee camp.

Within the framework of the Church of God reformation movement's polity, there is no stated creed to which all must conform. On a very few occasions, this has provided the basis for problems arising with missionaries. The Missionary Board in its Missionary Manual has never presented a statement of faith to which missionaries must subscribe before going to the field. Little wonder, therefore, that infrequently a missionary might disagree with the Board and terminate services or go independent. George and Minnie Tasker, after being with the movement for twenty-five years, left the services of the Board and separated themselves for some years from the Church of God. G. P.'s views on the church and sanctification were considered on the liberal side, and there was disagreement on methodology used in approaching Muslims. In retrospect, it could be said that George was a man ahead of his time. The Taskers continued missionary service independently and later renewed fellowship with the reformation movement.

One other example was E. Faith Stewart, a missionary for many years in India who served primarily at The Shelter. Her problem was basically administrative in nature, and she had difficulty in cooperating with other missionaries on the field. Her services with the Missionary Board terminated in 1929, and a year later she went to Cuba as an independent missionary. The Board has never desired to legislate arbitrarily or to force an issue when coming into disagreement with a missionary under its appointment. Usually through negotiation and the desire to keep the unity of believers, a solution can be found to the satisfaction of all. However, if an impasse ultimately develops, the Board will present to the missionary the concept that if he or she cannot agree with the teachings and practices generally held by the Church of God reformation movement, then the honorable thing is for the missionary to withdraw gracefully, thereby causing no disruption in the work.

One of the earliest attempts to withdraw a mission in favor of the national church took place when Adam and Grace Miller returned from Japan in 1927 after a five-year term of service there. The Millers were not to return to Japan, and it was recommended that since the Church of God in Japan was strong enough and had capable leadership no more missionaries should be sent. Frequent contacts were maintained with the Japanese church until all communication was severed during World War II. But the experiment in establishing a self-reliant church in a mission field had been for the most part successful. It should be observed that all during the twenties there was continued talk by missionaries about the churches in mission lands becoming self-supporting. Perhaps too much emphasis was placed on the financial aspect of the indigenous church and not enough on self-governing and self-propagating. In 1925 J. W. Blewitt, a highly honored member of the Missionary Board and head of the Church of God Missionary Home in New York City, made a trip around the world to see what could be done to encourage missionaries to lead the churches more rapidly into being the church and not responsible to a mission. As an MK (missionary kid), I remember our family's taking Blewitt to Palestine in the new Model T Ford that the Board had provided and narrowly escaping being robbed by bandits just before reaching Haifa.

The major financial situation that brought on the Great Depression began to develop in America. In 1926 there were 10-percent cuts in remittances to the fields. That was hard enough, but by 1928, 15-percent cuts were levied. In the course of those two years, something happened in the American church that must have reflected the need for more adequate financial support for the few general agencies of the movement. What became known as Associated Budgets was proposed, and after much deliberation the Missionary Board finally agreed to participate. This united form of fundraising among the churches by the national agencies of the church was the forerunner of World Service. The financial crash came on October 24, 1929, when the stock market on Wall Street collapsed. That marked the real beginning of the Great Depression. Millions lost their jobs; thousands, their homes. Payrolls declined, savings were used up, and banks closed their doors. There were soup kitchens and breadlines in every major city. Farmers were hard hit. The deepest years of the depression were 1931 and 1932.

This development in America caused a world economic collapse. Obviously, missionary contribution in America fell off rapidly. But hardships that missionaries experienced were only a reflection of the situation in the home church in America. Even though there were severe cuts of 50 percent and on occasion 75 percent in remittances, missionaries remained at their posts of duty. Little if any expansion took place, and the work took on a holding pattern. You could count on the fingers of one hand the number of new missionaries sent out by the movement during those difficult years. My wife Ruthe and I were among those few. I was appointed by the Missionary Board in 1933, and my annual allowance was $480. The following year Ruthe was appointed, and I made the trip by boat from Beirut to New York for a hundred dollars. We were married in Oklahoma, where scars of the depression were glaringly evident. A number of young people's groups in churches in the Tri-State area raised the amount for our fares for the journey to Beirut. On the field, native workers who had been receiving financial assistance from the Board found it necessary to take on other employment to keep bread on the table. Instead of continuing to rent residences, many missionaries conserved budget by living in homes of other Christian workers who were home on furlough. Yet with all these seemingly adverse circumstances there was scarcely any complaining. Everyone was in the same boat. Missionaries held on in faith, believing that God would provide the basic needs. And God did just that through a dedicated and influential woman in the church.

At the turn of the decade, Nora Hunter, a minister of long standing in the Church of God, made a trip to the eastern Mediterranean, visiting the missions in Egypt and Lebanon. Her heart was touched when she observed the effect of the Great Depression not only on the missionaries but also on the work, which was being severely curtailed. Her concern did not diminish upon return to America, but she began to visualize what the women of the church could do once they were mobilized. This was in spite of recognizing the reality of the depression. During the Anderson Camp Meeting in 1931, Nora Hunter gathered around her several capable women and they began to work on the possibility of organizing women of the church to raise the necessary funds to keep missionaries on the field. The records of the Missionary Board indicate the depression had really settled in by that time, and that year ten missionaries on furlough were waiting to be sent out again. The group of women headed by Nora Hunter came before the Board to seek its blessing and to discover how best to go about meeting their objectives.

In mid-1932 the National Woman's Home and Foreign Missionary Society was organized and a constitution and bylaws adopted. Nora Hunter began her travels throughout America, challenging the women of the church to raise money by making things and selling them. Women of the church all across the country caught the vision, put on their aprons and baked, and made all kinds of things to sell. As a result, funds began to be made available for assisting the missionary work of the church. Because of aid received, not one missionary left the field due to the depression. Every missionary recognized the tremendous effort and what it meant to the cause of missions. In 1934 the Board records read, "The National Woman's Home and Foreign Missionary Society is doing a superb job, keeping missionaries on the field." The missionary outreach of the movement had been saved, thanks to the women of the Church of God! By the following year, it appeared that America was slowly coming out of the depression, and hope was being expressed for the future. Later on, in 1946, the society's name was changed to the National Woman's Missionary Society, and in the seventies it was changed again to Women of the Church of God.

It should not be overlooked, however, that the financial effects of the depression were felt on mission fields right up to the beginning of World War II, which began in September 1939 when Germany invaded Poland. In fact, the first time during that decade when our missionaries received 100 percent of their budgeted allowances was in the November 1939 remittance. The genius on the field was the ability achieved by both missionaries and national church leaders to make maximum use of the limited funds available. Priorities emerged with major emphasis placed on direct evangelism and away from costly institutions.

The Beginning of the End

There were other more important issues that were beginning to capture the thinking and imagination of missionary leaders around the world. First of all, there was a growing unrest throughout the colonial system. During the late twenties and throughout the thirties, there were forces at work that would ultimately bring an end to imperialism and colonialism. This development was destined to have a major impact upon the missionary movement, especially as related to the emerging churches in mission lands.

First of all, more and more uprisings and revolts occurred throughout the colonial world, but especially in the Middle East, Africa, and India. Western-educated national leaders began to demand freedom and to organize resistance movements. Also, the masses came to realize they were living in a situation geared to profit imperialistic powers. An awakening, a kind of renaissance, took place among ordinary men and women. Political revolutions occurred more frequently and with increasing violence, all of which generated bitter antipathy and hatred toward Westerners. These revolts were fueled by a rising xenophobic nationalism. The love of their own country caused people to hate Western imperialism. They wanted freedom for their country wherein they could enjoy all the blessings of political independence. A national consciousness with definite aspirations emerged. And so tensions developed as people began and continued the struggle for political independence.

That period of time was charged with the words *freedom* and *human rights*. Many a young national leader was graduated from some mission school after being taught the following basic Christian concepts, which he readily transferred into his own national political arena: "You will know the truth, and the truth will make you free...If the Son makes you free, you will be free indeed" (John 8:32, 36 RSV). "There is neither Jew nor Greek . . . slave nor free . . . , for you are all one in Christ Jesus" (Gal 3:28 RSV). American missionaries also conveyed the spirit of a bold statement in our nation's Declaration of Independence that reads, "We hold these truths to be self-evident, that all men are created equal, and are endowed by their Creator with certain inalienable rights." Consequently, the struggle for freedom and human rights emerged not only from education and the abuses of colonialism but also from the spirit and teachings of missionaries over a period of several decades.

Because the people of the colonies thought the colonial powers came from Christian nations, a revival developed among some of the major world religions, such as Islam, Hinduism, and Buddhism. People began to take pride in their history and the ancient civilizations they had earlier enjoyed, including the beauties of their ancient religions. With this in mind, they thought they could offset the inroads being made by colonial missionaries from the West. Antiforeign nationalism coupled with religious fanaticism was a force difficult to combat. These combined forces gave anticolonial people great power as they struggled for political freedom and independence.

This spirit of nationalism and freedom certainly began to have its effect upon many of the national leaders of the churches in mission lands. Even though they scarcely knew how they could get along without the missionary and the financial resources made available from the missionary's homeland, they began to think in terms of how good it would be if they could enjoy the main positions of leadership in the church instead of the missionary. Many of these leaders were capable men and women, but for the most part Western missionaries considered them immature and not yet ready to assume responsible leadership in the church. Tensions therefore developed in many of the movement's missions between our missionaries and the emerging leaders of the church. The most adverse situations revolved around the question of who was going to have the final say in the distribution of funds from America for the support of workers and churches.

All of this together gave many sensitive missionaries the feeling that the days of colonialism were fast coming to an end and that the spirit of colonialism in missions must also come to an end because it was not right in the first place. Numerous missionaries around the world, especially the younger generation of missionaries, began a serious study of a biblical understanding and a methodology that would bring forth a truly indigenous church in lands where missions had been operating for a number of years. Books were written about the methods the apostle Paul used as he did his missionary work in Asia Minor and Europe and about the tremendous success a missionary by the name of Nevius had in Korea in bringing forth an indigenous church—self-governing, self-propagating, self-supporting.

The big question in those days was this: How do you help a church become self-reliant when it has only known relationships with the mission that were almost identical to those that colonies had with Western colonial governments? There was a real awakening among missionaries that the time had come to discover ways and means to lead the church that had been mission oriented and mission dominated into a vibrant indigenous church. I was among that number as missionaries were struggling with this very situation in mission-church relationships in Lebanon.

One more event took place that must be mentioned. The International Missionary Council, which had come into being in Edinburgh, Scotland, in 1910, had conducted two council meetings in 1921 and 1928, both of which were for missionaries only. My father, stationed in Beirut, attended the one in 1928 convened in Jerusalem. But in 1938 at Tambaram, just outside Madras, India, a revolutionary development happened. A few national church leaders from several countries were invited, although they were given no major responsibility. The chief topic of that IMC meeting was the development of the indigenous church. A considerable amount of material had been prepared in advance, and I was one of the many missionaries who read it all, even though I did not have the privilege of attending. All of us were searching for solutions to the situation in which we found ourselves, realizing quite well that the day of colonialism in missions had come to an end. We began to talk about fraternalism taking the place of paternalism. Little did we realize it would take years to bring about the transformation.

World War II emerged on the world scene, suddenly stopping any further development of the self-reliant church for almost a decade. In some places, however, the church began to realize that it could function without the presence of a missionary when the missionary was forced by the uncertain situations of war to leave the country where he or she was laboring. But now before we consider the effects of the war, we must return to the twenties and thirties to note important happenings in our movement's missionary outreach.

The Islands of the West Indies

The fast-growing work in Jamaica required more missionaries. A. E. Rather and family arrived in 1919; George and Maude Coplin, in 1923; and the

Frank and Jennie Steimla family, in 1924. George and Nellie Olson were still looking after the work on the Cayman Islands and had visited again in 1920 the new work in Panama City, Colon, and the San Blas Islands. Some properties were purchased and registered in Panama for the developing congregations. For the first time, the secretary of the Missionary Board, J. W. Phelps, paid a visit to Jamaica to see for himself what was going on and to encourage the church. Shortly thereafter, a missionary residence was built for the Olsons next to the High Holborn Street Church, and for years this "mother church" and home were the headquarters of the Church of God in Jamaica.

In 1926, Nellie Olson, feeling the need for a better-trained ministry, opened the Jamaica Bible Institute. She observed immediately that most of the students had not yet completed secondary school, and so the very next year she opened a high school department at the institute. During that same year, a young missionary, Edith Young, arrived to give full time to teaching at Jamaica Bible Institute, a position she held until her retirement many years later. Before the Great Depression became too severe, George Olson, having a real vision for the future of the work, was able to purchase a large tract of land facing Ardenne Road and Hope Road on the outskirts of Kingston. It was not long before a new school building was erected facing Ardenne Road and was named Ardenne High School. Later on, several other facilities were erected for AHS. It has become one of the outstanding secondary schools in Jamaica. During World War II, Jamaica Bible Institute was moved to a building facing Hope Road. Also during the war years, the Olsons' daughter, Mary, became headmistress of Ardenne High School, a position she held until retirement. When Mary began her work, there were only twenty-six students. Today there are over one thousand enrolled.

The One Hundredth Anniversary of Freedom from Slavery was celebrated in Jamaica in 1938. Naturally, there was great rejoicing throughout the island. Christian people became more enthusiastic in spreading the good news of freedom from sin. The Church of God continued to grow rapidly. By 1929 there were fifty congregations; by 1932, sixty-six; and by 1942, eighty-six. Unfortunately, there were only eighteen ordained ministers, plus local leaders. Jamaica has suffered through the years and even to the present time with an insufficient number of full-time trained pastors. In 1930 the ownership of all church properties belonging to the Church of

God in Jamaica was transferred to the churches under the General Assembly. Since Jamaica is as close as it is to America, quite a few leaders from the church in America visited the work to encourage the saints. These included E. E. and Lucena Byrum, C. E. Brown, and E. A. and Pearl Reardon, as well as Esther Boyer and Hester Greer. Of interest to me was that Edith Young was the first Church of God missionary to return to America for furlough by airplane. That required twelve hours from Kingston, Jamaica, to Miami, a distance of six hundred miles! By 1944 the church in Jamaica welcomed another missionary couple, Leslie and Nina Ratzlaff.

Over on the Cayman Islands, about two hundred miles west of Jamaica, several groups of believers were established through frequent visits by missionaries from Jamaica: the Olsons, the Steimlas, and Edith Young. A strong congregation in George Town, Grand Cayman, came into being, as well as a small congregation on the very small island of Cayman Brac. The small church building on Cayman Brac was destroyed by a hurricane and tidal wave in 1932, and then was rebuilt and destroyed again by hurricane in 1945. All the islands in the Caribbean are subject to the fury of storms that bring property damage and destruction. It is a way of life in the tropics, but when disaster strikes, the people need assistance immediately for rehabilitation. Harold Andrews was the first resident missionary under whose ministry two more congregations were started in Grand Cayman. Leslie and Nina Ratzlaff were sent to Grand Cayman in 1941 to Triple C School, and American teachers Caroline Glassman and Wilma Ryder were enlisted. Both of these teachers later married men from Grand Cayman and remained for many years on the island teaching in Triple C School and serving the church faithfully.

Far to the southeast in the Caribbean and out into the Atlantic the movement was gaining ground on the island of Barbados. By the mid-1930s, eighteen congregations had been established through the efforts of the missionaries serving during these two decades. It must always be remembered, however, that the real work of soul winning and establishing the work is done through highly motivated and consecrated national ministers and workers. So it was in Barbados. But like Jamaica, there was always a derth of full-time pastors. In 1928 Byron Chew married Zella, the Brookovers' daughter, and together with the Brookovers they served in both Barbados and Trinidad. During the early years of the church on both of these islands, apparently no major effort was made by the missionaries to develop in the people a sense of responsibility for the work there. Offerings even in the larger congregations consisted of only a few British pennies. The churches did not support the pastors, and so they had to work in secular jobs to live; they did not have to keep the church buildings in repair, for the mission did that. As a result of the total situation, a true understanding of evangelism and outreach was lost.

W. L. Brookover resigned and returned to America in 1937, and the Chews left in 1941. That left no missionaries in Barbados or Trinidad. That is when Ruthe and I were sent to the southern Caribbean as relief missionaries because we could not return to Lebanon due to the war. During the next three years as we served Barbados and Trinidad, the emphasis was initiated to bring the church to a position of self-understanding, leading ultimately to a position of self-reliance.

Growth in Trinidad was not as rapid as in Barbados, at least numerically. The situation was different. In Barbados, the population was predominantly West Indian, originally African. But in Trinidad, there was a mixed population of West Indians, Chinese, and East Indians who were originally from India. Only a relatively small work was ever developed by the movement among the East Indians. But a strong congregation came into being in the second largest city, San Fernando. Also, three congregations started on the island of Tobago, which is a part of Trinidad. In 1920 the Board made available a car for Thaddeus and Katrina Neff to use in their ministry. Annual Church of God camp meetings were initiated. All-day meetings each quarter were conducted to bring the saints together for inspiration and teaching. Baptismal services were always held during the quarterly meetings. Good, adequate church buildings were erected, and most of the ten congregations were pastored by full-time ministers. These were capable leaders, including one woman, and they should have been encouraged and instructed early on how to bring into being an indigenous church. The potential had been there for years. But remember, this is in retrospect. In those early years in the southern Caribbean, our missionaries seemed unaware of the necessity for missions to become churches so that the church could be the church without indefinite support from missions.

British Guiana (now known as Guyana) is a small country on the northeast coast of South America. It is the only English-speaking country in that continent, and its people are mainly West Indian and East Indian.

For these reasons British Guiana has always been closely associated with the West Indian islands. Therefore, in our missionary outreach the developments in Trinidad, Barbados, and British Guiana were considered as a whole. Missionaries from the two islands made regular evangelistic journeys to British Guiana. Soon several other congregations emerged, and when Adam W. Miller and Charles E. Brown visited there in 1935, there were three other ministers besides George Jeffrey. The John Street congregation in Georgetown became the "mother church." Jeffrey remained the dominant personality, with financial assistance received from America. He was known in the community for his welfare program on Bellaire Street, which was a "shelter for a motley collection of men, women and children who had fallen upon evil days."

The West Indian people many times moved about from island to island. Many of them made their way to New York City for temporary employment, and some went to Panama to help build the canal. This movement of people assisted in spreading the reformation movement. Significantly, Hannibal and Rose Boddie, who were originally from the island of St. Kitts, were converted in Elder Green's church in New York City. In 1932 they returned to St. Kitts and conducted open-air meetings in Basseterre and throughout the island. Two years later, Elizabeth Brewster, born in Barbados, arrived from New York City to join in the work. She purchased property and willed it to the church in Basseterre, and that is where the "mother church" in St. Kitts is located. Following her death, Wilhelmina Fraser came, held revival services, and became pastor of the Basseterre congregation. On the nearby island of Antigua, Wilfred and Christena Henry began services in the town of St. John's. They also had been converted under Elder Green's ministry in New York City. Francis and Mabel Lindo went from St. Kitts to the island of Curaçao of the Netherlands West Indies just off the coast of western Venezuela so that Francis could work with the Shell Oil Company. Mabel had come up under the tutelage of Elizabeth Brewster in St. Kitts, who encouraged her to start a work of God in Curaçao. She eventually did just that.

Central and South America

The reformation movement came to Panama primarily because West Indians arrived from several of the islands to seek employment as the Panama

Canal was being constructed. Some of these were Church of God people. They discovered each other and started meetings in their homes. There were the visits by George Olson from Jamaica and George Coplin from Barbados. But it was not until the mid-thirties when A. E. and Rebecca Rather became resident missionaries in Panama that the work took shape. Remember these were English-speaking West Indians developing a work in Spanish-speaking communities. And so the congregations remained English-speaking for the first and second generations of the group in Panama. It has required many years of effort to assist these good people in becoming a part of the country in which they are now permanently residing by using the Spanish language in their services. It reminds me of some of our German and Greek congregations in America taking considerable time to become English-speaking in their meetings. The transition in Panama only now has about been accomplished.

The McHughs from the Church of God in Jamaica moved to Costa Rica and took the gospel with them. Others joined them to work in the United Fruit Company. A. E. Rather, visiting them from Panama in the mid-thirties, found the saints worshiping in the McHughs' home at Cimarrones. A church building was soon erected, and the work continued among the English-speaking West Indians who lived on the plain near Puerto Limón on the east coast.

Cuba will be mentioned here because it is Latin oriented and not related to the English-speaking West Indies. Earlier in this chapter, I mentioned that E. Faith Stewart went to Cuba as an independent missionary because the Board had voted against her return as a missionary to India. She went to the home of an English-speaking Jamaican woman who was from the Church of God in Jamaica. Meetings were conducted in the English language in this woman's home. However, very wisely and deliberately the meetings were soon conducted in Spanish. Stewart began to learn Spanish, and when visitors came from America, their messages were translated from English into Spanish. The next year Ray Jackson came from America for a five-week evangelistic campaign. Many people were converted. A larger place for meetings was needed and was subsequently rented. Hester Greer arrived the next year, 1932, and remained as a missionary for many years. Greer worked in the city of Havana itself, and Stewart labored in the suburbs. A few years later, the movement reached the adjacent island of the Isle of Pines. Unfortunately, Stewart could not get along with Greer. Also,

Stewart refused to have the work in which she was involved placed under the supervision of the Missionary Board. Greer took the opposite position relative to the work she was developing. Stewart's work gradually separated itself and remained independent, while other missionaries arrived to work with Greer under the Missionary Board. Joseph and Grace Rodriguez and Manasseh and Gretchen Stephenson were among those. During the war years, the church was registered with the government under the Missionary Board and several permanent congregations were established.

To escape the results of the 1917 Communist take-over in Russia, Adolf Weidman and twenty-two families went first to Germany and then on to Brazil in 1923. This colony of German Church of God refugees settled in Santa Catarina. They formed a congregation and kept in touch with the German work in America centered in York, Nebraska. More German Christians, led by Edward Wagner, fled Poland and settled in Rio das Antas in Brazil. Others, such as the Bosserts, took up residence in the state of São Paulo, while the Koenig family found a home in the city of Curitiba.

The first Church of God camp meeting in Brazil was held by the German believers at Nova Esperanza in 1929. By 1931 the Church of God in Brazil became officially registered. David Meier, a German American, and his family felt called to missionary service among the German immigrants in Brazil and arrived there in 1935. For some time he was forced to teach school to provide food for his family. Meier was the first evangelist to go to Argentina, holding meetings in Alem in Misiones Province. His work was also among German immigrants. Solomon Weissburger, his son Heinrich, and their families fled Germany as Hitler began to persecute the Jews. They settled in Rio das Antas in Brazil. During World War II, all these colonies of German Church of God Christians had to remain quiet. For a time the German language was forbidden in Brazil, and on occasion some people endured imprisonment just because they were Germans.

In Argentina, Adolf Weidman became the strong leader at Alem. Under capable leadership, the work among these German-speaking people grew slowly but surely. And they were very German, reflecting their culture in almost every aspect of their lives. There were only rare attempts to do any evangelizing among the Portuguese-speaking people in Brazil or the Spanish-speaking people in Argentina.

More Happenings in Europe

Following World War I, the Church of God regained its strength and carried on quite an evangelistic outreach. In 1922 the *Evangeliums Posaune* (German *Gospel Trumpet)* was published in Germany instead of in America. A well-established work among the German-speaking people in Russia was one result of their labors. The Malzons and the Doeberts went into the Ukraine and the Caucasus again and again, revisiting and holding evangelistic meetings. When communization was enforced under Stalin, attacks on the church were increased. Also, contacts diminished between the brothers and sisters in Germany and those in Russia. Finally, when Hitler's armies invaded Russia in 1941, the German-speaking people in Russia were sent to Siberia. Earlier, a real spiritual awakening broke out among the German-speaking people in Poland. But inflation in Germany, which reached its climax in 1923, hindered the awakening a great deal. It has been said that it required a wheelbarrow full of German marks to buy a loaf of bread. A new missionary home was built in Kassel, and a Bible school was started for training ministers. But the economic crisis prevented growth that the church would have otherwise enjoyed. It should be observed here that this expansion of the reformation movement into Poland, Russia, Brazil, and Argentina was really a missionary-inspired outreach of the Church of God in Germany, even though it was primarily a work among people of German descent. Eventually, the church in Germany formed its own missionary board, known as Missionswerk. In the early twenties some penetration took place into Hungary. The first congregation was located at Tiszaszederkeny, and others were established at Kondoros, Gabrovo, Tschernitschevo, and Budapest. In 1938, on their way from Lebanon to America for furlough, my father and mother visited the churches in Hungary and Germany, encouraging the congregations as war clouds were gathering. They were amazed at the hold Hitler had on the minds and activities of the Christians of the movement.

The *British Gospel Trumpet* started under the editorship of Adam Allan in 1921 in Ireland, and a Bible training school enjoyed a brief existence in the mid-1920s under the guidance of F. C. Blore. In 1926 a young minister named John Larmour became pastor of the Belfast congregation, where he remained for a decade before moving to England. In Denmark,

J. P. N. Ikast and his family arrived from America in 1923. During the thirteen years Ikast labored there, major difficulties that killed the spirit of revival and brought division appeared among the churches. Pentecostalism had a devastating effect upon the Church of God, in spite of all the noble efforts of the Ikasts and Danish church leaders to reverse the trend. In 1927 Lars and Ellen Olsen were sent to Denmark to assist the Ikasts. Olsen edited the *Evangeli Basun,* the equivalent of the *Gospel Trumpet* in Danish. Somewhat discouraged with the church's situation in Denmark, the Ikasts left in 1936 and the Olsens in 1940, being evacuated through Italy during World War II.

J. Jeeninga began meetings in Waubach, Holland, in a remodeled barn in 1930. During the following ten years, small groups of believers were established in Treebeck and Ymuidan. Overall, the work of the Church of God in Europe appeared in a holding position, except for that in Germany. The direct effects of the oncoming war would be devastating, even though individual Christians remained true to their Lord and faithful to the teaching of the movement in spite of great suffering.

Growth in the Eastern Mediterranean

In Egypt, right after World War I, a woman by the name of Zaroohi Tabakian followed Ouzounian in the leadership of the large group of saints among the Armenians in Alexandria. During a five-year period following the war, three Egyptians—Hanna Arsanious, Habib Yousef, and Abdul Talut Michail—cared for a growing work among the Egyptians as it spread from Cairo to other cities. I mention these names because they labored faithfully and to the best of their abilities without the presence of any missionary from America. They profited from the visit of F. G. Smith and E. A. Reardon in 1920 and from the several weeks spent in Egypt by H. M. and Minnie Riggle in 1921 on their way to Syria. The first issues of the *Buk-el-Ingeel,* the Arabic *Gospel Trumpet,* came out in 1921. Strong requests for missionaries continued, but it was not until 1923 that Thaddeus and Katrina Neff landed in Port Said and went on to Alexandria, where they established headquarters for the mission in Egypt. Their arrival was a part of the new outreach following the war to assist in the eastern Mediterranean. The Neffs and their two children; John and Pearl Crose and their sons; Nellie Laughlin, returning to Syria following a furlough; Adele Jureidini,

a Lebanese minister who had been with Nellie Laughlin in America; and
Emil Hollander, a young missionary to Syria, were all on the same boat
from New York to Port Said. During the next ten years, the Church of God
in Egypt grew rapidly. Places of worship were erected in cities and towns
where congregations were established. Pastors to lead those congregations
were found from other groups. Armenian congregations were started in
Cairo as well as Alexandria. John Tabakian emerged as the Armenian leader
in Alexandria, and K. T. Sarian directed the work in Cairo. Work among
the Greeks in Cairo began, and Nicholas and Rose Zazanis arrived in 1928.
They developed a very large Greek congregation in Cairo and one of lesser
size in Alexandria. My father was invited by Neff every year to spend a
month in evangelistic meetings up and down the Nile. An Arabic printing
press was purchased, and one of the Egyptian brethren, Salib Farag, took
charge of publishing the *Buk-el-Ingeel* in 1924 as well as printing other
pieces of Christian literature, including a Church of God Arabic hymnal,
word edition only. All this Arabic literature was used not only in Egypt but
in Syria and Lebanon also. Nellie Laughlin was transferred from Lebanon
to Egypt in 1929 where she assisted until her retirement in 1931. The William A. Fleenor family was transferred from Lebanon to Egypt in 1932.
The following year the George Dallas and the William Conkis families arrived from America to assist in the work among the Greeks. Due to serious
illness, the Fleenor family returned to America in 1934. Thaddeus Neff
also began to have health problems. Nellie Laughlin was asked to return to
Egypt in 1937 and devoted the remaining five years of her life to a teaching
ministry in Assiut.

In Syria immediately following World War I, Nellie Laughlin made
a very wise decision. She felt impressed that for the future welfare of the
ministry of the Church of God in that country the work should be moved
from the small village of Schweifat to the city of Beirut. F. G. Smith and
E. A. Reardon visited the saints the next year and added their blessings
to the move to the city. Then in 1921 H. M. and Minnie Riggle arrived
from America in an effort to strengthen the work already begun. Riggle
traveled far and wide, calling people to repentance and winning quite a
few people to Christ. They remained in Syria while Nellie Laughlin took a
well-deserved furlough, having spent those difficult years of World War I in
Schweifat. H. M. Riggle completed his assignment by mid-1923, returning to America and writing of his experiences in a book entitled *Pioneer*

Evangelism. The Crose family and the Riggle family met in Anderson as the Croses were preparing to leave for Syria.

As an eleven-year-old boy I will never forget the journey by train across America. We stopped in several cities to visit churches on behalf of missions and spent some time in Anderson in the home of Russell Byrum. From there we moved on to New York, where the group was coming together at the Missionary Home. I also remember the boat trip from New York to Port Said. We traveled in the stern of the *S. S. City of Lahore,* where all the second-class passengers were missionaries going out after the war, many of them having had experienced missionary service before. These missionaries held nightly meetings on the boat, sharing their experiences in other lands. At Port Said the Neffs left the boat with Sister Neff critically ill. On the boat trip up the Palestinian coast to Beirut, we made a stop offshore at Joppa, where I believed I could see the house of Simon the tanner by the sea, and finally we were welcomed by the saints as we arrived early the next morning in the harbor of Beirut.

With an enlarged missionary staff, the influence of the Church of God in Syria increased and growth took place. Emil Hollander lasted as a missionary only one year. He stayed in our home, and I shared a room with him where we had a lot of fun together. I always thought it was not quite fair to have taken a young man just out of Anderson Bible Training School, knowing nothing except the sidewalks of New York City, where he grew up, and place him in situations where he would have to rough it, such as traveling by horse or donkey for hours while engaging in village evangelism. Beirut itself was nothing more than a broken-down Turkish port following the war, so life was still difficult even in the city. In those days, there was no form of orientation for new missionaries, and I had the idea that Emil really didn't know what he was getting into. He had been oversold on missionary service without proper preparation. In the end, he became frustrated both emotionally and spiritually and left the field. But Emil remained my friend, and I always saw him as I would come and go through New York City. The Missionary Board learned its lessons on recruitment the hard way.

In Beirut, funds were received from America to erect an excellent church building in the Ashrafieh District, using Armenian refugee labor. This also provided facilities for a Church of God elementary school. A congregation was maintained in the city of Tripoli, and farther north in Syria, village work was maintained by Ibrahim Maloof. William A. Fleenor and his family were sent to Syria in 1930 to relieve my parents, who returned to America for furlough after seven years on the field—the regular term at that time. I was appointed as a missionary to Syria in 1933, returning briefly to America during the summer of 1934 to marry Ruthe Hamon, who had been accepted by the Missionary Board. During the twenties and thirties, the work of the church grew to a point and then seemed to level off for a couple of decades. In retrospect, it appears the believers never really caught on to what their responsibility was as the church and in doing what the church under God should be doing. The work in Syria became too dependent upon the missionaries and the church in America, which supported the work of the mission. Several attempts were made to indigenize the work, but failure resulted time after time.

Constantine Nichols was a young Greek converted in 1915 in Cairo, Egypt, through the efforts of G. K. Ouzounian. He traveled to Chicago and began a work among the Greeks. While Nicholas Zazanis was attending Anderson Bible Training School he began editing the Greek *Gospel Trumpet*. At the same time, Greek brethren from Chicago visited the Peloponnesus in Greece, making contacts and some converts. In 1932 Zazanis, who was a missionary in Egypt by then, made a trip to Greece to contact the brethren there. And in 1936, the publishing of the Greek *Gospel Trumpet* was transferred to Athens under the direction of Athanasius Chionos. However, no organized work of the Church of God in Greece was to begin until after World War II.

And Now to East Africa

H. C. and Gertrude Kramer had been in Kenya for several years as American Quaker missionaries working with the South African Compounds and Interior Mission and were due a furlough. By then A. W. Baker in South Africa felt he could no longer sponsor and support his mission in Kenya, and so he asked the Kramers to seek out a church in America that would be willing to assume responsibility for the mission in Kenya. Baker said that mission should (1) not stress "the speaking in tongues"; (2) teach the Bible as the Word of God; and (3) teach the unity of God's people.

The Kramers had been receiving Gospel Trumpet literature irregularly for several years, and they had come to appreciate its teachings. So during their furlough in the spring of 1921, while visiting their sponsoring family in Pomona. California, they became acquainted with Abram and William Bixler, two brothers in the Church of God congregation there. Through the Bixlers' influence and that of the congregation, the Kramers embraced the truth. Upon hearing of the offer being made by A. W. Baker, William Bixler felt strongly that the Kramers should present the opportunity in Kenya to the Missionary Board. Correspondence with the Board took place, and the congregation in Pomona paid the train fare for the Kramers to be in Anderson for the camp meeting and the meeting of the Missionary Board. Baker's offer was presented to the Board, including what it would cost. The price was fifteen hundred dollars plus the cost of Mabel Baker's residence and a residence for another missionary family. Board members were obviously interested in this opportunity to enter East Africa. But before a final decision could be made, some investigation was necessary. Since Sam Joiner and his wife had expressed an earlier interest in Africa, the Board sent them to Kenya. Together with W. J. Bailey, they looked into the condition of the mission at Kima and sent back a favorable report to the Board. Transfer of the mission was negotiated and completed. In the end, Baker turned over everything without cost to the Missionary Board. He was well pleased with the attitude of the Board and the beliefs of the Church of God. During the 1922 meeting of the Board, Henry and Gertrude Kramer were appointed as missionaries of the Church of God, as were the Joiners. Also, Mabel Baker was accepted as a Church of God missionary. Ruth Fisher was appointed as a missionary to Kenya to teach the missionaries' children, and she went to Kenya with the Kramers.

Rapid growth took place. To the north, in the Butsotso tribal area, a mission was started at Ingotse by the Joiners before they were forced to return to the United States due to her health failure. In Bunyore, they had led a boy, Jairo Asila, to the Lord and he became one of the leaders of the church. In 1921 James Murray arrived in Kenya as a Salvation Army missionary, but he soon joined the Church of God mission. The William J. Bailey family was accepted by the Board in 1924 and stationed at Ingotse, where they labored as agricultural missionaries for five years. Kramer laid the foundation for the large "cathedral" at Kima. It was known as BKKB because the churches in Bunyore, Kisa, Kakamega, and Butsotso donated money for it. The building was completed later under the guidance of J. S. Ludwig. Many people were being converted and baptized. Elders were being appointed. Children needed education, and so Mabel Baker initiated "bush schools" or village schools, along with Sunday schools in each location. A school for children was started at Kima. In 1925 James Murray married Ruth Fisher, and they labored at Kima before being transferred to Ingotse when the boys' school that had been started at Kima in 1923 was transferred there. They taught in the school and assisted in village evangelism. African evangelists were successfully active and many village churches were started.

John and Twyla Ludwig were sent as missionaries to Kenya in 1927. They threw themselves into the work with tremendous energy. Soon Twyla started a girls' school at Kima, for she carried a burden for the women and girls of Kenya. She taught them how to fight prevalent diseases and to take care of their bodies. In 1929 the Ludwigs developed an Elders Council, which was composed of twelve elders. That same year the Kramers left for America, not to return to Kenya. They left two of their children buried in the cemetery at Kima. Henry Kramer had helped to build many village church buildings, and Gertrude had spent much time training "bush school" teachers and translating the New Testament along with Mabel Baker. A year later A. W. Baker from South Africa visited Kenya and was delighted with what he found developing at the mission he had helped to start and had turned over to the Church of God.

A young African, Musa Eshipiri, was converted in the Kisa tribal area and became an effective evangelist. He donated part of his land at Mwihila in 1934 for the beginning of a mission station. Homer and Vivian Bailey worked there first, followed by Jewell Hall, who started a clinic in 1939. This was a project taken on by the National Woman's Home and Foreign Missionary Society. In 1935 a maternity hospital was started at Kima. Missionary Freda Strenger was the nurse in charge, and a year later Lima Lehmer arrived to help in the nursing program. Soon afterward Rita Paulo became the first qualified African nurse.

Life was not easy for missionaries during that period of time because disease was prevalent—especially malignant malaria (blackwater fever) and typhoid. In 1936 Ruth Murray died from a severe attack of typhoid fever. James Murray continued his services at Ingotse for four more years until he died from blackwater fever. Their graves at Kima, along with those of their three children who died in infancy, bear witness to their sacrificial service to the Africans. Soon a beautiful church building was erected at Ingotse and called the Murray Memorial Church. Following the Murrays, Homer and Vivian Bailey assumed responsibility for the work among the Butsotso people at Ingotse.

The tempo of the work picked up during the last few years of the thirties. On December 20, 1936, a never-to-be-forgotten day by the church in Kenya, the missionaries and African church leaders gathered at Kima and opened the first case of New Testaments printed in Olunyore by the American Bible Society. That was the fruit of persistent and dedicated labor over a number of years by Mabel Baker, Gertrude Kramer, and several faithful African Christians. Printing of other literature became necessary, and as early as the mid-twenties a press was installed at Kima, where it remained until 1959. Highly dedicated pastors and school teachers were on fire for God. African Christians were indeed turning their immediate world around them upside down. Villages were established with a Christian atmosphere. Converts were learning to live what they were being taught.

Looking East into India

Immediately following World War I, the Floyd Heinly family was sent to India, becoming the first American missionaries of the Church of God to take up long-term residence in Calcutta,[1] where the headquarters of the mission was established. Mae Isenhart sailed with them but returned to America after three years due to health problems. Soon Mamie Wallace was sent to be the private secretary for Heinly. The Taskers arrived from furlough and worked in Calcutta. Josephine McCrie returned from furlough and brought with her Eva Goodwin, the first missionary to be sent out by the Church of God in England. Perhaps that was the first demonstration of partnership in mission. Both of these missionaries assisted the Taskers in Calcutta. When Faith Stewart returned from furlough in 1922, she brought with her two new missionaries, Mona Moors and Burd Barwick. When a home for boys was started the next year in Cuttack, Mona was put in charge. Mosir Moses and Floyd Heinly made a trip into Sikkim, a small country north of India, to see whether there were any possibilities of opening a work. That was not to be. In Calcutta, A. D. Khan organized a mission to students a short time before his death, which occurred on October 8, 1922. He died from a severe fever, probably influenza, when only forty-four years old.

That was a tremendous loss in leadership for the church in India. By all counts, Khan was considered by missionaries and Indian Christians alike as chief among them. What D. S. Warner was to the reformation movement in America, A. D. Khan was to the Church of God in India. Both were dynamic leaders, evangelists, writers, publishers, and true pioneers. Both died at an early age but lived long enough to see the work well on its way. Shortly before his death, Khan became greatly concerned about establishing a work in the general area of East Bengal, from which he had originally come. In consultation with the English Baptist Mission, it was arranged that the Church of God would evangelize the Kurigram Subdivision of Rangpur District, an area where there was no mission at work among the predominantly Muslim population. These, of course, were Bengali-speaking people, the same as in West Bengal State, in which Calcutta is located. The work was first started in Kurigram but soon centered in Lalmanirhat, an important railroad junction. It was decided that Floyd Heinly should be in charge, although his family did not move there until 1923. In the meantime, a financial campaign was launched in America on Christmas Day, 1921, to raise funds to build "A Station in a Day," and over ten thousand dollars was made available immediately. A church building was erected and soon after a missionary residence, both of which remain in use today. New ways were initiated for communicating the gospel to Muslims and some Hindus in that area. Homes and secular institutions were visited. Books were loaned and tracts distributed. Meetings were conducted and inquirers instructed. Workers preached in the bazaars and used a stereoptican lantern to show pictures wherever a crowd at night would give permission. Soon a primary school was started at the mission in Lalmanirhat. Out in the villages, Bible instruction was given along with moral lessons. There was preaching in the bazaars and visiting in the homes. There were meetings with the women and children and showings of lantern slides at night. In these ways the gospel was brought to bear upon the Muslims in a nonoffensive way.

Farther south in Cuttack, Orissa, seven acres of land was purchased at the edge of the city, and a new, adequate facility was built for The Shelter. This was the first of several buildings erected on the compound. At that time, there were 110 girls in The Shelter, each being educated through the seventh grade. Soon after Khan died, some adjustments took place among the missionaries. There remained considerable dissatisfaction because the

Indian leadership in the church thought they should make the decisions in the work and that missionaries were in India to assist the Indian church, whereas the missionaries felt they had been appointed by the Missionary Board to give leadership to the church and its Indian workers. There was also some difference of opinion between the Missionary Board and missionaries about methods to be used in the work. As a result, Faith Stewart and Burd Barwick left the field. Mona Moors took charge of The Shelter along with the Mundul sisters, Sonat and Nolini. E. L. and Martha Bleiler spent a term in Cuttack trying to make a success of the boys home, but that project died out. Josephine McCrie, who had been in India since 1904, resigned, as did G. P. and Minnie Tasker. This discontinued the work of the mission in Calcutta. Mosir Moses, the Indian leader and a convert from Islam, took charge of the congregation in that city, doing his best to carry on the work alone. And Andrew Shiffler, after twenty-five years of service primarily in literature work in northeast India, left for America at seventy-four years of age.

During this period of time, the Church of God in South India was gaining ground under the leadership of P. J. Philip and J. M. Spadigum. Following Khan's death, Field Secretary Floyd Heinly was in charge, and thereafter the work in South India was looked upon as a mission that was dependent upon the Missionary Board for support and direction. The congregations there were not considered self-reliant churches. P. J. Philip was ultimately appointed as a field secretary for the work in South India—another major blunder the Board made in its administration. Such an action perpetuated a mission complex. Far to the north in the state of Assam, today known as Meghalaya, the movement was growing rapidly among the Khasi tribal peoples under the leadership of Evalyn and J. J. M. Nichols-Roy. By 1926 it was reported there were over two thousand adults in the movement. Even though Nichols-Roy could not agree with many of the policies of the Missionary Board as related to the Church of God in India, he carried on in a self-reliant manner. Financially it was not easy, but the people were taught how to give. Nichols-Roy developed a fruit business of his own, while at the same time becoming a leader in the state government. Nichols-Roy was also a theologian in his own right, and he interpreted the New Testament from his own cultural perspective. Moore Wellson Laloo, a young Khasi man, was converted in 1933 and was destined to assume leadership of the work twenty-six years later. Unfortunately, "some strange teachings" were introduced to the work by Evalyn Nichols-Roy after she had been on furlough and had come into contact with the Foursquare Gospel, a Pentecostal movement in Southern California. This ultimately caused a split in the work in Assam in 1941 when Aquilla Seige led a breakaway of twenty-four congregations. They formed their own assembly and erected their own central church building at Mawkhar in Shillong. Both groups claim loyalty to the reformation movement of the Church of God, but the division has not been healed even to this day. Ellen High was appointed as a missionary to Cuttack in 1937, one of the very few new missionaries to go out during this period. With World War II already under way, Mona Moors returned to India following furlough in 1940. That same year the Heinlys left India, and my father and mother, John and Pearl Crose, were asked to go to India, as they were forced to evacuate Lebanon because of the war. They traveled constantly, visiting the churches and missionaries and endeavoring to create better relationships all around. The Taskers had returned to Bangalore, India, as independent missionaries, and Minnie Tasker died there in 1941. Soon thereafter George Tasker married Josephine McCrie, a longtime friend.

On the Rim of East Asia

When F. G. Smith and E. A. Reardon made their round-the-world trip in 1919, their first stop was in Japan. They sent an urgent message to the Missionary Board that someone must be sent immediately to relieve the Alexander family, who had been in Japan for more than ten years without a furlough. My parents, who were supposed to be in preparation for going to Syria, were approached, and they accepted the challenge. The events of that February sailing between San Francisco and Yokohama that stood out in my mind as a seven-year-old boy were the ice cream and fresh pineapple in Hawaii and the typhoon we encountered, during which I almost got swept overboard. The Alexanders soon left for America, having served the Japanese people faithfully. The center of the work moved from Musashi Sakai to the large two-floor Mission Home in the Hongo District of Tokyo. A. U. Yajima was pastoring the congregation that met in a large room on the second floor. He and his family of several children and grandmother lived in a wing of the first floor. Zuda Chambers, the single woman missionary, and Miss Shojima, the Bible woman assisting "Aunt Zuda," lived in a part of the first and second floors, while our family lived mostly on the second floor. The kitchen and Japanese bath were on the first floor. We all lived together, yet separate, with all things in common.

With all the potential present for developing a good work in Tokyo, the effects of overwork were soon noticed. My father spent many hours each day in language study, attending a language school in downtown Tokyo. In addition, he preached, conducted classes for university students, and visited among the people. In late 1920, a cable was received by the Missionary Board that declared, "Chambers and Crose overworked and underfed." After a year and half, my father suffered a complete nervous breakdown and was put on a boat where he was expected to die before reaching San Francisco. Axchie Bolitho was sent to Japan in 1921 to help Zuda Chambers, and Adam and Grace Miller went in 1922. Zuda Chambers returned to America later that year, having completed five years of service. During the early and mid-twenties the church grew and expanded. The Mission Home was only one mile from the Imperial University and many students were reached through English classes, some being converted to the Christian faith. Evangelism produced results, and there was effort put forth to develop church leadership. This wave of advance was quite unique in a predominantly Buddhist country, but many young people were searching for something other than the traditional religions in Japan. This provided opportunity to present the good news of salvation through Jesus Christ. Both the Millers and Axchie Bolitho began to feel the strain of heavy responsibilities by late 1925, and so in mid-1926 Bolitho returned to America, followed by Adam and Grace Miller in early 1927. There may have been some financial reasons why they could not be replaced, but it appeared to both the missionaries and the Missionary Board that the Church of God in Japan could be termed indigenous, no longer needing resident missionaries, as mentioned earlier in this chapter.

There were four congregations in the greater Tokyo area—Hongo, Mishigahara, Miyanaka, and Nerima—each having a Japanese pastor. Consequently, no more missionaries from America were sent to Japan until after World War II. At first there was some talk by the Japanese leadership about closing down the work, but through the faithfulness of A. U. Yajima, Choko Shimizu, and Shigetoshi Taniguchi, the situation started on the upward swing by 1930. Some financial assistance continued to be sent on a monthly basis by the Missionary Board. The Japan Bible Institute was opened, receiving official recognition from the Department of Education, and the first General Convention of the Church of God was held in 1931. When the people of China suffered from a great flood, the Church of God in Japan raised ¥6,111, which was a lot of money in those days, to send to the Hunnexes in Shanghai to help relieve those who were suffering. By 1932 there were ten meeting places, and the churches were beginning to use kindergartens as a means of reaching people with the gospel. That same year A. U. Yajima, a highly respected leader in all Christian circles in Japan, died. In the mid-thirties, contacts were made with the brethren in Korea. But late in that decade, the church in Japan began to face other difficulties as war against China developed in Manchuria. There was strong pressure from the Japanese government that only one Christian church be officially recognized. Danippon Kirisuto Kyodon, the United Church in Japan, generally known as Kyodon, came into being. There was considerable uncertainty in the Church of God as to whether they should join Kyodon. All through the thirties, correspondence was maintained with the Missionary Board. But that communication abruptly ended with Pearl Harbor, which put America at war with Japan. Nothing was heard from Japan until after that country's unconditional surrender in 1945.

Christian witness in China has traditionally been difficult, even though modern Protestant missions have poured millions of dollars and hundreds of missionaries into that country. Shortly after World War I, it was estimated that after 110 years of Christian witness, there were only a total of ten converts for each missionary engaged over that period of time. It was also estimated that it cost missions 558 gold dollars to convert one Chinese. But the Church of God was in China to stay, whatever happened to missionaries. Early in the twenties William and Gloria Hunnex left China permanently. Mission headquarters were moved from Chinkiang to Nanking, but Pastor T. C. Dong and his family remained in Chinkiang to shepherd the group of believers. Isaac Doone, a prosperous businessman in Hong Kong today, is a son of that family and remains loyal to the Church of God. A missionary home was started in Shanghai, with Pastor Lee giving Chinese leadership. Karl and Hazel Kreutz sailed as missionaries to China in 1923 and worked in Yangchow, fifteen miles from Chinkiang, where Daisy Maiden and Belle Watson were stationed. Strong emphasis was being placed upon self-support. This was fortunate because there were only a few times when missionaries were able to serve in China during the years ahead.

Civil war caused by a Communist-Nationalist takeover in 1927 made it necessary for all our missionaries to flee to the foreign concession in Shanghai: the Kreutzes from Yangchow, Maiden and Watson from Chinkiang, and Charles and Annabel Hunnex from Nanking. Belle Watson sailed for America, but the Hunnexes remained for a while in Shanghai. Daisy Maiden sailed home by way of India, Egypt, and Syria. She remained in Syria (now Lebanon) about a year, assisting in the Lord's work where she was greatly needed. That is where I as a youth in high school first knew Daisy. The Kreutzes went to the Philippines, where they lived for many years. A second evacuation occurred in 1937 when China was invaded by the Japanese military. Daisy Maiden was forced to leave again. The Hunnexes, who were on their way to China at that time, stopped off in the Philippines for nine months until they could get back into Nanking. Unfortunately for them, they remained in China too long and were held by the Japanese in an internment camp in Shanghai for two and a half years. The Kreutzes were caught by the Japanese in the Philippines during World War II and were held as prisoners in the Santo Tomas Internment Camp in Manila. But in spite of all this uncertainty of missionary presence, the ravages of civil war, and the presence of Japanese military forces, the Church of God continued to exist as a Christian entity, but with little chance for growth.

As mentioned earlier, the reformation movement spread to Korea. Some Korean ministers representing eleven congregations visited one of our churches in Tokyo. They became seriously interested in the Church of God and severed their relations with the Church of the Nazarene. At the request of K. Y. Kim, Adam W. Miller and A. F. Gray visited this group of people in Pyengyang during their tour of East Asia in 1937. That city is in what is now known as North Korea and was at that time the main seat of Christianity in Korea as a whole. These congregations were mostly self-supporting, and they carried on under their own leadership, encouraged through correspondence with the Missionary Board. It was not until the mid-fifties that Church of God American missionaries were sent to South Korea.

In the early thirties, a man in the Philippines by the name of Celestino Matitas contacted the Church of God in Montesano, Washington. He embraced the Truth and returned to his home at Laoag on northern Luzon Island and began a congregation. It was on the beaches of Laoag that the Japanese first landed in their attack on the Philippines during World War II.

Mattias died, but his son Fernando took over and tried for a while to enlarge the work. A small chapel was partially built in 1938. Encouragement was given by the Hunnexes and the Kreutzes, along with Adam Miller and A. F. Gray during their brief visit. But that little work all but died out during a period of twenty years, after which it sprang to life again.

"Man Is Destined to Die Once" (Heb 9:27 NIV)

By the close of this twenty-five-year period of time, several more of the reformation movement's first-generation missionaries had died. They included the following:

Mae Isenhart	192?	India
Zuda Chambers	1933	Japan
Opal Brookover	1934	Trinidad
Nels Renbeck	1934	Denmark
William Hopwood Family	1936	England
Ruth Murray	1936	Kenya
James Murray	1940	Kenya
Minnie Tasker	1941	India
Nellie S. Laughlin	1942	Egypt

We should also note the deaths of several national church leaders: A. D. Khan and Mosir Moses in India and A. U. Yajima in Japan. These, along with those mentioned earlier and even perhaps some I have overlooked, should be credited for having laid, for the most part, a good foundation in other lands for the Church of God reformation movement. I have stood several times before the tombstones of the Maidens, Opal Brookover, the Murrays, Laughlin, and Yajima and have prayed that I might be faithful to follow their examples. During the next period of thirty-five years, more fruit was destined to spring from the seeds that were sown by these early saints of God.

The Years of World War II

Contact with the church leaders in Japan was immediately lost when Pearl Harbor was attacked in 1941. Charles and Annabel Hunnex were interned for the duration in Shanghai by the Japanese. Mona Moors and Ellen High remained in Cuttack, India, but Floyd and Maude Heinly returned to America for a much-needed furlough. John and Pearl Crose had just returned to Lebanon when war broke out in 1939, and so they remained until forced evacuation in 1941 took them overland and by sea to India, a most hazardous journey, to cover for the Heinlys until they could return to India in 1942. Ruthe, our daughter Alta, and I, having completed one full term of service in Lebanon, sailed from Beirut in December 1939 on board one of the last American passenger boats to enter the eastern Mediterranean. This was at the advice of the American consul, who was anxious to get Americans with children out of the war zone. Caught in America by the war, we were sent by the Missionary Board to Barbados and Trinidad as relief missionaries for three years to relieve Byron and Zella Chew. The Ludwigs from Kenya were caught on furlough in America at the outbreak of war, but they were able to bring together a great deal of needed material and equipment, find a boat that would accept nonmilitary freight and a woman passenger, and reach Kenya, where they remained for the rest of the war. Thaddeus and Katrina Neff were forced to flee Egypt twice during heavy military attacks on Egypt, but each time they were able to return. During one air raid over Egypt the wife of one of the Church of God pastors was killed. The Zazanises fled Egypt, returning to America. In Germany, most of the work was destroyed; church buildings were reduced to rubble and church members were scattered. In other parts of Europe, church work as such came to a standstill, although individual Christians remained faithful, finding comfort and courage through their trust in God. Throughout the West Indies, the difficulties experienced took the form of scarcity of food and building supplies to maintain church buildings and living quarters. This was due to the presence in the South Atlantic and Caribbean waters of German U-boats, or submarines, whose commanders worked havoc with Allied shipping during the course of the war.

As fighting came to an end, most of the countries of Europe and Japan stood in dire need of all kinds of assistance as the people of the world struggled to bring themselves back to some form of peaceful existence. Tremendous adjustments were necessary, requiring several years of time to change from war to peace. A few countries, such as Lebanon, had profited, and its people came out of the war with far more economic blessings than was their status when war was declared six years earlier. This was in unbelievable contrast to the way in which the Lebanese people had survived World War I.

We will now look at what took place in the missionary enterprise of the Church of God immediately following VE and VJ Days. The Missionary Board had passed a resolution in the early forties "to hold all positions, even during the war" and that "missionaries would leave only if forced to do so." Now the Board was ready to go beyond a holding position.

CHAPTER 4
REGAINING MOMENTUM
(1945–1955)

Peace with some degree of normality does not come easily following five years of violent conflict such as the nations experienced during World War II. Japan and Germany lay devastated. Many other countries, such as England and Greece, showed to a greater or lesser degree horrible scars of war. Relief and rehabilitation assistance of all kinds were needed and activated. Many Americans felt a special burden for the family of God in Germany, and so food, clothing, and materials for rebuilding were made available. Christians of our movement demonstrated love and compassion especially for those of the reformation movement who were suffering as a result of the conflict.

The war had its effect on missionary activities and on the life of the church, particularly in countries directly affected. And there were indirect effects in countries where there was no actual combat. Unemployment and other economic problems abounded. Shortages of the necessities of life, especially staple foods, were experienced. Rationing had to be maintained in many places. Uncertainty about the immediate future caused many to lose hope. However, all of these factors put together provided a rare opportunity in many lands to present the "balm in Gilead" to suffering humanity. In America, the war effort had produced a degree of financial prosperity that made more funds for missionary outreach available to the church.

Adam W. Miller, first as executive secretary-treasurer of the Board (1933 to mid-1947) and then vice-president and finally president, had given wise guidance to the movement's missionary enterprise in bringing it out of the Great Depression, through the uncertain years of World War II, and on into a new and challenging era of missionary endeavor. The war's end presented an almost unparalleled opportunity to discover first the nature of the new world in which people now had to live and secondly the most effective ways to present Jesus Christ in such a world. C. Lowery Quinn served as executive secretary-treasurer (mid-1947 to April 1954) during this difficult ten-year period. More than five years of war brought changes in how people thought about themselves and the society in which they lived. How nations thought about one another had a direct effect on how missionaries would be received or not received in a growing number of countries. What did it mean to be an American missionary in this new world environment? That is what missionaries going out immediately after the war had to discover for themselves to make the necessary adaptations.

On the world scene, several colonial countries took up their struggle for political independence immediately after the war. The hatchets of xenophobic nationalism had been buried during the war in favor of joining the armed forces of the Western Allies in the struggle against their common enemies. But now with pent-up fury, the spirit of nationalism was revived and the struggle was renewed against colonialism and imperialism. India was a classic example. That nation's armed forces were loyal to Great Britain during the war, and its strategic geographical position provided many advantages for the Allies. In most colonies, the struggle for independence was accompanied with violence. But in India, Mahatma Gandhi led nonviolent protests that at times brought imprisonment to the leaders. Within two years, Britain gave India its independence. The only violence took place when Britain, to please strong religious elements among the people, partitioned India, creating a new nation known as Pakistan. The plan was to move all the Hindus living in West and East Pakistan into India and all the Muslims in India, especially northern India, into the two Pakistans, which were divided from one another geographically by over one thousand miles. The result was a bloodbath. Literally thousands of Indians were slaughtered on the roads and along the railways. Masses of people tried to move in one direction or the other, depending on their religion. They were not only in buses and trains but on top of them and hanging on the sides. The killing began when the vehicles in which the people traveled stopped at stations along the way. Blood literally ran alongside railroad tracks. Our new missionaries, Robert and Frances Clark, had just arrived in India, and they witnessed some of this. It should be noted that this division of India divided the work of the Church of God in that country geographically, for it was the state of East Bengal that became East Pakistan, and our mission work centered in Lalmanirhat found itself in a new country.

Other areas of the world experienced frequent outbreaks of violence. France was having difficulty in Indonesia, which led to France's withdrawal and ultimately to America's involvement in Vietnam. Egypt and other countries of the Arab world maintained their revolts against Britain and France until freedom was finally granted. Nationalist movements among the British West Indies colonies gathered strength. Colonial possessions in Africa began to give trouble to the imperial powers. Also, the British were handling the situation in Palestine somewhat clumsily. They were in a losing battle against the Jewish immigrants escaping from Europe, so in 1948 they partitioned Palestine, creating the state of Israel. This action brought immediate adverse reaction from all Arab countries, especially against America. Our missionaries in Cairo, Alexandria, and Beirut made themselves scarce on the streets for a number of days. However, all of these attempts to gain political independence from colonialism had only nominal influence on the work of missionaries. As a matter of fact, most missionaries sympathized with those who were attempting to gain their independence, for the era of colonialism had obviously come to an end. Indeed, most of the colonies were ready for their independence. This change of events also spoke to the feelings of Christians in the churches found in those countries and began to influence relationships between missionaries and national church leaders. As a whole, these developments challenged the missionary movement. Most missionaries, however, were optimistic.

The Missionary Board in America was also helpful. As it entered this decade of recovery and regained momentum, its members saw the opportunity for rapid advance in almost every area of the world where the movement maintained missionary activity. After picking up the pieces and sorting things out, the Board went on record "to start a new era of expansion after the trials of the past few years." Members felt "the need for a forward-looking program, well designed within the framework of present-day mission strategy." Early in the decade the president of the Board wrote in his annual report that if the gospel is to challenge the whole world, there are four imperatives:

1. Make clear the distinctive character of the Christian faith,
2. Explain the faith in terms people can understand,

3.   Discover new ways to make the Gospel effective in the lives of
     men and women, and
4.   Assist in the demand for unity.

Board members and missionaries alike began to see opportunities to serve
the people of the world through four general types of missionary endeavor:
evangelism, education, medicine, and agriculture.

The Church of God reformation movement in America was now
ready to send out a wave of new missionaries, a fourth generation. My
parents and their peers represented the second generation of missionaries,
and, as mentioned earlier, there were only a handful of third-generation
missionaries, due primarily to the Great Depression. As will be revealed
later on in this chapter, numerous missionaries were sent out during this
ten-year period from 1945 to 1955. There were volunteers, and there were
funds with which to send them. Ruthe, our two children, and I were, I believe, the first to leave America following the war, sailing from New York
in August on the second sailing of the *M. S. Gripsholm,* which was taking
American personnel into the Mediterranean. E. A. and Pearl Reardon were
on the same sailing, going to Kenya to help solve a major problem that had
been developing in that mission. The ravages of war were still very evident
as we stopped in Naples and Piraeus, the port for Athens.

Due to the influx of this new generation, a period of adjustment was
required on some fields between the older and the younger missionaries,
especially between some of those in the second generation and the new
fourth generation. This was due to new concepts emerging in postcolonial missions and to considerable change in attitudes and methods in the
American church. It was not easy for many of the older generation of missionaries to understand that where missions had been at work for several
decades there should now be a church emerging with its own identity to
be the church and to do its work. Paternalistically minded missionaries expressed fears that the national church was not yet mature enough to be on
its own without some kind of missionary oversight and that its leaders were
not yet ready for total responsibility.

Fortunately, many of those new fourth-generation missionaries who
went out soon after the war had been provided the opportunity by the
Missionary Board to prepare themselves for service. One of those places
of preparation was the Kennedy School of Missions, and before it closed

a number of years later, many of the movement's missionaries received training there. They went to the field, knowing something of what they faced in contemporary missions. They arrived on the field eager to aid the church through leadership training and to enter a transition period through which the mission would decrease and the church would increase in responsibility. In some countries, the transition was smoother than in others, as we shall see.

All the movement's missionaries were helped at this and many other points through a new Missionary Manual put out in 1947. This was the only new manual since the first one was printed in 1923. It brought numerous missionary concepts, strategies, and relationships up to date. Two quotations from the manual are worthy of note here.

> The supreme aim of foreign missions, therefore, is to make Jesus Christ known to all men as their divine Savior, and to persuade them to become His disciples; to gather those disciples into churches which shall be self-propagating, self-supporting and self-governing: to co-operate, as long as necessary, with these churches in the evangelizing of their countrymen and in bringing to bear on all human life the principles of Christ.

> The mission is not a permanent institution though it is a necessary one in the first stages of evangelization. It aims to build up as soon as possible an indigenous church which shall be self-supporting, self-propagating and self-governing, and it prepares and encourages the entire native church to complete the work of evangelization in the way best suited to its own national genius.

The significance of those statements was slow in being understood by some missionaries who maintained a colonial concept of missions, even some of the new fourth generation. The new Missionary Manual also made a change in name of the missionary on the field who was the liaison between the Missionary Board and the mission on the field. The old term was *field secretary,* and for a long time it had smacked of colonialism—the man wearing the white sun helmet. The new term was *mission secretary-treasurer.* Dropping the title *field secretary* was not appreciated by some who used it to indicate the authority they carried in the work and especially the privileged position with the church on the mission field. But the change was necessary in the new climate in which missions operated.

It was during this period that the Missionary Board lost the accumulative wisdom of several persons. In 1946 E. A. Reardon died soon after arriving in America following the year spent in Kenya. His wife Pearl had to bring his report to the Board. She had been with him in Kenya and had kept copious notes. Reardon was a charter member of the Board and had given valued service for thirty-seven years. J. W. Phelps also died in 1946. He had served earlier for sixteen years (mid-1912 to mid-1929) as secretary-treasurer of the Board. In 1947, F. G. Smith died suddenly. He had been a Board member for thirty-two years. The following year H. M. Riggle did not have his expiring term on the Board renewed. He was a charter member and had served thirty-nine years, three of which were as secretary-treasurer (1929–1932). In 1950, C. E. Brown resigned as president of the Missionary Board. He had held that office since 1931. Brown was elected as a Board member in 1921 and remained as such until 1958. It is always good to have new blood on the Board, but those first few years following the war showed an unusual turnover and the loss of considerable continuity. The Board, however, was existing in a new day in missions and needed new members to introduce fresh concepts commensurate with the changes in mission policies and strategies in the postwar world.

A number of the second-generation missionaries were reaching the age of retirement. Contemporary feeling in the church required that something be done to provide for its missionaries in old age. Three things developed. In 1949 the Board worked out a Retirement Allowance Schedule to care for those missionaries already retired. At the same time, all active missionaries were placed in the newly established Pension Plan of the Church of God. Some were near retirement when they entered the plan, so they still required some supplement from the Retirement Allowance Schedule. Then came Social Security as it was made available to missionaries who were eligible. It was entered on a voluntary basis and would ultimately take the place of the supplemental retirement allowance. That was a great boost for the morale of the third- and fourth-generation missionaries. It meant they would more likely make missionary work a career. This also demonstrated the church's expression of loving concern for the welfare of its missionaries. It was in keeping with trends in American society.

The offices of the Missionary Board found a new home in 1949. The National Woman's Missionary Society, World Service, the Board of Christian Education, and the Missionary Board of the Church of God cooperated in building the Missions Building just east of the Gospel Trumpet Company. This structure provided much more adequate facilities for the Missionary Board as it moved from very small quarters in the old tower of the Gospel Trumpet Company building.

In 1950 the National Council of Churches of Christ was formed and the Foreign Missions Conference of North America became the Division of Foreign Missions within the framework of NCCC. The Missionary Board reconsidered its relationship carefully, for the general feeling in the movement was opposed to relationships with the NCCC. However, involvement in DFM provided the opportunity to give and receive valid services and to experience many helpful relationships with other missionary boards. Our Board decided to retain its membership with the Division of Foreign Missions. Later on, when the NCCC was reorganized, requiring church bodies to be members in the NCCC before they could be full members in any of its divisions, the Missionary Board became an associate member of the DFM. Furthermore, in more recent years since the National Association of Evangelicals has within it a missions department, the Missionary Board has also gone in that direction to serve and to be served on behalf of the cause of missions.

Another united move took place in 1951. Instead of publishing three separate magazines, the Board of Church Extension and Home Missions, the National Woman's Missionary Society, and the Missionary Board of the Church of God combined their efforts and came out with a jointly controlled and supported *Church of God Missions* magazine. That publication has been a great informative and educational tool within the movement ever since. Another good thing happened in 1953 when the General Ministerial Assembly voted that it must ratify the names of all chief executive officers of the general boards and agencies, following their election by their respective bodies. The Missionary Board voted in favor of this move, which indicated quite well the excellent relationship always maintained between the Assembly and that Board.

As the church in America entered the decade of the fifties, its men, sparked by the enthusiasm of Everett Hartung, an outstanding layman residing in Anderson, Indiana, organized themselves in a campaign called

Mid-Century Building Fund. The goal was to raise two million dollars, primarily for special capital fund needs demonstrated by the Missionary Board of the Church of God, the Board of Church Extension and Home Missions, Anderson College, Pacific Bible College (now known as Warner Pacific College), and the international campgrounds in Anderson. There were included some noncapital fund needs for the Board of Christian Education and the Board of Pensions. Men of the movement rallied around the slogan "We Build for the New Age." Banquets for men were held in strategic places across the nation where they were challenged by dynamic speakers such as W. Dale Oldham and Everett Hartung. Many volunteers were involved in getting men to sign pledge cards. Enthusiasm ran high. Never before in the history of the reformation movement had such a large sum of money been raised. What the women of the church had done during the Great Depression its men were now doing to help the movement with capital funds at this important time when the Church of God was beginning to regain its momentum following World War II.

The Missionary Board needed capital funds desperately to meet financial obligations it could not include in its regular operating budget. Over five hundred thousand dollars was ultimately made available for overseas missions. Numerous church buildings and missionary homes were erected and some ten automobiles were supplied that otherwise could not have been made available. Generous amounts were given for building needs at Bible schools in Trinidad, Jamaica, and Germany. A mission center in Alexandria, Egypt, was made possible. The first main unit of the Hunter Memorial Hospital at Mwihila, Kenya, was erected and a large generator was installed to provide electricity for that station. Considerable assistance was given to the completion of the new church building in Athens, Greece. All in all this was a major demonstration of what the church could do once it was informed, for the financial potential was there. The campaign did not impinge adversely upon the giving to World Service. It was a real victory for the men of the church!

Ruthe and I came to America on furlough from Egypt in the late spring of 1952. We had been out for seven years and it was good to be home again among relatives, friends, and leaders of the church. I had the exhilarating experience of being caught up in this unprecedented Mid-Century Building Fund campaign at two points: (1) In the fall of 1952 I was loaned by the Missionary Board to the project to assist in setting up the campaigns in numerous places and, at times, to take part in some of them as a missionary to tell about the needs, and (2) in the spring of 1953 I was asked to become director of the campaign from an Anderson office. These two assignments provided me with considerable exposure to the movement across the country, and I was delighted to make what little contribution I could to such a successful happening in the church.

An interesting phenomenon emerged during the late forties and early fifties. Several younger men of the church decided on their own to travel out into the world and visit Church of God mission stations. They wanted to see for themselves what was being done and to be "missionaries to the missionaries." Some of them took it upon themselves to present reports to the Missionary Board. Among the several were Maurice Berquist, Ralph Starr, Frederic Pinyoun, and Wade Jakeway. I speak from my own viewpoint and experience by saying that these visitors were able for the most part to be a blessing to the family of God wherever they went, and they were in an excellent position to bring back to the church in America a different perspective about what was going on out there. This was the beginning of a time when Church of God pastors and laypersons would make their own trips or join tours to visit mission stations. This has done much to stimulate a greater interest in missions.

An administrative transition in the Missionary Board took place in 1954. C. Lowery Quinn resigned as executive secretary-treasurer after having served for seven years. Those were difficult years administratively, as the missionary cause of the Church of God was quickening its pace. Quinn had never been a missionary and it was therefore difficult for him to comprehend all the factors in difficult situations in other cultures. But he was faithful and dedicated to his work. The Missionary Board elected the writer to succeed Quinn, and I came into the office April 1, 1954, not being quite sure about the significance of the date. I was ratified by the General Ministerial Assembly that June. In Egypt, Wilbur Skaggs was appointed as mission secretary to succeed me in that responsibility. I mention all this to let you know how difficult it is to determine God's will in such matters. I had spent twenty-one years as a missionary and was just beginning to feel at home with the Arabic language. Ruthe and I were in a position to make our greatest contribution on the mission field. But others thought differently, and they seemed to feel they had the mind of the Lord in requesting that we remain in America in a new administrative position so vital to carrying on the church's obligation to take the good news to the whole world.

Now we must turn from the general to the more specific developments on the mission fields during this decade from 1945 to 1955. Through it all you will notice the hand of God leading his people on to greater involvement in missions.

The English-Speaking West Indies

The Church of God in Jamaica was still growing. By 1947, when it celebrated the fortieth anniversary of the Olsons' arrival on the island, Jamaica had ninety-one congregations with approximately twenty-five hundred members. Sixty-seven pastors were assisted by seventy-six evangelists and helpers. Visitors from America continued to give encouragement, among them C. Lowery Quinn, Nora Hunter, W. Dale Oldham, Ross Minkler, Maurice Berquist, and Frank Towers. The Olsons moved out of Kingston to a residence called Mount Joy located on the hillside just outside the city. George Olson tried to develop better interisland relationships by attending the Annual Convention of the Church of God in Barbados and Trinidad. In 1951 Hurricane Charlie hit Jamaica, destroying ten chapels of the movement and badly damaging six more.

This was also a period of transition in missionary leadership on the island. Quinn, present for the 1952 Annual Assembly, publicly announced the resignation of George and Nellie Olson as missionaries, although they were granted a brief extended period of service. Nina and Leslie Ratzlaff arrived back from furlough, and Leslie was to be the new mission secretary. Those changes did not come easily. The Olsons elected to remain in Jamaica, for it was thought George Olson could assist Leslie Ratzlaff when asked. This period of transfer had its effect on the Church of God in Jamaica. With considerable uncertainty pastors and lay leaders alike experienced this "changing of the guard," which was the first of its kind in the movement's history in Jamaica. The following year Edgar and Mildred Williams arrived to strengthen the missionary force. They had been evacuated out of China and visas could not be secured for them to enter India, so they graciously accepted the call to Jamaica. In December of that year, George and Nellie Olson went into full retirement after having given forty-six years of leadership in Jamaica.

Good things were happening in the two institutions in Jamaica. In 1946 Charles and Florence Struthers arrived as missionaries to teach in the Jamaica Bible Institute along with Edith Young, already there. The Strutherses remained for twelve years in that very important task of training leaders for the church. Ardenne High School had become a government grant-aided secondary school by 1948, and in 1950 a new science laboratory was built. The school enjoyed 100 percent passes in Cambridge examinations in 1951 and again in 1952. And 1952 marked the twenty-fifth anniversary of Ardenne High School, with 345 students enrolled. Mary Olson was headmistress, being assisted by very capable Jamaican teachers.

Two hundred miles to the northwest on the Cayman Islands, more missionary teachers were being sent to assist in the work of the church and Triple C School (Creative Christian Character). Emilia Blaskowsky arrived in 1947, remained for two and a half years, and was transferred to Barbados. Max and Neva Hill and Ethel Jeffcoat gave full time to teaching. Raymond and Elna Mae Hastings helped the church from 1951 to 1954. Numerous persons gave leadership for special occasions as they came from America and Jamaica. Finally in 1954 the first long-term missionaries were sent, Arthur and Mary Kluge, with the assignment to help the church become self-reliant as quickly as possible.

In Trinidad, not too long after the arrival of Clair and Retha Shultz in 1945 and Ralph and Ruth Coolidge in 1947, plans were set in motion to begin a Church of God training school. For many years this had been a need throughout the southern Caribbean. The churches were in dire need of trained leadership. In the beginning, it was necessary to accept dedicated students where they were educationally, for most had not completed the equivalent of high school. A vocational department was a necessity from the beginning to provide training in woodwork for the students as well as income so that they could pay their way. In 1952 Oakley and Veryl Miller were sent as missionaries so that he could head up the vocational department and she could teach Christian education courses. In that same year, land with a good residence was purchased at La Pastora in a valley over the mountain from Port of Spain. Also, a building program was soon under way for housing the vocational department and a combined dormitory-classroom unit. The West Indies Bible Institute became a going institution and is known today as West Indies Theological College. This was the beginning of a most effective training program for the church's leadership in the central and southern Caribbean. Regular visits were made by the missionaries to the island of Grenada, where a work of the Church of God had started.

Further out in the Atlantic, the Church of God on the island of Barbados was enjoying increased missionary leadership. Lars and Ellen Olsen, missionaries to Denmark who had been caught in America during World War II, were sent as relief missionaries to Barbados to relieve Ruthe and me in 1944 so that we could be ready to leave America for Lebanon immediately at the war's end. The Olsens left Barbados in 1946 and were soon back in Denmark. They were followed by William and Hope Livingston and then Walter and Margaret Tiesel in 1947. The Livingstons moved on, but Emilia Blaskowsky arrived in 1949 from Grand Cayman. Aaron and Kathryn Kerr were also in Barbados for a brief time. It was Walter and Margaret Tiesel who remained for a number of years and strengthened the church, leading them toward complete self-reliance. While I was working in Barbados during the war, I discovered that even though all the properties of the Church of God on the island were registered in the name of the Missionary Board of the Church of God, the Missionary Board was not registered on the island as an alien not-for-profit corporation That placed the eighteen or nineteen properties in jeopardy. I began the legal process immediately to rectify the situation, but it was not until 1949 and through the persistent efforts of Walter Tiesel that, by an act of the legislature signed by the governor of Barbados, the Missionary Board legally owned those properties. All of this was in preparation for the transfer of the properties to the General Assembly of the Church of God in Barbados more than a decade later.

The West Indian and East Indian work in British Guiana took on new life. George Jeffrey, the strong national leader who had come with the Church of God a number of years earlier, died in 1959. Aaron and Kathryn Kerr were transferred from Barbados in 1950 to give leadership to the work but were transferred to East Pakistan after a year. When Herman and Lavera Smith returned home from Kenya, they were sent as long-term missionaries to British Guiana. When they arrived in Georgetown, there were only three congregations of the movement in that British colony.

Soon things began to happen. Out in the Corentyne District an East Indian Hindu, Ramalingum Armogum, was converted. He soon became a Christian leader and pastored in that area among the East Indians for many years. The Smiths remodeled the old home for the needy at Bellaire Street in Georgetown, making it into a church with numerous rooms for a large Sunday school. Lavera Smith developed the first departmentalized Sunday school in the entire colony. The Yussig Abdool family, East Indians living in Georgetown, were converted to Christianity from Islam, and they remained faithful down through the years. Training institutes for Sunday school teachers were started as were vacation Bible schools. The concept was to reach children, have them grow up in the church, become converted as young people, and later establish families in the church. British Guiana was one of the first colonies in the Caribbean to have the *Christian Brotherhood Hour* broadcast over government radio. The broadcast was heard throughout the colony. In 1955 a very successful youth revival was conducted in the John Street Church in Georgetown. It was led by a young student from St. Kitts named Theodosia Francis who was studying in the West Indies Bible Institute in Trinidad. She later became the wife of Carlton Cumberbatch, who was destined to become the first West Indian president of the West Indies Bible Institute. By 1955 there were six congregations of the movement in British Guiana.

The small works on the islands of Antigua, St. Kitts and Curaçao began to develop under the assistance of the Missionary Board of the National Association of the Church of God headquartered at West Middlesex, Pennsylvania. These efforts were sponsored by many of the black churches in America. Bernice and Monroe Spencer emerged as the strong national leaders in Antigua. Both were ministers, although Monroe devoted considerable time to his very profitable business through which he was able to assist in meeting the financial needs of the growing church. By 1953 there were five congregations. That same year the Brewster house in Basseterre, St. Kitts, was demolished and the present church building erected. Willa Davis from Dayton, Ohio, was appointed by the National Association as a missionary to St. Kitts in 1948, but unfortunately she died two years later. In Curaçao, David Wade began a second congregation of the Church of God. This was the beginning of a situation destined to give trouble over many years. The Wades developed loyalty with the National Association in America while the Lindos, who had started the first congregation of the Church of God in Curaçao, chose to remain closely associated with the Missionary Board of the Church of God.

Central and South America

From the very beginning, the work of the Church of God in Mexico had its leadership from very short-term evangelistic ventures out of America, especially from the Spanish-speaking congregations that had grown up in Texas and Southern California. Because of this the Board of Church Extension and Home Missions looked after and gave direction to what was taking place in Baja California and northern Mexico. By 1953 that Board sent the first long-term missionaries, Maurice and Dondeena Caldwell, to Saltillo. Within a year they had seen the need for and had started La Buena Tierra, the first Bible training school of the movement among the Spanish-speaking people of Latin America. And by the following year there were brought together in united fellowship and organized effort nine congregations of the movement in Mexico. In addition to receiving training in the Bible, the students learned about small animal husbandry, which would help them as they went out from the school to live in village situations where the churches were at the time.

To the south of Mexico, in Guatemala City, there was a young Costa Rican student studying in a Presbyterian seminary. As a dynamic evangelist he visited America, seeking Christian fellowship. He happened to attend a camp meeting in the Northwest where Max Gaulke was the evangelist. Isai Calderon's heart was moved. Entirely on his own he then attended the International Convention at Anderson, observing, praying, and feeling very warm toward the fellowship convened there. Calderon then decided he would become identified with the Church of God reformation movement. Therefore, he returned to Guatemala City, where he had already married a Guatemalan named Cheney, and they began an independent work in that city. Under their leadership, the work grew and spread to Puerto Barrios, Delores, and San José de las Minas. Contacts were made with Max Gaulke in Houston, Texas, and with the Missionary Board. Fortunately, by the mid-fifties the opportunity was seized upon to allow this new work to grow as an indigenous church from the beginning. Even though there has never been a resident missionary of the Church of God in Guatemala, the church in America through the Missionary Board has been able to assist Latin leadership so that the church could function as a church and not as a mission. In future chapters, the results of this bold attempt will be seen as having been very successful.

In 1948 in Costa Rica, "Mother" McHugh, who really began the work of the Church of God on the coastal plain, died. Although seven persons were baptized that year, the small group of English-speaking West Indians was left without any kind of leadership except as the missionary in Panama might make a visit once or twice a year. In 1945 Ralph and Mary Collins were sent to Panama, and in 1947 Ernest and Grace LaFont were commissioned as missionaries to Panama After three years, the Collinses retired from the field because of ill health. The responsibilities in Panama and the Canal Zone were so great that very little contact was maintained with Costa Rica.

The Latin work in Cuba and the Isle of Pines continued to take shape, although the congregations that were predominantly West Indian continued to use the English language in their services. Several of the local leaders were bilingual, and this helped communications. While doing some missionary service in Cuba in 1946, Ellsworth Palmer met a young lady named Hilaria, who soon became his wife. By 1950 they were appointed as missionaries to Cuba and were starting a new group in Matanzas. It was entirely Spanish speaking. Another missionary couple, Earl and Freda Carver, was soon sent, adding to the emphasis on reaching the Spanish-speaking people of Cuba. Within a period of four or five years, all the congregations of the movement in Cuba were using the Spanish language. The work had now reached the center of Cuba at Cascorro, and there were three congregations on the Isle of Pines. Several church buildings were erected. Good progress continued until the end of the decade when something happened about which you will read in the next chapter.

During World War II the German immigrants in Brazil maintained a low profile. When peace came, however, they renewed their efforts to evangelize, primarily among their own ethnic group. During this time there were periodic attempts to reach the Portuguese-speaking people of Brazil. David Meier returned from America and decided to start a new work in São Paulo, and within two years a building was going up in a newly developing area of the city. Heinrich Weissburger began a Bible training school in Rio das Antas, and soon a printing press was purchased and a magazine named *Missionsbote* was being published. By 1955 there were twelve congregations in Brazil, eleven outreach missions, and ten meeting houses. These were served by eleven ministers and ten helpers.

Rebuilding in Europe After World War II

The people of Europe were in a state of shock when the carnage and dev-astation of war finally ended. It would require considerable time for them to emerge from war's rubble to normal life again. It took most of a decade for those related to the Church of God reformation movement to regroup their people, begin earning a livelihood, rebuild their churches and homes, and start functioning as a church. This was especially so in Germany. But the leaders of the church led the people through a realistic rehabilitation program as quickly as possible. In 1948 Ernst Kersten began the new Bible school at Fritzlar. Gerhard Klabunde in Essen served as pastor of the first church to reconstruct its building in 1948. The Missionary Board sent Wick and Grace Donohew to Europe for two years to give whatever as-sistance possible. That was a great encouragement. In the basement of the new building in Essen, Klabunde founded the printing shop called Wick-enburg Press. By 1955 the first World Conference of the Church of God was held in Fritzlar. It astonished the delegates to see what the church in Germany had been able to accomplish in ten years by extreme sacrifice and plain hard labor.

In other parts of Europe, it was also a struggle to regain momentum in the life and work of the church. Lars and Ellen Olsen, after their stint in Barbados, were sent to Karlstad, Sweden, where they spent three years before transferring to Aalborg, Denmark. The situation in Sweden seemed hopeless, and the work of the Church of God there has never recovered. However, the Olsens were able to start a small Bible school in Denmark, endeavoring successfully to train several young men for the ministry. This was the first step toward the movement's becoming completely self-reliant in that country during the years to come.

The year after the war ended Adam Allan died in Ireland, leaving his daughter Naomi to carry on the publication of the *British Gospel Trumpet*. A wooden Quonset-type structure was used as a church building in Belfast. In 1953 Pastor McCloy withdrew from the work after having served for seventeen years as pastor in Belfast. Sam Porter, a stable layman in the con-gregation, assumed responsibility. John Larmour, originally from Belfast, was in England endeavoring to revitalize the congregation in Birkenhead. Meanwhile, across the Channel, one new group in Leeuwarden was added to the small work in Holland.

When Stalin died in 1953, the German-speaking people held prisoner in Russia were released from the Siberian concentration camps. Many of those in the Church of God fellowship returned to their former homes in the Ukraine and the Caucasus. To the credit of our brothers and sisters living in Europe at that time, having survived the horrors of war, they accomplished an almost unbelievable comeback during that first decade immediately following the conflict. This was done with what I would call a minimum amount of assistance from outside.

Recovery in the Eastern Mediterranean

After a wartime holding pattern throughout the congregations of the Church of God in Egypt, everyone was ready to move forward. Egypt was still smarting under some remnants of British colonialism, but within the new decade complete independence from Great Britain would be achieved, and through a bloodless coup the monarchy overthrown in favor of an elected president. This change did, however, bring less freedom for Christian witness because Islam became the official religion of the government, whereas under British rule considerable religious freedom had been enjoyed by the Christian community. This was to affect the activities of the church and mission for years to come.

Thaddeus and Katrina Neff were back in Egypt several months before the end of the fighting, and William Fleenor went out alone from America in the spring of 1945 to assist them. Wilbur and Evelyn Skaggs were appointed to Egypt, arriving in November of that same year. Nick and Rose Zazanis also returned to Egypt. Missionary leadership appeared adequate. But William Fleenor soon returned to America to be with his wife, who was very ill. The Kenneth Crose family was in Egypt for about a year. In 1948 a training center was started in Cairo, but it had an on-and-off history until 1954. That summer the Neffs went to Italy for a time of complete rest due to Thaddeus's poor health. In the spring of 1949, I was called to Egypt from Beirut to help in some difficulties that arose in the mission. That summer Ruthe and I and the family went to Egypt to live in the Neff residence in Alexandria while the Neffs spent the summer in America on health leave. We endeavored to care for the responsibilities carried by them. Thaddeus Neff had been able to purchase good properties in the Camp Cesar District of Alexandria and the Shoubra District of Cairo for the further development of the work in those two cities. The Zazanises were forced to leave Egypt in 1946. They became persona non grata because the Greek Orthodox archbishop in Egypt brought pressure on the government to expel the Zazanises. It was felt that too many Greeks were being converted. There was a very large congregation of Greeks in Cairo and a smaller one in Alexandria, and so the archbishop used the only method he knew to stop this work of evangelicals. Panayote Dendrinos, a capable layman in the congregation in Cairo, assumed pastoral oversight of the congregation. He maintained this leadership until most of the Greek people left Egypt, including Dendrinos, due to pressure from the government a few years later.

In 1950 Ruthe and I were transferred from Lebanon to Cairo. We had closed out the mission in Lebanon, for the church had become self-reliant. But instead of returning to America at the end of that five-year term in Lebanon the Missionary Board asked us to spend another two years in Egypt before taking our furlough. We agreed to do this to help in the transition taking place in the mission in Egypt. The Neffs retired from the field in 1951 just prior to the return of the Skaggses from furlough. Accompanying the Skaggses was William Fleenor, who was being sent to Egypt for a three-year term. His wife Vada had died earlier. Youth centers developed in both Cairo and Alexandria and turned out to be a new approach to reach university students and young professionals. Downtown offices in Cairo were rented, providing facilities for leadership training. Two missionary residences were purchased in Maadi, a suburb of Cairo. The former residence of the Neffs in Alexandria was remodeled and named Neff Christian Center. Another missionary couple was considered necessary to have a well-rounded staff, with the new personnel to devote full time to leadership training. Consequently, the Missionary Board transferred Ernest and Grace LaFont from Panama to Egypt. In 1954 Jean and Ruth Kilmer arrived in Egypt as numerical missionary replacements for Ruthe and me. I had been asked while on furlough to become the chief executive officer of the Missionary Board. The future of the Church of God in Egypt was looking up, and there was enthusiasm expressed throughout.

Back up now to Lebanon right after World War II. This little country had gained its political independence from France during the war. When Ruthe and I arrived back on the field in mid-1954, we found the church doing well with a large number of younger people, some with leadership potential. Fouad Melki was among that group. My parents were badly in need of a furlough, and so they were in America from mid-1946 to mid-1947. It could be said that during the five-year period following the war the Church of God in Lebanon was being led toward and prepared for becoming a self-reliant body. It was a period of struggle and uncertainty for both missionaries and the church. Careful and continuous review of what an indigenous church was and the potential the church possessed toward being one indicated the possibility was present. But the will was lacking on the part of some. Then in May 1948 the world gave birth to the state of Israel. That provided the setting within which it would be possible to initiate a planned withdrawal of missionaries from Lebanon. Americans became an embarrassment instead of an asset in Lebanon. Consequently, negotiations began between the Missionary Board, the mission in Lebanon, and the Church of God in Lebanon, believing that then was the time for the church to become self-reliant without the presence of resident missionaries. It was decided that John and Pearl Crose would leave Lebanon in mid-1949 and that Lester and Ruthe Crose would remain one more year to close out the mission before transferring to Egypt.

One should understand the combination of reasons leading to this decision, for when we arrived home on furlough in 1952, I found the church in America to be quite unaware of what was taking place in the world of missions following the war. Many people still thought that nothing could be done in the work overseas without the presence of an American missionary. Here are six reasons why it was thought imperative that the church in Lebanon be allowed to be on its own: (1) It would give the native church opportunity to assume the initiative in leadership. (2) Continued political unrest, resulting in tensions, made it difficult for the missionary to work. This was especially true for smaller missions that were engaged primarily in evangelism. (3) Lebanon and Syria continued to be unproductive fields compared to worldwide missions. Permanent visible results were not commensurate with efforts expended. (4) There was a trend on the field by larger missions to turn over church work to native administration. (5) Operational costs for the mission in Lebanon were high compared with other fields. (6) There was an apparent lack of funds with which to expand, such as for a student center and equipment for the two mission schools.

Although this appeared to be a bold step and quite unprecedented in the work of Church of God missions, the plan was carried out and the experiment was successful. The last resident missionaries were out and the church in Lebanon became from that moment entirely self-governing, self-propagating, and self-supporting. God has blessed the church there with success. The movement in Lebanon has maintained contact with the worldwide church in an interdependent relationship.

It had long been the desire of Nick and Rose Zazanis to start a work of the Church of God in Greece. So when they were forced to leave Egypt, it was only natural for them to be transferred to Athens. The Greek people suffered much during the war, and so for several years relief was necessary. In 1946 Church of God congregations in America sent to Greece more than eight tons of clothing, which the Zazanises distributed among the needy. A centrally located hall was rented in Athens. Four groups of Christians were soon found in the Athens area. A place was rented in Patas, and Nick Zazanis was preaching in numerous places. Since the Greek Orthodox church is the state church in Greece, persecution against evangelicals materialized. The Zazanises were thrown in jail in Corinth at one time. Three of the four places of worship were closed in Athens. But Nick Zazanis persisted. He finally got the Evangelical Church of God registered with the government. Then he began the arduous task of buying a lot and erecting a church building in Athens, a project that everyone said could not be done in that Greek Orthodox-dominated country. But it was, and in mid-1955 a beautiful three-story church building was dedicated in downtown Athens. There were many converts. Zazanis edited the *Greek Gospel Trumpet.* Literature of all kinds was distributed, and there were signs that the work was on the verge of expansion.

Building on Foundations in Kenya

Postwar conditions in the East African British colony of Kenya provided opportunity for a new face-off in our missionary activities; therefore, numerous new missionaries were sent. A period of transition was required. The postwar missionaries saw situations differently from earlier missionaries. There were differences in approach, methods used, organization of the growing church, and appreciation for the postcolonial attitudes rapidly appearing among the Africans. In mid-1945 immediately after the war E. A. and Pearl Reardon were sent by the Missionary Board to Kenya to rectify a situation that had developed around John and Twyla Ludwig. It was not until 1947, however, that the Ludwigs returned to America on furlough, during which time the Missionary Board voted that they should not be sent back to Kenya because John Ludwig had reached retirement age. In 1945 the first teacher training class was started at Kima to provide qualified teachers for a growing number of Church of God elementary schools. By the next year Frank and Margaret LaFont and Herman and Lavera Smith were serving at the Kenya mission, the Smiths having been transferred from Trinidad. More nurses were needed, and so Ruth Sanderson and Lima Lehmer were appointed. The boys' school was moved to Ingotse, where Ruben C. and Nora Schwieger were to work. The Teacher Training School was moved to Mwihila with Jewell Hall in charge, soon to be joined by James and Glenna Yutzy. Irene Engst was sent to the Mwihila station and lived with Jewell Hall. Both of these moves were a disappointment to the Bunyore African Christians around Kima due to tribal jealousies. Evangelism was producing many strong village churches. The newly formed Woman's Missionary Society in Bunyore raised funds to send their own missionary, Obed Kutera, to another tribal area, Kisii, in southern Kenya. A station was started at Ibeno. Lydia Hansen was sent to Kima, and she and Lima Lehmer formed a strong team at that station.

When the Ludwigs left for furlough in 1947, Herman Smith was appointed as mission secretary. He was the first to provide a democratic organization for the church by developing a General Assembly with appropriate bylaws. This encouraged a much greater involvement and more cooperation by the many pastors and elders. It became a delegated assembly. When the Smiths went on furlough to America and were then transferred to British Guiana, Wick and Grace Donohew were transferred from Europe to Kenya and Wick became the mission secretary. These were good moves by the Board. Both Smith and Donohew, over a longer period, gave stability to the mission and to the church. By virtue of his office and according to the bylaws of the General Assembly, Donohew was chairman of the Assembly. It required twelve years before the church was ready to accept an African chairman. But change had to come.

One of the first achievements by Donohew was to start a Bible school, which was the first attempt at providing regular training for pastors. When I made my first visit to Kenya at the end of 1955 to participate in the Fiftieth-Year Jubilee of the Church of God mission in Kenya, I was introduced to the first twelve students who were to graduate from the Bible school. These fine men had to be accepted and taught from where they were educationally. Not one had more than a second-grade education, and one was illiterate. That was no discredit to them. But teaching had to be at that level. Within a few years, the picture changed completely due to the rapid advance in general education in Kenya.

Education was indeed given priority throughout Kenya. Christian missions were much involved by request of the British colonial government. Many of the Church of God village churches began elementary schools. Calvin and Martha Brallier were sent out and stationed in Mwihila, and from there Calvin gave supervision to these elementary schools. Velma Schneider was sent to Kima to teach in the girls' school, which was an intermediate school. Margaret LaFont had become headmistress after the Ludwigs left.

In 1951 the Missionary Board voted to establish a hospital in Kenya, and within a short time David and Elsie Gaulke were on their way there to oversee the project. Nora Memorial Hospital was sponsored by the Woman's Missionary Society and the Mid-Century Building Fund. Hazel McDilda and Vera Martin were sent as nurses to be ready when the first two units of the hospital, a duplex for American nurses and a doctor's residence at Mwihila, were ready for occupancy in early 1956. In these two areas of education and medicine, the mission worked very closely with the government. Much of it was subsidized by government grants, for the colonial power at that time had a policy of working through the various missions in caring for the needs of the people, especially those in the interior provinces. That relationship was to be modified in subsequent years.

The Asian Sub-continent: India and East Pakistan

After one hundred fifty years under British rule, India gained its independence from Great Britain in 1947 but remained a member of the British Commonwealth. At the same time, as mentioned earlier, two states of India became a new country named Pakistan. The work of the Church of God mission in India centered at Lalmanirhat found itself in East Pakistan with an Islamic government. Floyd and Maude Heinly discovered that they and the mission were responsible to new authorities. This left only Mona Moors and Ellen High as missionaries in India, giving most of their time to the care and education of the girls in The Shelter at Cuttack. Mosir Moses, the only capable Indian leader in Calcutta[1], had died during the war. Also, there were very few contacts with the Nichols-Roys in the northern state of Assam.

In the southern state of Kerala, P. J. Philip was in control, having almost no contact with the two groups of the Church of God centered in Cuttack and Shillong. The entire mission in India came out of the war in a weakened condition. In 1949 P. J. Philip made a journey to America to be present during the International Convention in Anderson and to meet with the Missionary Board to secure more financial aid for South India. Actually, there were only two strong leaders of the Church of God in India at that time: J. J. M. Nichols-Roy in the northeast and P. J. Philip in the south. Nichols-Roy was a leader in government, in business, and in the church. I recall the time he showed me a large picture of the special congress convened by the government to draft the constitution for the newly independent country of India. There were only a half-dozen Christians in that large assembly of Hindus and Muslims. Yet their influence as Christians was strong in demanding religious liberty in India, a secular state. And so it is found yet today in India's constitution. P. J. Philip in the early fifties was selected as chairman of the Malayalam (the language of Kerala state in South India) Bible Revision Committee of the Indian Bible Society. He was also chosen as the vice-president of the Kerala Christian Council. But both Nichols-Roy and Philip, though able men, were getting on in years, and there was need for younger leadership. In 1950 the doors of Miller Bible Institute were opened in Chengannur, South India, but it had an up-and-down history and finally closed, due primarily to lack of qualified and continuous leadership.

After having served in East Pakistan for a year, Aaron and Kathryn Kerr moved to South India to work with P. J. Philip. The Kerrs were the first American missionaries of the Church of God to reside in South India. At that particular juncture, relationships did not work out too well for the Kerrs. Three men were ordained to the Christian ministry: P. C. Zachariah, P. D. Varughese, and K. K. Mathai. All three gave many years of leadership to the movement in South India. The Bodhini Press began operation in Chengannur, printing many kinds of Christian literature, including the church paper called *Atma Bodhini.* Philip was editor. After three years in South India, the Kerrs left the country; their replacements were Gordon and Wilhemina Schieck from the Church of God in Canada. P. J. Philip soon turned over administrative responsibility to Schieck and shortly thereafter died. One should keep in mind that he was one of the young men who had been converted and had enjoyed contact with A. D. Khan in 1907. He had been been with the Church of God for forty-nine years, and his death was a loss to the entire Christian community in South India. P. C. Zachariah then became the new editor of *Atma Bodhini.* Up to the northeast in Cuttack, a chapel was built for The Shelter. Mona Moors, after giving thirty-one years of service to India, retired from the field to marry G. P. Tasker, whose estranged relations with the Church of God had been resolved ten years earlier. Also, permits were finally received from the Indian government to allow Sidney and Jean Johnson to take up missionary service at Cuttack. It appears to have taken almost a decade following the war to regain some momentum in India.

But a new day had dawned for Christian missions in India. Soon after gaining political independence, the government of India began to bring pressure on all Protestant Christian missions by restricting the entry of American missionaries. In fact, India was being flooded with many independent missionaries, and unethical means were frequently employed to gain converts. As a result of the government's adverse reactions, long-standing missions in India suffered along with the offenders. The movement was fortunate to have qualified Canadians whom the Missionary Board could send to India. Canadians did not need an entry visa because they were members of the Commonwealth and therefore could not be denied entry into India. Gordon and Wilhemina Schieck were the first of several Canadian missionaries of the Church of God to be sent to India during the next decade. The government also brought great pressure on long-standing missions in India to transfer their property holdings to the Indian church of their respective denominations. In 1955 the Missionary Board went on record with a resolution to make such a transfer of properties it held in India to the Church of God in India as soon as a representative body of the church became a legal entity capable of holding property. And that, as we shall see, required a number of years.

East Pakistan was even slower in picking up after the war. The mission station at Lalmanirhat had been requisitioned by the United States Air Force during the last two years of the war as a base for flying "the hump" into China. Robert and Frances Clark, however, arrived in India (soon to be East Pakistan) early enough to have about a two-year overlap with the Heinlys before the Heinlys' retirement from the field, which for them was necessary due to poor health and age. As mentioned earlier, Aaron and Kathryn Kerr were with the Clarks at Lalmanirhat for about a year before going to South India. The Clarks labored diligently, and by the time of their first furlough, they felt they were beginning to experience some breakthrough in reaching Hindus. There had been ten baptisms, and four Sunday schools were being conducted. A little later they had their first preaching mission among Muslims. But the going was difficult and visible results were small. Considerable relief work was also necessary on a perennial basis due to floods and other natural causes. At one time considerable feeling was generated in the Missionary Board to close out this nonproductive field. Fortunately, good Christian common sense prevailed. Regardless of the small number of converts to Christianity, the Hindus and Muslims need the witness of Christian faith in their midst. That is explicit in the Great Commission.

Out of Dust and Ashes in East Asia

The Japanese people were badly shaken by the time the peace treaty was signed with America. The atomic bomb used by America ushered in a new era for the world. Thousands of Japanese had been killed and many more wounded. Their homes and factories lay in ruins. Here was presented to the Western church the opportunity to demonstrate mercy and love. And, strangely enough, American missionaries were to be readily accepted. But the question was how to regain contact with the few scattered Japanese Christians. One of the Church of God servicemen stationed in Japan, Ralph Morton, wrote to Adam Miller, secretary of the Missionary Board, asking for information on how to find any Church of God people. He was given an address. By December 1945, Morton was able to discover Choko Shimizu.

It was learned that the large building at Hongo had been destroyed as well as every other church building except that at Nerima. Almost unbelievably, no Japanese of the Church of God had been killed during the war, although some almost lost their lives. Many had lost their homes and businesses. Direct contact with the main Japanese church leaders was established. Shigetoshi Taniguchi called for many missionaries to come to Christianize Japan. Shimizu-sensei wrote about being visited by five Christian Americans of the occupation forces. One of these was Nathan Smith, who within five years was out of the armed forces and back in Japan as a Church of God missionary. In spite of all the problems encountered in entering Japan at that time, it was unfortunate that the church in America was not prepared to do what, in retrospect, could have been accomplished in Japan when the time was ripe for salutary Christian evangelization. We can be thankful, however, for what progress was made during the ten-year period immediately after the conflict.

Policies must be flexible to meet the needs of changing times. Even though the church in America had sent no missionaries to Japan since 1927, the Church of God in Japan was now in desperate need of missionary assistance and encouragement. Early in 1949 Kyodon (the United Church of Japan) was building a model community in Shinjuku District of Tokyo and approached Shimizu-sensei to have the Church of God start a congregation there. A good location on top of a hill was offered, and this became the Toyama Heights Church of God. Obstacles were overcome, and by November 1949, Arthur and Norma Eikamp reached Tokyo. At first they had to live in the YMCA, but when the new church building was erected at Toyama Heights, they were able to live there in a couple of rooms.

Within a year and a half, Nathan and Ann Smith were sent to join the missionary family. A new church building was erected at Nerima, another district of Tokyo. To show the resilience of the Japanese Christians and also their way of demonstrating their appreciation to the American church, the Church of God in Japan sent seventy dollars as a contribution to Christ's World Service Day in 1951.

Nathan and Ann Smith started a work in Tachikawa near an American military base where some Church of God members of the American armed forces had made contacts with several interested Japanese. Within three years, Philip and Phyllis Kinley reached Japan and assumed responsibility for the work at Tachikawa, leaving Nathan and Ann Smith free to move southward to the island of Kyushu, where a beginning had been made at Imajuku by Church of God military personnel. Also nearby in the city of Fukuoka another congregation was developing under the leadership of Morito Tajima and his wife, both professors at a university. They were ably assisted by Nakahara Chikatsu, one of the leaders from Tokyo dating back to the mid-twenties. The son of the late Japanese pioneer of the Church of God, Keiji Yajima, a businessman in a large department store, was transferred to Osaka, the second largest city of Japan located about halfway between Tokyo and Fukuoka. He initiated children's meetings out of which grew a congregation. At Toyama Heights Shimizu-sensei, a very capable pastor and leader, was willing to get along without missionary assistance, and so Arthur and Norma Eikamp moved to Tamagawa, another district of the great city of Tokyo. A mission home was built for them, and soon the congregation was large enough to warrant a building. And it was at Tamagawa that Arthur Eikamp, encouraged by the Japanese church leaders, began what is known today as Tamagawa Seigakuin, a school for girls, through which it was hoped homes in the area could be reached with the Christian message. A five-year plan was sponsored by the Missionary Board, during which time the school became well established and was soon to become one of the best and most well-known intermediate and secondary schools for girls in Tokyo.

There were other educational approaches to the Japanese people through which the gospel could be communicated. As local congregations began again after the war, they started kindergartens for small children in the community. This provided ready access into nearby homes and provided some partial support for the pastor, who was always head of the kindergarten. Christian teachers were employed, and the overall influence in the communities through the children was significant. The American church's missionaries in Japan and the Japanese churches were further assisted during this period of time by another influence. While American occupational forces were in Japan, the United States government provided what were known as Dependents' Schools for the children of American families. These schools required American teachers, and some of them, such as Alfred Lange and his family, were from the Church of God. The Langes requested to be placed in the Dependents' School in Fukuoka so that they could assist in the work of the church. Their ministry was a real blessing. One of these teachers, Freda LaFoe, became a full-time missionary after completing her assignment with our government when the schools for dependents were closed out. She taught in Tamagawa Seigakuin for a number of years. A new training school was felt necessary for educating potential leadership for the church. This was a night school and only religious subjects were offered. As we shall see later on, this was not adequate training for the otherwise highly educated Japanese young men, and another form of training emerged. Another missionary couple, Donald and Arlene

Goens, arrived in Japan to become involved in direct evangelism, helping to develop new congregations. Contacts were maintained with America through infrequent visitors, such as Adam and Grace Miller and Dale and Polly Oldham.

With all of these efforts, and especially through the hard work of the Japanese Christians, the work of the Church of God in Japan came out of complete chaos in 1945 into a growing church through the subsequent decade. That growth is best seen through these statistics:

	1949	1951	1952	1953	1955
Congregations	4	4	7	9	11
Sunday Schools	4	5	8	14	16
Church Attendance	90	145	230	310	350
Sunday School Attendance	170	575	900	1,500	2,000

On the mainland in China, the missionary endeavors of the Church of God got off to a good start immediately after World War II but came to an abrupt end when the communists invaded and took over China in 1949–50. In Shanghai, Charles and Annabel Hunnex were released from the internment camp where they had been held captive by the Japanese for two and a half years. Their health was somewhat impaired, but they remained in China to assist and give guidance to the new missionaries arriving. Daisy Maiden returned to work in Soo Chow. David and Elsie Gaulke, along with Milton and Eleanor Buettner, were taking special courses at the University of California at Berkeley in preparation for their assignment in China and in 1946 found themselves in Yunnan Province of West China as Christian witnesses at the Peace Memorial Hospital in Tengchung. Lovena Billings arrived shortly thereafter.

David Gaulke was the first medical missionary doctor to be commissioned by the Missionary Board of the Church of God. Elsie Gaulke and Eleanor Buettner were nurses, and Lovena Billings also assisted in the hospital. Milton Buettner did evangelistic work and also taught English in the government middle school. The following year Edgar and Mildred Williams were appointed to China, where they were involved in leadership training and administrative work in East China. Just when some encouraging results were beginning to appear through the efforts put forth in both East and West China, the communist invasion of those areas began, ending in subsequent take-over. This meant immediate evacuation by all American missionaries. Charles and Annabel Hunnex and Daisy Maiden left immediately for America, and all three retired from active missionary service. About the same time Edgar and Mildred Williams left for America.

While studying in a Peking[2] language school, Lovena Billings had met a young medical doctor from Bristol, England, P. K. Jenkins. He was preparing for missionary service in China. They were married in July and in December evacuated to Hong Kong. There they began working in a medical clinic through the Emanuel Medical Mission. David and Elsie Gaulke and Milton and Eleanor Buettner evacuated West China southward to Burma[3]. The Gaulkes then went to Kenya to check on the possibilities of enlarging the medical services of the Kenya mission, and the Buettners served for several months in Cuttack, India, before returning to America. From that point on in China our only contact with our Christian fellowship has been through the underground.

The year following the end of the Second World War, M. C. Sergeant, a major in America's armed forces, made contact with the group in Korea who had earlier identified themselves with the Church of God. Several Church of God chaplains also encouraged the group, who were already beginning to suffer from Communist pressures. By 1950 severe persecution of the Christians in what we now know as North Korea had set in. Many were killed. Seventy-five to eighty percent of the Christian ministers were either captured or killed by communists, and many churches were burned. Christians fled by the hundreds to the southern part of the country. Then came the Korean War with the subsequent division of Korea into North and South. After the conflict was over, two Church of God chaplains, Gerald Weaver and Ralph Adamson, made contact in and around Seoul with the Christians of our fellowship. Arthur and Norma Eikamp went over to Japan to give encouragement. The Korean church was requesting missionary assistance as they were starting life all over again. They especially wanted someone who could teach in the Bible school they were beginning. The Missionary Board brought John and Pearl Crose out of retirement and sent them to Korea to offer the mature guidance needed at that time. They remained in South Korea only one year.

Another gradual change was taking place in the movement's missionary outreach. Practically all of the second-generation missionaries of the Church of God had by 1955 made their contribution in overseas service.

They had served faithfully and well during very difficult years of the world's history from the end of World War I to around a decade following World War II. The few third-generation missionaries, among whom were Ruthe and I, were still much involved, acting as a bridge between the colonial and postcolonial eras of missionary history. But it was primarily the new wave of fourth-generation missionaries who were now to carry the burden of taking the good news to people around the world. Naturally the process of change from one generation to another is always gradual and has a great deal of overlap.

CHAPTER 5
CHURCHES EMERGE FROM MISSIONS
(1955–1965)

Both excitement and concerns were generated during this particular decade as congregations of the Church of God reformation movement extant in countries other than America began to recognize and cherish their identity as something quite unique and different from the foreign missions that brought about their existence. As suggested earlier, these dynamic feelings within the overseas churches ran parallel with the rapid appearance of new nations as they gained their political independence from colonial powers. In Africa alone during this ten-year period, thirty-seven new states or countries representing two hundred million people emerged from colonialism to gain control over their own destinies. An atmosphere conducive to the indigenization of churches was created. If these countries could do it politically, why couldn't the churches do it in their relationships with the "mother" church? I had gone through this experience in Lebanon shortly before assuming responsibility in the Missionary Board, and I was aware of what could take place in Barbados, Trinidad, and Egypt. Indeed, the possibilities that appeared to be present in most countries where the Church of God had missions were very exciting.

The entire missionary outreach of the reformation movement in America was entering a period of its history when a new understanding of its mission surfaced, especially as it related to churches in mission fields that had been in existence from ten to fifty years. As the church was growing and maturing in each country, the mission had been acting as a kind of scaffold around the structure from which missionaries helped shape the church. Now it was time for the scaffolding to come down, allowing the church to stand alone as a biblical entity, an indigenous church.

The Indigenous Church

What is indigeneity? A clear understanding of this term is necessary to visualize what was happening in missions during the 1950s and 1960s. Most people in the American churches had only a very nebulous concept of the meaning of the indigenous church as applied to mission churches. Many missionaries considered the major goal to be self-support. Mission churches usually perceived it as being a plan perpetrated by colonial missions to withdraw financial support and missionaries. If there was any degree of understanding, it was always in terms of the three selfs, as they were called: self-supporting, self-governing, and self-propagating. Self-support always came first in the eyes of American Christians. I consistently maintained that self-government and self-propagation were primary. Once any new group of Christians was able to govern itself according to the Word of God and was experiencing new births into the kingdom of God, the third "self" would come naturally and with greater ease than by having the monetary factor stressed first, as so many missions were doing.

Look at it more closely. A plant is indigenous when it grows naturally in the soil of the country where it is planted, takes root, and flourishes. The same is true in church planting. When the seed of the gospel is planted by missionaries in the hearts of the people of another country, it dies but later springs forth in the lives of new Christians of another culture. Another reflection of the incarnation of God among people takes place. Jesus becomes one of or identifies with the believers found in that particular culture. And the gospel becomes relevant only when this incarnation takes place. A church becomes indigenous only when this becomes a reality. But this is not all. When incarnation occurs in another culture, certain adaptations or adjustments are necessary—cultural adjustments, to be precise. The seed of the gospel planted in the new soil of another culture will spring up as the gospel, but it will not be identical in every respect to the seed originally planted. The Christian faith will make the necessary accommodations to the new culture but without losing its absolute identity with the gospel.

There must be limits, however, to these adjustments or accommodations. A core of basics representing the pure faith or pure truth as revealed through the Holy Spirit will always endure as the Word of God is studied diligently. When any accommodation would do damage to that core of truth, it should not be considered. If an accommodation does not damage the core, it could be accepted as a cultural adaptation. If this is properly understood and practiced, it is possible to avoid syncretism or the union of Christianity with paganism. On the other hand, to understand this principle is to assist in achieving indigenous Christianity wherever missions go. True, the gospel is above culture, but it must be presented in meaningful cultural patterns to be effective. Who decides what adaptations to make and not to make? It is not the responsibility of the missionaries, although they could very well be resource persons if they are wise and have the confidence of the people among whom they are working. Primarily the decisions should be reached by the Christians living in a specific culture, guided by the Holy Spirit as the Word is studied.

All of this removes the colonial approach as a missionary introduces the gospel into new cultural patterns. Some new religious forms or ways of doing things in the church will gradually emerge. For instance, church architecture will reflect local cultural styles. Hymns will not merely be translations of Western hymns using Western music, as is sometimes necessary in the beginning, but will in due time be born from the soul of Christian poets and musicians within the culture. Musical instruments reflecting the culture will be used during the meeting together of believers. There are indeed different ways each culture has to express the feelings of the Christian life and experience. These accommodations relate the gospel to people and not to a "foreign" religion.

Missionaries who find themselves in fields where totally Western cultural patterns have been used in planting the church can use these concepts in providing opportunities to discover and implement whatever accommodations should take place to allow the church to become truly indigenous. But that takes time. The missionaries themselves will probably retain most of their cultural likes and dislikes, at the same time making the necessary adaptations to the culture in which they live in order to exist comfortably and effectively among the people. But they must not impose their own cultural forms on the Christians of the other culture. Furthermore, we must also recognize that cultures do change with every age, at every level, and with each generation. This occurs as new conditions emerge that naturally create change in the culture of any society.

I have spent considerable time explaining the indigenous church, because without a correct understanding it is impossible to comprehend what was taking place on the mission fields during this decade of time. During the twenty-one years of my administrative ministry in missions, I made many trips to the countries where the movement existed and to the American church. I tried to explain to the church in the United States and its leadership, to our missionaries on the field, and to national church leaders in other countries the biblical concept of the indigenous church and the manner in which the church should become indigenous. I tried to impress upon the American church that the day of colonialism in missions had passed and that our missions in other countries had to maintain the initiative during a transition period to the end that an indigenous church would emerge from a mission church. I tried to indicate that the American church must learn not to violate the integrity of the indigenous church coming into being, but rather it should relate to the church in a spirit of fraternalism, not paternalism.

In more recent years, a new term has come into good usage: *self-reliant.* A church that is self-reliant depends upon itself and not upon a mission from another country. I wish we could have had this term in popular usage in the late 1950s as the attempt was being made to help the church of the reformation movement in other countries to be the church and not to depend on a mission from America to do the staffing, supporting, and administering. The American church had to understand that as indigenous churches came into being, it did not mean the end of missions. Crosscultural missions will remain imperative to the end of time, for there will always be in some parts of the world those who have never heard the name of Jesus. A proper concept of the self-reliant church is necessary to understand some of the situations that developed in mission-to-church and church-to-mission relationships. These will be observed as we continue in this chapter.

The goals set and reset in all these undertakings were not achieved overnight. They required the diligent effort of all persons concerned throughout the time span of 1955–75, roughly twenty years, or a generation of time. That is just about what it required—a new generation in the church—to bring the Church of God reformation movement into being in countries around the world. But at this point I must bring to your attention some concepts and plans that were linked closely with the indigenization of the mission church.

General Assemblies Come Alive

In most countries where our missions had functioned for a number of years and where there were several congregations, the emerging church followed the general congregational polity of the Church of God reformation movement. During the decade of the 1950s, General Assemblies became evident—some for the first time and others showing themselves for what they indeed were. But in most situations where resident missionaries were present, those General Assemblies assumed a secondary position. Unfortunately, the mission held the primary position. The 1947 Missionary Manual called for the organization of the mission staff to carry out the objectives of the mission. When this happened, as it did in most countries, it turned out that the mission staff on each mission field fairly well controlled the affairs of the church. This was not a common practice at the local congregational level, but rather at the point of the overall work of the Church of God in that country. Instead of the mission's working with the church that had come into being, as was the intent of the statement in the Missionary Manual, the church worked with the mission.

I sat in many mission staff meetings in Kenya, Jamaica, Japan, India, Barbados, Trinidad, and British Guiana during the late 1950s and early 1960s when the missionaries would strategize and plan the implementation of all the efforts to be put forth by the church. The mission would report the thinking and decision of the missionaries to the General Assembly. The church had no national representative present in mission staff meetings. But many times missionaries held most of the key positions in the General Assembly, serving as chairmen, secretary, treasurer, and chairmen of committees.

In retrospect, perhaps all of this happened as part of the evolution of the indigenous church. But it should not surprise anyone that this method of operation would be challenged. Colonialism in missions had to cease. I was asked by national ministers at that time what was going on behind closed doors of a mission meeting that should eliminate the presence of a national church representative.

This was indeed the beginning of the end of mission control of the church in countries where there was a church large enough to be organized. But the process of demissionizing was not easy and in most cases required several years of transition. To make the change suddenly and completely by mandate of the Missionary Board would have been disastrous. Most missionaries were not ready for it. They thought the church leaders were not mature enough. Some were afraid of the "young rebels" or the "radical element" in the church wanting to gain control. And strange as it may seem, most people at the local church level were not wanting it. Missionaries thought they were doing what they had been sent to accomplish. Church people, particularly the older ones, were afraid of being on their own and still wanted the last word on any issue to come from missionaries, especially from the mission secretary. It was generally agreed that the treasurer must be a missionary, since there was a lack of confidence in a national Christian by both the people of the church and by the missionaries. But the times demanded change, which was soon to come.

The first move was to strengthen the General Assembly, allowing it to function according to its own bylaws, representing the voice of the church. This was not always easy. I observed in 1957 in South India that the church was known as the "Church of God Missions." I told the leaders that it should be called the "Church of God in South India." But it required years for the congregations there to reach that objective, with a viable General Assembly. In several other countries, missionaries took the initiative by declaring that they would refrain from serving as officers of the General Assembly or as chairmen of committees. That became a process extending over several years until national leadership was finally in control of the General Assembly. However, it did not entirely eliminate missionary presence. Missionaries agreed to serve on committees and boards if elected by the church to serve, the same as any other person, and not because they were missionaries.

This was the beginning of the period when the official position of the organized mission would decrease in influence and the rightful position of the church would increase. The mission began to carry less and less responsibility for the work of the church with missionaries performing major functions. The church began to assume more and more responsibility for its own life and activities, since national ministers and church workers were being trained to carry on. All the functions of the church were now to be looked after not by the mission but by the General Assembly. It was interesting to note that most of these General Assemblies became members of the national councils in their respective countries, such as the Kenya Christian Council, the Assam Christian Council and the Kerala Christian

Council in India, and the Jamaica Christian Council. This was to give General Assemblies of the Church of God considerable strength as a part of the total Christian population in their respective countries.

It must also be noted that from the very beginning and by choice of the church in each country, the General Assembly of the Church of God was a delegated body. Furthermore, it represented through its membership the laity of the church as well as its pastoral leadership. Our Christian brothers and sisters in other countries experienced no theological problem at this point, but it did tend to make these General Assemblies more official with greater influence over local congregations. Part of our recognizing the validity of the overseas General Assembly was to understand and develop proper relations with it. If the General Assembly had integrity, it should have the privilege of making its own decisions, which the mission, its missionaries, and the Missionary Board should recognize and respect. Within a few years, the Missionary Board began to seek the feelings of each General Assembly relative to the kind of assistance the church wanted from the church in America and the type of missionary it might want. This was not always easy for the Missionary Board or for the missionaries to accept. It was a shock to a few missionaries to hear from the General Assembly that their services were no longer needed. And it was difficult for members of the Missionary Board, for example, to understand the General Assembly thought differently from them about how an institution should be operated or staffed. But let it be said here that in every situation the spirit of Christ was demonstrated within the framework of mutual love and respect.

Employing the Concept of Grant-In-Aid

One of the major problems as the church on mission fields moved toward being indigenous was that of finance. The problem was how to become self-supporting when the church had been so dependent financially on the mission for so many years. In most situations the mission had supplied the total or partial support of ministers and other church workers as well as amounts required for the activities of the church through institutions or other services. Could the problem be solved by the Missionary Board's giving notice that as of an early date all financial assistance would be cut off abruptly and entirely? Hardly. There were a few who advocated that approach saying, "Let the churches sink or swim. They have received financial assistance long enough." But when reviewed carefully, that plan appeared inadequate to reach the desired goal. In fact, it could have well destroyed what had already been achieved on the mission field after many years of diligent and sacrificial labor. Even colonial governments continued assisting through financial grants the new independent nations that had formerly been their colonies. Survival was important and necessary.

Therefore, during the late 1950s and early 1960s the General Assemblies of the Church of God in countries where our missionaries had labored for many years were approached one by one to enter into an agreement with the Missionary Board on a plan called "Grant-In-Aid on a Decreasing Subsidy Basis." It was a simple concept that would allow the Missionary Board to continue financial support where actually needed, but the amount would be decreased each year over a period of ten or fifteen years until the time would come when the church would indeed be self-supporting. Each agreement had to be worked out with each General Assembly. There was no rigid pattern to follow. The situation in each country was different from that in another.

It was not long before the movement's churches in Japan, Kenya, Egypt, Denmark, Jamaica, Barbados, Trinidad, and Panama were well on their way in the plan. When the shock of the first or second year's decrease of income from the Missionary Board was survived, it became obvious that a strong emphasis on all-of-life stewardship must be implemented. In countries where most of the pastors' support came from the Missionary Board, pastor-congregation relations were being strained. The pastors much preferred receiving their support from a trustworthy foreign mission rather than being dependent on their congregations. The congregation was slow in accepting responsibility for its pastor, feeling it was the mission's responsibility. Most pastors thought it was begging to ask their congregations to support them. The solution required a strong educational program aimed at both the pastors and the congregations. And that could best be done, although with problems, through the General Assemblies.

To help the churches feel responsible to their General Assembly and to assist the General Assembly in feeling responsible to aid the churches, both of which were necessary if the Grant-In-Aid plan was to be successful, the Missionary Board suggested that the entire amount of the monthly Grant-In-Aid be sent to the treasurer of the General Assembly and not to the mission secretary-treasurer for disbursement. The General Assembly would then use the funds according to an agreed-upon budget schedule. As a matter of fact, the General Assembly could probably determine more accurately the needs of pastors, churches, and programs. This placed a great deal of responsibility upon the General Assembly, but that was good. It was no longer the mission or the missionaries who were managing the finances of the church. This plan liberated the mission secretary-treasurer from one of the most difficult tasks in relation to the people. I was made aware of this after having served in that position in four different countries. Now members of the General Assembly through its various committees had to determine how the Grant-In-Aid would be distributed to persons and programs.

But adverse situations were not over. It was soon learned that the Grant-In-Aid plan had to be flexible in order to be practical. On occasion, I had to sit with a General Assembly or its Executive Council to review the possibility of adjusting the amount being sent or to extend the number of years over which the decrease of amounts was to be made. Those were always difficult sessions. It was not always easy to determine the accuracy of presentations. A certain degree of pressure had to be maintained to indicate to individuals who were not living up to agreements that the Missionary Board meant business. And yet undue suffering could not be tolerated. The question of how to be hard-nosed and compassionate at the same time is not an easy one. And there were valid reasons for adjustments or for declaring, on occasion, a moratorium on the decrease for one or two years. Sometimes, economic problems in the country were of such a nature that the common people were actually suffering. Disasters such as severe drought, famine, flood, or even war made it imperative to grant certain considerations. One or two specific situations presented special concerns. Sometimes the cost of living in a country would increase tremendously. To impose the agreed-upon cut in salary or program would amount to a double blow. Or if additional pastors or workers were taken on as the work was growing, they would not always fit into the Grant-In-Aid scheme without adjustments. Much grace and wisdom were required by all involved, and I always found the members of the General Assembly to be understanding and willing to make adjustments and concessions if the Missionary Board would do the same. In some countries, it required more grace than in others.

What happened to the funds that were withheld by the Missionary Board each year when the decrease was made in remittances sent to

General Assemblies involved in the Grant-In-Aid scheme? Naturally that question would be raised by members of those Assemblies. At first they felt the amount of the decrease in any given year should remain in the country for some special need or project. On the other hand, the Missionary Board was being hard-pressed to start new missions in new countries, and the increase in income in America was not permitting much, if any, expansion. Therefore, funds released through the decreasing subsidy plan helped the Missionary Board, but not sufficiently. It was during this period that demands were made for expansion and more missionaries were sent out. But overextension brought about deficit spending. That soon came to an abrupt end as reserves were depleted. For two or three years, what was known as an austerity budget was implemented, although neither missionaries nor the Missionary Board appreciated it. Hence, any savings through the decreasing subsidy plan to General Assemblies was desperately needed at that particular time to maintain fiscal integrity.

Toward the Transfer of Properties

The Missionary Board began to encourage each of the various General Assemblies to become a legal entity recognized by its respective government. This was stressed to allow the church in each country to hold its own properties rather than the Missionary Board's holding them. Up to this time when the Missionary Board was responsible for the work of the church, the Board had registered as an alien corporation in that country and therefore held church properties in its name. But related to the indigenization of these churches was the desire expressed by both the Missionary Board and the General Assemblies that in a country where the church existed that church should own the properties. Consequently, each General Assembly revised its constitution and bylaws to allow for the holding of properties and became a legal entity in its own country. That process required time—in some countries much longer than in others. Then the transfer of all the church's properties could take place. But eventually it happened. Occasionally, there was discussion about the possibility of including movable properties such as automobiles, house furnishings, and equipment. As a rule, movable properties were not transferred. The Missionary Board, however, did turn over all office equipment to the offices of the General Assembly when the transfer of responsibility was made from the mission to the church. It also made available at a token price mission-owned automobiles. There was always a deliberate attempt on the part of the Board to be as generous as possible at such times. Of course, the transfer of church properties itself provided the church with assets running into thousands of dollars. Furthermore, it was understood that once the transfer had been made, the church would be responsible for the maintenance and upkeep of those properties. Since in most situations there were no vast institutional buildings to maintain, no major problems evolved at that point.

Indigenous Churches from the Beginning

As the Church of God reformation movement began to spread into new countries, opportunities prevailed to start these new works as indigenous churches from the very beginning. In order to grow, they would not require a mission to be established by the Missionary Board. At the same time, however, the Board could relate and assist as mutually agreed upon by sending an occasional missionary to perform some specific and needed function. Financial assistance could also be provided without violating the integrity of the church. This could be done without giving the young church the idea that it was being controlled by the church in America through the Missionary Board. There were times and places where the people of the country were actually very poor and required some form of assistance from the affluent American churches. But the giving had to be done in such a manner that it did not make the recipient subservient to the donor.

A new set of relationships materialized with these fresh and enthusiastic beginnings in other countries even though they were not initiated by the Missionary Board. For instance, we began to have good relations with the start that Carl and Lova Swart were making in Australia, a country that had not been considered a foreign mission field. The start in Guatemala and the Philippines was made by nationals of those countries who became burdened for their people and who desired to begin a work of the reformation movement. In Denmark, a Grant-In-Aid scheme continued even after a resident missionary was no longer necessary. In Germany, the church had moved to the place where our relation with it was one of church to church. There was the unique situation in Okinawa where Church of God American military personnel started a children's work that quickly developed into an adult program. They wanted the Missionary Board to come in and take over. Instead, since Okinawa had belonged to Japan, the Board encouraged the Church of God in Japan to send one of its ministers to assist in Okinawa. The Japanese gave the young minister ten years to build an indigenous church. Later on in this chapter, more details will be given about each one of these situations. The point to make here is that in all of these new starts, the attempt was made not to burden the young church with a mission, but rather to assist it to be the church from the very beginning. This allowed for the formation of General Assemblies, the registration of those legal entities with their respective governments, and the handling of any church properties from the beginning. This bypassed the earlier route of establishing a mission, developing a church, and then demissionizing that church so that it might become indigenous. When the young indigenous church was given guidance by the Missionary Board, the possibility of fragmentation or anarchy was avoided.

By now the Church of God reformation movement was beginning to be seen, heard, and felt around the world. Not only was the missionary outreach gaining momentum, but individuals and groups were interested in starting a work wherever they might happen to be.

As I visualized the world and the work of the movement around the world, I developed the concept that there were certain spheres wherein the Church of God had influence. I called them *orbits of the Church of God.* Beyond the American and Canadian sphere, there were seven orbits of Church of God influence: the English-speaking Caribbean, Latin America, Europe, the Middle East, East Africa, South Asia, and East Asia. We will now look at what was going on in each one of these orbits during the late 1950s and the early 1960s.

The English-speaking Caribbean Orbit of Influence

The Church of God in Jamaica after fifty years of growth on the island was entering a period in its history when the influence of American missionaries and the Missionary Board was decreasing and the leadership and authority of the General Assembly and the leadership of the Jamaican church was increasing. And that was good. Years before, missionary George Olson had led the church in assuming ownership of all church properties. The Missionary Board still held title to the land and buildings of Ardenne High

School, Jamaica Bible Institute, and missionary residences. Except for a very small grant from the Missionary Board to assist in the support of pastors, the congregations were assuming major responsibility for the support of their leadership, although the pastors were poorly paid. Also, most of the pastors shepherded from four to six congregations in a circuit system, assisted by sometimes very capable lay leaders.

But difficulties were encountered as control and administrative responsibilities of the General Assembly, Ardenne High School, and Jamaica Bible Institute shifted from the Church of God mission to the Church of God in Jamaica. These situations required face-to-face consultations. I visited Jamaica twice in 1955 and then again in 1956, 1957, 1958, 1959, 1960, 1962, and 1964. Many days were spent each time in discussions with the church's leadership and the missionaries. Most of the older believers, especially those in the country churches, did not want change. They preferred authority within the church to remain with the missionaries. There were highly qualified and loyal laypeople in the church, especially in the Kingston area, who were having an increasing influence in the churches and in the General Assembly. The Assembly was lay delegated. Because there were so few qualified fulltime ordained pastors, compared to the large number of congregations, the laity began to have greater influence. But, in retrospect, I can say that this was a challenging and interesting period of time during which the church was readying itself for complete indigeneity within the next ten to fifteen years.

Nellie Olson, who had come to Jamaica with her husband in 1907 to begin the work of the Church of God, did not live to enjoy the Jamaican Church of God's fiftieth anniversary celebration. She died April 23, 1956, one of the few missionaries who spent their entire careers in one place, contributing so much toward the growth of the church. In July of that same year, a large assembly hall was dedicated at Ardenne High School and named Olson Hall. That same month a new church building was dedicated at Constant Spring Road within the Kingston corporate area, its first pastor being missionary Edgar Williams. During the annual Assembly in 1957, the fiftieth anniversary celebration took place. Adam W. Miller represented the Missionary Board, and Ocie Perry, Hallie Patterson, and Nellie Snowden represented the National Woman's Missionary Society. In July a special service was conducted at Port Antonio on the north coast of the island to celebrate the landing of the Olson family fifty years earlier. I was present and felt something of the pioneer spirit as I stood on the now broken-down wharf where the boat carrying the Olsons docked.

There was now talk of reorganizing Jamaica Bible Institute to initiate an accelerated program. But that, along with some other situations, required some changes in missionary personnel. It was agreed that Charles and Florence Struthers and Edgar and Mildred Williams would leave, to be replaced by Raymond and Elna Mae Hastings and Clair and Retha Shultz. The General Assembly wanted a change in mission secretaries, but some members were somewhat fearful about Clair Shultz's being transferred from Trinidad. They thought he might try to use the "big stick." But upon arrival the Shultzes calmed that fear and were able to help the church on toward complete indigeneity. William and Emilia Fleenor, evacuated from Egypt during the 1956 Suez crisis, were sent to Jamaica to assist a number of congregations in evangelistic efforts. As a means of strengthening Jamaica Bible Institute, a vocational department was established so that the students could earn their way through their educational programs. Ralph and Helen Little were sent so that Ralph could direct the work at the shop. Further strength was given to JBI as Kenneth and Elizabeth Jones were sent to Jamaica so that Kenneth could teach in the school's ministerial training program.

A large science building at Ardenne High School was dedicated in 1961. That was also the year when the government of Jamaica voted against the West Indies Federation, which was an attempt to develop a new nation by uniting several of the British West Indies islands, chiefly Jamaica, Trinidad, and Barbados. Jamaica's decision to go it alone spelled failure for the federation. I mention this to indicate the influence political events have on the people even within the body of the church. The fires of independence were being fanned.

The big event the following year in Jamaica was the celebration of independence from Great Britain. That did something to the entire population and helped to stimulate the desire within the church to go it alone. After all, if it could be done politically, why not within the church? That same year Clair and Retha Shultz were transferred to Kenya where he would replace retiring Wick Donohew as mission secretary. The vacancy in Jamaica was filled by the arrival of Tom and Dorothy Pickens.

On April 25, 1963, George Olson died, having given fifty-six years of service to the people of Jamaica. Kenneth and Elizabeth Jones had left

Jamaica and were replaced by James and Gwendolyn Massey. But time was running out for our missionaries in Jamaica. Edith Young retired after thirty-seven years of teaching at Jamaica Bible Institute. The Masseys were to remain for only three years. The Littles were on their last term. Also, someone had to be found to replace the Pickenses, who were being transferred to London, England, to pastor a West Indian congregation of the Church of God. Meanwhile, there was a move on to replace Mary Olson with a Jamaican headmistress at Ardenne High School. By now there were 730 students enrolled in the school. In terms of the Jamaican work as a whole, there were eighty-eight congregations of the Church of God but only fourteen full-time ministers to care for that number of churches.

On the Cayman Islands, Arthur and Mary Kluge were endeavoring to fulfill their assignment by encouraging the congregations and the one institution, Triple C School, toward indigeneity. Missionary Vivian Phelps, principal of the school, was urging a better school organization. It was a mission school, but Phelps thought responsibility should rest with the church. There was some question whether the school should be a private school or one responsible to the church. It required several years to get all of this settled, including the school's relationship to government and to the one other secondary school on the island. On Grand Cayman, the church had no legal entity to hold the properties of the four congregations on the island. They were held under a trusteeship, and some of the trustees had moved away or had died. It was necessary, therefore, for the General Assembly to be regularized and duly constituted to hold its own properties for the church. Vivian Phelps was transferred to Kenya in 1959. A five-year plan was initiated to make Triple C School entirely indigenous but responsible to the Church of God General Assembly in the Cayman Islands. One of the most severe problems for the Caymanian church was related to pastoral leadership. For some reasons very difficult to understand, the church appeared unable to produce its own ministers, let alone teachers for the school. When Dewey and Thelma Johnson replaced Arthur and Mary Kluge in 1963, it was understood that the Johnsons would be the last resident missionaries for Cayman. And the Johnsons did remain until 1970. During the 1960s, every attempt was made to assist the Church of God in the Cayman Islands to develop and employ Caymanian pastors. Even to the present time, any attempt on the part of the church to do that has been unsuccessful and North American pastors have been asked to serve. There has been a rapid turnover of these expatriate pastors because the congregations do not pay adequate salaries, even though they have the potential for doing so.

Farther south in the Caribbean, on the island of Trinidad, missionaries and national church leadership began thinking in terms of the indigenous church and how to achieve it. Donald and Betty Jo Johnson were transferred from British Guiana in 1956 and assumed roles of leadership in the West Indies Bible Institute. By 1958 William and Emilia Fleenor had come down from Jamaica to provide evangelistic emphasis among the fourteen congregations on the islands of Trinidad and Tobago. Meanwhile, Clair and Retha Shultz were transferred to Jamaica. It was becoming obvious that the official position of the mission was beginning to diminish. In fact, in Trinidad both missionaries and leaders of the General Assembly talked in terms of the integration of the mission and the church. Questions were raised, such as to what extent the missionary was subject or responsible to the national church. It was a time of testing several approaches to the situation and learning from the process.

When Clair Shultz left Trinidad, it provided opportunity to consider a West Indian as president of WIBI. Fortunately, Carlton Cumberbatch agreed to accept that position. He was the son of the first ordained minister of the Church of God in Trinidad. By the early 1960s, graduates coming out of WIBI were assuming roles of leadership in the Church of God throughout the southern Caribbean. The General Assembly in Trinidad and Tobago accepted a scheme for Grant-In-Aid on a decreasing subsidy basis over a ten-year period of time. Throughout that decade, the church was faithful in carrying out the plan. In 1959 a new chapel was dedicated at WIBI and named the Houston Memorial Chapel in honor of the First Church of God in Houston, which had donated the funds. Walter and Margaret Lehmann served as missionaries from 1961 to 1964. In 1963 Donald and Betty Jo Johnson left missionary service at the end of a term, and Walter and Margaret Tiesel were transferred from Barbados to Trinidad. The General Assembly in Trinidad began the process of incorporation so that it could be recognized as a legal entity to hold the properties of the church. It was obvious to all that the time was soon coming when the Church of God in Trinidad and Tobago would be indigenous and the West Indies Bible Institute would no longer be a school administered by the mission but a school responsible to the Church of God in the southern Caribbean and administered by a board of trustees representing the area.

Further out in the Atlantic, the Church of God in Barbados continued to mature. In the late 1950s, the General Assembly and the Missionary Board worked out a ten-year plan for decreasing financial subsidy through the Grant-In-Aid concept. At the same time, work began to incorporate the General Assembly so that it could become the legal entity to hold the properties of the church. In order to change the image of the missions, the Grange building was sold. This large building, formerly the residence of the postmaster general, had been purchased earlier as a residence for our missionaries. But it always appeared that the missionary was living in a luxurious place compared with the homes of the church people. Also, it was costing the Missionary Board too much money to maintain the building. From the sale of the Grange, two modest residences were purchased, one for the one remaining missionary family in Barbados and one next door to the Chapman Street Church in Bridgetown to be used as a manse as well as for headquarter offices for the General Assembly.

The fiftieth anniversary of the Church of God in Barbados was celebrated in 1962 during the annual Assembly. An island crusade was conducted with Dale Oldham as guest speaker and Doug Oldham as song leader. At the appropriate time, a special service provided opportunity for me to hand over all the deeds of church properties to Augustus Banister, chairman of the General Assembly, thus transferring those properties to the church. They represented seventeen pieces of land, nineteen church buildings, and four manses, with a value totaling approximately one hundred thousand dollars. Here as well as in other countries where transfer of property took place, I explained that it was never the intent of the Missionary Board to take its investment in properties back to America when the mission ceased to exist in any given country. Rather, the investment by the American church in properties was part of the total contribution made in order to help establish the church.

About this time, the General Assembly was experiencing difficulty in keeping up with the decreasing subsidy of the Grant-In-Aid plan. A revision was necessary, which the Missionary Board accepted. When Walter and Margaret Tiesel were transferred to Trinidad, Lavern and Darlene Root were sent as replacements. One very positive outreach by the church in Barbados materialized. The people became vitally interested in their own missionary project on the island of St. Vincent. I was amazed when I saw the manner in which the offering plates would be filled with contributions for supporting their own missionary outreach. That brought new enthusiasm and vigor to the church. Such a method will do it every time wherever it is tried!

During this period of time in British Guiana, missionary leadership was undergoing change while at the same time several attempts at expansion were initiated. In a small village called Whim and farther up the Demerara River at a settlement called Wismar, there were small groups of believers associated with the Church of God. For health reasons Herman and Lavera Smith left the field in 1959 and were replaced by Aaron and Kathryn Kerr. Within two years, the Kerrs left and Raymond and Elna Mae Hastings were sent, followed by Edward and Meriam Oldham when the Hastingses were transferred to Saltillo, Mexico. With such a rapid turnover in missionary personnel, it was not easy to maintain stability in the work. The church leaders were never quite certain whom to follow.

It was during this time, however, that British Guiana was in the last stages of gaining its independence from Great Britain and that provided the right atmosphere in which to encourage the church toward becoming indigenous. Racial and political tensions produced strikes and riots between the East Indians and the West Indians. In the church, for the most part, racial tensions did not surface, although most of the East Indian congregations were found in the Corentyne, a district to the east of Georgetown. The church was still in a season of growth. Ralph and Ruth Coolidge were sent to the colony to give additional missionary support. Several young women and young men were returning from the West Indies Bible Institute, prepared to work in the church. The big question discussed in the General Assembly was how to carry on planned expansion and with whose financial support.

There were now thirteen congregations of the Church of God in British Guiana and twenty-five Sunday schools. Only six congregations had church buildings. The greatest growth was among the East Indians in the Corentyne. Up the Demerara River, real potential existed for a strong work at MacKenzie and Wismar, centers of the lucrative bauxite industry. Farther into the interior, two attempts were made by the church to start a work among the Amerindians, the primitive people of the jungles. Mr. Dover, who was a corporal in the police force, and his wife—members of the Bellaire Street Church of God—were sent to the Northwest Territory to keep law and order among primitive peoples and those who were coming in to open up the area. Mrs. Dover started a Sunday school in their home. Unfortunately, a severe border dispute between British Guiana and Venezuela forced the Dovers to leave the interior—a move that closed the opportunity there.

The Church of God in British Guiana was making strides toward self-reliance. The General Assembly adopted a revision of its constitution and bylaws, giving it strength and authority. For the first time, a national minister became chairman of the Assembly in place of a missionary. A Grant-In-Aid scheme was adopted, even though there were fears that it would not succeed due to the terrible state of the country's economy. Also, the fiftieth anniversary of the Church of God in the colony was celebrated. As in the other countries celebrating the year of Jubilee in the church, I was privileged to be present to assist in the joyous occasion. At the end of their first term of three years, Edward and Meriam Oldham returned to America, but Ralph and Ruth Coolidge remained to give encouragement to the church.

The Latin American Orbit of Influence

Sustained efforts were maintained to keep the small yet growing work in Guatemala indigenous from the beginning. As the small group of believers began to enlarge and reach out under the dynamic leadership of Isai Calderon, the question was raised as to what extent the American church should assist. The Missionary Board did not want to inject a mission with a resident missionary. But there were needs that the American church could provide through the Board. Frequent visits by American church leaders assisted in revivals and conventions. Missionaries provided encouragement through visits by Earl and Freda Carver from Cuba, William and Emilia Fleenor from Trinidad, and Keith and Gloria Plank from Costa Rica.

By 1962 there were ten congregations of the Church of God, and those had come into being in less than ten years. There was a lack, however, of trained leadership for these groups of believers. Isai Calderon recognized the need for doctrinal teaching and strong moral support. Occasional grants were made available. By 1963 land was purchased on the Pan American Highway where it passes through Guatemala City, and a year later construction began on a beautiful and adequate church edifice, primarily sponsored by the First Church of God in Houston and the

Missionary Board. It became necessary for the Missionary Board to hold the properties of the church in Guatemala until such a time as its organization would become strong enough to be a legal entity. But the reformation movement in Guatemala was well on its way as a viable indigenous group of believers.

The time came when resident missionaries were needed in Costa Rica if the English-speaking West Indian believers were to be encouraged to expand into the Spanish-speaking community. Consequently, in 1958 Keith and Gloria Plank were sent as missionaries. They lived in the capital city, San José, where they studied Spanish at a language school. They started meetings in their home as well as making occasional visits to the two small congregations on the plain. Another missionary, Paul Ashton, was sent to assist in reviving the congregation in Puerto Limón. Also, a new work in Siquirres came into being. The Planks and Paul Ashton left in 1964, and Sidney Bennett, a Costa Rican returning from his studies at West Indies Bible Institute, along with his Trinidadian wife, assumed responsibility for the two congregations of Cimerrones and Siquirres. Leroy Nicholls, a Trinidadian who had just graduated from WIBI, and his wife from Barbados came as missionaries to care for the work in Puerto Limón. Leroy and Monica Nicholls went through all the culture shock and the necessity of learning Spanish the same as any missionary from America.

In Panama, the reformation movement was still primarily among the West Indian people with all the meetings being conducted in English. A move was on, however, to shift from English to Spanish, for now second and third generations were coming along who had been educated in Spanish. English was the language still spoken in the homes and church services. There was also the desire to reach out to the Spanish-speaking people. A new face-off in the work took place when Dean and Nina Flora were sent to Panama as missionaries, replacing William and Hope Livingston. Strong emphasis was placed on the need for the church to move toward indigeneity. The church began to organize itself in a more responsible fashion, and it was not too long before the General Assembly accepted a Grant-In-Aid scheme over a ten-year period. A new spark of enthusiasm was generated in the church when contacts were made with a number of converts among the primitive people the Cuna Indians on several of the small San Blas Islands. This was to mature into a strong segment of the total work of the Church of God in Panama.

Progress continued in Cuba during the late 1950s, but difficult days were soon to be experienced. A Woman's Missionary Society was organized, and a Spanish-language broadcast entitled *Light from Heaven* was started. Four young men of the church were in training at an interdenominational Bible school at Placetas. A National Assembly of the Church of God in Cuba became a reality, and a new church building in the Finlay section of Havana was erected. The first youth convention in Cuba was held with great success. But political conditions began to bring adverse pressure on all Christian work on the island. Unsettled conditions prevailed as Fidel Castro began his takeover. There were mixed feelings about Castro, as the population was glad to be rid of the Batista government. The church, however, began to suffer. The government closed the Placetas Bible School. Earl and Freda Carver were forced to leave, followed by Ellsworth and Hilaria Palmer. The Palmers settled in Miami, Florida, and began to work among the Cuban refugees who were streaming into America to escape the Castro regime. This was the beginning of a Spanish Church of God in Miami.

Back in Cuba, the Church of God continued with almost no interference from the government. Meetings continued and properties were maintained. There were, however, certain regulations to abide by, and secret service men attended meetings regularly. All evangelical pastors had to register with the government and had to pay 11 percent of their earnings. Fortunately, there was a good core of capable leadership for the church: Remberto Ortiz at Matanzas, Arturo Fumero at Cascorro, Gerino Blanco at Finlay (Havana), Jaime Beil at Diezmero, and Andres Hines on the Isle of Pines. As time went on, fewer and infrequent contacts with the church leaders in Cuba were enjoyed, even by way of correspondence.

At the beginning of the 1960s, German immigration into Brazil remained high, including people from the Church of God. The Missionary Board knew almost nothing of what was taking place among the German believers in the Church of God in Brazil and Argentina. The Church of God in Germany took on the work in both countries as a missionary project, sending evangelists and pastors as needed. Publication work was under way in Rio das Antas and Bible classes began in Joinville. As David and Lillian Meier returned to Brazil, they soon found themselves in the new settlements in and around Rondon in western Brazil. The general headquarters of the work seemed to be in Curitiba. As early as 1960, the Missionary Board was giving some consideration as to what might be done to assist in the work in Brazil and Argentina. Approaches from certain German people were received, but during that decade, prime responsibility remained with the Church of God in Germany. There were only feeble attempts to reach the Portuguese-speaking population.

Something new was started in Peru by Paul and Mary Butz and their family as they felt called of God to leave America and take the gospel to the people in the interior of Peru. Paul hired on with Le Tourneau, which had developed a center at Tournavista and was developing agricultural projects south of Pucallpa for the government. Paul and Mary were self-supporting missionaries. They had visited with the Missionary Board on their way south and wanted to keep in touch. During the first four years, the Butzes worked with the settlement of American Christians at Tournavista. They wanted, however, to reach out to the people of the country. When Paul lost his job with Le Tourneau and became employed by Zachry Construction Company, he launched out on his own in doing gospel work. He built his home at Campo Verde and began a congregation. Soon a church building was erected, and a Peruvian worker by the name of Salomon Cabanillas was assisting. A little later on, 125 acres of land was purchased between Campo Verde and Pucallpa where eventually a Bible school would be established. Here is a classic example of what individuals can do in missionary service with the knowledge and blessing of the Missionary Board when the Board is unable to extend its financial commitments.

The European Orbit of Influence

Something out of the ordinary was taking place in England. Due to severe economic pressures in many of the British West Indian Islands of the Caribbean, many West Indians were emigrating to England to seek employment. They could enter Great Britain easily, for they were citizens of the British Commonwealth. Included among them were many Church of God people from Jamaica, but there were also several from Trinidad and Barbados. As they discovered one another in the great city of London, they came together to form a new congregation of the Church of God reformation movement, the only one in London. The other two older congregations were further north in Birkenhead and Liverpool. The group started in 1960 in a rented Anglican church hall and was led by one of its number, Shirley Miller.

Lars and Ellen Olsen left Denmark in 1957, having assisted greatly in training several young Danes for Christian service. Their replacements were James and Esther Fair. Esther was the daughter of J. P. N. Ikast, who had served earlier in Denmark. She knew the Danish language, having grown up in Denmark. The Fairs had a five-year goal to develop an indigenous church. Six major activities occupied all their time. First, the Bible school was expanded. Consequently, effective church leadership emerged. Carl Carlsen and David Anderson, who became the two main leaders of the church in Denmark, were the first two graduates. Second, since the only religious materials available were those printed by the Lutheran church, the state church of Denmark, translation of some basic materials for the Church of God was undertaken. This was a laborious job, but it was well worth the time and effort expended. Third, a new hymnal in Danish for the Church of God was printed in 1962. Fourth, to break down the isolation of the Church of God in Denmark, interchurch cooperation was encouraged with evangelical groups. In 1960 the Church of God became a member of the Danish Free Church Council and the Danish Sunday School Association. Fifth, James Fair invited Church of God pastors in Denmark, England, and Germany to meet in Denmark to discuss ways and means whereby there could be more cooperation in the Church of God in Europe. By 1960 the first European Ministers' Conference convened in Bochum, Germany, with ministers present from Denmark, England, Greece, Holland, Germany, and Switzerland. This conference now meets every two years and is a unifying factor for the reformation movement in all of Europe. And finally, Fair encouraged the Church of God in Denmark to become a freestanding body. A lay-delegated General Assembly was organized, Guds Meinghed's, with an Executive Council, Representantaskak. The Fairs returned to America at the end of their first five-year term, having accomplished the goal. The Church of God in Denmark was self-reliant, with a revised scheme of Grant-In-Aid that would be decreased over a fifteen-year period.

Progress continued throughout the Church of God in Germany. In fact, the movement in Germany became the focal point for all the work in Europe, mainly through the biennial European Ministers' Fellowship, which I have mentioned before, but also as a result of the second and third World Conferences of the Church of God convened in Essen in 1959 and in Bochum in 1963. More about these World Conferences will be mentioned later in this chapter. In West Berlin, which was like an island stranded in the midst of communist East Germany, the Church of God maintained a congregation under the leadership of F. Besteck. As I stood at the church one day in 1963, I could almost feel the strong pressures militating against the Christian forces in West Berlin. In Essen, the publishing work of the Church of God under Gerhard Klabunde was given the opportunity to build a new facility for the printing of gospel literature. It was on the same property in Essen that a beautiful new church building had been erected two years earlier.

Continuing to exist under numerous handicaps, the movement in Hungary maintained its viability under the leadership of Janos Vigh in Budapest and Attila Vigh in Tiszaszederkeny. One new work came into being at Imaeden, Holland. And in Switzerland, the congregation in Zurich came under the pastoral care of younger people, Willi and Edith Krenz, who soon brought more youth into a congregation composed of mainly elderly persons. Enthusiasm was also generated in that congregation to work toward the time when it could have its own property, for up until that time it had always convened in rented quarters.

The Middle Eastern Orbit of Influence

It does not happen very often to missionaries, but just as the apostle Paul experienced shipwreck so did Ernest and Grace LaFont and their son Leland as they were returning to America for furlough from Egypt in mid-1956. The passenger ship *Andrea Doria,* on which the LaFonts were sailing, suffered a collision with a Swedish liner, the *Stockholm,* and sank. The accident occurred not too far out of New York. Most of the *Andrea Doria's* passengers were rescued, among whom were the LaFonts, and many were brought into the harbor on board the crippled Swedish boat. Upon hearing the radio news of the disaster at sea, I boarded an airplane to New York and caught up with the LaFonts just as they arrived at their hotel in New York. They had escaped, of course, with only what they were wearing at the time of the accident. Fortunately, Ernest had the family passport in his pocket. So before closing time that afternoon, we went out on a shopping spree to buy toothbrushes and toothpaste, combs, brushes, shaving equipment, and clothing for further travel to Anderson. Everyone in New York was kind and considerate toward the survivors of this major sea disaster.

In November of that same year, the crisis over the Suez Canal exploded and all nonessential American citizens were advised by the American embassy to leave Egypt at once. Jean and Ruth Kilmer, William and Emilia Fleenor, and Evelyn Skaggs with her two children were evacuated by the United States Navy to Italy, along with most of the other missionaries in Egypt. It was agreed by the mission staff that only Wilbur Skaggs would remain in Egypt to look after the work of the church and the affairs of the mission. Since there was need in Kenya, the Kilmers were sent there from Rome. The Fleenors and Evelyn Skaggs with her two children were brought home to America. The Fleenors were then sent on to Jamaica to assist in evangelistic work.

The Suez Canal crisis proved to be a turning point in the political life of Egypt—a turning point felt by both the church and mission. There was a strong upsurge against imperialism, colonialism, and the state of Israel. With a revival of the state religion of Islam, many legal requirements were laid upon Christians and churches, including the holding of meetings only by royal decree. Missionaries suffered in the backlash. Because it appeared the days of missionaries in Egypt were numbered, strong emphasis was placed upon the nationalization of the church in that country. The Missionary Board felt the work should go on in Egypt but with a change in emphasis by the missionaries. They now had to expend every effort to prepare the church for complete self-reliance. Therefore, within a year Jean and Ruth Kilmer were returned to Egypt from Kenya. Also, Evelyn Skaggs and the two children returned from America. Unfortunately, Evelyn suffered a severe illness that terminated the missionary career of the Skaggs family. Ernest and Grace LaFont returned to Egypt. Antiforeign and anti-Christian forces gained momentum throughout the valley of the Nile. It was a time of testing through subtle persecution experienced by all Christians.

In an attempt to maintain a helpful missionary staff in Egypt, James and Sybil Simpson were sent to Cairo, but they remained only three years. Difficult situations were developing within the General Assembly of the Church of God in Egypt. The decreasing subsidy schedule of the Grant-In-Aid scheme had failed and adjustments in the plan were required. In Egypt, this always brought tension between the missionaries and the leaders of the church. At the end of their term on the field, Jean and Ruth Kilmer returned to America to stay. James and Elizabeth Royster, however, were transferred from India to Egypt. The Indian government had refused to renew the Roysters' resident visas.

After two years, a need developed farther to the south in Kenya, requiring the services of James Royster; so when the family was transferred from Egypt to Kenya in 1964, it left only one missionary couple in Egypt, Ernest and Grace LaFont. Because of the uncertainties of the future, all Church of God properties in Egypt remained under the ownership of the Missionary Board. These were uneasy months and years for the Arabic-speaking congregations. The Greek and Armenian congregations were dying due to emigration to other countries. Foreigners saw no future for themselves in Egypt. But all was not dark. The youth centers in both Cairo and Alexandria were booming. University students and young professionals from various ethnic backgrounds came together in these places in Christian fellowship to strengthen one another and to minister to others. Out of the group in Alexandria, Franco and Beatrice Santonocito felt called to the ministry, went to Lebanon for training in a Bible school, and returned to Alexandria to assume leadership of the youth center there. In 1965 the Church of God mission in Egypt joined in partnership with three other evangelical missions in Egypt to operate the Nile Christian Bookstores, taking over a British-sponsored Nile Mission Press, which had been asked by the government to leave the country. This proved to be an unprecedented opportunity to witness in a Muslim land through literature.

To the north in Lebanon, the work was really beginning to grow as a self-reliant entity. Fouad Melki and Adel Masri were ordained to the Christian ministry. A campsite was purchased in the Lebanon mountains by some of the church members in Beirut, and a small colony of believers began development of a community that is now called Theopolis. Evangelistic efforts fired the body of believers to involvement in Kingdom work and the Church of God in Lebanon began to receive the attention of the entire Protestant community. To the northwest in Greece, a revival broke out among a group of Gypsies in Tragano, which is located in the southern Peloponnesus. The Zazanises needed help, so Dan and Aleta Dallas were sent to Greece. The Dallases encouraged a large youth group in the Athens congregation and assisted greatly in Tragano. Unfortunately, that work among the Gypsies collapsed because an opportunity opened for them to emigrate to Germany, where employment was available. Following the Dallases, Savas and Olive Joannides were sent to Athens to replace the Zazanises, who were retiring, It was a moving experience for me to be present with the congregation when Savas Joannides was installed as pastor and the farewells were being said to the Zazanises. It should be noted that in Greece, where the Greek Orthodox church is the state church, it was most difficult for any evangelical group to grow. In fact, the strength of the Greek Orthodox church politically was such as to prevent by force any major growth of any evangelical group.

The East African Orbit of Influence

The fiftieth anniversary of the Church of God in Kenya celebrated in 1955 was the beginning of a decade of very rapid growth. Evangelistic efforts of the church resulted in many village congregations springing up, worshiping in large grass huts for the most part. Many times elementary schools began in connection with and at the birth of the local church. To keep up with the opportunities and needs of this growth, the Church of God mission in Kenya was enlarging numerically and broadening its services. Missionaries were laboring with a passion to bring into being a church worthy of the name, although many times rather strong colonial methods were employed.

In Kenya, more than in any other country where the Church of God had missionary activity, the Missionary Board employed the institutional as well as the evangelistic approach. This was due no doubt to the educational and medical needs of the people. Most certainly they also had urgent spiritual needs because of the strong hold animism had on the people.

The British colonial government showed considerable interest in giving direction and financial grants to Christian missions involved in education and medical services, for the people would thereby be enabled to develop their country more rapidly. Missionaries entered into these services motivated by a spirit of Christian love and compassion, feeling that many people would thereby be reached with the good news of salvation. By the early to mid-1960s, the American Church of God reached its largest investment of missionaries in Kenya, averaging around forty-five for any given year. Roughly one-third of these were involved in educational work, one-third in the medical program, and one-third in direct church-related work. It was not always easy to maintain a balance in these various kinds of services, for institutionalism has a way of demanding personnel, equipment, and an operating budget that, although necessary, tends to leave lesser amounts for direct church-related expenses. At one point we had so many institutional buildings and so many missionary residences in Kenya that a full-time maintenance missionary was required.

But the rapid advancement of the African people of Kenya could never have taken place without all of these combined efforts. With all the criticism leveled at colonialism, and most of it justifiable only in retrospect, it must be said that the British more than any other colonial power endeavored honestly to prepare developing peoples for political independence. Independence came to Kenya on December 12, 1963, when the Union Jack was replaced by the national flag of Kenya. The British had trained public servants for government offices as well as provincial and district officers for governing the interior of the country. It should also be noted that a parallel situation existed in the Church of God in Kenya during this period of time. Missionaries were involved in basic services of all kinds that would prepare Christians for the time when the church would become indigenous—a time not far away.

As I look at the record, I am amazed at the rapid growth of the mission's medical department. Over a very few years, numerous buildings were erected, especially at Mwihila. Nora Memorial Hospital, generally known as the Church of God Hospital, started with only the main unit of the facility, an outpatient clinic, one doctor's residence, and a duplex for American nurses. Within less than ten years, the investment included a men's ward, a women's ward, and a maternity wing as units attached to the main unit of the hospital, in addition to rooms for surgery, X-ray, offices, and classroom space. Then two more residences for missionary doctors, an African nurses' residence, an African male dresser's house, a kitchen and dining hall, a laundry, a chapel, a morgue, and a graduate nurses' home were built. Added to that was a larger outpatient clinic, including offices for two doctors.

All of this plus missionaries who were living at the same station involved in educational work created a small village in itself, for which adequate water supply had to be found and electricity generated by the mission's own generator brought in from America. The American church invested close to a half-million dollars in this one project. In addition, there was development at the Kima Hospital, which offered mainly maternity service as well as excellent clinical attention. There were at least six clinics scattered out in other parts of the Western Province, staffed by American and African nurses and visited regularly by the doctors stationed at Mwihila. A strong nurses' training program was established at the hospital at Mwihila.

Missionaries who worked in the medical program during this decade, although not necessarily the entire period of time, were Deloris Beaty, Darlene Detwiler, Rosa Bollmeyer, David and Elsie Gaulke, Lydia Hansen, Candace Heinly, Merlene Huber, Harold and Donna LaFont, David and Joan Livingston, Vera Martin, Hazel McDilda, Jene Nachtigall, Ruth Sanderson, Richard and Donna Smith, Naomi Sweeny, Edna Thimes, and Arthenia Turner.

Elementary education spread rapidly by way of the church and mission and was subsidized by the government. Intermediate schools sprang up at Kima, where the girls' school was located, and schools for boys were established at Mwihila, Ingotse, and Emusire. For a number of years, our mission provided the Teacher Training Center at Mwihila and staffed it with missionaries to provide qualified graduates to teach at the elementary level. A few of our missionaries were involved in intermediate education, for there were not enough Africans prepared to teach at that level.

Within almost no time, pressure was on for more secondary schools (equivalent to our high schools) due to the demand from students graduating first of all from elementary schools and then from intermediate schools. Competition to enter the very few secondary schools throughout Kenya was fierce. The government hastened to make the necessary provision. The Mwihila Teacher Training Center was changed to a secondary school for boys; the Bunyore Girls' School at Kima was changed to a secondary school for girls; the intermediate school at Ingotse was changed to a secondary school for boys, and the intermediate school at Emusire was changed to a secondary school for both boys and girls. These and similar changes throughout Kenya created staffing problems, for there were only a few Africans in Kenya who had a bachelor's degree in education.

As Africans went forth to Europe and America to train, having completed secondary education in Kenya, American short-term teachers by the scores were required immediately. Many Church of God teachers responded and made a marked contribution at a very critical time in the overall development of Kenya, but especially within the Church of God in Kenya. African Christians were so intent upon providing education for their children that *harambee* schools were started. This African word means that the people pulled together to start their own schools, struggling for a few years until they could qualify for government grants.

Missionaries who were in the educational program during this decade, although not necessarily the entire period of time, were Alta Abrams, Esther Beaty, Calvin and Martha Brallier, Olive Fiscus, Jewell Hall, Harry Nachtigall, Carl and Eva Kardatzke, Margaret LaFont, Velma Schneider, Ruben Don and Jenny Schwieger, James and Dorothy Sharp, Richard and Georgia Woodsome, and James and Glenna Yutzy.

While all this was going on, rapid developments also took place in other institutions related more directly to the church and mission. The Kima Bible School was upgraded rapidly so that as young men came out of intermediate and then secondary schools, feeling the call to the ministry of the church, they could be adequately trained on a commensurate level. More space and buildings were required. By 1962 the name was changed to Kima Theological College, and adequate facilities were being provided over a period of years. It joined the East African Theological Association. This institution was a definite asset to the development of the Church of God in Kenya.

A self-help program brought forth a tannery and leather-craft industry where Christians could find employment in a local business and thereby become self-reliant more quickly. Unfortunately, this experiment did not end with success, and this brief attempt at self-help went out of existence. As the extremely outdated printing press was abandoned at Kima, a modern offset press was installed in a building at Mwihila, and through the efforts of Douglas Welch, a strong literature program called Church of God Publications was started. An African church paper was initiated.

One more institution, which was strictly American, was born. Within the numerous Church of God missionary families stationed in Kenya, there were many children who were too young to be sent off to boarding school at Kijabe, where the Africa Inland Mission maintained an excellent school for American children. Consequently, the Church of God mission started the Baker Elementary School at Mwihila, where missionary Vivian Phelps, transferred from Grand Cayman, taught in a modern one-room school for children in grades one through six. After that they would go to Kijabe. Baker Elementary School remained open for almost fifteen years and then closed its doors, for there were no longer any missionary children in that age bracket to educate.

A new mission station was opened at Ibeno in Kisii. It was to provide additional assistance beyond what had been given by the African missionary, Obed. Lima Lehmer and Lydia Hansen were especially helpful in getting this station started, serving there for a time. Soon medical and educational facilities were established, and the work of the church in the Kisii area expanded. Roy and Magaline Hoops, who were independent Church of God missionaries stationed in Shitoli to the northeast of Mwihila, were appointed by the Missionary Board, bringing the few congregations in the Idakho area into the mainstream of the Church of God in Kenya.

Other missionaries who served in church-related work were Samuel and Jane Betts, Irene Engst, Lew and Wanda Goodrick, Frank LaFont, Vivian Phelps, Simon and Mae Robinson, Ruben and Nora Schwieger, Clair and Retha Shultz, James and Beth Royster, and Douglas and Ruth Welch.

Each one of the numerous missionaries who served in Kenya during this period of unusual development and expansion deserves the highest praise for work well done. Many times adverse circumstances prevailed. Language had to be learned. Malaria was still prevalent. Dirt roads made travel difficult during the rainy season. It was not always easy to make the necessary adaptations to fit into the African culture, but there was always the positive side. Satisfying joy was found in service, and gratification came from an unusual dedication to the task assigned. God supplied the missionaries with physical strength and spiritual graces beyond the ordinary. And above all, the African Christians were always grateful and showed their appreciation in so many gracious ways.

By 1965 real signs of a self-reliant Church of God began to appear. The General Assembly of the Church of God in East Africa was making the necessary adjustments and approaches to the government to become a registered legal entity in order to hold property that the Missionary Board was soon to transfer to the African church. For the first time, an African, Daudi Otieno, became chairman of the General Assembly, replacing a missionary. He was the son of the chief who gave the land in the beginning for the Kima mission station. The Kaloleni Church of God had been established in that section of Nairobi on the plot of land given by the government for the establishment of the only Protestant church. Also, the Mariakani Christian Center was erected in another part of Nairobi on land given by the government. Altogether, there were twelve congregations of the Church of God in Nairobi, the capital city.

The Church of God was being established in other urban areas, such as Nakuru, Eldoret, and Mombasa. Africanization was well on its way in the institutions. Boards of governors were placed in administrative control of the four secondary schools, the hospitals at Mwihila and Kima, and Kima Theological College. The manner in which members were appointed to these boards provided the possibility for the Church of God to maintain control, thus making them truly institutions to serve the church in East Africa. Throughout all this administrative development, the Church of God in East Africa was primarily evangelistic in character, resulting in church growth. Much of this direct evangelism was done by Africans, making it especially effective.

The year 1958 found Stanley and Marion Hoffman and Ralph and Gertrude Farmer in Kenya as independent Church of God missionaries from Canada. They were being sponsored by the World Missionary Fellowship with headquarters in Medicine Hat, Alberta. For a time the couples worked with J. S. and Twyla Ludwig in Nairobi. Early in 1959, however, the Hoffmans began a mission station in a primitive place in Tanzania called Kaiti. Later that same year, the Farmers moved to Tanzania to start another station not too far from Kaiti near the small town of Mbulu.

Two years later, Stanley Hoffman began another station farther south at Mirambo. These were strictly pioneer missionary ventures of faith requiring much hard work. Slowly but surely over the next five years the stations at Kaiti and Mbulu became centers of Christian nurture and outreach. Missionary residences were constructed, and several other buildings were erected on each station to facilitate the work. Following evangelistic efforts, small congregations came into being in surrounding villages. Limited clinical services were provided. Training classes developed into Bible schools at Kaiti and Mbulu. At Mbulu, the school was called ABLE, which stands for African Bible and Leadership Education. A few other persons from Canada came to both stations on very short terms of service. Before long, there were a number of pastors and evangelists. God was blessing the efforts of these missionaries in spite of some of the difficulties inherent in independent missionary outreach.

Missionaries and a few African church leaders from Tanzania visited the Church of God in Kenya, attending an annual convention there. It dawned upon all that the work of the Church of God in East Africa should be one. This seemed to suggest that the mission in Kenya and the mission in Tanzania ought to be one. In 1965 Clair and Retha Shultz and I were invited to visit this development in Tanzania. That was a beautiful experience of fellowship and sharing concepts related to the unity of God's people and the missionary work in which they are engaged. A tentative schedule was agreed upon, pointing toward the time when the work in Tanzania would come under the administrative guidance of the Missionary Board of the Church of God. This subject, however, takes us into the next chapter.

The South Asian Orbit of Influence

On the Indian scene, the government was struggling with its political independence. This decade of time that we are now considering encompassed three five-year plans through which the nation was attempting to improve communications, industry, and agriculture. The British were forgotten, but English was the only common language of India, where more than four hundred languages and dialects are spoken. An attempt was being made to enforce the teaching of Hindi in all schools. The aim was to eventually make it the common language of the country, but it did not work.

Within the Church of God in India, this was also a time of change and progress, including the ways in which Church of God missionary efforts in that country related to it. To the south, in the state of Kerala, Gordon Schieck was endeavoring to bring the church together in a unified approach. The first General Assembly of the Church of God in South India convened in Chengannur, with the three ordained ministers and Gordon Schieck forming the Executive Committee. A number of the church properties were held in the name of the late P. J. Philip, and so the first step was to have them transferred to the Missionary Board of the Church of God and then to wait until the All-India Assembly of the Church of God formed a legal entity to which all the properties held in the name of the Missionary Board of the Church of God could be transferred to the Indian church. Farther north, in the state of Orissa, Sidney Johnson was feeling his way and gaining confidences. The main emphasis in Cuttack was placed on the institutional work of The Shelter and the schools. The one congregation claimed to be indigenous, and so little assistance was given by the missionaries. It was not long before Sybil Holmes became the first Indian home superintendent at The Shelter instead of a missionary. The small group in Calcutta[1] had dwindled. In Cuttack, the Sonat Nalini Girls' High School was dedicated, and in place of a missionary being responsible to give guidance, a management committee assumed control. Farther to the north, in the state of Assam, I had the privilege of spending several days renewing relationships with James and Evalyn Nichols-Roy. This opened the door for future contacts to be made with them by our missionaries in India. It was a period of reaffirming fellowship within the one body of Christ.

At the very southern tip of India lived a seventy-two-year-old man named D. M. Devasahayam. He was the leader of a group of three thousand Christians called the Bible Faith Mission. They were looking for fellowship and affiliation with a larger group and had been recommended to the Church of God because their beliefs were almost identical to those held by the reformation movement. In 1957 it was my joy to be with Gordon Schieck when the first official contact was made with the twenty congregations. My notes reveal a few exciting moments wherever Schieck and I appeared and were honored in processions with horns, flutes, drums, and garlands. At one place, a public address system played Sousa's "Stars and Stripes Forever." It was like a wedding ceremony at times. In fact, Devasahayam expected the marriage of the two groups to take place immediately. But obviously more time was necessary for complete understanding. A year later an affiliation agreement was signed, integrating the Bible Faith Mission with the Church of God in South India. It reminded many people of the Day of Pentecost when three thousand persons were added to the body of believers.

There were other signs of advancement by the Church of God in India. In the state of Orissa, the government granted permission for the Church of God to enter Keonjhar District, which was 99.64 percent Hindu. This challenge was taken up by the congregation in Cuttack. The small group in Calcutta again began meeting under the leadership of Hridoy Mundul. Later the congregation was assisted by Glenn and Alice Beach, Canadian missionaries appointed to India.

A feeling was growing among our missionaries and a few of the Indian church leaders that it would be good to bring all the work of the Church of God in India more closely together. It was said, "How can we believe in unity and live in isolation? Something similar to the early camp meetings held in Cuttack from 1905 to 1920 should be revived." So it happened in October 1961 that the first meeting of the All-India Assembly convened in Cuttack, Orissa, with Church of God delegates present from the states of Assam, Kerala, Orissa, and West Bengal. This brought about a feeling of oneness and strength throughout the Church of God in India. Only a provisional committee met in 1962 due to Chinese infiltration into northeast India, severe food rationing, and difficulties in transportation. But the scope of the Assembly was outlined. A planning and coordinating committee was formed, and an outline of some basic beliefs of the Church of God was reviewed.

By 1963 the first draft of a Trust Memorandum was considered as the initial step toward the formation of the All-India Trust for the holding of properties. Four very important papers were presented to the Assembly, designed to develop a oneness in understanding major issues in the church. Also, a monthly periodical, *High Calling*, was started for the English-speaking ministers of India and East Pakistan.

The result of all this was that the missionary force of the Church of God in India was strengthened in spite of mounting restrictions and difficulties in securing visas. Glenn and Alice Beach were in West Bengal assisting at Calcutta; Clifton and Mary Morgan were in Orissa soon to help at the new outreach at Keonjhar after land was purchased and a multipurpose building erected; and James and Elizabeth Royster were in Kerala with an assignment to study carefully the problem of theological training for upcoming Church of God leaders in India. As a result of that study, the All-India Assembly decided to use primarily Union Biblical Seminary, located at Yeotmal in the geographical center of India. The Missionary Board concurred and became a member of the Cooperating Home Board in America, which gives assistance to the seminary. When Ellen High left India for furlough in 1958 after eleven years of service, she did not return to India under the auspices of the Missionary Board. During this period of time, there were losses in Indian leadership. J. J. M. Nichols-Roy died in Shillong, November 1, 1959, after fifty-five years of service in the ministry. In 1960 Banchu Sahu, pastor of the Mount House Church of God in Cuttack, retired after fifty years of labor. Four years later in Cuttack, Jonathan Mohanty died. He was a dedicated lay leader, an educator, and early pioneer in the Church of God. That same year, in September, Evalyn Nichols-Roy died in Shillong. You will remember she had come to India as a young missionary in 1904, married young J. J. M. Roy in 1906, and had given her entire life to the Khasi people over a period of sixty years.

In September of 1962, I met in Calcutta in the Red Shield Hostel of the Salvation Army with twelve of our missionaries in India and East Pakistan. This was the first and last conference of its kind, but it was necessary at that juncture. Understanding and consensus were necessary as relationships of missionaries to the Indian church were experienced. My notes taken at that time reveal several items discussed: the development of the indigenous church, the All-India Assembly, Grant-In-Aid on a decreasing subsidy basis, the possibility of an All-India Trust to hold properties, ministerial training and theological education, ecumenical relations, institutional work, and the development of the local congregations. These topics were carefully studied over a period of five days. A ten-year plan emerged, outlining certain strategies, one of which was that by the year 1972 the Missionary Board would have no more resident missionaries in India. But observe that in the Calcutta conference there was not one Indian church leader present. It was agreed from that time forward that the All-India Assembly should be the body to strategize and plan. And so during the next few years, the missionaries worked closely with that body regarding all the issues at hand. Each time I visited India, I did business directly with the Assembly and had wonderful Christian fellowship. The church indeed, was emerging from a mission.

Some signs of progress appeared in the Church of God mission in East Pakistan, but pressures from an Islamic government were keenly felt. An indigenous church was extremely slow in forming. Paul and Nova Hutchins were new missionaries living at Lalmanirhat while Robert and Frances Clark moved into a rural area at Kakina, endeavoring to identify with the Pakistanis by adopting their lifestyle as much as possible. In 1960 the Hutchinses moved to Nilphimari to help build the work. Just across the border in India is a frontier town called Siliguri, and a new group was developing under the leadership of P. K. Misra. Since this was so close to Nilphimari, it was thought best to have the missionaries in East Pakistan give encouragement. Of course, as the work grew in Siliguri, it became an integral part of the Church of God in India.

About this time there was a discovery in the Sylhet District of northeast East Pakistan. A number of years before, when East Pakistan was the East Bengal state of India, a large number of Church of God Khasi Christians from Assam settled in the Sylhet area, But no contact had ever been made with them after the partition of India took place and Pakistan became a new and separate nation. So it was with a great deal of enthusiasm that this large group in the Sylhet area was brought into the fellowship with the Church of God in East Pakistan. They spoke the Khasi language rather than Bengali, but this did not prevent regular contacts being maintained with them.

When Robert and Frances Clark returned to America at the end of their term in 1961, they terminated their services in East Pakistan. In order to keep at least two missionary families in that mission, Joseph and Ramona Spires were sent by the Missionary Board. They resided at Lalmanirhat. On that mission station, the Lalmanirhat Mission Middle English School was providing elementary education through the eighth grade. There were 287 pupils, 12 percent being from Christian families, 74 percent Muslim, and 14 percent Hindu. The school had been operating for ten years without a government permit, but there was never any question from the authorities. One of the pressures that finally had to be obeyed, however, was the teaching of the religion of Islam to the Muslim students only. Christian mission schools in all countries where Islam was the state religion struggled with this pressure, but they agreed that it was still worthwhile to keep the schools with an overall Christian influence open rather than to have them closed and thus lose all contact through children. The Missionary Board, therefore, authorized the missionaries in East Pakistan to comply with the law.

There were basic weaknesses in the work of the Church of God in East Pakistan. Traditionally, the people were dependent upon the mission. Poverty prevailed, making it easy to fall into a system of "rupee diplomacy" whereby almost everyone received financial assistance in one way or another from the mission. Considerable thought was given to developing some kind of a self-help project in this rural area, and sometime later a large fish pond for raising fish to market and a small cooperative farm were tried. For reasons difficult for Westerners to understand, both projects never really reached the goals set for viable self-help projects.

The East Asian Orbit of Influence

By the beginning of this decade, Donald and Arlene Goens and Philip and Phyllis Kinley were new missionaries in Japan. Through the efforts of the four missionary couples then present in Japan and the enthusiasm of Japanese church leadership, the Church of God continued to grow. New church buildings were erected in Imajuku, Fukuoka, and Osaka. Nathan and Ann Smith moved southward to Kyushu Island, where there was potential for Christian growth, with starts that had been made at Imajuku and Fukuoka. Donald and Arlene Goens helped Japanese leadership at Fukaya and Menuma north of Tokyo. Another new work in Tokyo was started in Nishi-Kunitachi. At the request of Renmei, the Japanese church's General Assembly, Arthur and Norma Eikamp moved from Tamagawa in Tokyo to the Osaka area. The Church of God in Japan was beginning to have three points of emphasis: the greater Tokyo area, the Osaka-Kobe area, and Kyushu Island to the south.

Instead of starting a Church of God seminary for theological education in Japan, it was finally decided to use excellent Christian seminaries already in existence in Tokyo and start what was called a Seminary House. This would be a kind of hostel where the few Church of God seminary students would live and from which they would attend the seminary chosen. Philip Kinley was requested by the Japanese to head up this program. The Kinleys would live next to the Seminary House and offer guidance and fellowship to the students. Two important courses would be taught by Philip Kinley: Church of God Doctrine and Christian Education. Kinley always worked closely with the dean of the seminary where the students attended, particularly at the point of field work in Church of God congregations. This Seminary House program provided excellent theological training commensurate with the level of education enjoyed by Japanese young men who felt called to the Christian ministry. The number of those called, however, was not great, and so the number attending seminary through the Seminary House during any given year was anywhere from two to six students. But this was felt adequate for openings available in the Church of God in Japan.

Tamagawa Seigakuin, the school for girls, was enlarging its enrollment from 450 pupils in 1960 to 515 in 1962, and was reaching for 750 students. This required additional building and equipment facilities as well as additional faculty. Freda LaFoe left teaching in United States military schools in Japan and became a full-term missionary, teaching English in Tamagawa Seigakuin. This school provided great opportunity for Christian witness not only in Tamagawa District but also in Tokyo as it became known for its excellence in education. Quality leadership was found in Shigetoshi Taniguchi-sensei, who was principal for a number of years.

As I sat in the meeting of Renmei in 1962, I heard individual reports, translated quietly into English by Arthur Eikamp, from fourteen congregations and preaching places. These represented a total of 422 adults attending morning services and an average of 1,090 attending Sunday school. That is a very good record of achievement considering the church started from zero immediately following World War II. In Japan less than one-half of 1 percent of the population is Christian, including Roman Catholics and Protestants. It is not easy and requires considerable time to bring a person reared in the major non-Christian religion of Japan to an understanding of Jesus Christ. It should be observed, however, that for a number of years following World War II, there was an interest expressed by many Japanese to discover a better way. But culture and society continued to have strong influence, preventing many from following Christ.

Near the end of World War II, one of the bloodiest landings by American forces took place on the little island of Okinawa as General Mac-Arthur's forces moved closer to the mainland of Japan. Once taken from Japan, it remained under the control of the United States Civil Administration of the Ryuku Islands for many years. The island was considered the keystone of the Far East. About 1960, interest on the part of several Americans stationed on Okinawa seemed to converge. These were persons of the Church of God who were interested in winning people to Christ. First of all, there was Mr. McGarvey's wife, who was of Japanese background. McGarvey was employed by the occupational forces, and his wife had been converted to Christianity in the Church of God in El Paso, Texas. Somehow she made contact with William Caylor of the air force, Richard Rudman of the navy, and John Williams of the army, along with their respective families, all of whom were Church of God people. Altogether, they were interested in starting not only a Sunday school but also a congregation. They had gone into Ameku, a suburb of the capital city, Naha, and started work among the children of the community. Almost all of the homes they visited were Buddhist. Among this group of Americans only Mrs. McGarvey knew the Japanese language.

I was invited to stop at Okinawa during one of my trips to East Asia, and there I observed a real opportunity to do something for God. Members of the American armed forces stationed in Okinawa were already supporting the activities with their finances. In fact, they had already purchased a small lot in Ameku and were hoping to gain assistance to build. Nathan

Smith was asked to come down for a visit from Japan. Okinawa is about halfway between Japan and Taiwan, and so it was not far from where Smith lived on Kyushu Island. I suggested that perhaps the Church of God in Japan would like to take on this opportunity as a missionary outreach, especially since the people of Okinawa were Japanese speaking. Renmei, the Japanese General Assembly, accepted the challenge, and Masahiro Orita was sent to Okinawa as their first missionary. It is interesting to note that the church in Japan gave Orita-sensei ten years to bring about a totally self-reliant work in Okinawa or they would consider his efforts a failure. By 1964 all of these Church of God Americans had left Okinawa, but they continued to support the work as best they could while on the island. Orita-sensei carried on the work as it grew and spread to several other locations on the island.

Following the Korean War, the leaders of the Church of God in Korea began requesting assistance from the American church. Perhaps as a result of a guilt complex, the Christians of America began pouring millions of dollars into that country. The Korean Church of God established the Seoul Bible Institute, known in Korean as Han Yung Shin-Hak-Won. The main leaders at that time were H. C. Ahn in Seoul and Jai Kun Kwak in Mok Po. The church had established two large orphanages in Mok Po and Suwon as well as a boy's high school in Mok Po. Many Church of God people in America gave liberally to the support of the widows and orphans in Korea.

The Missionary Board decided to provide thirty thousand dollars to get a resident missionary to Korea and to assist in capital fund needs at the Bible school. Kenneth and Sue Jo Good were sent in 1961. First, they spent two years in language school and then devoted the remainder of that five-year term to teaching at the Bible school and assisting in general church work as the church leaders desired. A Grant-In-Aid plan was set up to assist in the support of the Bible school, where there were twenty-five students and nine faculty members, although they were not all full-time. Everything appeared to be going smoothly, and the work was growing as students began to graduate from their training programs. It was unfortunate, therefore, when seeds of division were sown by an independent American by the name of Carl McIntyre. This was certain to affect not only the Church of God in Korea but every other Protestant group. In another chapter you will read what happened.

In Hong Kong, P. K. and Lovena Jenkins were serving the Chinese people in that British colony. He had become medical superintendent of the Junk Bay Medical Relief Council, which supervised the Haven of Hope Tuberculosis Sanatorium, Rennie's Mill Christian Medical Center, and the Sunnyside Children's Hostel. Staff was secured from evangelical Christians in Europe and America. Following several visits to Hong Kong I was being encouraged to have the Church of God contribute a staff person. But it required several years for this to materialize. Contacts were made with Isaac V. Doone, the son of one of the early pastors of the Church of God in China. Doone was and still is a successful businessman. Through him and other underground sources the Missionary Board was able to maintain some contact with the believers in China.

Rolando Bacani, a Filipino working on an American base in Guam, became a Christian under the influence of William Rife, went to Gulf-Coast Bible College in Houston, Texas, to complete his education, and returned home to Manila, capital of the Philippines, to begin a work of the Church of God. This proved to be another successful attempt at starting a church that would be indigenous from the beginning. That is to say, there would be no long-term resident missionary sent to oversee the development. In 1959 Bacani started meetings in his home and within two months moved to a larger rented place. During those early years of the work, I stopped by occasionally to provide encouragement. Nathan Smith made a visit or two from Japan. Bacani made contact with the earlier congregation of believers in Laoag to the north. By 1962 there were three Church of God congregations in the Philippines, and the following year the Pacific Bible Institute was initiated.

Vacation Bible schools flourished in both Manila and Laoag, and the Church of God in the Philippines incorporated so that the congregations could hold their own properties. By 1964 a chapel and parsonage were built for the First Church of God in the Valenzuela District of Manila. Rolando Bacani proved to be a very capable leader. The people were willing to work hard and to sacrifice, and so there was really no need for the Missionary Board to become involved officially. However, it did not violate the concept of indigeneity to encourage and assist from time to time. Financial grants were also in order. But this aid did not make the people of the congregations dependent upon the church in America.

During World War II, Japan conquered Guam, a small island in the southwest Pacific. Three years later, William Rife landed with the United

States Marines under heavy gunfire. Rife's buddies fell all around him as the invasion force waded ashore and dug foxholes in the sandy beach. He felt his life had been spared for a purpose under God. I have stood with Bill on that beach and have heard him tell the story with tears running down his cheeks. It is not surprising, then, that in 1955 William Rife returned with his family to Guam to preach the gospel. He also taught school in order to earn a living. Rife and his family were met by Denny Armey, a member of the armed forces with whom contact had been made through the *Gospel Trumpet,* now *Vital Christianity.* The Rifes began a work among the Filipinos who had been hired by American contractors building for the United States Air Force and Navy. By this time, Guam was a possession of America. Guamanians were American citizens, but without the right to vote. The population was 96 percent Catholic. At first, groups of interested persons met in a camp where the Filipinos were billeted. By 1958 the group of believers was large enough that property was purchased in Barrigada just outside the town of Agana. The First Church of God was incorporated in Guam to hold property. Tropical storms played havoc with the wood frame building, and so in 1963 a new steel-framed building was erected. A minister by the name of Wilbur Miller, who was from the Northwest, flew to Guam with his family to assist in the work. To support himself, he operated the A & W Root Beer franchise on Guam. It was about this time that Rife left his teaching at the local high school to begin giving full time to the ministry, and the one congregation flourished.

On the island of Hawaii in 1955, Curt and Carole Loewen went to Honolulu from Pacific Bible College, now Warner Pacific College, and enrolled in the University of Hawaii. They soon met other Church of God people from the mainland, such as William and Dolores Wright, and house meetings were conducted in their homes. The group soon grew to about twenty persons and Carl Riley responded to their plea for a pastor. Regular services were first held in Kenneth Smith's residence and then in the M's Ranch Restaurant in the Aina Haina District of Honolulu. Soon there were about eighty attending. There were Japanese, Chinese, Filipinos, and mainlanders, including a few from the armed forces.

When Carl Riley resigned, my parents were taken out of retirement again and sent by the Missionary Board to Hawaii for two years. Since there was quite a turnover of persons in the congregation because of changes in military personnel and people going and coming from the mainland, it was thought good for the Missionary Board to assume responsibility for the work for a few years. In 1959 Hawaii became a state of the United States of America. Some conversation began with the Board of Church Extension and Home Missions to see if it would be interested in assuming responsibility for the work in the new state. Later you will read what happened. The following year a large residence was purchased on Mona Street in Aina Haina, and one part was remodeled for use as a small sanctuary. After the Croses returned to the mainland, two pastors served for brief periods of time. Then Proctor and Virginia Barber began a four-year ministry, during which time the church was strengthened. During the Croses' ministry, a number of Hawaiians of Asian background were converted from non-Christian faiths.

Even though Australia is a separate continent from Asia, I am arbitrarily including it in the East Asia orbit of the Church of God. As you read in Chapter 2, contacts with E. P. May were broken in 1924, and the Church of God ceased to exist in Australia as a reformation movement until 1958 when Carl and Lova Swart reached Sydney as independent missionaries but with the Missionary Board's blessing. It was a venture of faith, and God rewarded their efforts. After purchasing a car and a small trailer, the Swart family spent the first couple of months touring the eastern part of the continent to discover the best place to begin. During their travels, they discovered some Church of God people from Germany, the Hermann Siebert family, who had settled in Warners Bay and had started a small congregation. The greater Sydney area was chosen by Swart as a starting point. The first meeting was convened in mid-1959 in the Masonic Hall in Canley Vale. Soon land was purchased in Canley Heights and a small house on it was renovated. By 1961 a new brick sanctuary was built. Annual camp meetings were conducted on the large grounds.

Not too long after meetings were started at Canley Heights, the Swarts discovered the Harold Chilvers family, who had remained loyal to the reformation movement from the days of E. P. May. Chilvers and his married son, Lloyd, were successful dairy men. Both Harold and Lloyd Chilvers and their families were real assets to the Church of God as it was growing again in Australia. It was not long before Lloyd and Ruth Chilvers moved to Canley Heights, and they became vitally involved in the work. God called him to the ministry and he began to pastor. Several persons arrived from the United States to assist the Swarts, and most of them were self-supporting through teaching school. It was about this time that E. P. May was discovered and by invitation attended one of the large camp meetings at Canley Heights.

Another congregation was started at Green Valley, a new and growing subdivision. Then God led the Swarts to the state of Queensland, where land was purchased on the Isle of Capri in Surfers Paradise. But it was to be a few years before the first Sunday school was conducted. Edward and Leona Schweikert, from Michigan, and Gilbert Swart and his wife, from Ohio, both couples being experienced pastors, were valuable self-supporting additions. By 1965 the leaders of the Church of God had organized and the Association of the Church of God of Australia was legally formed. All church properties were held by the association.

Special Events and Significant Landmarks

World Missions Conventions. This was a period of increased interest on the part of the Church of God in missions. The National Woman's Missionary Society, the Board of Church Extension and Home Missions, and the Missionary Board of the Church of God were working together in missions education to assist the church in its desire to learn more about and to do more for the cause of missions. One of these attempts to inform was through World Missions Conventions. Guest leaders presented challenging messages, missionaries on furlough conducted conferences, and displays provided colorful information. Here is where the first three were held: Dayton, Ohio, in September 1955; Wichita, Kansas, in September 1957; Oakland, California, in August 1959.

Following the third convention, a careful evaluation was done. Concern was expressed at the point of effectiveness. The same group of convention goers in the Church of God were being reached at each convention. Little helpful information was getting back to the local congregations. It was then decided to attempt to take these meetings to more people by having several conventions about the same time. Therefore, the fourth World Missions Convention in 1961 was conducted in three cities in the East and three cities in the West. The fifth convention was held in Anderson, Indiana, in 1963 in the new Warner Auditorium. A final attempt at this kind of convention was to conduct almost simultaneous meetings in eight cities: Atlanta, Georgia; Sikeston, Missouri; Detroit, Michigan; Pasadena,

Texas; Denver, Colorado; Walla Walla, Washington; Edmonton, Alberta; and Pomona, California. From that time forward, better methods were employed in missions education within the church.

World Conferences of the Church of God. By the mid-fifties, the time was ripe on the international level for bringing world representatives of the Church of God together for fellowship and sharing. Sponsorship at first was by the Board of Christian Education in America and was soon broadened to include the Missionary Board and the Executive Council of the General Assembly in America. Ultimately, representatives from the Church of God in other countries were brought into the World Conference Planning Committee. Following is where these important meetings have convened: Fritzlar, Germany in 1955; Essen, Germany in 1959; Bochum, Germany in 1963; Zurich, Switzerland in 1967; Oaxtepec, Mexico in 1971; Beirut, Lebanon in 1975 (canceled due to civil war); Anderson, Indiana in 1980.

Through these very productive efforts, world leaders of the movement became acquainted with one another, discussed important issues, and shared valuable information from around the world. These conferences have remained strictly nonlegislative. They have not been considered a world General Assembly for the Church of God. Multiple and valuable blessings have come out of each one of these World Conferences. They caused people to think in terms of the Church of God all around the world.

Inter-American Conferences. A growing interest on the part of the church in America in Central and South America prompted W. E. Reed, the executive secretary of the Board of Church Extension and Home Missions, and me to visit almost every one of the Spanish-speaking areas where the Church of God was extant. So in mid-1960 we stopped in Miami, Florida, on our way south to determine the possibilities for ministry among the Cuban refugees. Then we went on to Cuba, where we heard firsthand how the church was being affected by the revolution. In fact, Dr. Reed and I just got out of Havana in the nick of time. Then we met with churches and their leaders in Panama, Costa Rica, Guatemala, Mexico, and those involved in the Spanish-speaking work in Texas.

We picked up four definite recommendations that became the combined concern for both the "home" and the "overseas" boards. Leadership training and skills were number one. The drastic need for more literature in the Spanish language was the second recommendation. Because of that need, a Spanish publication committee emerged. Number three was evangelism. And finally, everywhere we went we were urged to initiate some kind of annual meeting for the entire area that could provide opportunity for sharing and encouragement. Out of this last expressed desire came the Inter-American Conference, to be conducted every other year. The two Boards assumed responsibility at first for these biennial meetings, but now the gatherings are entirely in Latin hands. Following are the places where the Inter-American Conferences have convened: Mexico City, Mexico, in 1962; Guatemala City, Guatemala, in 1964; Mexico City, Mexico, in 1966; Guatemala City, Guatemala, in 1968; Mexico City, Mexico, in 1971 (back-to-back with World Conference in Oaxtepec); San José, Costa Rica, in 1973; Panama City, Panama, in 1975; Caguas, Puerto Rico, in 1977; Curitiba, Brazil, in 1980.

The Church of God throughout Latin America has been greatly strengthened as a result of these times of fellowship and inspiration enjoyed by both nationals and missionaries.

Fiftieth Anniversary of the Missionary Board of the Church of God. A golden anniversary is always a time for celebration. The Missionary Board was fifty years old in 1959, and appropriate expressions of gratitude were provided. A dramatic presentation titled *Fifty Years of Missions* was presented during the International Convention in Anderson. A special banquet for the Missionary Board was prepared at each of the six regional ministers' meetings in America. A large fiftieth anniversary cake was served and appropriate speeches given. Weekend celebrations were conducted for clusters of congregations across the United States. The National Woman's Missionary Society promoted "Greenleaf" teas among local societies. A very well-done brochure was prepared that described the fifty years of service the Board had given on behalf of the church.

Lastly, the Missionary Board launched a special project, having cleared it through World Service, to raise one hundred thousand dollars for some special needs on the mission field. The theme for the entire celebration was "Because We Care." And because the people of the church did care, the goal was reached. Twenty thousand dollars was designated to Japan to be used in helping to build small church buildings; thirty thousand dollars was given to Korea to help in the building program at the Seoul Bible Institute and to place a resident missionary in that country; and twenty thousand was earmarked for Kenya to help establish the new

Kisii station, with an additional thirty thousand dollars set aside to add a maternity wing to the hospital at Mwihila as well as to build a kitchen and dining hall. Finally, it should be reported that the Missionary Board was making plans for advance during the decade of the 1960s and prepared a film titled *Our Mission for the Sixties* for missionary education.

Missionary Education Committee. Very early in the 1960s an ad hoc committee was formed by the leaders of the National Woman's Missionary Society, the Board of Church Extension and Home Missions, and the Missionary Board of the Church of God, to include persons from each agency responsible for promotion. It was named the Missionary Education Committee and quickly became the focal point through which cooperative efforts were made by the three agencies to place before the church in America informative, educational, and inspirational material related to the mission of the church. It published the monthly *Church of God Missions* magazine and prepared various kinds of study materials. It introduced the concept of schools of missions, which later on were simply called missionary conventions. The MEC has continued through the years in a most effective manner, making a tremendous contribution to the missionary cause of the movement.

All-Board Congress. As America entered the decade of the sixties, revolutionary changes were taking place within its society. In fact, the entire world was being shaken with radical social, economic, political, and cultural upheaval. It was a new era that forced the Church of God in America to take a hard look at the situation and reach some conclusions as to how the church might fulfill its obligation to the peoples of the world. Therefore, members of all Church of God national boards and agencies, along with representative ministers from across America, came together in Anderson for four days in 1963 to think and pray about certain objectives. Specific goals emerged for the Missionary Board: (1) to develop a dynamic program to further the church in other lands; (2) to take advantage of specific missionary opportunities in the 1960s, such as in major urban areas of the world and among the unreached primitive peoples wherever found; and (3) to develop a "new breed" of missionaries to carry out the responsibility of the sending church as well as to prepare better missionary education materials and methods for use by the church at large. By involving many leading pastors from across the country, stimulating feedback to the boards and agencies was achieved.

Living Link Program. Edgar Smith, assistant secretary for the Missionary Board for many years, began work immediately following the All-Board Congress to bring together in a more personal way the church in America and the missionaries it was supporting. Merely giving to a missionary budget seemed quite impersonal and left many donors cold regarding how their contributions were being used. The result was the Living Link Program, whereby a congregation could take one or more missionaries to support and have direct contact with those missionaries. It was possible to support a missionary totally or only in part. Rules were drawn up, the concept was cleared by World Service as a valid way in which to raise funds in the church, and numerous pastors were approached for their reaction to possible involvement of their congregations. At the very beginning, eighty congregations signed up, and the program has been a success ever since. The program underwent several revisions, all for the good, eventually including the partial support of national pastors wherever Grant-In-Aid funds were sent for that purpose.

Growth in Number of Missionaries. At this juncture, it is of interest to note the manner in which the number of missionaries under appointment of the Missionary Board increased, for it was in 1964 that the number reached the maximum. The following statistics present the growth:

Year	Number of missionaries
1909	19 plus 8 evangelists in Europe
1920	32
1930	41
1945	60
1953	73
1967	96

Following 1964, the number of missionaries sent out by the Missionary Board declined to the low eighties and the high seventies. The reasons for this will be presented in the next chapter. It must always be remembered that the quality and extent of the missionary movement of any group is not measured simply by the number of its missionaries. More important factors enter in. The numbers game is important only within Western culture.

Theological Education. In a country such as Kenya where secular education was being upgraded so rapidly and made available to almost all children, it was only natural that within a few years Kima Bible School would be upgraded to Kima Theological College with entry requirements becoming gradually more demanding. As more young people with a secondary education were available in the Church of God in the Caribbean area, both Jamaica Bible Institute in Jamaica and the West Indies Bible Institute in Trinidad were upgraded. The Seminary House in Japan changed only slightly in how it functioned to facilitate Japanese young men in their quest for theological education. The Bible Institute in Korea maintained a level of education commensurate with the needs of those training for the ministry. La Buena Tierra in Mexico served the church's youth well. The Church of God in Germany continued to upgrade the courses offered by the Fritzlar Bible School. And in India, young persons desiring to be trained for the ministry were being encouraged to attend Union Biblical Seminary if they were academically prepared.

But there remained the need for training at the postsecondary level. The Missionary Board felt that theological education was one very important contribution it could make, even in countries that were becoming self-reliant. Also in response to this need, the National Woman's Missionary Society made available a limited number of scholarships to worthy students recommended by their respective responsible church bodies, feeling it was much better to train students in their own country rather than to bring them to America.

CHAPTER 6
THE THIRD-WORLD CHURCH
IN DEVELOPING NATIONS
(1965–1975)

The Church of God reformation movement wherever extant throughout the developing nations continued its growth during the decade beginning with 1965. This was in spite of continued unrest at home and abroad. In America, student demonstrations on numerous college and university campuses many times ended in violence. There were marches of many descriptions. Feelings of revolt against institutions had an adverse effect even on the institutional church. And around the world, numerous factors were casting their influence on the missionary scene: population explosion in many countries, continued rabid nationalism, violent revolution, resurgence of ancient world religions, new theologies within the Christian church at large, and sudden social and political developments with the balance of power shifting from the so-called white world to other people.

These general characteristics of the sixties made it imperative to discover fresh and meaningful guidelines for determining the missionary response to the world's life and the church's life held in tension. These would take us beyond the traditional in missions to more dynamic and effective ways of bringing to bear upon human need the fact of redemption through Jesus Christ. The Missionary Board was faced with the ever-present problem of determining priorities. Strategy in the midst of contemporary events demanded an unusually careful deployment of personnel and funds to demonstrate good stewardship. Policy required that somewhere between the reactionary right and the revolutionary left the Board must maintain a radical middle of vital conservative evangelical thought and action, emphasizing both the evangelization of individuals through the proclamation of the gospel and the expressions of social concern through service.

I emphasized that throughout all our missionary endeavors we must maintain a consistent historical perspective. The year-to-year political vicissitudes are not the criteria by which we judge success or failure in missions. Doors close and doors open, so we roll with the punches, maintaining long-range planning and strategy with a flexibility to meet the necessity for adjustments. It was also my simple thesis that regardless of methods used and policies followed, the theological imperative of the irreplaceable task of evangelism must remain uppermost. Our missionary efforts must be found in the right location within the magnetic field between the two forces of revolution and reconciliation.

Through all of the previously described situations, my feeling was that the cause of missions should always serve with a practical extension of Christian love and compassion performed with responsibility and integrity. However, the missionary work of the Church of God is, I declared, a movement, not an establishment. It is and always will be the work of the Holy Spirit working through consecrated persons but not the work of people alone. Therefore, great things continued to happen. There were challenging developments during this period of time, as we shall now observe.

Proliferation of independency. For a period of more than fifty years, the reformation movement in America had been looking to the Missionary Board as the focal point to give expression and direction to its missionary outreach into other countries. The Board had been formed by the Ministerial Assembly in 1909 to provide purpose, meaning, and coordination to former independent expressions of missionary activity. This mandate from the responsible body of the movement was taken seriously by both the Board and the entire church body. But now, in the mid-sixties, there began to appear again an increasing proliferation of missionary independence. This well represented the mood of the times in America. And it was not all bad, although it did generate some situations requiring careful thought and cooperative effort for solution. Individual volunteerism, independent crusades, work camps, and paramissionary organizations became active, involving within a few years hundreds of missionary-minded persons from scores of local congregations across America.

There was still another situation that seemed to lend credence to this growing missionary independency overseas. The Missionary Board was one of the general agencies in World Service, the national united fund of the movement for the support of the work of the agencies. As such, the Board was committed to operate within its budget approved by the General Assembly. It could not go to the church and promote nonbudgetary projects or solicit nonbudgetary funds. As a result, the Missionary Board was experiencing great difficulty at that time in enlarging its missionary outreach, even though there was increasing demand from the church to do so because of numerous opportunities in other countries. Through missions conventions being conducted in an increasing number of local congregations, there was a growing desire on the part of numerous individuals to engage in some form of missionary service. Consequently, if the Missionary Board could not send them, some of these who felt led by the Holy Spirit went about raising their own support from one or more local churches and departed on their own to serve in a country where they felt there was need. Sometimes these persons partially supported themselves. It is true that many times these individuals would review their plans with the Missionary Board, seeking its blessing.

Independent ventures of faith appeared in Guam, Australia, Peru, Puerto Rico, and Tanzania. There were attempts on the part of some to provide special services of one kind or another in the Philippines and Guatemala where the church was maintained on an indigenous basis from its beginning. Paramissionary organizations became active within the movement. Two such organizations were Vacation Samaritans, headquartered in San Diego, California, and Project Partner with Christ, headquartered in Wichita, Kansas. There were those who considered the National Woman's Missionary Society and Church of God Men, International, as paramissionary organizations, but that was not quite correct. Both of those organizations have always been considered to be auxiliaries to the work of missions, for they have not sent out missionaries or engaged in any form of administration in missionary outreach. Some have thought that the Tri-S (Student Summer Service) Program at Anderson College was paramissionary. But it was primarily an academic activity with a strong emphasis in contacting and serving in areas of need in other countries. Whenever a group of students completed a project related to the Church of God in another country, that was it; there were no sustained relations with the church.

The result of all this was much the same as that that led up to the appointing of the Missionary Board in 1909. Many church leaders in America began to wonder what kind of a church was being developed in countries where it was being started by independent individuals. The fragmentation of financial support was seen as a hindrance to any united effort to promote the missionary cause. By 1970 there was a general call for a clarification of relationships. During the 1974 General Assembly, action was taken to coordinate all independent activities with those of the Missionary Board. A Missions Study Committee was appointed, and the following year it submitted its report with an outline of helpful expectancies. The trend was to bring these independent efforts within a working relationship with the Missionary Board, recognizing as valid the mandate given to the Board by the Ministerial Assembly in 1909.

World relief. The specter of world hunger was brought to the attention of Americans, especially Christian Americans, when in 1966 India suffered the worst drought in seventy years, resulting in 80–100 percent crop failure. Millions of people faced starvation unless immediate assistance reached them. The Missionary Board and the General Assembly passed resolutions that year calling upon the movement's people to cooperate with efforts to alleviate world hunger. Contributions for world relief were sent to the Missionary Board and distribution was made immediately through Church of God missionaries involved in relief or through Church World Service. Compassionate Christians responded immediately. Thousands of dollars were distributed effectively. By the following year, a real concern for refugees was developing around the world. By the beginning of the seventies when all of our brothers and sisters in Christ in East Pakistan suddenly found themselves as refugees in northeast India, it was not difficult for people of the Church of God in America to contribute several thousand dollars. That kept our fellow Christians alive in refugee camps and assisted in their repatriation and rehabilitation in what became known as Bangladesh. In 1973 our people were again moved to respond to the tragic famine in the Sahil region of sub-Sahara Africa. They were encouraged to give through Church World Service or through the World Relief Commission. In 1974 a Disaster Fund became a part of the World Service budget, providing funds for suffering resulting from natural disasters as well as from starvation. Later, in 1975, the Church of God in America became more serious in meeting world needs as a result of a resolution sponsored by the Missionary Board and passed in the General Assembly, placing one hundred thousand dollars in the World Service Disaster Fund. This provided funds for immediate use in time of need without having to wait for funds to be sent in.

Continued progress by third-world churches toward self-reliance. The third world is generally known as those countries that are developing in every aspect of their lives. So it was with the Church of God reformation movement in countries where missions from America had been working for several years. There was a growing consciousness on the part of the people in congregations that they were the church. A trend was observed in the change from a "mission complex" to that of "church consciousness." With the obvious devolution of our American missions in a number of countries, the Missionary Board became particularly sensitive to what the indigenous church in those countries was saying. The integrity of the church was recognized, along with the responsibility that it carried as a body with a unique identity. For instance, it was found necessary to work with the responsible body of the church relative to American missionaries. What missionaries did the church want, for what use, and where were they to be placed?

The word *flexibility* was in vogue among missionaries, recognizing the fact that they might well be asked by the church to serve in some capacity other than that for which they had been assigned when sent to the field. *Redeployment* became another word well understood among missionaries when their services were no longer needed in one country and they would work with the Missionary Board in finding another field in which to offer their services. There were some countries wherein the number of our missionaries was decreased, such as in India, Kenya, and Jamaica. But there were other countries in which the number of missionaries remained constant, such as in Japan.

It is important to observe that relationships were never broken between the Western churches of the movement and the new self-reliant churches in the third world. Everyone within the fellowship felt they were a part of the worldwide Church of God reformation movement. And it became apparent that the "developing churches" and the "developed churches" must cooperate as partners on equal terms. This was especially true when the Church of God around the world was faced with the evangelization of the fourth world. This was a new term to denote the peoples in the world who had never heard of Jesus Christ as Savior. All signs pointed to a time in the near future when self-reliant churches of the movement around the world would be cooperating in Kingdom work.

In this connection, recognition of Church of God congregations in several third world countries was accorded. These groups, such as in Guam,

Australia, Peru, Bolivia, Uruguay, Nicaragua, and Tanzania, had been established through some form of independent effort. Now it was time to acknowledge these Christians as part of the worldwide fellowship of the reformation movement.

Integration of the two Missionary Boards. The presence of two missionary boards of the Church of God was first brought to my attention by students attending the West Indies Bible Institute in Trinidad. They had become aware of the existence of the Missionary Board of the Church of God with offices in Anderson, Indiana, and the Foreign Missionary Board of the National Association of the Church of God with headquarters at West Middlesex, Pennsylvania. They wondered why there was a "white" board and "black" board. Also the Study Commission on Race Relations set up by the Executive Council of the Church of God in America suggested that where there might be duplication of boards of the Church of God on a racial basis an attempt should be made to effect integration. This was another reflection of the mood of the times in America.

During this time I had numerous conversations with Evans B. Marshall, chairman of the Foreign Missionary Board. Beginning in the mid-1960s, a total of five joint meetings were convened in which official representatives of the two missionary boards reviewed the situation, agreed that something should be done about it, and came up with a schedule pointing toward the time when the two boards could be integrated. Missionaries working in the missions of the National Association on the islands of Bermuda, Antigua, St. Kitts, and Curaçao were given the opportunity to discuss the proposed integration. A joint visitation to these islands was conducted by Evans Marshall and his wife; the Butlers, a leading black couple from Toledo, Ohio; Adam W. Miller; and me.

Upon the approval given by the General Ministerial Assembly of the National Association of the Church of God and the Missionary Board of the Church of God, the merger of the two boards took place by the signing of an official agreement on June 21, 1967. This agreement called for only one board, the Missionary Board of the Church of God. The Missionary Board would assume all administrative, financial, and church-related oversight of the work of the Church of God (Anderson, Indiana) then existing on the islands of Bermuda, Antigua, St. Kitts, and Curaçao. The three missionaries who had been serving under the National Association, Wilhelmina Fraser in St. Kitts and Carl and Mayme

Flewellen in Bermuda, were appointed by the Missionary Board to continue their services under its auspices. The agreement also provided for at least a second black member on the Missionary Board, with the possibility of a third. All of this was looked upon with great favor by the church in general across America and wherever the black church existed in other countries. But this was not the end of the race problem facing the Missionary Board.

Confrontation with black/white issues. The Executive Council of the Church of God in America convened a consultation in May 1968 to have discussion between twelve black leaders, generally known as the Black Caucus, and the executives of the national boards and agencies of the church. This provided opportunity for the black representatives to present their convictions relative to race relations within the Church of God and how to bring about improvements. Feelings ran high, but the grace of God prevailed. It was obvious some changes within the boards and agencies were appropriate. A resolution was presented requesting that the Church of God be made a fully integrated and equal opportunity church through the appointment of men and women from various ethnic groups to several executive positions in the national agencies, plus a more equitable policy for hiring agency employees. By request, one of the black representatives presented the main burden of the Black Caucus to the annual meeting of the Missionary Board in June. The Board took the matter seriously and by a resolution adopted a position paper that promised specific action in three areas: (1) to include more black representation in Board membership; (2) to put forth every effort to consider persons of competence from the black constituency of the church for possible addition to administrative and office staff; and (3) to continue what is both proper and urgent in the appointment of missionaries representing the whole church. The result? By 1970 there were three black members of the Missionary Board: Leonard Roache, Donald Williams, and C. T. Boyd. In 1973 the minutes of one of the meetings of the board of directors included this statement: "It was observed that the new associate secretary or the fifth staff member, if hired, should be a black person if possible." When the second associate secretary was appointed by the Missionary Board, it was a black brother, Thomas Sawyer. Perfect solutions to all the race relations problems found within the Church of God in America have not as yet been achieved. But the Missionary Board endeavors honestly to cope adequately with situations within its jurisdiction through which racial equality in all aspects of its work can be maintained.

Administrative transfer of the Mexico mission and the Hawaii mission. Over the years, the Board of Church Extension and Home Missions and the Missionary Board of the Church of God have cooperated well in assisting the church in its missionary endeavors at home and abroad. During the decade following the visit of W. E. Reed, executive secretary of the Home Missions Board, and me to several Latin American countries in 1960, the two Boards worked together in those countries in the areas of education of leadership, literature production, evangelism development, the use of national and missionary personnel, and the Inter-American Conferences. Since the Missionary Board was planning a major missionary thrust into Latin America during the decade of the 1970s, and since both Boards were committed to good stewardship of leadership and finance in the total mission to Latin America, and as a result of preliminary discussions between the executive staffs of the Home Missions Board and the Missionary Board, the Board of Church Extension and Home Missions by a resolution adopted in its April 1969 meeting proposed to the Missionary Board that the work of the Mexico mission be placed under the administrative responsibility of the Missionary Board. This would have the effect of making the work of the Church of God in Mexico a part of the total mission to Latin America. The Missionary Board, during its annual meeting in June, agreed to assume that responsibility. This agreed-upon administrative transfer for the work of the Church of God in Mexico was favorably considered by the Executive Council of the Church of God and given enthusiastic approval by the General Assembly of the Church of God that same year. Missionaries who were serving in Mexico and involved in this transfer were Albert and Irene Bentley, Maurice and Dondeena Caldwell, George and Marie Geiwitz, Luz and Carol Gonzales, Ronald and Ruth Shotton, and Amelia Valdez. This was the first of two vivid illustrations of how the two missionary boards cooperated in sincere attempts to maintain the kind of unity required to allow the work of the church to go forward.

The following year another transfer between the two Boards took place involving Hawaii, which had recently become a state of the United States of America. It appeared to the administrative staff of both Boards that since Hawaii was now a state it should more logically be under the administrative responsibility of the Home Missions Board. The development of the work of the Church of God among people of Asian heritage and an ever-increasing number from the mainland commended itself to the program of Home Missions. Conclusive exploratory work was accomplished between staff members of both Boards. Therefore, during its April 1970 meeting, the Board of Church Extension and Home Missions voted to accept the transfer of the work in Hawaii from the Missionary Board of the Church of God. Subsequently, in its annual meeting in June 1970, the Missionary Board passed a resolution transferring the administrative responsibility for the work of the Church of God in Hawaii to the Board of Church Extension and Home Missions. This was favorably received by the Executive Council of the Church of God and enthusiastically approved by the General Assembly. The transfer involved one missionary family, Brice and Nancy Casey.

In both of these changes, there were numerous considerations requiring appropriate solution. One was the holding of nonmovable properties. Another was adequate budgeting so that the work could continue growth uninterrupted. Personnel had to be informed and consent gained from them. This included both missionaries and national leadership of the churches. In fact, the responsible bodies of the church in each place had to be consulted. But no problem is unsurmountable when leaders are totally committed to the well-being of the church, which was the case in both of these transfers.

Missionary Board of the Church of God reorganized. An obvious and urgent need was seen for a major revision of the bylaws of the Missionary Board. This was to update the relationships and work of its officers and Executive Committee. The size of the Board and the time and place for its annual meetings required review. Further study was needed to determine whether or not the Board's Articles of Incorporation should be revised to conform with the Indiana General Not-For-Profit Corporation Act passed in 1935 by the Indiana General Assembly. This act had superseded the Act of 1901 under which the Missionary Board was originally incorporated in 1914. If any revisions were to be made of its Articles of Incorporation, they would of necessity be made in conformity with the Act of 1935.

A committee under the leadership of Adam W. Miller was appointed to study the matter and to report at intervals to the Executive Committee and to the entire Board for guidance. Something of this importance required and benefited from legal advice. The final draft of the committee's work was presented to the Missionary Board during its annual meeting in 1970. The Articles of Reorganization were adopted by the Board and subsequently obtained the consent of the General Assembly. The bylaws were adopted that contained the provisions for the regulation and management of the affairs of the Missionary Board of the Church of God under its newly adopted Articles of Reorganization. To some this item of business may seem somewhat irrelevant to the task of missions. But on the contrary, the Missionary Board was in need of updating the rules and regulations that governed its effective operation in a considerably different world from that in which it was originally incorporated.

1970 Consultation of the Church of God. One hundred seventy-two delegates convened in Anderson at the invitation of the Executive Council of the Church of God to sense the times and to determine God's will for the movement during the 1970s. Roughly half of the delegates were state representatives, with the remaining number being representatives from each of the national boards and agencies. The purpose was to consider projections or goals that would help give guidance to each of the general agencies. Consequently, there was much thinking and praying together. It is always good for the Missionary Board to have this form of close relationship with the movement across America. One of the six groupings considered missions, and it was broken down into three work groups. The results were brought together in the form of missions projections and reflections. I was pleasantly surprised that most of the projections were an affirmation of what the Missionary Board was already endeavoring to do. But there were suggestions about how to get the church in America to respond knowledgeably, concertedly, and adequately. The delegates also considered how to capture individual initiative and interest while at the same time uniting instead of fragmenting the work in lands of other culture. Emphasis was given to short-term missionaries going on specific assignments and to reeducating the church as to the meaning of missions. All of this and more served as a point of reference for several years.

World economic forces provide challenge to missions. Especially during the period of time covered by this chapter (1965–1975), unanticipated situations presented grave obstacles to be overcome by missionaries and the Missionary Board. On the one hand, the American church was experiencing a fresh awakening to its missionary obligation, with a decade of advance in Latin America coming into focus. Also, the Missionary Board was assuming additional responsibility for missions in Puerto Rico, London, Hong Kong, Peru, Tanzania, Mexico, Bermuda, St. Kitts, Antigua, and Curaçao. On the other hand, however, the devaluation of the dollar on the world market resulted in a growing loss on exchange when remittances were changed into local currencies. In addition, inflation was rampant in many countries, causing a very rapid rise in the cost of living. This meant missionaries were receiving less local currency when more of it was required to overcome inflation. Pastors of supporting churches in America insisted on sizable increases in a missionary's personal allowances. The Missionary Board promised missionaries that their personal allowances would be adjusted to maintain reasonable buying power. But these steps became necessary regarding other allowances. All unnecessary expenses had to be eliminated. If that did not balance the budget, program would have to be reduced. That was more difficult. If neither of these brought the desired results, the number of missionaries would have to be cut. There was excellent cooperation on the part of the missionary personnel.

Fortunately, an increasing number of American pastors were conducting annual missionary conventions in their local congregations along with a Faith Promise emphasis. Many wanted to support specific missionaries through the Living Link Program. Many requested that their support of the Missionary Board budget be nonleveled on the World Service budget. This gained such wide acceptance that it ultimately had to be regularized. But it did provide more dollars to offset the world situation described previously.

Mission to Latin America during the decade of the 1970s. It was an annual occurrence, but something very unusual happened in February 1968 when I went before the Budget Committee of the Executive Council of the Church of God to present the budget asking of the Missionary Board for the 1968–69 fiscal year of World Service. Going back a little, most Americans had considered Middle and South America in terms of revolution and threats. But during more recent years those same Americans had increasingly understood that there was a great continent to the south of us that demanded our best attention. The Alliance for Progress initiated by President John F. Kennedy did much to stimulate the notion that the United States could be of help without being motivated by colonial overtones.

This aroused enthusiastic interest in Latin America on the parts of numerous pastors of the movement in the United States, who in turn sparked a strong desire within their congregations to do something worthwhile for God especially in South America. Traditionally the Church of God reformation movement had never been very deeply involved in that continent. And we knew very little about the few Church of God congregations located there. Some of the previously mentioned pastors had made trips on their own into some of the Latin American countries. I began to feel the gentle but ever-increasing pressure to discover ways and means to initiate a viable outreach of some magnitude into that vast area south of our American border. This brings me back to my meeting with the Budget Committee.

Beyond the asking budget requested for the Missionary Board, the main burden of my heart was presented to the committee. All five members appeared sympathetic with my feeling that then was the appropriate moment to lead the movement in America in a special emphasis toward developing a mission to Latin America. This would require a special project to raise anticipated capital fund needs. Almost before 1 knew what was taking place, I had outlined to the committee what I considered those needs to be. The committee then agreed to recommend to the Executive Council meeting the following week and then to the General Assembly convening in June 1968 that the Missionary Board be provided a special project through the World Service budget to raise $150,000 over two budget years beginning July 1, 1969. This would give the Missionary Board time to make necessary preparations.

During its annual meeting in June 1968, the Board voted to launch a special emphasis called "Mission Latin America" during the decade of the 1970s, including a special project to raise $150,000 in capital funds. The Board further authorized a survey team to visit Middle and South America during the first six weeks of 1969. Donald Johnson, David Lawson (representing World Service), and I visited Guatemala, El Salvador, Costa Rica, Panama, the Canal Zone, San Blas Islands, Colombia, Peru, Uruguay, Argentina, Brazil, Guyana, and Puerto Rico with our eyes, ears, and minds open to what work the movement already had and what the opportunities were. Studied evaluations and recommendations were presented to the Missionary Board, and in June 1969 it authorized its Executive Committee to proceed with "Mission Latin America" during the 1970s. The special project was increased to $165,000. Leadership training, literature development, planting churches in strategic centers, and providing limited missionary personnel when necessary became priorities. As promotion for "Mission Latin America" began among American congregations, it stirred again the fires of evangelism within the church to give expression in cross-cultural missionary effort. Further on in this chapter and in the final chapter you will observe the results of this decade of advance in Latin America.

But I will now turn to a review of what was transpiring in the third-world church of the reformation movement found in rapidly developing nations of the world. Attention will be focused on progress toward self-reliance being made by many of the third-world churches as well as on some exciting expansion in the American movement's missionary outreach, especially as "Mission Latin America" got under way in the first half of the 1970s.

The Caribbean Orbit of Influence

Even though it required a number of years to reach the goal, the Church of God reformation movement in Jamaica became self-reliant. Relationships between the church, the missionaries, and the Missionary Board always remained at a high level in spite of some difficult situations to work through. A revision of the bylaws for Ardenne High School and the Jamaica School of Theology provided administrative authority to rest with the church and not with the mission. For the first time, there was a full-time Jamaican instructor, Eugenia Campbell, at JST. Legal changes were made so that the mission secretary-treasurer would no longer be the attorney for the Society of the Church of God in Jamaica. A Jamaican would now hold that very important position. There was a noticeable effort on the part of the smaller mission staff to become thoroughly integrated into the Jamaican church program.

Staffing problems plagued Jamaica School of Theology. Since they could not return to Korea, Kenneth and Sue Jo Good were redeployed to Jamaica for a term to assist at JST. George and Eva Buck, assigned to theological education, replaced Tom and Dorothy Pickens as they transferred to England to give pastoral care to the new venture in London. Mary Olson resigned as headmistress of Ardenne High School in 1969 and a highly qualified Jamaican named Claire Gayle assumed that position. A review of the vocational department of Jamaica School of Theology indicated it was no longer needed for the self-support of students of that institution, and so it was given to Ardenne High School to provide vocational training for boys in that school. Therefore, Ralph and Helen Little soon left Jamaica, since their services were no longer needed in the vocational department. Plans were indeed in their final stages to close out the American mission in Jamaica.

The movement in Jamaica appointed its first full-time executive secretary, Rupert Lawrence, for the Executive Council of the Church of God. He and his family lived in a former missionary residence at 35A Hope Road. During this time, the opportunity presented itself for the church in Jamaica to begin a missionary outreach of its own in Haiti. A new work of the Church of God was needing guidance and help, and the church in Jamaica was seeking some form of missionary outreach. One of the Haitian leaders, Jean Surin, and his wife came to Jamaica to study in the Jamaica School of Theology. Through strong efforts to educate the people of the Jamaican church in stewardship, the finances were such that very few funds were required from America. But guest speakers, Tri-S programs, and Project Partner work camps were of great encouragement.

Two situations had been under advisement for a number of months, the first of which gave considerable concern to both the General Assembly of the Church of God in Jamaica and to the Missionary Board. This was related to theological education for Church of God leadership on the island. For some time, the trend had been toward "buying in" at the United Theological College of the West Indies University in Kingston, allowing the existing Jamaica School of Theology to be the base under the supervision of one or two missionaries for feeding students into UTC. After much study and discussion by the church, the Executive Council of the Church of God voted to cooperate with UTC in the training of its ministry. This appeared to be best for the church and was approved by the Missionary Board. The second situation had to do with the church's membership in the Jamaica Christian Council. Many years before, under the guidance of George Olson, the Church of God in Jamaica had become a charter member of JCC and had made a considerable contribution to the council in many ways as well as having profited much through this relationship with the total Christian community on the island. But now there was an element within the movement's congregations, especially those located outside the Kingston corporate area, that was bent on withdrawing the Church of God from the council. In 1971 the General Assembly elected a very conservative Executive Council, which immediately reversed the earlier decision to cooperate with the United Theological College and voted to withdraw from the Jamaica Christian Council.

The decision had already been made for George and Eva Buck to be transferred to Trinidad, leaving no missionary in Jamaica. In light of this decision, Jamaica School of Theology closed its doors since there were no missionaries to carry it on and the church was unable to staff it. That was a serious blow. Until the church could find some way to reopen the school, Jamaican students would be attending an evangelical seminary nearby.

But other signs were more encouraging. That same year a home for the aged was opened in Kingston, primarily by the Woman's Missionary Society in Jamaica. Church of God Men, International, organized in Jamaica. When the World Conference of the Church of God convened in Mexico, there were thirty-five delegates from Jamaica. The Executive Council sent an official request to the Missionary Board for a missionary couple who were specialized in the field of Christian education and who were willing to serve one three-year term. Within a few months, Alva and Bernadean Dean were working well under the direction of the church. And finally, Jamaica's first missionary, Phyllis Newby, was appointed to Haiti. This also was primarily at the request of the Woman's Missionary Society.

By 1965 the work on the Cayman Islands was requiring more and more American personnel, for the congregations were not producing their own leadership. The Missionary Board maintained one missionary couple in Grand Cayman until 1970. Dewey and Thelma Johnson from Canada were the last missionaries. After that the General Assembly of the church was responsible—not the mission. Each congregation supported its own pastor, although it was not easy to find American pastors who could live on what was received. A five-year Grant-In-Aid was arranged by the Missionary Board to provide some additional finances. Triple C School became an institution responsible to the church and was soon self-supporting. In the early seventies, the leadership situation became desperate, but the Missionary Board was able to assist without taking over. Other kinds of assistance continued from America. For instance, in 1975 seventeen men and women from the Pennway Church of God in Lansing, Michigan, converged on the little island of Cayman Brac to build a parsonage.

Across the Caribbean to the southeast, the General Assembly of the Church of God in Barbados was finding its answer to a difficult question: To what extent is a missionary subject to the General Assembly in

Barbados? They were not the first assembly to wrestle with the problem. Does the missionary do what the Missionary Board directs or what the General Assembly says, especially at the point of where and how he or she will serve? Lavern and Darlene Root were missionaries in Barbados at the time, and they were very open to the feelings of the church. But, like many other missionaries of that period of time, they also felt they had some responsibility to their sending and supporting church. The church in Barbados desperately wanted to be independent, but at the same time it was in many ways dependent upon the mission. Following the Roots, Ron and Marcia Howland spent a three-year term, and even though they had some frustrations, their enthusiasm was contagious. As part of their program, they introduced the Faith Promise concept to aid the people of the churches in supporting the work more adequately. But when the Howlands left Barbados in 1970, there was no missionary replacement, and the scheduled Grant-In-Aid scheme was soon to be completed, making the Church of God in Barbados self-reliant. The church also maintained its missionary outreach to the island of St. Vincent.

The year 1965 was the beginning of a new era in Trinidad from the perspective of mission-church relationships. Progress was being made toward the incorporation of the General Assembly of the Church of God in Trinidad to make possible the transfer of church properties from the Missionary Board to the church. That legal and public transfer did take place in a special meeting in the Port of Spain church, and I was present to do what was needed on behalf of the Board. All Grant-In-Aid funds were now to be sent directly to the treasurer of the General Assembly. Also, all correspondence about the church was to be between the secretaries of the General Assembly and the Missionary Board. This eliminated the strategic position of the mission secretary in Trinidad.

The constitution and bylaws of the West Indies Bible Institute were revised, making it responsible to and under the control of a board of trustees representing the churches in the southern Caribbean area rather than the Missionary Board. Walter and Margaret Tiesel (Walter had been missionary secretary-treasurer) retired from the field in 1966 and Oakley and Veryl Miller (Oakley had been director of the vocational department of WIBI) left in 1967. To better the financial situation of WIBI, one of the Trinidadian pastors became its manager, and soon afterwards its vocational department formed its own registered company called Master-bilt Products.

Unfortunately, the company experienced financial difficulties within two or three years.

Tragedy struck the Trinidad mission in January 1967. A telephone call from Trinidad was received one night by the Coolidges in Georgetown, Guyana, informing them that William Fleenor had been killed in an automobile accident. At the time, I was speaking in a youth rally during a Church of God convention in Guyana. I learned the sad news immediately following the meeting and made arrangements to fly to Trinidad the next morning in time for the funeral in San Fernando the following day. I delivered the funeral sermon, which was a personal privilege, for I had known Bill over the years since 1930. He had accidentally stepped off a curb without looking and was struck by a taxi, living only a few hours afterward. No charges were filed, for it was obviously Bill's error. Emilia soon returned to America.

When the Millers left Trinidad that summer, there was no longer a mission per se from America. However, the church was continuing in its attempt to get off dead center and requested a missionary to come to assist in evangelistic outreach. Tom and Jean McCracken were sent, arriving in mid-1967. They stirred the fires of evangelism, and things began to happen. George and Eva Buck came from Jamaica to help while the McCrackens were on furlough in 1972. By 1974 the McCrackens were redeployed to Brazil, leaving the self-reliant Church of God in Trinidad on its own. However, Eugene and Margaret Fehr were sent as area missionaries to the southern Caribbean, making Port of Spain, Trinidad, their place of residence.

It was an honor for me to be present in British Guiana in 1965 when the Church of God celebrated its fiftieth anniversary. The following year the colony received its political independence from Great Britain and became known as Guyana, an old Amerindian word meaning "land of waters." Guyana was the first South American country to become independent since Venezuela in 1830. The Union Jack had waved over the colony for 152 years, and so the celebration was nationwide. There was almost immediate "Guyanization" at every level. New missionaries were prevented from entering, and it was with great difficulty that a visa was secured for Paul and Noreda Kirkpatrick to enter in 1970 when Ralph and Ruth Coolidge retired from missionary service.

Guyana was rich in natural resources, but the masses of people in the few cities and towns were extremely poor. Hence there was little financial potential for the church, and it suffered greatly from a serious lack of leadership. As many of the young men and women returned from training at West Indies Bible Institute in Trinidad, they soon left Guyana for Canada or the United States. The work of the movement entered a holding situation. However, there was a move toward the incorporation of the Church of God in Guyana so that church properties could be transferred, with the belief they would be more secure when owned by a local corporation instead of an alien organization like the Missionary Board. The Kirkpatricks ran into visa problems and were redeployed ultimately to Peru. Tom McCracken made frequent visits of encouragement from Trinidad. When Eugene Fehr became the area missionary, he also made regular visits to Guyana, but there were no resident missionaries in Guyana. The church was on its own, and the struggle for survival was not easy, in spite of valiant efforts on the part of several national leaders of the church.

As a result of the merger of the two missionary boards as described earlier in this chapter, the transfer of administrative responsibility to the Missionary Board had been accomplished quite well, but much remained to be done to lead the churches on the islands of Bermuda, St. Kitts, Antigua, and Curaçao toward self-reliance. Fortunately the potential was there. In 1969 Wilhelmina Fraser retired from St. Kitts, and Allen and Clovis Turner were sent as replacements with the specific assignment to develop indigenous leadership on the island. The following year Carl and Mayme Flewellen completed their term of service in Bermuda, and they were replaced by Raymond and Noreen Chin. It is of interest to note that Raymond came originally from Jamaica. In Antigua, where there were no resident missionaries, Monroe and Bernice Spencer had emerged several years before as the strong national leaders.

In Curaçao, repeated efforts continued to encourage intercommunication between the two groups of the Church of God, one led by the Lindos and the other by the Wades. Their united witness was being hampered by their unwillingness to work together on that small but oil-wealthy island of the Netherlands West Indies. The work of the movement on the island of Grenada not too far from Trinidad had been cared for by the Trinidad mission. However, it was now being encouraged to form its own General Assembly and to receive its own Grant-In-Aid. Both missionaries and church leaders from Trinidad continued to visit, giving guidance and encouragement.

The Latin American Orbit of Influence

From what was said earlier about the emphasis on "Mission Latin America" during the decade of the 1970s and the special project to raise capital funds beginning in mid-1969, it should surprise no one that there was marked growth in the American church's interest and activity in the Latin world to the south of it. The special project had a goal of $165,000, and $216,000 was contributed. The Woman's Missionary Society continued to give further grants, such as $15,000 for expansion into Amazonia. Also, thousands of bequest dollars made available to the Missionary Board were designated to "Mission Latin America".

For some time there had been increasing interest in starting a work of the Church of God reformation movement in Puerto Rico. By 1966 Earl and Freda Carver, former missionaries to Cuba, were reappointed as missionaries to Puerto Rico, and they began by working closely with the Evangelical Council of that island to determine the area on the island where the movement could make its greatest contribution. Turabo Gardens, a new urbanization project in Caguas, just south of San Juan, was chosen. The following year a missionary residence was purchased, along with a nearby strategically located lot for future church facilities. A carport ministry was started immediately at the residence. A Sunday school and a daily vacation Bible school brought in many children and provided contacts with their parents.

The group grew so rapidly that within a year another residence had to be rented across the street to provide adequate facilities. By 1969 a new church facility had been erected on the land originally purchased. In addition to regular services, a nursery school was provided for the community. Growth continued among these middle-class people, and it demonstrated what could be accomplished in Latin American urban areas. A strong emphasis was placed on literature, and Carver purchased a Davidson press to make quantities of Spanish-language materials possible.

Early in the seventies, the congregation at Turabo Gardens was looking for its own pastor. Marciano Yates, originally one of the young men in Cuba the Carvers helped train for the ministry, was chosen to serve. Due to growth, adjoining lots were purchased at the church site until the entire cul-de-sac was owned. This provided opportunities for expansion. A kindergarten and then a first grade were started, eventually becoming a thriving elementary school. The church grew also. Laypeople held prayer meetings in homes, and a Bible class was started in the community center. By 1974 a new work was started in Mariolga, another urbanization development. In another year, a third group was being established in Tomas de Castro.

Throughout the 1960s very little was known about what was happening in Cuba. The Missionary Board was able to send about eight thousand dollars a year through the World Council of Churches in Geneva and on through the Swiss Embassy in Havana, Cuba. This was part of a joint effort on the part of several church groups in America to send funds to their respective church bodies in that Communist-controlled country. Sometimes this worked, but not always. By the early 1970s, we began to have infrequent correspondence with Jaime Greene, the main Church of God leader, and by 1974 it was possible for Canadians to visit Cuba. Gordon Schieck, former missionary to India and now member of the Missionary Board, and A. D. Semrau, administrative director of the Canadian Board of Missions, were able to visit the Church of God in Cuba and observed that it had survived the Castro regime quite well. They attended a convention in the Finlay Church of God in Havana and meetings in all three of the Havana congregations but were unable to visit the two congregations in Matanzas, the one in Camaguay, one in Oriente, and one on the Isle of Pines. Schieck and Semrau found five ordained ministers serving 193 baptized persons over twelve years old. The regular attendance in the eight congregations was 380, and all services were conducted in the Spanish language. In spite of many obstacles, the children of God had remained faithful. This provided a good example of what could happen in a communist country.

As the Missionary Board assumed administrative responsibility for the work of the Church of God in Mexico, it was observed that Mexican leadership wanted to carry more direct responsibility. But the relationship of the missionaries was still quite paternal. This was not a negative reflection on the missionaries but rather on the current structure of the mission. In fact, there was a sincere attempt on the part of both national leadership and missionaries to determine and carry out proper church-mission relationships. La Buena Tierra, the training school located at Saltillo, was being upgraded. A change in leadership brought in Eliu Arevalo as the school's new director, the first Mexican to hold that position. Juan Cepeda became director of CBH-Spanish and the Spanish literature department.

There remained the need to bring the movement's activities in Baja California and Central Mexico more closely together. The Church of God in Mexico had the honor of hosting the first World Conference of the Church of God held in the Western Hemisphere. It convened in Oaxtepec, just south of Mexico City, in 1971. All of these contacts with the church in other countries provided the Mexican church leaders with a better understanding of what it was to be a self-reliant church.

Because there was the attempt to allow the growing work in Guatemala to be indigenous from the very beginning, it provided opportunity for numerous unilateral contacts from the American church. And not always were Americans understanding and sympathetic with Latin culture. As a result, some questions began to be raised regarding the activities and methodology of Isai Calderon as he gave leadership to the development of the congregations. Raymond Hastings from Houston, Texas, and I were requested to make a special trip to Guatemala to determine the exact nature of the situation. We found Calderon to be functioning well within the bounds of Christian ethics as interpreted within Latin culture, which is a perfectly normal procedure as the gospel is planted in country after country. In this situation, that interpretation was not being controlled by a resident missionary.

I use this as a classic example of what can happen at times when sharp differences in cultural patterns are not taken into consideration and leaders from different cultures find themselves at odds over some question of ethics. But it was suggested to Calderon that a stronger group consciousness, loyalty, and involvement should be promoted within the movement's existence in Guatemala. In the late 1960s considerable growth was noticed as the church reached out as far as Quetzaltenango as well as to the Cackchiquel Indians. Also, an Inter-American Conference convened in Guatemala City helped give more stability to the church in that country.

Just to the south of Guatemala is the little country of El Salvador. In 1969 a group of Christians made contact with Isai Calderon in Guatemala and expressed desire to become affiliated with the Church of God reformation movement. Over the next few years, numerous contacts were made with those congregations. An independent effort on the part of Joe Salinas helped to solidify relationships. This work was followed by the combined efforts of Luz Gonzales and Harry Nachtigall, who were conducting institutes for leadership training in Costa Rica. There were six congregations.

When a devastating earthquake hit Managua, Nicaragua, in 1972, Project Partner hastened to the rescue with relief for the suffering. As assistance was given in a rehabilitation program, contact was made with an evangelical group under the leadership of Misael and Amina Lopez. This was the beginning of a growing relationship with the Church of God. Now there are twenty-four congregations with some two thousand members affiliated with the movement. This is another group that was indigenous from the very beginning.

As a result of interest shown by some brethren in Florida, something new was developing in Honduras. On Roatan, a little island off the coast, a Christian by the name of Philip Allen began a work of the Church of God in 1972. Meetings were conducted under the trees and in his small home. Now there are three congregations with three pastors. Regular contacts are maintained with this group of believers. Honduras, like El Salvador and Nicaragua, was entered as a result of the growing interest in Latin America by Christians in North America.

What was taking place in Costa Rica? After the Planks left, a young Costa Rican woman named Millicent McLaren, a Christian education graduate from West Indies Bible Institute in Trinidad, gave tremendous assistance to the group of Christians in San José. She supported herself through a good job in the same city. To strengthen this congregation in the capital city, a pastor, Rafael Campos, was employed. He resigned, however, in 1967. In addition, Sidney Bennett resigned at Cimarrones and Siquirres, and Leroy Nicholls resigned at Puerto Limón. Those three resignations were devastating. Even though Jorge Moffat, a young Costa Rican who had just completed his training at La Buena Tierra in Mexico, was returning to his homeland to work for God, the church sent a desperate message to the Missionary Board requesting a missionary immediately to save the situation.

Edwin and Carol Anderson were sent but remained for only one term of three years. They were new missionaries finding their way, and the complexity of the situation only frustrated their efforts. Another attempt was made to give assistance by redeploying Luz and Carol Gonzales from Mexico to Costa Rica. Luz, a dynamic personality, had the tendency to take over everything. That did not prove to be good for the situation, for it was not in any manner developing national leadership for the congregations. Harry and Jene Nachtigall assisted for a longer period.

All through these few years a location was being sought upon which a Christian center could be constructed to provide facilities for the potential development in San José. Through all this time of uncertainty, there remained the hope that something good would emerge. The Gonzaleses left in 1974, and the San José Christian Center was completed in 1975. The fact that this entire episode covered a decade of time vividly illustrates that there are occasions when the best of plans, seemingly God directed, simply do not work out.

Quite another situation was in progress in Panama and the Canal Zone. Throughout the mid 1960s, there was phenomenal growth. A strong new congregation came into being in Villa Guadalupe, a large urbanization project on the edge of Panama City. A new church building was erected in Colón, and a missionary residence was constructed in the Canal Zone. Rapid expansion took place among the Cuna Indians on the San Blas Islands, and a leadership training center was established at New Providence. More and more emphasis was placed upon Spanish-speaking work. Other primitive peoples were being reached up the Indio River. The emerging leadership of the church felt itself capable of administering the affairs of the movement. Dean Flora began to experience major difficulties in maintaining *Pap Igar Ulu* (The Word of God Boat), the boat being used in the work among the San Blas Islands.

Other administrative and relational problems existed. Harry and Jene Nachtigall were transferred from Costa Rica for a year to assist in the situation. By 1975 Dean and Nina Flora left Panama after sixteen years of dedicated and helpful service. Local church properties were transferred to the Church of God in that country. "Mission Latin America" funds were being used to assist such projects as the building of the church edifice at Villa Guadalupe. Ronald and Ruth Shotton moved from Mexico, where they had given twelve years of service, to guide the church in Panama on toward complete self-reliance. That was a big assignment, but the church was ready for it.

As Paul Butz left his employment with the Zachry Construction Company to give full time to the work of God, trusting God for support through interested congregations and friends in America, he and his wife Mary devoted themselves unstintingly to starting a work of the Church of God in Peru. Their modest home at Campo Verde was the place of beginning. The need for leadership training was recognized, and La Buena Tierra

Peruana was started. This project was greatly assisted by Tri-S work camps from Anderson College as students helped to develop the campus by erecting several buildings over several summers. By 1967 the first General Assembly of the Church of God in Peru convened, and plans were under way to incorporate the Church of God in that country. Paul and Mary Butz had, as independent missionaries, started a very good work. But by 1969 they began to feel the need for being a part of a larger organization for guidance and support, especially since a major thrust into Latin America appeared imminent. The following year they were appointed missionaries by the Missionary Board, coming under its administration and support.

The first graduating class came out of La Buena Tierra in 1971, providing some leadership for expansion into other small communities surrounding Pucallpa, the main city on the eastern side of the Andes. Paul and Noreda Kirkpatrick, after spending time in language school in Costa Rica, arrived to give full time on the campus of La Buena Tierra. The Spanish *Christian Brotherhood Hour* was being heard over one station in Peru. Part of the emphasis in Latin America during the 1970s was to develop appropriate outreach in major urban areas. An urbanization project in Zarate outside of Lima, the capital of Peru, caught the attention of Salomon Cabanillas. Therefore, a lot was purchased with funds from the special project and plans were prepared for a building. Robert and JoAnn Tate gave paramissionary service at La Buena Tierra.

An opportunity to enter Bolivia came in an unexpected manner. Independent missionaries Homer and Elvira Firestone had been working for over twenty years among the Aymara and Quechua Indians. They would make regular trips to America, and during that time Homer would teach in some college to earn their support. During several of these visits in southern California the Firestones became acquainted with the Church of God and discovered commonality in beliefs and practice. The Missionary Board was approached by some of our pastors in Southern California requesting the Board to study the possibility of accepting the Firestones as missionaries. The Firestones, in turn, approached the over ninety congregations and their leaders in Bolivia to secure their favorable reaction to being associated with a larger group. By 1974 this Bolivian work of God became associated with the Missionary Board. This included Homer and Elvira Firestone's appointment as missionaries by the Board as well as that of their son Ronald and his wife Violet. Ronald, a medical doctor, was carrying on clinical work in La Paz. This rather large group of approximately seven thousand Christians was indigenous from the beginning, and remains so even today. The Holy Spirit leads about seventy pastors and leaders, encouraged by missionaries and the backing of the church in America.

As mentioned earlier in this chapter, the church in America became vitally interested in reaching out to Latin America during the 1970s. Wherein the Church of God in Germany through its Missionswerk was assisting the work in Brazil and Argentina, the Missionary Board desired to give further help only in areas not covered by Missionswerk. By 1970 there were twenty congregations of the Church of God in Argentina, mostly in Misiones Province to the north. Most of the work was among German immigrants, who were pioneers in developing the country.

Floreal Lopez began a group of Spanish-speaking persons in the 1950s. The Missionary Board used "Mission Latin America" funds to help complete the church building in Alem for this Spanish-speaking congregation. Many of the young people were three generations removed from Germany, and they had been educated in Spanish. Therefore, there was a definite trend toward using the Spanish language in the church, including reaching out beyond the German community. By request from the Assembly in Argentina the Missionary Board in 1973 redeployed Albert and Irene Bentley from Mexico to develop theological education by extension, thus setting up a leadership training program.

Over several years, evangelistic meetings were conducted across the Parana River into Paraguay. In 1974 a lot was purchased in Colonia Obligado as house meetings were being established. As can be seen, the work of the Church of God in Paraguay really started as a missionary outreach by the church in Argentina.

By 1970 some thirty-five congregations had been established in Brazil by the German work headquartered in York, Nebraska. Now the Assembly of the Church of God in Brazil requested the Missionary Board to assist them at two main points: leadership development and literature. Brazil is the only South American country to use the Portuguese language, so in breaking away from the German-speaking community, Portuguese had to be used.

In 1970 Maurice and Dondeena Caldwell were transferred from Mexico to Brazil. They spent time in language school to shift from Spanish to Portuguese. Then they took up residence in Curitiba. Construction of a Bible school began in nearby Guarituba, and in 1972 the Caldwells were requested to assume the leadership of Instituto Biblico Boa Terra. Since Maurice Caldwell had been editor of *La Trompeta,* the Spanish *Gospel Trumpet,* he was asked to be editor of *Trombeta* in Portuguese. These two contributions helped to unify the Church of God in Brazil and to point toward its outreach beyond the German Community.

Farther to the north, in Amazonia, the Missionary Board cooperated with the church in establishing at Itaituba a bridgehead for a growing work in the great Amazon basin. In 1972 the Missionary Board sent William and Betty Mottinger to work at Itaituba following language study, and the church in Brazil sent missionaries from among the first graduates of the Instituto Biblico Boa Terra to Amazonia. In 1974 Thomas and Jean Mc-Cracken were ready in São Paulo to inspire the Church of God to launch an urbanization program to reach out into several districts of that tremendous metropolis of eleven million people.

Finally, one more opportunity opened in Uruguay. An independent Slavic Gospel Mission had been established in San Gregorio by Emma Spitzer. In the late 1960s she was in Canada and was invited by friends to attend the International Convention in Anderson. Emma was deeply impressed with what she saw and heard and decided to turn over her work in Uruguay to the Church of God. That took place in 1973. Short-term missionary service has been supplied through the Missionary Board with missionaries in Brazil giving some assistance.

The European Orbit of Influence

Major urban areas of the world were targets that the Missionary Board had in mind when considering expansion. There was a unique opportunity in London, England. The group of Church of God West Indian immigrants that had come together was requesting assistance. In 1965 plans were prepared for the London project, which was initiated the next summer following a Billy Graham crusade in London. Marvin Hartman, pastor of the church in St. Joseph, Michigan, agreed to spend a year in London. He was replaced that year in St. Joseph by Philip and Phyllis Kinley on furlough from Japan. Hartman made preparations for a Church of God campaign to be held in the town hall in the area of London where the church gathered in rented quarters. The speaker would be Dale Oldham. This generated considerable enthusiasm and set the stage for growth. Thomas and Dorothy Pickens were redeployed from Jamaica, having been chosen to pastor the congregation in London. They were not considered missionaries. That proved to be a good move.

The congregation was international and interracial in name and design, bringing in Church of God people from various countries of the British Commonwealth, but in reality it continued to be composed primarily of West Indians from the islands of the West Indies. In 1970 an old church building was purchased and a down payment on a manse was made. There was a very rapid decrease in the temporary Grant-In-Aid that the Missionary Board had provided. When the Pickenses returned to America in 1972, the church chose Martin Goodridge, a member of the congregation, to be pastor. He had graduated from the West Indies Institute in Trinidad some time back, and he and his wife originally came from Barbados.

In Denmark, the movement was learning very well how to maintain itself as a self-reliant church. The people were no longer dependent upon the leadership of missionaries. But several contacts each year were maintained with the Church of God in Germany, and this helped make them feel a part of a larger group. In the late 1960s, however, there was one major disappointment. Two brothers, Jorgen and Kresten Norholm, had gone to America to train for the ministry in two of our church's schools. They married American girls and returned to their homeland of Denmark, where they assumed pastoral responsibility in Church of God congregations. Their wives learned the language and made excellent adjustments to a new culture. But both Jorgen and Kresten became impatient with the slowness of growth in the Church of God in Denmark. They tried using methods in evangelism that they had learned in school in America, but those methods did not produce results in the Danish culture. I appealed to them as young Danes to be patient and discover under God methods based on New Testament teachings that would bring results. Unfortunately for the work in Europe, they returned to America with their families where they are serving well. This is not to discredit these fine young men, but it is to show how the proclamation of the gospel must be done in such a manner as to make its claims understandable within the culture of the hearers.

There is one more reflection on the work in Europe during this period, and it is a sad story. During the late sixties, the small congregation in Belfast, North Ireland, tried another time to find pastoral leadership. A young man named Fred Murdock was chosen, but he remained for only two years. So again Sam Porter, a dedicated layman in the congregation, endeavored to give leadership. But the group was growing smaller and there was not one young person there. For some reason that I was never able to discover, the believers from several decades back had never been able to hold their young people. Consequently, when civil strife broke out in North Ireland, it practically destroyed the existence of the movement. Politically, the Catholics representing Ireland, and the Protestants representing North Ireland were at each other's throats. The Irish Republican Army, representing freedom for North Ireland, was fighting a guerrilla war with the British Army, which was presumably protecting the rights of the Protestants. Doers of evil took advantage of the perilous times, and loss of life and destruction of property were daily occurrences. Whole sections of downtown Belfast were burned and destroyed. During one visit I looked upon what was once our congregation's church property. It had been totally destroyed. Roadblocks were maintained and it was difficult to move about. There were no more meetings for our people. Sam Porter continued to visit the very few elderly persons. The work of the Church of God in North Ireland had, for all intents and purposes, ceased to exist. Yet there were a half-dozen persons still claiming loyalty to the reformation movement.

The Middle Eastern Orbit of Influence

With only one missionary couple in Egypt, the mission was in a holding pattern. Ernest and Grace LaFont spent much time assisting in the work of the youth centers in Cairo and Alexandria, but as much as they tried, they did not feel their influence was doing much to help the Egyptian church. Time after time the LaFonts endeavored to bring to bear upon members of the General Assembly of the Church of God in Egypt the necessity of becoming self-reliant so that they would not be dependent upon the mission or the missionaries. An outstanding Greek named Christo Psiloinis, who had not as yet left Egypt, gave yeoman service. He had been reared in Egypt in a Church of God family, knew Arabic very well, and was a good leader in the Cairo Youth Center. For a time he was both vice-chairman and treasurer of the General Assembly. Unfortunately, he soon moved to Cyprus.

Then the 1967 War broke out between Egypt and Israel. The LaFonts had to evacuate and remain out of the country for some time. Upon their

return, they faced tremendous difficulties. Franco and Beatrice Santonocito were leaving the work in Alexandria to go to Italy, the move being necessitated by Franco's dangerous health situation. There were pressures on all
American missionaries in Egypt. They were followed by secret service men.
The reason? America was behind Israel, the enemy of Egypt. The Church of
God in Egypt had broken relations with the Protestant body known as Ma-
glis-el-Milli, which represented evangelicals before government. That was
a miscalculation on the part of our people and was the cause of problems
later on. The church's leadership had reached a stalemate in relationships.

Early in 1971 the Missionary Board encouraged Nasser Farag and his
wife Marilyn, an American, to go to Egypt as laypersons to help the situation. Nasser was the son of the late Salib Farag, the Church of God printer
in Alexandria. The LaFonts decided to leave Egypt as the last resident missionaries, move to Beirut, and become missionaries for the eastern Mediterranean area. Farag's ministry, though not totally successful, highlighted
some of the glaring difficulties that were hindering growth. In 1973 the
Farag family left Egypt, being sent as missionaries to Kenya. That left the
Egyptian church at a very low ebb. On occasion the LaFonts would give
some encouragement through a brief visit. Also, Lebanese leaders tried to
provide inspiration and guidance through infrequent visits.

Into the seventies the Church of God in Lebanon continued to pros-
per spiritually and materially. God was blessing the efforts of all the believers and they worked together to spread the gospel. Not only was there
evangelistic outreach into other parts of Lebanon, including new districts
of Beirut, but there was also missionary outreach into other countries.
Fouad Accad, now retired from a career with the United Bible Society and
a second-generation member in the movement, was encouraged to go as a
missionary to Bahrain in the Persian Gulf to witness in his unique way to
Muslims. Amol Boudy, another second-generation person in the church,
went to Nabi Othman in the Arabian Gulf, supporting herself as a mid-
wife. She built her own tent of palm leaves and ministered both physically
and spiritually to the women. These were encouraging signs of vitality.
However, the people of Lebanon were about to enter an unprecedented
time of suffering and trial. In the spring of 1975, a civil war erupted that
was so severe that the leaders of the church in Lebanon recommended that
the planned World Conference to convene in Beirut that summer be canceled. What followed takes us into the next chapter.

The future of the reformation movement in Greece was becoming uncertain. The relationship the Greek people of the Church of God in Chicago, Gary, and Detroit had to the work became somewhat nebulous. Savas and Olive Joannides felt a lack of cooperation as they endeavored to strengthen the congregation in Athens, feeling they would soon be leaving, which indeed they did in 1968. The Missionary Board was ready to phase out the work in Greece, selling the valuable property in Athens to perhaps the Oriental Missionary Society. But that did not work out. The Greeks in the American church objected vehemently. Nick and Rose Zazanis came out of retirement and arbitrarily returned to Athens. But there was little enthusiasm for the future. Failing health forced the Zazanises back to America within three years, having performed a holding position. The Missionary Board had second thoughts about selling the property and decided it might become a center in the eastern Mediterranean orbit, especially with the growing uncertainties developing in Lebanon. Consequently, Panayote Dendrinos and his wife were sent to Athens in 1973 to carry on. You may recall that they were the ones who followed the Zazanises in Cairo, caring for the Greek work until all the Greeks emigrated due to political pressures.

It was a sad time for Franco and Beatrice Santonocito when they left Egypt for Italy in 1968. Franco required surgery by a specialist in Rome. The future was uncertain. But God was merciful, having something more wonderful in store for the Santonocitos. During his convalescence, Franco began to see God's hand leading them to begin a work of the Church of God reformation movement in Rome. By 1971 the possibilities were definite. As I was going to India that year, I met with Franco and Beatrice at Rome's airport during an hour-and-a-half plane stop. On the basis of that conversation, the Missionary Board decided to assist in making the project possible. Consequently, in October 1972, following careful study on where to begin, a start was made in Ostia, a suburb of Rome located by the sea. It was clear to all that this development was not to be a mission from America but that it should grow naturally within Italian culture, using ways and means commensurate with the understanding of the Italian people. Success was almost immediate, and by the end of two years, two young men had completed their training for the ministry and another suburb of Rome, Dragoncello, had been entered. You will note that even though Italy is really a part of Europe, as is Greece, it seemed appropriate to consider the work in these two countries as part of the eastern Mediterranean orbit of influence. However, this new development in Italy soon attracted the attention of Church of God leaders in Europe and lasting contacts were established.

The East African Orbit of Influence

Continued movement toward self-reliance was the pattern followed in Kenya during the last half of the sixties and the first half of the seventies. Kenya's president, Jomo Kenyatta, declared that his government was "committed to support the churches and stand back of the work that they are doing." The concept of gradualism was no longer valid. Rapid Africanization had to take place, including the transfer of authority. For both the church and the mission, this meant, as one leading African Christian said, a "flexible capacity for rapid change in the days ahead." And indeed there was great progress in the work during this period of time.

In spite of some observable weaknesses in church leadership and in the life and work of the church, the responsibility for the work in Kenya and its functions was actually passing from the mission to the church. All departments and committees now functioned under the General Assembly: evangelism, stewardship, radio publications, women's work, youth, education, religious instruction in schools, Christian education, and the boards of governors responsible for the four secondary schools, Kima Theological College, and the two hospitals. Almost all the department and committee chairpersons were Africans. The headmasters of the secondary schools were now Africans. And the chairman and the treasurer of the General Assembly also were Africans. The General Assembly had by 1970 a full-time African executive secretary, Byrum Makokha. And there was a phasing out of the short-term teaching program for secondary school teachers from America, for by this time Africans began to to return to Kenya, having earned their bachelor's degrees in education.

All of this required a review of the function of the mission and the role of its missionaries. What were the implications in mission-church relations? What, if any, redeployment of missionaries would be necessary? It became obvious that the large and powerful Church of God mission in Kenya should be phased out. It was also obvious there was a trend toward more specialized missionaries as might be required to assist the church. The General Assembly appointed an Overseas Personnel Recruitment and

Placement Committee (generally known as OPRPC) to work with the Missionary Board in the selection and placement of missionaries. The Assembly appointed two or three missionaries to the OPRPC. Missionaries were appointed or elected to committees and boards of the church not because they were missionaries but because of their individual skills and abilities, which Africans saw as desirable.

In place of a mission in Kenya, with all the negative overtones the word *mission* carried with it, there came into being the East African Ministries of the Missionary Board of the Church of God. The name was almost frightening. Usually "East African Ministries" was used. The former position of mission secretary-treasurer became that of coordinator. And to make it easier for the new African executive secretary to function with an office at Kima, the new coordinator's place of residence was moved from Kima to Nairobi. Instead of funds from America being sent through the mission, all Grant-In-Aid funds and special grants for the church were to be sent by the Missionary Board directly to the bank account of the General Assembly.

In 1966 the church in Kenya, the mission, and the Missionary Board grappled with a situation in the mission staff in Kenya that brought heartache to many. Lew and Wanda Goodrick, excellent missionaries with nine years of fruitful service behind them in Kenya, became enamored with and involved in the charismatic movement. Since Lew was then principal of Kima Theological College, this became a real problem for the church's leadership. Missionaries on the field were disturbed, and as a result the Missionary Board had to deal with a public relations problem. Following considerable discussion in Kenya between the Goodricks and both African and American personnel, and after much frank and open correspondence between the Goodricks and the Missionary Board, the Goodricks gracefully resigned as missionaries to Kenya, seeing they could not accept the position generally held by the Church of God reformation movement relative to the charismatic movement. This was the honorable way out of a delicate situation and left no permanent scars on the work of the church in Kenya.

As the educational and medical programs began to receive more and more government aid and the church was carrying administrative responsibility for those related institutions, the missionaries were giving more time to direct church-related work. Whatever the Missionary Board might

do for Kima Theological College or even for the medical program would
be through their respective boards of governors. The government was not
interested in subsidizing KTC, and so the Missionary Board had considerable responsibility to see that KTC functioned well in providing leadership
training for the African church.

During this period of time, it was difficult to find medical personnel to serve. A Canadian physician named Larry Hoogeveen, with his wife
Verna, served two years, and a Mennonite doctor named Ron Loewen was
seconded for a brief time. They were followed by the first African doctor at the hospital, Geoffrey Ingari. African nurses began to be employed,
although Caroline Ackerman remained by request as a missionary nurse.
Clair and Retha Shultz were withdrawn in 1970 so that he could join the
administrative staff of the Missionary Board. Shultz was replaced by Douglas Welch as coordinator. The publication work that had been assisted by
Welch was now directed by Africans. Jewell Hall retired in 1972 and was
not replaced. Irene Engst retired in 1974, and an African woman replaced
her in women's work. Edgar and Lima Williams left the field in 1970, and
the board of governors elected Dennis Habel to succeed Williams as principal of KTC. Vivian Woods served for one term. Nasser and Marilyn Farag
arrived from Egypt and served in the Kisa, Idakho, and Butsotso areas by
request of the church.

Two of our missionaries, with the church's approval, served for several years in strategic ecumenical positions. Aaron Kerr was seconded to
be executive secretary of the Protestant Churches Medical Association at
a time when he could give much needed advice to our church's medical
program. David Crippen was seconded to the Christian Churches' Educational Association with the specific assignment of working on the curriculum for religious education courses being taught in both elementary and
secondary schools throughout Kenya. Both of these families lived in Nairobi. In February 1972, a great gathering convened at Kima to witness official ceremonies through which all nonmovable properties were transferred
to the Church of God in Kenya. These properties included all missionary residences and all buildings of the institutions and were conservatively
valued at $356,800. Certain valuable pieces of equipment found in the
institutions were also given to the church. Government officials, numerous church leaders from various communions, and many friends made the
occasion a memorable one. I was privileged to be the representative of the

Missionary Board to sign the transfer documents. In the following chapter you will read how the church managed, having achieved indigeneity.

As mentioned in the last chapter, it had become the desire on the part of the independent missionaries serving in Tanzania under the auspices of the World Missionary Fellowship based in Canada to have the mission come under the administration of the Missionary Board of the Church of God. This was primarily to help the church in Tanzania become a part of the Church of God fellowship in East Africa and to achieve indigeneity. It required over two years of working with the Executive Committee of the World Missionary Fellowship and the Canadian Board of Missions to arrive at a suitable agreement, which was signed by representatives of the three agencies in 1968. Four main points in the agreement were the following: (1) the entire mission and church in Tanzania (including evangelism, teaching in the two Bible schools, present and future lands and buildings and present and future missionaries) would immediately come under the administration and financial arrangements of the Missionary Board; (2) the World Missionary Fellowship would remain registered with the government so that properties could be held and visas and work permits could be secured for missionaries; (3) all properties would still be owned by the World Missionary Fellowship until such a time when the Church of God in Tanzania should become a legal entity to hold property, at which time properties would be transferred to the church; and (4) the present missionaries would become missionaries under the appointment of the Missionary Board.

The church was strengthened and a stronger national leadership was being developed. The church was reaching out with greater spiritual vitality. Simon and Mae Robinson gave a year of service, being transferred from Kenya. Roy and Magaline Hoops were also transferred from Kenya to work long term at Mirambo, an assignment that was cut short by Roy's sudden death during furlough in 1980. When the Farmers left Tanzania in 1973 after thirteen years of service, they were replaced at Mbulu by Robert and Janet Edwards. By 1972 the church had organized its General Assembly with an executive secretary, Eliazer Mdobi. He began to have direct relationship with the Missionary Board. There were by then thirty-three congregations.

By the end of 1974, the Church of God in Tanzania had officially registered with the government and incorporated as a legal entity. The government, eager to Africanize the church as it became registered, automatically and unilaterally transferred all the properties from the World Missionary Fellowship to the Church of God in Tanzania and canceled the registration of the World Missionary Fellowship in that country. The government also understood that any missionaries coming in at the invitation of the church would be sponsored by the Missionary Board. The terms of the 1968 agreement had been fulfilled. This was not easily understood by the Fellowship, but the mission was now the church in Tanzania.

A number of Church of God Africans from Kenya had crossed the border into Uganda for employment. They began to come together in Jinja, Kampala, and two or three smaller places. The church in Kenya sent and supported as its missionary to Uganda Jackson Amule and his family. Frank and Margaret LaFont were loaned by the Missionary Board to go to Kampala, not to form a mission from America but to assist in establishing the work. In 1971 a political upheaval took place and all Kenyans were forced to leave Uganda. The LaFonts were evacuated, and the church in Kenya asked them to reside in Mombasa to assist in two church building projects. Jackson Amule remained for a while but ultimately had to leave. These events just about ended the presence of the Church of God in Uganda.

The South Asian Orbit of Influence

The Church of God Mission in India continued to experience difficulties in securing visas for American missionaries. This was also true for endorsements for Canadian missionaries. However, it was made possible for Canadians Bertram and Marian Steers to be sent to South India so that Bertram could, by request of the South Indian church, be administrator of the Church of God in that area. Another Canadian couple, Eugene and Margaret Fehr, accepted appointment to South India to reside in Trivandrum, where opportunities were present for beginning a new work, especially among university students. On the minus side, however, Gordon and Wilhemina Schieck left India in 1967 after twelve years of service. In addition, the sudden and unexpected death of Marian Steers brought sorrow to those who had known her for only a brief time. She was buried in Nagercoil. Bertram completed a three-year term, after which he returned to Canada.

The All-India Assembly continued to meet annually, bringing the movement's leaders together from the northern, central, and southern parts of India for fellowship, inspiration, and business. Outstanding Indian and American guest speakers provided helpful insights to assist in the strengthening of the church. During one of these annual meetings in Cuttack when groundbreaking ceremonies for a guest house took place, I brought gifts from the Woman's Missionary Society in Barbados and from the Church of God in Japan to assist in financing this project. Such a gesture reflected a good church-to-church relationship in those days. The Assembly annually reviewed the progress that was being made toward the registration of the Church of God Trust Society of India, which finally was incorporated in 1972. Then the amalgamation of the Missionary Board of the Church of God with the Church of God Trust Society provided the transfer of properties conservatively valued at around $250,000 to the church in India. That procedure had taken seventeen years!

The church in South India finally made the necessary adjustments and agreed to form its Coordinating Council with P. V. Jacob as chairman. Area assemblies were structured. The Church of God in India was now in a position to "go it alone." Eugene and Margaret Fehr left South India at the end of their five-year term. Clifton and Mary Morgan left their responsibilities in the state of Orissa after ten years of service. And Sidney and Jean Johnson left India in 1972, the last of our resident missionaries to leave. They had given seventeen years of their lives to India and were not ready to leave southern or southeast Asia, as we shall see later on. Church of God expansion was led by enthusiastic Indian leadership. Evangelistic outreach began afresh with results, especially in South India, where the motto was "Double in a Decade." And they did! A radio program aired from the Seychelles in the Indian Ocean provided P. V. Jacob with thousands of contacts as the message went out in the Malayalam language. In view of this enthusiasm, the Missionary Board promised its continued interest in assisting and working with the Indian church in its endeavors to evangelize and to do missionary work.

Political disturbance in East Pakistan in 1965 required the sudden evacuation of Joseph and Ramona Spires and their children along with Nova Hutchins and her children. Paul Hutchins remained in a caretaker situation. The evacuation was to Manila. From there the Spires family went on to America and did not return to East Pakistan. Nova Hutchins

remained in Manila until Paul could come to get her, and the family returned to East Pakistan. Since there was continued refusal to grant visas
for new missionaries, more responsibility was carried by national leadership. The work in the Sylhet District grew. There were now Church of God
congregations in seventeen of the sixty Khasi villages. The main church was
at Lumpangad Pungee with B. Lyngdoh as pastor. Twenty-eight acres was
purchased and named Balang U Blei Lumdonbok (Church of God "Hill of
Good Fortune"), whereon several excellent projects were to develop. I will
long remember the gathering on top of one of the hills on a very hot Sunday
morning when the land and concept were dedicated to God.

On Easter Sunday, 1971, the West Pakistan Army entered Lalmanirhat and the surrounding countryside. About 150 of our church
people escaped, although a few were killed and a number of women
molested. All the mission property in Lalmanirhat was taken over by
the army. There was considerable destruction and damage. The people
fled across the nearby border into West Bengal of India and settled in a
large refugee camp at Cooch Behar that was being operated by the World
Lutheran Federation under the direction of a Norwegian doctor named
Olav Hodne. Relief funds were immediately sent from America. Almost
a year was required before our people could return to Lalmanirhat. East
Pakistan had proclaimed its independence and was known as Bangladesh.
Olav Hodne gave personal assistance in developing a tremendous rehabilitation program at Lalmanirhat. Property and buildings were repaired
and our people's homes were reconstructed. Various kinds of work were
provided to aid persons financially. Several thousand dollars was donated
by the movement in America and sent to make this relief project a success. Late in 1972 Paul Hutchins was able to visit Bangladesh for a brief
period. That was a great encouragement. The younger leadership of the
church had learned much through the tragedy and were now giving more
adequate direction.

Something new and significant was happening in Thailand. During their year's furlough following their departure from India, Sidney (Mac) and Jean Johnson were seeking guidance for their next appointment. Inspiration came in the spring of 1973, and it was decided that they should live in Bangkok, Thailand, and be missionaries at large to serve the movement's interests in India, Bangladesh, the Philippines, and Hong Kong. That fall they entered language school in Bangkok and made initial contacts in the area as well as with the Christian communions present in Thailand.

When I met Mac in Bangkok in January 1974, I spent an entire day with him working on his visa problems. At that time I also met Wichean Watakeecharoen for the first time. He held a responsible position with the Church of Christ in Thailand and was giving valuable assistance to the Johnson family. I was deeply impressed with him. The next time I met Mac was in January 1975 at the Calcutta airport. His enthusiasm was overwhelming as he shared in detail the information that Wichean Watakeecharoen was available to lead the beginning of a Church of God in Thailand. Space will not permit the recording of all the details that led up to this recommendation, but the Holy Spirit was obviously at work. The Board of Directors of the Missionary Board gave its approval to the plan, and that June, with Watakeecharoen present, the Missionary Board voted to establish a work in Thailand with Watakeecharoen in charge in the hope that the work could be as self-reliant as possible from the beginning. Johnson and Watakeecharoen had developed a ten-year plan, setting goals along the way. It appeared practical and possible. So in August 1975 a new work of the reformation was born in Thailand, where 98 percent of the population is Buddhist. The area chosen for the New Life Center in Bangkok contained four hundred thousand persons who were without any Christian witness. Our missionaries were playing a supportive role.

The East Asian Orbit of Influence

With each visit made to Japan, I was increasingly aware that the Church of God there seemed to know where it was headed and how it was going to achieve its goals. Missionaries and Japanese church leaders were working well together. They were constantly searching for new forms of ministry through which non-Christian persons could be reached with the gospel. Short-term Church of God teachers from America were being encouraged to teach English in various institutions while at the same time sharing their Christian witness. Arthur and Norma Eikamp started a "coffee house" approach, along with teaching English, in the Tarumi District of Kobe, a large city next to Osaka. Nathan and Ann Smith were in the process of developing a Christian center in Futsukaichi, not too far from Fukuoka. And not far away another congregation began in Saga. Orlo and Carol Kretlow were aiding in new developments at Nishi-Kunitachi in Greater Tokyo. My impression was and still is that the Church of God in Japan is a vital force, although relatively small, with which we must cooperate to evangelize East Asia.

Because the Japanese church had so few leaders, it was unable to take advantage of opportunities it had in joint missionary efforts in Brazil, Taiwan, and Guam. The one experience it had in missionary endeavor in Okinawa was very successful, for by 1972 there was a strong and self-supporting congregation at Ameku, as well as several preaching points on the island. When America returned Okinawa to Japan, it became a prefecture, and the church became integrated into the total work of the movement in Japan.

By 1967 the Church of God in Korea had thirteen churches, two primary schools, two junior high schools, one high school, one Bible institute, and two orphanages. Unfortunately, its leaders had been influenced to join the International Council of Christian Churches headed by Carl McIntyre. Some of the reasons might be considered valid, but mercenary motivations were evident. At the end of Kenneth and Sue Jo Good's first furlough in America, the Missionary Board was advised by the Koreans not to return the Goods to their country but to send the church the money it took to support and maintain them on the field. The Board transferred them to Jamaica, where their services were needed, requiring their total allowances. During the late sixties and early seventies, I made several visits to Seoul. The door was also kept open through correspondence. It was not too long before the "middle generation" of Korean leaders (those who had received training in the Bible institute) became disillusioned with McIntyre because he was not producing all he had promised. A period of establishing cordial relations was entered. Hong Mook Yoo, a young man who was now president of the Korean General Assembly of the Church of God, made a visit to America, stopping in Anderson. The time would soon come when the Church of God in Korea would again be united with the movement around the world.

Hong Kong is always a place of opportunity. Even though originally the Missionary Board did not desire to add to the scores of evangelical missions working among the Chinese, Ethel Willard was sent in 1969 as a missionary to serve the Junk Bay Medical Relief Council as a private secretary while studying the Chinese language. After her first term, she became secretary-treasurer and later business manager. She cast a spiritual influence through several opportunities in that British colony. In 1971 P. K. and Lovena Jenkins officially came under appointment of the Missionary Board. Growing pressure from government to nationalize all positions, brought about the retirement of Jenkins as medical superintendent. He was replaced by a Chinese Christian doctor, David Lum. The search was on to find a Chinese person to replace Willard. Considerable thought was being given in the mid-seventies about the kind of witness the Church of God could make in the rapidly growing sections of high-rise apartments by these Church of God missionaries who were qualified for the task.

By 1965 the sixth anniversary of the Church of God in the Philippines was celebrated. Eduardo Viray, the first graduate from the Pacific Bible Institute, started a new work in Tondo, an economically depressed area of Manila. About this time, Bacani's brother-in-law, Greg Federis, began to show signs of leadership. Contacts were maintained with the original work far to the north at Laoag. Year after year an additional grade was added to the elementary school at Valenzuela. A school was started at Tondo. In 1970 a General Assembly of the Church of God in the Philippines was organized by twenty-three delegates from four congregations. Later a Woman's Missionary Society was formed, generating missionary outreach by these four congregations. This particular self-reliant church overused, not always to its advantage, Western methodology and actively sought Western financial support.

In 1966 William and Frances Rife incorporated the Pacific Ocean Mission in Guam and established an interdenominational congregation at Barrigada. Wilbur Miller failed in the A & W Root Beer business and had to withdraw. Rife hoped to evangelize all the Trust Territory islands, but as an independent he could not gain permission. Phillipe Marioles, a Filipino who attended Gulf-Coast Bible College the same time as Rolando Bacani, married an American girl and arrived in Guam to start another congregation. But that effort failed. Finally, in 1976 the Rifes resigned and returned to the mainland. The Missionary Board was then asked to send missionaries.

The first commissioned missionary pastors to Hawaii were Brice and Nancy Casey. While they were in Honolulu, a second congregation was started at Waipahu pastored by Ernesto Babas. But it was discontinued after a couple of years. Also during the Caseys' time in Hawaii, the administrative transfer took place from the Missionary Board to the Board of Church Extension and Home Missions. In Australia, Austin and Nancy Sowers arrived to start the Australian Bible Training School. After ten years of work in that country, the Church of God had produced only Lloyd and Ruth Chilvers as pastors. The work was still very much dependent upon American leadership. While visiting Australia in 1972, I endeavored to discover with the help of those in the work there exactly what plans could be employed in the future and what the role of the Missionary Board should be in assisting. The answer came later.

CHAPTER 7
PARTNERSHIP IN WORLD MISSIONS
(1975–1980)

By now the disturbances of the 1960s in American society were almost a thing of the past. Within our movement, people were ready to move out and discover afresh how to work more closely together. Believers in the third-world church were ready to act in taking the gospel to the fourth world. In the Missionary Board office, a "changing of the guard" was due. By action of the Missionary Board and ratification by the General Assembly, Donald D. Johnson became the new executive secretary-treasurer. He came to the office in 1975 after six years of missionary service and seven years as my associate secretary. For one year I continued service as secretary of research and development and then was loaned to Anderson School of Theology to initiate the Department of Missions, developing and activating a curriculum of studies leading to a master of arts in religion with emphasis in Christian missions. In 1977 I retired from the employ of the Missionary Board after forty-four years of service. My second retirement was from the School of Theology after two years of teaching. Douglas Welch, adequately qualified academically and with fifteen years of missionary experience in Kenya, was chosen as my successor. The transitions were accomplished with ease.

The coming of Donald Johnson as chief executive officer of the Missionary Board provided a new face-off in missions for the movement, and several developments were forthcoming. He came in with a dynamic and ability that led the Board through some helpful situations and changes. Encouragement was given to the Board's Long-range Study Committee, which had been formed in 1973. By 1979 it had completed its assignment but not before it had grappled with the theology, philosophy, strategy, and methodology of missions. On the practical side, Johnson urged the building of the Crose Missionary Residences on Tenth Street in Anderson,

Indiana. This project was designed to provide a condominium of six well-furnished apartments that would provide "a sense of dignity and well-being to our missionaries," showing that the church really cared for them as they at times lived in Anderson. The apartments were dedicated in 1977.

Picking up on what was mentioned about world relief in the last chapter, the Missionary Board was given more responsibility in administering disaster funds. Major relief and rehabilitation required $144,000 in Guatemala following a major earthquake in 1976. Fifty-five thousand dollars was sent to help our fellow Christians in Lebanon during the civil war. A small amount was given to Antigua following an earthquake that damaged some church buildings. Several thousand dollars was remitted to the Philippines after a severe fire in the Valenzuela church school badly burned a number of students. Eight thousand dollars was yet needed in Nicaragua for rehabilitation. Funds were sent to St. Vincent following the eruption of a volcano. In Jamaica, severe flood damage required eleven thousand dollars in aid to our people. And in 1980, twenty-five thousand was sent to Southeast Asia to help care for Cambodian refugees. Also, one hundred Haitian and Cambodian refugees were settled in Church of God congregations in America through efforts administered by the Missionary Board offices.

In 1979 the Missionary Board adopted a revised missionary manual. You will recall the last manual was issued in 1947. Obviously a great deal of upgrading was required to bring regulations and policies up to date. Several new programs were developed through which individuals could perform some missionary service. Among them were VIM (Ventures in Mission), wherein groups could go to a specific country to perform some needed task, and spot missionaries, who would go to a country at their own expense where their particular skills were needed. During the 1977–78 fiscal year, the Missionary Board for the first time received over two million dollars. But continued inflation of between 30 and 40 percent in most countries and the devaluation of the dollar continued to work havoc on the field and make it difficult to increase the number of missionaries. It was estimated that during the prior ten years the buying power of the American overseas missions dollar had been reduced by 128 percent! That is why in its 1980–81 budget the Board was spending $941,000, or 45 percent of its budget, for the support of seventy-eight missionaries.

During its seventy-first annual meeting in 1980, the Missionary Board made some major revisions in its operation. It enlarged the Board's membership from fifteen to twenty. The term of the executive secretary-treasurer was changed from three to five years beginning in 1981. A pilot experience was launched: the naming of Sidney Johnson as a Southeast Asia liaison, meaning he would represent the interests of the Missionary Board in that area wherever there were no resident missionaries. The Missionary Board agreed to assume administrative responsibility for the Church of God Refugee Program. A year earlier the Board passed a resolution honoring Hallie Patterson as she retired from its membership, having served thirty years, twenty-five as a member of the board of directors. Shortly after that Board meeting, another valued member, David Gaulke, was lost by death.

Four Consultations on Missions Strategy

Covering two years, 1976–77, consultations were held in Michigan (September), California (November), Oklahoma (February), and Georgia (April). They were designed to listen to what the church was saying about missions as well as to challenge delegates with what was going on in other countries. Attention was given to methodology and strategy in the movement's missionary enterprise. But inevitably, some consideration had to be given to the theology and philosophy of missions. These consultations helped both the churches and the Missionary Board during the immediate years ahead.

Inter-American Publication Consultation

Serving under the direction of the Inter-American Conference, the Inter-American Publication Committee had been meeting each year during the 1970s to fulfill one of the objectives of "Mission Latin America": more Spanish and Portuguese literature to aid in the advancement of the movement as it reached out into new areas. To add impetus, an Inter-American Publication Consultation convened in Oaxtepec, Mexico, in 1978, representing not only members of the Inter-American Publication Committee but also delegates from the Board of Church Extension and Home Missions, Warner Press, Women of the Church of God, and the Missionary Board. This was to bring more cooperation and better coordination in literature publication. Throughout the decade thousands of tracts, books, and doctrinal booklets were published and distributed. *La Trompeta* (Spanish) and *Trombeta* (Portuguese) were widely used in evangelistic outreach and in keeping the Latin American churches informed. A Spanish Church of God hymnal with notes was a major publication funded by Warner Press.

Caribbean Consultations

Throughout the English-speaking West Indies, the people of the Church of God reformation movement had moved from dependence to independence to interdependence in their relations with the Missionary Board. In twelve territories, as these island countries are called, there were 170 congregations in the movement with around seven thousand believers. They had their own problems related to interterritorial cooperation. Throughout the transition from independence to interdependence, the movement in the entire area experienced difficulties related to theological education, suitable literature, capital funds, and ways of meeting socioeconomic conditions. The West Indian church coveted the cooperation of the Missionary Board as they struggled against low wages, high inflation, and government pressures. Consequently, with a determination to press on, four consultations convened during the decade of the 1970s.

Consultation I met on the island of Antigua in 1971. The role of the Church of God in contemporary West Indian society was reviewed. Theological education was discussed. Relations between the churches and the Missionary Board were reviewed, with the Board expressing sincere willingness to be of service. Consultation II congregated on the island of Grenada in 1973. The emphasis was on stewardship and theological training. Helpful suggestions were presented on the first subject, but little cooperation was evidenced on the second. There was talk about drafting proposals for a regional body of some kind. Consultation III convened in Trinidad in 1975. Discussion took place on whether or not the Church of God in the Caribbean area should join the Caribbean Conference of Churches. A committee was appointed to work on a regional hymnal and a yearbook.

Unusual headway was made during Consultation IV when thirty-five Church of God leaders from eleven territories came together on the island of St. Kitts in 1979. These delegates convened to do business. Only the delegate from Haiti could not be present. Four main issues were carefully presented and discussed: West Indies Theological College, missions, family life, and area organizations. The first three were dealt with quite adequately, but there was an organizational breakthrough relative to the fourth topic. It was thought that the entire area could be divided into three zones. Zone A would include Cayman Islands, Jamaica, Haiti, and Bermuda. Zone B would include St. Kitts-Nevis, Antigua, Barbados, and St. Vincent. And Zone C would include Trinidad-Tobago, Grenada, Guyana, and Curaçao. It was recommended to the General Assemblies in each of the territories that a regional assembly be formed, having a full-time regional director. The organization would be called Caribbean-Atlantic Assembly of the Church of God. Delegates were to return to their respective territories seeking the approval of the General Assemblies. A pro tem director was elected, and the first meeting of this vital area Assembly was to meet in the near future. This was a great step forward, pointing toward a period in which greater witness and growth would be achieved through united efforts in the Caribbean.

Centennial of the Church of God Reformation Movement

It was a great celebration in Anderson, Indiana, June 20–29, 1980! More than thirty-five thousand of the reformation movement's believers came together from all over the world to give serious and joyful expression on the occasion of the one hundredth birthday of this Church of God reformation movement. It's heritage was celebrated and the future projected. This was all done during the ninety-first International Convention, convened in Anderson. The Missionary Board and church leaders in many countries of the world looked forward to this year of 1980, the centennial year, for some very specific reasons: (1) to celebrate the Decade of Advance in Latin America, (2) to launch a Decade of Special Emphasis in Asia, (3) to give thanks for what would be accomplished through the raising of the special project, Million for Missions, and (4) to be involved in the World Conference, especially with the possibility of developing a World Forum. These must now be considered in greater detail, for they represent important landmarks in the missionary movement of the Church of God throughout the world.

The Decade of Advance in Latin America

The capital fund drive at the beginning of the 1970s provided "Mission Latin America" with finances to assist in building as the church in these

countries began to expand. At the beginning of the decade, the Missionary Board was involved in only six of the twenty-two countries of Middle and South America: Mexico, Guatemala, Costa Rica, Panama, Cuba,
and Puerto Rico. Seventeen missionaries were involved. By 1980 eleven
new countries had been entered as part of the Missionary Board's outreach
for the American church: Honduras, El Salvador, Nicaragua, Colombia,
Venezuela, Bolivia, Peru, Brazil, Uruguay, Argentina, and Paraguay. This
made a total of seventeen countries in which thirty-four missionaries from
America were involved, although American missionaries were not found
in all of these countries. By 1977 the Missionary Board's budget for Latin
American countries had multiplied five times since 1970. By the end of
the decade, the number of Bible schools had doubled, the two new ones
being started, in Brazil in 1972 and in Argentina in 1977. A radio ministry through CBH-Spanish was being broadcast in several countries and
CBH-Portuguese was broadcast in Brazil. The first Christian Community
Center was established in San José, Costa Rica. A strong urban emphasis
was placed in such major cities as Mexico City, Guatemala City, Panama
City, Lima, Saõ Paulo, and Buenos Aires. People had been reached with the
good news, and by 1980 there were twenty-two thousand believers in the
movement in Latin America gathering together in 340 congregations. All
of this means that the work of the Church of God in that part of the world
doubled in a decade! This was because of the Holy Spirit working through
the lives of hundreds of God's children. Leaders were looking forward to
entering Chile and Ecuador.

Asia in the 1980s

As early as 1974, Sidney Johnson and I began to have dreams about a decade of special emphasis in South Asia and Southeast Asia immediately following the Decade of Advance in Latin America. This was later expanded
to include East Asia. What a staggering thought! For that is where masses
of people reside who have never heard of Jesus Christ. If you draw a line
from Bombay[1] to Peking[2], two-thirds of the world's population resides below it. One-half of the world's people are Buddhist, Hindu, and Muslim,
and most of them live in Asia. In Asia, only 2 percent of the population
is Christian, including Roman Catholics. The Asian countries are where
most of the 2.7 billion people live who have never heard of salvation from

sin through belief in a Savior. And that is where the population is growing faster than anywhere else in the world. Indeed, this is a difficult area in which to witness. But what a challenge it is to the reformation movement to become a viable part of the total missionary task force operating in Asia. By 1975 the Missionary Board had taken action to launch in Asia in 1980 a strong united evangelistic and missionary outreach by the Church of God.

To determine what plans the Missionary Board should make to become correctly involved during the decade of the 1980s, two consultations were conducted. The first was a five-day Consultation in Tokyo in July 1978. Twenty-seven long-term and short-term missionaries were present, along with nine delegates from America. This was primarily to hear what missionaries in Asia were thinking about the possibilities for outreach and what the Missionary Board's involvement should be. The second was a three-day Consultation in Bangkok convened in February 1979. Seven church leaders representing the Church of God in Korea, Japan, Taiwan, the Philippines, Thailand, Bangladesh, and India met with three persons from America to review what the reformation movement's believers in Asia considered to be the approach in evangelism and missions among non-Christians and what would be the most appropriate assistance from the Missionary Board. Later that same year, the Missionary Board itself gave serious thought to recommendations coming out of both consultations.

It appeared a number of emphases would be most helpful, working with the Church of God extant in Asia. Here are some of the guildelines considered appropriate: (1) an Asian identity for the movement to be created by fostering interrelationships between the churches extant in various countries, (2) specialized long-term missionaries to be invited to serve, (3) short-term missionaries to play an increasing role, (4) Missionary Board assistance in the training of leaders to be given, (5) literature to be produced in greater quantity, and (6) Board partnership in missionary outreach into new countries to be encouraged, the Board being at times the initiator and coordinator. All the way through the decade of the eighties, the American church, being supportive, must recognize that results come slowly and not in great numbers. Such a concept is difficult to understand in American culture where immediate returns for investment made are almost demanded.

Million for Missions Special Project

Million for Missions was a joint project approved by the General Assembly for the Missionary Board and the Board of Church Extension and Home Missions. The sum of $750,000 was to be raised for the Missionary Board and 250,000 for the Home Missions Board for a total of $1,000,000. This was a capital fund project to cover three budget years beginning in July 1977. For the Missionary Board, this was to provide nonbudgetary needs especially for Asia in the 1980s, although some vitally needed projects in other parts of the world would be included. By the end of the three years, approximately $750,000 had been raised, giving the Missionary Board about $560,000.

The project was hoping to raise a total of at least $900,000, which would give the Missionary Board $675,000. This would mean a project curtailment but certainly would meet many critical needs. For Asia, Million for Missions was providing an outreach program in Bangladesh; missionary outreach, leadership training, and contribution toward the relocation of Union Biblical Seminary in India; a new multipurpose church building at Tamagawa in Japan; facilities for the new development in Singapore; assistance in high school facilities in the Philippines; a Christian center in Taipei, Taiwan; and assistance in small church buildings and a new missionary outreach into Cambodia from Thailand. These and many other very important projects were being cared for through Million for Missions. The church in America responded well.

Sixth World Conference of the Church of God

The Worldwide Strategy and Planning Consultation convened in Kenya in 1977 to plan for the joint meeting of the sixth World Conference and the International Convention to celebrate the centennial of the Church of God in 1980. This would be the first World Conference to meet in the United States of America. Plans for the World Conference were coordinated with the Centennial Celebration Committee and the International Convention Program Committee. The first three days of the joint meeting were designed for the World Conference. Co-chairmen were Willi Krenz from Germany and Carlton Cumberbatch from Trinidad. Leading speakers from nine different countries brought challenging messages. In addition, there were conferences, Bible study groups, prayer and testimony meetings, and plenty of time for fellowship and sharing. Many leaders became acquainted with each other for the first time. Names became faces! For the first time, hundreds became aware of the great strength of the Church of God around the world and the tremendous task before it to present the good news to the world.

World Forum of the Church of God

I was one of several who had been thinking for some years about the necessity for a kind of world gathering for Church of God leaders where more definite planning for the Church of God in mission could be done on a scale never before possible through the World Conferences. A World Forum was proposed during the Worldwide Strategy and Planning Consultation in 1977, to have its first meeting during the centennial celebration in 1980. The World Forum would not be administrative or legislative but rather consultative as world leaders would gather from time to time to consider topics of vital concern affecting the life and work of the movement worldwide.

In June 1980 some fifty-five delegates gathered during two sessions of the first World Forum. Organizational business was cared for. But the main topic for consideration was "International Partnership in Mission," an appropriate starting point due to the interest in missions on the part of the third-world church. Papers presented by Donald Johnson and Douglas Welch created discussion and considerable consensus regarding the future. Indigeneity is not achieved until the gospel takes root in the culture of the people where it is planted, or until a missionary outreach of the new church is established. The mission church must become a missionary church. Then and only then can there be real partnership in mission by the Church of God around the world. But that partnership must be based on mutuality. At this point some big words were introduced: *reciprocity, complimentarity,* and *interdependence.* But they were properly defined, and they added up to the concept of the internationalization of missions. Missions on a global scale would involve persons from the "developing churches" and from the "developed churches." It was thought that a linkage system could be maintained through the World Forum.

The Church of God: A World Movement

During the immediate years preceding 1980, the third-world churches of the movement continued to show signs of strength and growth and a determination to join with one another and first-world churches to evangelize the fourth world. This will be illustrated in the closing pages of this book. You will note that the need for missionaries from America remains, involving redeployment at times.

The movement in Jamaica, Barbados, and Trinidad had come of age. West Indies Theological College was functioning well. Eleven out of fifteen pastors in Trinidad and Tobago were alumni. The school had incorporated in 1979 and properties were transferred. In St. Kitts, Clarence and Bernice Glover replaced Allen and Clovis Turner. Vernon and Ruth Lambe had come to Bermuda. When Jamaica withdrew its missionary involvement in Haiti, the work continued to grow with some assistance from America. There are now twenty congregations with fifteen hundred believers and three day schools, one clinic, and an orphanage.

When Warren and Devie Kinion completed a term of service in Mexico, Aaron and Kathryn Kerr were redeployed from Guam to serve in Baja California, and Nasser and Marilyn Farag were redeployed from Kenya to serve in north central Mexico. A rapid growth of the church in Guatemala took place after the severe earthquake and there were now more than sixty congregations. The Christian Center in Costa Rica provided a kindergarten, gymnasium, coffeehouse, library, and a place for the congregation to worship. Ronald and Ruth Shotton retired from Panama in 1979 and were replaced by Vernon and Cathy Allison. That same year Earl and Freda Carver retired from Puerto Rico and Joseph and Elva Mattox continued serving the Academy, which then had 193 students. Paul and Mickey Zoretic were redeployed from Peru to pastor the congregation at Turabo Gardens. Mendoza and Daisy Taylor in Panama heard the call from Colombia and responded. Within a brief time, there were six congregations with pastors. Even with visa problems, Thomas and Mary Lou Walls finally found themselves in Ciudad Guyana, Venezuela, beginning a work there. Albert and Irene Bentley left Argentina, and Bill and Kay Konstantopoulos served a term there. Appointed to the Instituto Biblico Boa Terra in Brazil were Willi and Esther Kant. And the work in Amazonia expanded to Santarem and several settlements.

By 1980 the work in Italy was seven years old and there were two new groups, making a total of four congregations in the suburbs of Rome. An FM radio station was purchased and broadcasting began. Donald Johnson made contact with a work in Poland, bringing encouragement through the Missionary Board. More was learned about the fifty congregations of the Church of God in Russia. A consultation for leaders in the eastern Mediterranean convened in Cyprus in September 1980—the first expression of interdependence following the World Conference in June. Delegates strategized regarding evangelism among non-Christians and recognized the need for a place in the area where leaders could be trained. Egypt received new missionaries, James and Betty Albrecht, introducing a new era for the church. The Church of God in Lebanon had been under fire during five years of civil war. Thirty-five families had lost their source of income, but not one believer was killed, nor did one pastor forsake the flock. Now almost all have been rehabilitated and the churches are self-supporting again. During this period of time, Ernest and Grace LaFont terminated their services in the eastern Mediterranean.

Further south in Kenya, Douglas and Ruth Welch terminated their services. His position as coordinator was not refilled. But George and Eva Buck were sent so that George could serve as administrative assistant to the executive secretary of the Church of God. By 1979 the missionaries present in Kenya reorganized so that they could care for missionary problems with which the church did not wish to bother. There was a strong outreach among the Maasai in south Kenya. Eugene and Barbara VanAlstyne began service at Kima Theological College. Heidi Froemke went as a nurse to replace Edna Thimes, who retired in 1979. Robert and Evelyn Lindemuth spent two short terms assisting in the business of the church. David and Margaret Montague left the field. Church of God headquarters in Tanzania were established in Babati. New missionaries Stanley and Patricia Desjardine were stationed in Arusha, and Sherman and Kay Critser in Mirambo. The Emerald Avenue Church of God in Chicago had made several contacts with a group in Ghana, and Donald Johnson and Paul Hutchins found this to be a viable work of the Church of God when they made a brief visit.

The movement in India remained in a period of growth in Kerala, Orissa, and Meghalaya. An Asian Bible college was opened to train workers to reach the villages in Kerala. Eighty-eight percent of the population of India lived in villages. Self-help projects continued to assist the people and the church. Indian music and the art of meditation enhanced worship services. The church in Meghalaya was longing for another expression of interdependence by joining with the Missionary Board in some missionary outreach into an Asian country. Kinderhilfswerk, from the movement in Germany, was assisting in schools and orphanages in both India and Bangladesh. For months, the Missionary Board tried to secure visas for Raymond and Nina Martin to enter Bangladesh, but it was unsuccessful. However, more and more people were accepting Christ in non-Christian communities. The ten-year plan was right on target in Thailand. The New Life Center was opened in 1975 and the Gospel Training Center in 1976, both in Bangkok. Already young graduates from the training center had successfully established five new churches in the Buriram Province near the Cambodian border. In 1977 Marvin and Karen Helsel were sent to assist in the Bible school. And in 1979 a new work came into being in Singapore under the leadership of Neville Tan. It was incorporated as Asian Missionary Outreach, with a subtitle of The Church of God in Singapore.

Japan was enjoying the services of several short-term teachers who assisted the church. To show good faith in the reconciliation process in Korea, Nathan and Ann Smith were redeployed from Japan, and they were soon joined by David and Greta Reames. Following language study, all four were assisting the movement in Korea, which had by then grown to twenty-seven congregations with fifty-five hundred believers. The missionaries in Hong Kong were still working on how to establish a Bible study center in a new high-rise apartment complex. The church in Australia had been reduced to three congregations. The Missionary Board assumed administrative responsibility by request, and the three missionary couples, Kenneth and Sue Jo Good, Andrew and Rebecca New, and Jack and Bonnie Dunn, were officially appointed by the Board. As mentioned earlier, Aaron and Kathryn Kerr left Guam and were replaced by Steve and Maxine Igarta. And finally a new work developed in Taiwan. The first congregation, located in Taipei under the leadership of Thomas Lo, came with the Church of God in 1976. The second group, also in Taipei, came to the movement in 1977 under the leadership of Joseph Loh. They were hoping for a third congregation in southwest Taiwan.

The Missionary Board commissioned a sizable number of missionaries during its annual meeting in 1980: Will and Patsy Kline to Brazil, Charles and Evelyn Wilson to Kenya, Cova Ricketts (actually a Jamaican trained as a nurse in England) to Kenya, Mark and Sherrie deFelice on short-term assignment to Italy, David and Barbara Miller to Bolivia, and Keith and Gloria Plank to Costa Rica. A number of short-term teachers were also recommended to serve in Asian countries.

After Ninety Years of Missionary Activity

The Church of God reformation was now found in sixty countries with the Missionary Board carrying responsibility in forty-two of them. The sun never set on Church of God missions! Growth had taken place and was indicative of sustained activity. In 1979 there were 177,736 members in the movement in America (including Canada) and 150,778 members in the sixty other countries. There were 2,308 congregations in America (including Canada) and 1,715 in the other countries. Since there is more rapid growth in the churches in the third world, it was believed that before the end of the decade there will be more believers in the movement in other countries than in America. The results in years to come would inevitably be much greater than anticipated. Why? Because of the partnership then rapidly developing to hasten the bearing of the good news to the millions in Asian countries who have never heard of God's love for them.

Passports were being issued not only to missionaries of the first world but also to an increasing number of third-world missionaries. One example was the sending by the Church of God in Meghalaya, India, of two of its members, Leaderwell and Rivulet Pohsngap, as missionaries to Kenya, where he taught Old Testament in Kima Theological College and she, a nurse, worked in the Kima Maternity Hospital. Exciting opportunities were anticipated to be just around the future's corner. China was one example. The institutional church died during the ten-year Cultural Revolution under Mao Tse-tung and his little Red Book. But the resurrection came through the house-church movement involving some one million Christians. This would provide a unique opportunity for our movement. It would not be the traditional entry of Western missionaries; instead it would happen as a result of Chinese and Southeast Asian Christians entering China as professionals for the purpose of witnessing. However, various forms of partnership would be required to cope adequately.

Unreached people remained a challenge to modern-day apostles from many countries to join together as contemporary pioneers of the reformation movement in cross-cultural missionary service. As the church's sons and daughters went out to proclaim Christ as Savior and Lord, the statement of the apostle Paul continued to be a reality: "All over the world this gospel is producing fruit and growing" (Col. 1:6 NIV). We were indeed on the threshold of entry into an exhilarating missionary era as the Church of God reformation movement entered its second century.

CHAPTER 8
EXPANDING THE PARTNERSHIP
(1980–1989)

It was no small celebration in Anderson, Indiana, from June 20–29, 1980. Six months into a new decade, the Church of God celebrated its one hundredth birthday, its ninety-first International Convention, its sixth World Conference, its first World Forum, and the first International Dialogue on Doctrine, all within the span of ten days. More than thirty-five thousand representatives of sixty-two countries where the Church of God was at work gathered for the party, many in national costumes, including native American headdresses, Japanese summer kimonos, colorful African turbans, and embroidered Philippine dress shirts called barongs.

Centennial Celebrations Look Backward, Forward

While there were many tributes to what had been accomplished during the church's first century, the convention theme—"Let the World Know"— helped focus attention on the future. Willi Krenz, of Germany, and Carlton Cumberbatch, of Trinidad, World Conference co-chairs, and other convention planners recognized that what had already been accomplished was only a stepping stone to what must be achieved during the second hundred years if the Church of God would continue fulfilling the biblical mandate to "go into all the world."

It was an unspeakably large assignment for a movement as small as the Church of God. At the dawn of the decade, statistics showed 177,736 members in 2,308 Church of God congregations in North America and 141,738 members in 1,574 sister congregations elsewhere in the world.[1] How could this relatively small band of believers even begin to take the gospel to the 4.5 billion people of the world in 1980? This question must have captivated Missionary Board thinking even as the church celebrated.

Two words answered this vital question: *partnership* and *mission*. They also helped the Missionary Board focus on plans for the coming decade, including "Asia in the '80s," a new thrust into the most populous but mostly unreached region of the world. While there had always been partnership in missions, it had often been a lopsided partnership: North America sent, provided, and frequently directed, while many countries simply received. At best, only limited results could be expected. However, a fresh definition and practice of partnership in mission would prepare the church to turn the corner and enter a new, more productive century for Church of God missions.

At this crossroads, two papers on "International Partnership in Mission" by Douglas Welch and Donald Johnson urged interdependence in missions.[2] Then executive secretary-treasurer of the Missionary Board, Johnson wrote this challenge: "The time has come for us to undertake a partnership in mission. We thank God for what we have done in the past, separately or together. We look to God for our future. We recognize our dependence upon each other. The first one hundred years of the Movement have only prepared us to undertake the second century together."[3]

In addition to challenging the church about the need for partnership, Welch and Johnson suggested practical handles for creating a structure that would produce a more effective international collaboration. These included (1) encouraging each national church to develop its own national missionary board and (2) creating an international consultative committee to help foster mutual learning, mutual strategizing, and mutual sharing of resources, including personnel and finances. Additionally, evangelism and leadership training were identified not only as the reason for the church's existence but also as the foundational goals for its international ministries. These and other weighty issues were considered by fifty-five delegates to the first World Forum just prior to the centennial celebration in Anderson.

It was not long before practical results of the two days of discussions could be identified. Among these was a conference in Cyprus and the launch of a Bible college for the Mediterranean basin, the formation of the Asian Conference, and a new evangelistic thrust into Asia.

Conference on the Work of the Church of God in the Mediterranean Area

Only three months after the conclusion of the historic events of June 1980 in Anderson, Indiana, another historic meeting was convened at Ayia Napa,

Cyprus, September 29 to October 3. The Conference on the Work of the Church of God in the Mediterranean Area brought together nineteen people from Greece, Italy, Lebanon, Egypt, and the United States to discuss how better to accomplish ministry in the Muslim context. Seed money for this consultation was given by Women of the Church of God; its national director, Nellie Snowden, was in attendance. Dr. Harold Vogelaar, then teaching at the Center for Islamic Studies at the Evangelical Seminary in Cairo, served as a resource person and helped conference participants understand both the Muslim culture and the modern world of Islam.

Accomplishments of the five-day meeting seemed to illustrate and carry out the stated desire for greater interdependence in missions. Oral Withrow, assistant to the executive-secretary of the Missionary Board and conference coordinator, declared, "The Missionary Board took another giant step in an effort to encourage area leaders to assume key roles in planning for future ministries in their area of the world."[4] He called the Cyprus consultation one of the most noteworthy of all planning conferences that had been organized by the Missionary Board as the Church of God entered a new century.[5]

Particularly significant was the statement of priorities that emerged to guide the work in the Mediterranean region. A committee of three national leaders—Fouad Melki (Lebanon), Franco Santonocito (Italy), and Mounir Riskallah (Egypt)—was named to begin work on the three priorities: (1) establishing a post-high-school training institution for ministers and laypersons and developing a continuing education and extension training program for leaders already serving the church; (2) developing a strategy for evangelism "to discover and open new fields and possibly reenter areas where the Church of God is no longer ministering," which would include such things as printing and distributing literature and radio evangelism; and (3) developing "a model for interdependence by establishing a coordinating body to research and implement our mutual concerns and to suggest continuing structures for cooperation."[6]

Birth of Mediterranean Bible College and a Mediterranean Assembly

The implementation team was soon hard at work on the first priority. Actually, Melki already was dreaming of an area leadership training school before attending the Cyprus meetings. His concern was that qualified young people were leaving the Middle East for education and not returning. Now, after the pivotal consultation, progress could begin on addressing this concern and making the dream become reality.

Consequently, a second meeting was convened in October 1982 in Athens, Greece. Melki, Santonocito, Panayote Dendrions (Greece), and Lester Crose and James Albrecht (United States) made significant progress in forging ahead. They adopted the name Mediterranean Bible College (MBC) for the new school, chose a board of directors, and agreed to locate the facility in Beirut, Lebanon, an unlikely setting considering that civil war had been raging in that country since 1975. Plans also were made to launch the academic program four years later with Melki as the founding president and Walter M. Doty as the academic dean. At the time, Doty was a faculty member and dean of external studies at Gulf-Coast Bible College in Houston, Texas (now Mid-America Christian University, Oklahoma City, Oklahoma).

Remembering the landmark decisions being made by the committee, Melki asserted, "We agreed to join in prayer and ask for a last sign: 'If five students will register by April 1984, we will open [in] the fall of 1984.'"[7]

The prayers were answered beyond expectation. Twenty-two students enrolled in the school, which shared facilities with the Ashrafieh Church of God. At the end of that first academic year, President Melki reported, "On June 1, 1985, we had a song in our hearts and prayers of thanks on our lips as we praised God for bringing to a close the first year at Mediterranean Bible College, with nineteen students finishing the second term. Faculty, staff, and students met together to thank the Lord for this wonderful year, in spite of the war situation in our country."[8]

Continuing on that high note, twenty-six students registered for classes at the start of the second year. By 1986, new land was purchased for the eventual relocation and expansion of the school on the outskirts of Beirut. (This land would also become the new location of Cedar Home Orphanage for girls—many of them Palestinian refugees—operated by the Church of God in Lebanon.)

With an eye towards helping MBC develop its curriculum, faculty, student body, financial base, and regional outreach, the Board of Directors also was concerned about other priorities identified in the 1980 Cyprus conference. During its November 1985 annual meeting, the directors explored how to form an area assembly of the Church of God in the Mediterranean basin. Subsequently, whenever leaders gathered in connection with MBC, they also informally discussed area-wide issues until the birth of the General Assembly of the Mediterranean Area (GAMA) in 1999. During its first official meeting in Rome, July 12–17, 1999, delegates from Egypt, France, Greece, Germany, Italy, Lebanon, Spain, and the United States elected Franco Santonocito as the regional assembly's first chairman.

New Hope for the Church in Egypt

Another result of the 1980 Cyprus conference was new hope for the Egyptian church. Roots there extended back to 1904 and a preaching mission by E. E. Byrum, followed in 1907 by a lengthier visit by George P. Tasker and Hiram A. Brooks. Later, Thaddeus and Katrina Neff became the first long-term resident missionaries (1923–51). Other missionaries served in Egypt and neighboring countries until the mid-1970s, but by 1980, the work seemed dormant. However, the decision in Cyprus to revitalize Church of God regional outreach began to change that. James Albrecht recalls:

> When we went to Egypt as missionaries in 1978, we found a nation recovering from four wars with Israel. This devastated the economy and isolated Egypt from the West. But with the September 1978 Camp David Peace Accord brokered by Jimmy Carter and signed by Anwar Sadat and Menachem Begin, a new door was opened to the world. This included renewing the mission of the Church of God.
>
> At the time, there were only seven existing churches, all in various stages of neglect and decline. Four new pastors were called, and Mounir Riskallah Soliman assumed national leadership. The church started some new ministries, including evangelism to some five hundred children, led by Morgan Ibrahim Fam in the Alexandria area. In Cairo, children were reached first through World Vision and later Children of Promise, and missionaries Russ and Sharon Skaggs worked with several churches and home Bible studies in the city.
>
> A national conference center opened in 1987 and hosts leadership conferences, including the first Mediterranean Bible College extension institute in August 1989. As many as fifteen hundred children and youth attend summer camps there. The intentional

thrust of the 1980s opened a window to the world for Egyptian churches and pastors who had been isolated and parochial in their experience and practice. Several began traveling abroad for conferences and conventions, gaining an awareness of the wider Church of God. Today there is new life in Egypt, with thirteen congregations and fifteen hundred members.[9]

Launch of an Assembly for Asia

During the Church of God Centennial celebrations in 1980, Nathan and Ann Smith, former missionaries to Japan and Korea, had opened their home for informal conversations about how greater cooperation among Asians might help further Church of God work in their vast region. Among those present were Kozo Konno (Japan), Thomas Lo and Joseph Loh (Taiwan), Hong Mook Yoo (Korea), Wichean Watakeecharoen (Thailand), Rolando Bacani (Philippines), Neville Tan (Singapore), and Borman Roy Sohkhia and Asim Das (India).

While Ann Smith, the Missionary Board's liaison to Asia, facilitated the meeting in Anderson, it was the Asians who decided to organize a gathering for Church of God leaders in Asia. Subsequently, the first Asian Church of God Leaders' Conference was convened in Taipei, Taiwan, November 9–11, 1982. It was hosted by Thomas Lo and Joseph Loh, brothers (despite the different spellings of their last names) and pastors of the first two Church of God congregations in Taiwan. This historic assembly was followed two years later by a second gathering in Hong Kong. It was chaired by Japan's Konno, chosen as first chairman of what would eventually be called the Asian Church of God Conference. (This name was to change again in 1996 and become the Asia–Pacific Church of God Conference.) Seventeen delegates, including both national leaders and missionaries, assembled from eight Asian nations where the Church of God had organized work. Regrettably, the hosts of the 1982 meeting could not attend because of visa issues that highlighted the difficult relationship between Hong Kong and Taiwan.

Notably, these leaders' conferences spelled a significant change in the manner of earlier regional meetings, which seemed to gather either missionaries or national leaders, but not both.[10] Perhaps for the first time, the 1984 Hong Kong gathering united both leadership groups and highlighted attempts at true partnership in evangelism and mission in the region.

Building upon the rich fellowship enjoyed in Anderson and Taipei, two working committees of the area assembly were established in Hong Kong. First, a Communications and Education Committee was formed with Rolando Bacani as its chairperson. Activities of this committee would include publishing the *Asian Church of God Magazine*, to be edited by Asim Das and produced by Neville Tan in Singapore. Second, a Missions Committee was formed with Wichean Watakeecharoen as its chair. Bylaws also were drawn up stating that every missionary in the region was invited to participate as an observer, once again illustrating the intent of living out partnership in mission. (These were formalized a decade later in a document written in another meeting in Hong Kong stating that membership was composed of "all members of Church of God congregations in Asia–Pacific and missionaries of the Church of God serving in Asia–Pacific, subject to approval of the Executive Committee of the Conference."[11])

"A dream is coming true. The Church of God in Asia is finally coming of age," Das enthused in his first editorial. Citing the births of the regional assembly and the magazine, Das thanked God for the "vision and tireless effort of Rev. Kozo Konno, chairman of the Conference, and Rev. Sidney Johnson, missionary for Asia."[12]

Looking back upon early activities of the newly-founded assembly, Konno, pastor of Nerima Church of God in Tokyo, wrote in the inaugural issue of the *Asian Church of God Magazine*:

> I believe that these developments signify the great change of our attitude. It signifies, first of all, that fellowship beyond national boundaries exists. A cooperative missions program by Asians is being carried out. As I have mentioned before, the Church of God mission in Asia has been promoted mainly by the churches and missionaries of North America. Now the Asian churches are participating in that program. It is time for us to go forward from 'participation' to 'cooperation.' . . . When we develop this healthy and mutually constructive relationship with the Missionary Board, the Asian Church of God will grow strong with God's help and his blessing.[13]

Similarly enthusiastic about the birth of the Asian Conference, Johnson called it "perhaps the most significant development during the 'Asia in the '80s' decade."[14] In addition to Taipei and Hong Kong, biennial meetings during the decade were conducted in Bangkok, Thailand (1986), and Cuttack, India (1988). The stated goal of "mutual fellowship, mutual prayer, and cooperation in mission"[15] was being lived out in Asia.

Formation of the Caribbean–Atlantic Assembly

What was happening in the church in Asia was being mirrored in the Caribbean region at the start of the decade. Like the movement in Asia, church leaders in the zone closest to the United States were eager to work together more cooperatively and effectively.

Setting the stage, missionaries during the 1960s had stressed that the Caribbean church should become self-governing, reflecting a philosophy that missionaries were responsible to work themselves out of their jobs. This played out in the completion of many missionary terms in the Caribbean during the decade of the 1960s, including the departures of Donald and Betty Jo Johnson and William and Emilia Fleenor from Trinidad and Tobago, and of Mary Olson, Clair and Retha Shultz, Harold and Barbara Johnson, James Earl and Gwendolyn Massey, Tom and Dorothy Pickens, and Ralph and Helen Little from Jamaica.

This exodus of missionary personnel prompted an area-wide meeting of Caribbean leaders in October 1971 on the island of Antigua. It was the first of four consultations convened to discuss the future role of the Church of God in contemporary West Indian society. In addition to regional leaders, participants included W. E. Reed, executive secretary of the Executive Council, and Donald D. Johnson, Missionary Board executive secretary-treasurer.

Perhaps the most significant outcome of the final consultation in St. Kitts in July 1979 was the birth of the Caribbean–Atlantic Assembly in 1980 "to enhance fellowship, communication, encouragement, and continued outreach to all the islands."[16] Victor Babb was named the part-time executive director of the assembly in 1981, with the regional office located in his homeland of Barbados. By 1986, his responsibilities had become a full-time assignment. They would expand even further when he was invited by the Missionary Board in 1991 to become regional director of the Caribbean–Atlantic region. Significantly, Babb became the first national to head up one of the five regions where the Missionary Board was at work around the world (Africa, Asia, Caribbean–Atlantic, Europe–Middle East, and Latin America).

1980 Inter-American Conference

While Asia and the Caribbean–Atlantic were just beginning to organize their area assemblies, the church in Latin America had been at work regionally since its first area-wide meeting in 1962 in Mexico City. Now, at the start of the new decade, six hundred delegates from sixteen of seventeen countries in the region where the Church of God was at work met in January on the campus of Boa Terra Bible Institute in Curitiba, Brazil, for back-to-back assemblies: the ninth Inter-American Conference, attended by fifty official delegates, and the Brazilian National Convention, drawing participants from the nation's thirty-four congregations. [17] Both conferences celebrated what had been accomplished during the decade just completed when the Missionary Board had conducted its first-ever major thrust into one geographic area.

Called the "Decade of Advance in Latin America," the 1970s special emphasis had doubled Church of God membership in that region to more than twenty-two thousand people as the Missionary Board had entered eleven new nations: Brazil, Peru, Argentina, El Salvador, Honduras, Uruguay, Bolivia, Paraguay, Nicaragua, Colombia, and Venezuela. Participants in the two January meetings celebrated as they heard other exciting reports: more than five hundred delegates attended a national youth convention in Argentina in 1979; some congregations in Bolivia had grown to more than one thousand people; thirty-two hundred Bolivians participated in their 1979 national convention; new church buildings had been dedicated recently in Argentina and Brazil; and the Church of God in Guatemala had grown to sixty-one congregations (thirty-eight with church buildings) and ten new preaching points, with more than five hundred Guatemalans converted in Church of God congregations during 1979.

Particularly exciting were the national churches that reported missionary activity outside their own borders. These included Argentina, reaching out into Paraguay, Uruguay, and Chile; and Puerto Rico, working in the Dominican Republic. Additionally, in cooperation with the Missionary Board, Panama was ministering in Colombia.

Although North America had given enthusiastically to support the "Decade of Advance in Latin America," the Inter-American Conference was "the major unifying force," explained Maurice Caldwell, then Missionary Board associate secretary with special responsibility for Latin America. He noted the Board's support for the biennial conference in his annual report and announced the new officers chosen in the January meeting who would help lead the Inter-American Conference into the new decade. These officers were: Isai Calderon (Guatemala), president; Hector Lopez (Mexico), secretary; and Nelson Junges (Brazil), treasurer. Significantly, Junges was the first South American officer in the eighteen-year history of the Inter-American Conference. Conference delegates also voted to convene the next biennial meeting in Argentina in 1982.

Million for Missions

There could have been no doubt in anyone's mind that the Church of God was inaugurating the most ambitious fundraising campaign ever in its history when a new budget year began on July 1, 1977, launch day of the Million for Missions campaign. Responding to cries across the church that more should be done for missions, the 1976 General Assembly approved Million for Missions as a "unique three-year special effort to raise an added one million dollars, beyond our normal World Service ministry, for expansion of missions outreach at home and overseas."[18]

What was unique about the campaign? David Lawson, associate director of World Service, noted that it was a capital funds thrust that would provide more money for home missions outreach through the Board of Church Extension and Home Missions and for foreign missions projects through the Missionary Board. One-fourth of contributions, or $250,000, would be earmarked for home missions, with three-fourths, or $750,000, to make possible increased overseas missions efforts. New projects at home and abroad were pegged by a survey team during two trips in 1977. In the spring, they examined home missions needs among Native Americans in Scottsbluff, Nebraska; Wounded Knee, South Dakota; and Klagetoh, Arizona; and an inner city mission in Denver, Colorado. Later in the fall, the group toured international sites that might be included in the special fundraising budget.[19]

In order to achieve its amazing million-dollar goal, Lawson remarked that the campaign might better be called "A Million *More* for Missions."[20] Unless the church responded with giving that was over and above regular World Service support, the other agencies of the Church of God in North America and ongoing support needs for what already was being done in home and foreign missions would suffer.

The church's response was enthusiastic. At the end of the first year (June 1978), $187,000 had been given to Million for Missions. Although receipts did not match one-third of the million dollar target, many congregations were just getting involved. There was much optimism because Million for Missions had already generated a greater dollar response across the church than any previous special project.

Momentum and excitement were building. By the end of June 1979, the response during the second year was even more remarkable with more than $300,000 given toward the goal. Once again, a special-project giving record had been broken, and there were thrilling reports of what already had been accomplished as a result. Among these, the Church of God in San Benito, Texas, a new Hispanic congregation launched in 1976, was able to construct a church building thanks to Million for Missions funds raised by Women of the Church of God. On the international scene, an apartment and a parking garage in Ostia, Italy, outside Rome, were purchased and renovated to become the home of the Church of God congregation there.

However, the challenge was greater yet at the start of the third year. Half a million dollars remained to be raised in order to declare victory. Was it possible to match what had been given in the previous two years with even more extraordinary giving during the campaign's final year? Concerted promotional efforts outlined exciting projects in more than fifteen nations, including Antigua, Bangladesh, Brazil, Colombia, Egypt, India, Malaysia, Mexico, Tanzania, and Thailand.[21] While many of these were construction projects for schools, churches, hostels, camps, and offices, some funds were to support national churches in their own outreaches. Among other examples, $25,000 was earmarked for Singapore to reach out to neighboring Malaysia and Indonesia, and $20,000 would help Brazil develop an urban outreach in São Paulo.

Congratulating the church on its meritorious Million for Missions efforts, World Service reported that a record $717,000 had been received by June 1980, including $227,726 during the final 1979–80 budget year. Unfortunately, receipts during the third year fell short, so the campaign was extended for a fourth year. Subsequently, the 1980–81 World Service budget included $225,000 to wrap-up up the special effort. Perhaps the church had wearied of Million for Missions by this time, however, because only $121,600 came in during that final year. This was barely half of the hoped-for amount and the smallest contribution of the four-year campaign.

Consequently, a number of projects were curtailed, among these the Jericho Project in Nairobi, Kenya. It was finally completed in the mid-1980s after significant fundraising efforts by the Kenyan church and a promotion at the 1983 Nairobi World Conference that resulted in a six-thousand-dollar offering for the church building project.[22]

Although the million-dollar goal had not been reached, the church in North America deserved commendation for its overwhelming response. In four years, it had given an outstanding $838,600 to Million for Missions. Many noteworthy accomplishments had resulted, including these construction projects: missionary residences in Tokyo, Japan, and Seoul, Korea; the Crose Missionary Residences in Anderson, Indiana, to house furloughing missionaries; a church headquarters building in Cochin, India; school units in Bangladesh and the Philippines; church buildings in St. John's, Antigua; Santarem and São Paulo, Brazil; Diego Martin, Trinidad; Ostia, Italy; Cairo, Egypt; Bangkok, Thailand; and Singapore; and Christian centers in Taiwan and Tanzania.

Additionally, Million for Missions had helped launch new ministries to Hispanics in San Benito, Texas; Toledo, Ohio; Brooklyn, New York; Phoenix, Arizona; and Fresno, California; to Native Americans in Anchorage, Alaska, and to persons of Asian descent in Hawaii. New outreach ministries also had begun in Siliguri, India; Malaysia; and Indonesia. Finally, since the Missionary Board helped support Union Biblical Seminary, the premier leadership training institution in Asia, Million for Missions money assisted in the school's relocation from Yeotmal to Pune, India.[23]

Evaluating the campaign, David Lawson, by then executive director of World Service, wrote in his 1980 ministry report, "'Million for Missions' has enabled us to possess new territory for Christ. We have joined together in accomplishing what could not have been done otherwise." However, he also challenged the church not to be satisfied and issued a call to an even more exciting future. "Boundless opportunities await an adventurous people willing to courageously follow God," he stated.

"Asia in the '80s"

What were some of those "boundless opportunities"? With well over half of the Million for Missions projects located in Asia, that continent had moved into the forefront of the church's missions thinking by the end of the four-year campaign. "The task remains for us to join God in helping… so that the good work begun by 'Million for Missions' can flourish and grow," Lawson declared in his call to action, which supported the Missionary Board's decision to promote a new decade of emphasis called "Asia in the '80s."[24]

With two-thirds of the world's population, including a vast non-Christian majority, Asia also represented the birthplace of all the world's major religions. In addition to its predominant Muslim, Hindu, and Buddhist populations, Asia was also home to the world's largest officially atheistic nation, China, and many governments that formally or informally supported the persecution of the Christian church. Not only would Asia provide thrilling new open doors for missions, but it also would challenge the Church of God as never before.

At the dawn of the new decade, the Church of God was evangelizing in eight Asian nations. The second-oldest work outside the United States (Mexico was the first) had begun in 1896 in India. In Asia, the Church of God was also resident in Japan, Bangladesh, Korea, the Philippines, Thailand, Taiwan, and Singapore. Interestingly, the church in each of these countries was introduced by a national worker, not a missionary.

Shortly before the new decade began, Singaporean Neville Tan had agreed in March 1979 to begin the work of the Church of God in his country during an historic strategy meeting in Bangkok attended by Wichean Watakeecharoen, national leader in Thailand, Marvin Helsel, a missionary to Thailand, and Sidney Johnson, Missionary Board liaison to Asia. To satisfy government requirements, the work in Singapore was initially registered as the Asian Missionary Outreach, a missions organization. However, the first congregation was established shortly afterwards, in July 1980.

While it could not be verified, it seemed that the Church of God was also present in China at the start of the 1980s, although it did not have any international ties if it was. William and Gloria Hunnex began the work in Chinkiang, China, in 1909, but when all ten Church of God missionaries were expelled in 1949 with the Communist takeover, communication with the national church was lost. Nevertheless, contacts with several people, including Isaac Doone in Hong Kong (son of T. C. Dong, an early Church of God pastor in mainland China), supported the growing belief that both the Christian church and the Church of God had survived an era of great persecution that was still in effect.

Not only was Doone eager that his homeland be evangelized, but he also had a passion for helping establish the Church of God in Hong Kong before the British territory would revert to China's sovereignty in 1997. Consequently, he served on the organizing committee for "Church of God Hong Kong Ministries," founded in 1979. Then, in 1984, the government registered the Church of God as a legal entity called Christian Fellowship (Church of God). Missionaries Michael and Debra Kinner and national worker K. K. (Kin-Keung) Mak connected with this committee to launch an outreach into a heavily populated high-rise apartment complex in the New Territories district.

Considering the vastness of the continent, however, Church of God work at the launch of "Asia in the '80s" was barely a drop in the bucket of what was needed for Asia to be evangelized. India then represented the third-largest Church of God constituency (behind the United States and Kenya), with 436 congregations and forty-four thousand believers. However, this openness to the gospel—particularly in Meghalaya and Assam, states in the northeast, and Kerala, in the south—was not at all typical of countries elsewhere in Asia. Rather, Christian populations of less than two percent in such countries as Japan, Thailand, and Bangladesh were the norm.

Was the Church of God up to the challenge? Not if the North American church attempted it on its own. Sidney Johnson explained, "It is a fact of life today that if Asia is to be evangelized, it will have to be done primarily by Asian leaders. In some Asian countries today, North Americans/Westerners are not allowed to enter. In a few countries, no workers from outside are able to work. However, in some countries, Asians can enter and minister to other Asians."[25]

If ever there was a case for partnership in missions, this was it. It was also a call to interdependence and mutuality in missions, a philosophy of seeking to meet needs through cooperatively using the resources of all parties. While Asians might be able to enter other Asian nations, they might not have sufficient finances, education, or training to enable their service there. So the Missionary Board was always looking for open doors for advancement that could be entered through interdependence and mutual cooperation with the church in Asia and its strong leaders. Consequently, by the end of the decade, five more Asian nations had been entered—Indonesia (1981), Nepal (1983), Myanmar (1985), and Malaysia (1988)—with groundwork completed for the beginnings of the Church of God in Sri Lanka in 1990.

Two Good Examples

What does partnership in missions look like? One good example is related to the Church of God in Meghalaya, northeast India, home of Borman Roy Sohkhia, Leaderwell and Rivulet Pohsngap, and Amos and Semper Moore, whose stories are, in part, those of partnership, interdependence, and mutuality in missions. Initially, this partnership began with educational support from North America for Sohkhia at Anderson School of Theology and for the Pohsngaps at Union Biblical Seminary in India.

Recalling the early days of the partnership, Sidney Johnson shares, "In January 1978, Borman Roy Sohkhia enrolled in Anderson School of Theology. After completing his degree, he said to me, 'I am returning to India and Asia, and together we will light a fire that will burn until Jesus comes.' Subsequently, he was instrumental in organizing a Missions Committee of the Church of God in Meghalaya, India, in 1979–80."[26]

As this committee began dreaming about outreach opportunities, it approached the Pohsngaps about a possible missionary assignment in Kenya, where Leaderwell would teach at Kima Theological College (now Kima International School of Theology) and Rivulet, a registered nurse, would work at the adjacent Kima Hospital.

"The church in India and the Missionary Board in the United States came up with the idea of a pioneering joint venture in missions. At the time of the discussion, we were at Union Biblical Seminary for further studies. Borman Roy Sohkhia approached us and asked if we would consider this assignment," Pohsngap explained, his wife adding that they spent two years praying before they could move to Kenya on January 1, 1981.[27]

But this was only the beginning. After three years in Africa, the couple enrolled in Asbury Theological Seminary, Wilmore, Kentucky, to continue graduate studies that would prepare them for later ministry in the Church of God in Meghalaya. Specifically, Leaderwell pastored and became founding president of Nichols-Roy Bible College while Rivulet organized the state women's association as its president. In the wider church, Leaderwell served two terms as president of Union Biblical Seminary (UBS) from 1997 to 2004. Working alongside him, Rivulet helped students' wives prepare for their own future unofficial, but nevertheless important, ministry roles as pastors' wives. Additionally, Leaderwell was on national and international boards of World Vision from 1994 to 2007. Following their UBS tenure, the Pohsngaps returned to Meghalaya in 2004. Leaderwell became international director of Global LEAD Alliance, a parachurch organization focusing on leadership development, and Rivulet began working with Church of God Sunday school curriculum development and teacher training on a statewide basis.

"These are certainly examples of partnership, interdependence, and mutuality," declares Donald Johnson, who has fond memories of conversations in which he was involved as executive secretary-treasurer of the Missionary Board, leading to the unique arrangement whereby personnel from Meghalaya and financial support from North America resulted in a practical example of partnership.

Another example comes from the beginnings of the Church of God in Nepal in 1983. Sidney Johnson is outspoken in attributing this to the vision and action of the Church of God in Meghalaya and Assam, India, organized following Sohkhia's return to his homeland in 1979.

> In 1983, the [newly organized Meghalaya Missions] Committee sent a survey team to Nepal to determine if work could be started in that mostly unevangelized Hindu kingdom. As a result, Amos and Semper (Manners) Moore went from Meghalaya to Kathmandu, Nepal, in May, 1983, when it was yet illegal for a citizen of Nepal to change religions. One would be imprisoned for up to seven years if found to have brought a person to faith in Jesus Christ. Despite these difficult circumstances, the Moores labored hard and faithfully to establish the Church of God movement in Nepal.
>
> The significant thing about the beginning of the work in Nepal is that it was totally under the Church of God in Meghalaya, India, as their outreach. The Missionary Board in America fully supported the idea, but was not involved administratively or financially.
>
> In 1984, the Church of God in Japan began giving some support for the work in Nepal. However, these funds were used for missionary outreach and not for the salaries of workers or missionaries. Later the Missionary Board in the United States became involved in some financial help, but from the beginning until the present the Church of God in Nepal has been fully the responsibility of the Church of God in Meghalaya.[28]

"Meghalaya sent and supported the Moores, and the church in the United States and Japan were financially involved in supporting projects identified by the Meghalaya missionaries. This is an example of international partnership," Donald Johnson states, applauding the church in Meghayala and Assam for their eagerness to plant the Church of God in neighboring Asian nations.[29]

Practicing a Biblical Theology of Mission

The partnership lived out in the relationships between the Church of God in northeast India, Japan, Kenya, Nepal, and the United States did not occur by happenstance. Rather, they were an expression of the philosophy of the Missionary Board as it attempted to practice biblical missions. This philosophy was explained by Douglas Welch in "Toward a Biblical Theology of Mission," a thought-provoking three-page paper he wrote for discussion at the 1982 annual Missionary Board retreat.

Noting that the mission of the people of God is a mission of reconciliation—that is, calling the nations to repentance and reconciliation with God and with each other—the Anderson University School of Theology missions professor pointed out that this task must be carried out in international community if it will achieve God's purpose.

> Mission in its truest biblical sense is a community function. It is the whole People of God involved in the whole world in God's mission. A broader fellowship of God's People should not undertake mission on behalf of another national fellowship. Rather, all should unite together in mission on behalf of the nations. So mission is essentially international in its nature. We assist each other in mission. We depend upon each other. Just as Paul believed it necessary to seek the partnership of the churches in Rome for a missionary thrust to lands to the West (Romans 15), so should a national fellowship of the People of God seek to unite with all similar national fellowships in discipling the nations, and in many respects unite with even those of somewhat dissimilar traditions. Both international and inter-confessional unity and cooperation should be sought for the sake of the nations.[30]

In addition to the cooperation with Meghalaya and Assam, there are numerous other examples of how the Missionary Board tried to practice partnership in mission and international reconciliation during the 1980s. Among these is the story of the planting of the Church of God in Ecuador.

Delia Rodriguez was living in Ecuador's Amazon jungle in 1986 when, listening to the radio, she heard the gospel proclaimed on the Spanish-language *Christian Brotherhood Hour* (CBH). Responding, she wrote to Anderson to request a World Calendar of Prayer that had been offered on the broadcast. Since there was no Church of God in Ecuador then, CBH sent her name to missionary Paul Butz in Peru, who passed the information along to Narciso Zamora, a Peruvian pastor who had become interested in missions outreach into the neighboring country after learning that the Inter-American Conference had targeted Ecuador as a new nation to enter. After fasting and praying, Zamora traveled by bus into Ecuador, searching for Delia. Overjoyed that someone would go to such lengths to respond to her inquiry to CBH, Delia accepted Christ as her Savior.

The story wasn't finished yet. The first Church of God convert in Ecuador wrote a letter to her sister in Quito asking her to give Zamora lodging for one month so that he could explore church-planting opportunities there. Upon arriving in the capital city, the Peruvian missionary prayed for God's guidance. He recalls, "I stood under a street light at a corner bus stop, sang my choruses, and preached. One woman accepted Christ."[31] By month's end, ten people had accepted Christ and the small room Zamora had rented as an evangelistic site was filled to capacity.

Confident that God was working to establish the Church of God in Ecuador, Zamora returned to Peru to move his family—his wife Udelia and their two sons—back to Ecuador as missionaries in January 1987. Another partnership country entered the mix when Mendoza Taylor and a group from Bogotá, Colombia, visited the Zamoras to encourage the new church and offer support as fellow members of the Inter-American Conference. Shortly, financial assistance from both the Inter-American Conference and the Missionary Board were added to the congregation's regular tithe and money-raising efforts to enable the congregation to buy property for an eventual church building. Partnership was alive and well in Ecuador!

Partnership Examples in Africa

On the African content, another partnership brought together Kenya, Uganda, Canada, and the Missionary Board to relaunch the church in Uganda. Initially, the Church of God in Uganda was planted in 1964 through the outreach of Frank and Margaret LaFont, missionaries in Kenya who made evangelistic trips across the border into the northern region. When the increasingly horrific activities of President Idi Amin precluded the LaFonts from continuing that outreach, the young church retreated into the safety of dormancy. But the situation began to change when Amin was overthrown in 1979 and freedom of worship was restored.

Testing the waters in 1980, a small group of believers began meeting together by lantern light in one room on a back street in Kampala, Uganda's capital city. When a man from the small Church of God congregation in the north arrived in Kampala, he shared the good news that a Canadian couple was interested in coming as missionaries to Uganda. Excited, the back street group requested to affiliate with the Church of God.

Back in Canada, Stan and Marion Hoffman were equally excited as they waited for God to open the door fully. Paul Hutchins, Missionary Board liaison in Africa, subsequently visited Uganda and met with the growing group in Kampala. Their excited welcome of the Hoffmans by name was a prelude to their enthusiastic greeting of them in person at the airport in July 1983.

Soon the work in Uganda was expanding once again. The Canadian missionaries, sent through the Missionary Board, purchased land in Kampala to become the headquarters of the Church of God. They also launched a theological education by extension (TEE) program that helped the church expand quickly into the rural areas. The cooperative church planting efforts of the Hoffmans and Rufus Akhonya, of Kenya, saw the expansion of the church to 160 congregations by 1985.

Another country entered the mix when the Missionary Board sent Tim and Colleen Stevenson, the Hoffmans' daughter and son-in-law, to Uganda as project missionaries in 1986. Among the projects they would represent was a sponsorship program for Ugandan children through the German Church of God. By 1989, the number of Ugandan churches had more than doubled to 331, a testimony to the effectiveness of the five-nation partnership in missions. The partnership expanded even further

when the Hoffmans moved to Zambia in 1989 and linked up with regional evangelists to launch the church in Zimbabwe (1992), Mozambique
(1994), Malawi (1995), and Angola (1999).

Likewise in Latin America

Across the Atlantic Ocean from the African continent, partnership was
also alive in other Latin American nations, in addition to Ecuador, whose
story of collaboration was already shared. The following short history of
the Church of God in the Dominican Republic illustrates another success
story of partnership.

In July 1983, Pastor Gerardo Taron traveled from his home in Obera,
Argentina, to lead evangelistic services in Santo Domingo, Dominican Republic. While he was away, his wife Olga dreamed twice that her husband's
first words upon returning would be, "Viejita, let's go to Santo Domingo."
Indeed, when Olga met Gerardo's plane, he excitedly blurted out those
exact words.

Much had happened in Gerardo's life during his month in the Dominican Republic. Along with Isai Calderon of Guatemala, Taron was an
officer of the Inter-American Conference. The two Conference representatives were in the Dominican not only for the evangelistic outreach but also
to help a Shreveport, Louisiana, missions team construct a church building, conduct evening gospel meetings, and make arrangements to welcome
a career missionary family from El Salvador. But the plans were threatened
when the government refused to issue visas to the Salvadorans.

"We were very worried because now there was no one who wanted to
be a missionary and we had searched all over Latin America," Taron recalls.
"It was during those days that the Lord touched my heart. In the beginning it scared me. I thought I was making a mistake. But…the call became
clearer and clearer. I told the brothers and they immediately felt the Lord's
confirmation. However, I warned them that I would only come as a missionary if my wife was completely in agreement. I had imagined that she
would say I was crazy, but without hesitation, she answered, 'Let's go!' No
doubt remained that this was God's will."[32]

Eight months later, Gerardo, Olga, and their three small children
became the first missionaries commissioned by the Inter-American Conference in a wonderful example of partnership in missions. Support for the

Argentineans came from the Inter-American Conference, the Missionary Board, local churches in the United States, and national assemblies of the Church of God in Latin America. Eventually, the Dominican church also became active giving partners—not just recipients—by helping support the family. Within twelve years, the Santo Domingo church had grown to two hundred members and had launched a school where more than nine hundred children were enrolled.

Partnership in Radio

Another exciting partnership linked the Church of God in West Germany, a German pastor who was raised in Russia, the Mass Communications Board, Women of the Church of God, and several congregations in the United States in producing the Russian-language *Christian Brotherhood Hour*. Known in the former Soviet Union as *The Voice of the Gospel*, CBH-Russian was launched on June 7, 1984. Within four years, it was being aired weekly in five different time zones, proclaiming the gospel in an area wider than the distance from New York to San Francisco. While the Missionary Board was not specifically linked in this partnership, there is no doubt that seeds were planted through it for a significant evangelistic thrust from the Board into Russia during the next decade after the fall of the Berlin Wall in 1990 and the breakup of the Soviet Union in 1991.

At the time, it was estimated that there were more than forty thousand radio churches in the USSR. Although the Soviet government restricted access to church buildings, pastors, songbooks, and Bibles and persecuted those who practiced their faith, shortwave radio was able to reach out evangelistically. "Congregations" would gather around radios in homes as the center of their worship. As a result, despite harassment, the Christian church was growing in the 1980s.

Enter Walentin Schüle. Born in 1951 in what is now Kazakhstan, Schüle gave his heart to Christ as a ten-year-old boy, thanks to the influence of his parents—particularly his mother—who were among the first generation of Church of God Germans who had emigrated to the Russian Caucasus. Almost immediately, he began helping in the Sunday school. By the age of fifteen, he was translating sermons in his German-language church into Russian so the congregation could reach out to its Russian neighbors.

In 1974, Schüle moved to West Germany and, with his wife Irma, planted a Church of God congregation in Pforzheim to minister to the many German immigrants in the area who had returned from Russia. "Russia was always on my heart," he declares of his decision to become the Russian-language radio broadcast speaker even while pastoring in Pforzheim until 1988. He continues the radio ministry today while also pastoring in Calw and doing missions work in the Ukraine and Siberia.

Illustrative of partnership in missions, seed money for the Russian-language broadcast came from Westwood Church, Kalamazoo, Michigan, and Sherman Street Church of God, Fort Wayne, Indiana; the church in West Germany paid the program's production costs; and Women of the Church of God gave a one-time grant of $10,000 for expanding the broadcasting region. At the end of the first year of CBH-Russian, gospel broadcasters were reporting that as many as 90 percent of Christians being baptized behind the Iron Curtain were coming to Christ through evangelistic radio broadcasts such as this one.

Partnership in Publications

Greater partnership in missions also was taking place within the United States between the various agencies of the Church of God and even extending to other church groups. Back in 1969, an example between agencies had emerged with the administrative transfer of the work in Mexico from the Board of Church Extension and Home Missions to the Missionary Board. This had opened the door for a more unified missions thrust into Latin America during the upcoming 1970s "Decade of Advance in Latin America."

A few years later, as editor-in-chief of Warner Press and *Vital Christianity*, Arlo F. Newell would play a major role in the expansion of another inter-agency partnership in missions, this one between the publishing house and the Missionary Board.

Newell recalls the incident that launched this expanded partnership:

> During my first term in office (1977–82), I was asked to lead a conference for the North American Convention on missions outreach. Having covered the general areas being addressed at that time, I shared with the small group my vision of what could be

accomplished by publishing doctrinal books in Spanish and other languages. Unbeknown to me, a layperson named Jack Wilson (a furniture dealer in the Tulsa area) was present. Following the convention, he corresponded with me, asking what it would cost to publish F. G. Smith's book *What the Bible Teaches* in the Spanish language. Having lived in Oklahoma where a large number of Hispanics had settled, he sensed a real burden for this type of outreach. I have referred to this as the "mission miracle" through the burden and vision of one man. Presenting this possibility to [Warner Press] President Donald Noffsinger, it was approved and became a reality.[33]

According to Newell, Warner Press later published a number of other doctrinal books in Spanish. Among these were two that he authored: *The Church of God as Revealed in Scripture* (1972) and *Receive the Holy Spirit* (1978). Distribution of this literature further extended the partnership as the Missionary Board, Project Partner, the Spanish-language periodical *La Trompeta*, the Inter-American Conference, and the Spanish Council joined hands to circulate the materials as widely as possible.

But Spanish wasn't the only language of publishing partnerships. Many missionaries were requesting permission to translate and publish Warner Press materials in such languages as Portuguese, Swahili, and some dialects in India and Egypt. In 1985, Warner Press also published three thousand hymnals in Russian. These were shipped to West Germany and hand-carried into Russia without any Warner Press imprint in order to protect the original source. Later, cooperation helped publish *Egermeier's Bible Story Book* in Russian, although not by Warner Press, and in Spanish through the efforts of a Spanish/Portuguese Publication Network. Established in 1987 with representatives from five churches (Nazarene, Wesleyan, Free Methodist, Missionary Church, and Church of God), the Network was directed by Maurice Caldwell, the Missionary Board's liaison to Latin America.

"As editor-in-chief of the publishing house of the Church of God, I carried a passion for producing materials to support the missionary outreach of the church," Newell declares. "To my knowledge, Warner Press had not been involved in this type of [cooperative] publication prior to that time."[34]

A Growing Emphasis on Refugee Work

One basis for greater partnership in missions was Jesus' prayer that his followers would be one. But international events of the 1970s and 1980s also had a significant impact upon Missionary Board activities. Even as the Church of God was focusing on "Asia in the '80s," all of America was being exposed to the region as well, thanks largely to the Vietnam War, the longest military conflict in United States history. Although it had come to its bitter end in 1975, the war was continuing to affect the United States well into the 1980s as Vietnamese were escaping into neighboring countries, especially Hong Kong. Over a million Vietnamese would enter the United States before the end of the twentieth century, becoming the single largest ethnic group of refugees to be resettled during that period.

Cambodians also were fleeing their Southeast Asian nation. After spending time in refugee camps, particularly in Thailand, they were being resettled in many other countries, including America, as they tried to forget the atrocities of the Pol Pot regime of 1975–79, responsible for the slaughter of two million of their countrymen.

But the refugee problem was not limited to Asia. Ever since Fidel Castro assumed power in Cuba in 1959, Cubans had been escaping that nation. Most had their sights set on Florida, a dangerous ninety-mile voyage in rickety boats. Nearby in Haiti, political instability and economic privation in one of the poorest nations in the Western Hemisphere were pushing thousands to risk their lives on unsafe boats they hoped would prove worth the gamble. On the African continent, war and drought in Eastern Ethiopia were sending refugees into neighboring Somalia at the rate of one thousand a day. By the mid-1980s, relief agencies were calling the Horn of Africa the world's worst refugee crisis. Even Europe was experiencing an unprecedented rise in third-world refugees during the 1980s. Indeed, this was an international crisis, with an estimated ten to fifteen million refugees adrift in the world.

The Church of God was not deaf to the crisis. In 1974, World Service added a disaster fund to its budget.[35] Six years later, realizing that the scope of the problem was greater than a small committee representing each agency could handle adequately, the Disaster Committee of the Executive Council resolved that the Church of God Refugee Resettlement Program become "part of the organization and task of the Missionary Board of the

Church of God."[36] Consequently, Gwendolyn Massey, coordinator of the program since October 1979, moved her office into the Missionary Board suite in the Church of God Executive Office building and became a member of the Missionary Board staff.

Massey's annual reports for 1980–81 indicate hers was a busy office as the national church joined the ranks of sympathetic Americans eager to help alleviate the suffering of refugees. In 1980, the Refugee Program resettled 101 individuals from Vietnam, Cambodia, Laos, Cuba, and Haiti. This number more than quadrupled in 1981, when 446 refugees were placed with the help of thirteen cooperating congregations and individuals. These included Rev. Noah and Mrs. Carolyn Reid, of Philadelphia, Pennsylvania, Mr. and Mrs. Robert Edson, of Flint, Michigan, and Howard and Ruth Wood, of Spokane, Washington, who were honored by the Commission on Social Concerns on June 18, 1981, for their outstanding efforts in finding new homes for sixty-five refugees.

Among these refugees were two Ethiopian men who arrived in Philadelphia in 1981. Massey shared their story in her annual report:

> Their stories of flight are typical of all refugees, whether Vietnamese, Cuban, or Ethiopian. These two men fled their homes, from Eritrean province of Ethiopia, because of the civil war there and their fear of being killed. Eritrean men, especially the well educated English-speaking men who do not support the Communist-backed army in their country, are killed or tortured. These two men traveled by foot, making their way to the Sudan. There they found passage on a ship going to Rome, where they sought asylum at the office of the United Nations High Commissioner for Refugees. After their stories were reviewed by the United States State Department, these two men were accepted for resettlement in the United States."[37]

Subsequent reports showed that 1981 was the peak year for the Refugee Resettlement Program. Afterwards, the number of placements continued to fall annually.[38] Nevertheless, a total of 1,105 refugees from twelve different countries were resettled by 1986 as Church of God congregations in nineteen states as far away as Alaska and Washington sponsored refugees and provided for their critical needs.

Despite this significant work, Missionary Board budget cuts implemented in 1986 reduced the coordinator's position to half time. Massey
subsequently resigned because she believed she could not be effective on
that basis. Accepting her resignation, the Board asked her to phase the
program out in order to care for any resettlements already in progress. Her
last placements were with Mt. Scott Church of God, Portland, Oregon, in
September 1987. On July 1, 1987, the Executive Council's Disaster Committee once again assumed responsibility for refugee concerns.

The Seventh World Conference, Nairobi, Kenya

If the world was coming to the United States in the form of refugees and
immigrants, the United States was also going to the world. By 1980,
seventy-eight missionaries were under appointment by the Missionary
Board. This number had grown to one hundred and one by 1983, the
year Nehiel and Joanna Rojas were commissioned to Uruguay, becoming
the first Missionary Board missionaries assigned to that South American
nation. In addition to Uruguay, the Church of God was then at work in
sixty-one countries, including nineteen where North American personnel were serving.

Also in 1983, 430 delegates from the United States set their sights
on Nairobi, Kenya, where they joined delegates from thirty different nations around the globe at the seventh World Conference. This was the first
time this international meeting was convened outside of Europe and North
America.[39]

With the Kenyan church's one hundred thousand members—the
largest Church of God constituency outside the United States—delegates
and guests from the host nation and continent helped swell attendance to
some four thousand people at each general service. Presentations by enthusiastic African choirs, Bible studies, prayer meetings, and worship services were built around the conference theme, "Partners in God's Action,"
a slogan selected by the ten-member planning committee whose work had
been chaired by Isai Calderon of Guatemala. Interviews with international
church leaders before each service helped illustrate various partnerships
taking place around the world. Characteristic of these was a conversation
with Fouad Melki, who spoke of God's faithfulness to the Church of God
in Lebanon as his homeland was enveloped in civil war.

Particularly memorable at the start of the August 11–14 conference was the address by His Excellency Daniel T. arap Moi, Kenya's president, who praised the Church of God in Kenya for its involvement in evangelism, education, and social services. President Moi also took opportunity to denounce the system of apartheid in South Africa, asserting, "As Christians we are opposed to apartheid because it is an evil system…in which one race assumes superiority over another. To say the least, this is not in the service of God."[40]

Keynote speaker Edward L. Foggs, associate secretary of the Executive Council, lifted up the "Partners in God's Action" theme as he admonished participants, declaring, "If we do not understand we are partners, if we do not act as partners, we are without justification for claiming that we are the body of Christ."[41] Other messages were delivered by Franco Santonocito (Italy), Neville Tan (Singapore), Samuel Hines (United States), David L. Lawson (United States), Victor Babb, (Barbados), and Borman Roy Sohkhia (India).

Meeting immediately prior to the Nairobi World Conference, the World Forum convened for the second time and considered the theme "Strategies for Interdependence in Mission." During the two-day forum, a thesis titled "A Biblical Basis for Interdependence in Mission," written by Douglas Welch, guided forty-six delegates from thirty nations to discuss such topics as "How Do We Evangelize Together?" "How Do We Respond to Personal Needs Cooperatively?" and "How Do We Relate to Persons or Groups Seeking Affiliation with the Church of God?"[42]

Crisis Management in East Africa

The Nairobi meetings were not the only venues where serious consideration was being given to how better to engage in missions. The question was raised often by the Missionary Board as it endeavored to help missionaries successfully navigate their relationships to the Board, the congregations that supported them, and the receiving church in the nations where they served. "It was a very difficult time for me as executive secretary-treasurer. It seemed I was trouble-shooting one crisis after another," recalls Donald Johnson.

The retired missions executive cites a particularly difficult problem brewing in Kenya in the late 1970s and spilling over into the next decade.

Some East African missionaries were criticizing insufficient accountability in the national church for its use of Missionary Board support funds. As a result, Johnson and Oral Withrow, his associate, went to Kenya in January 1979 to hear these concerns directly and to meet with members of the national church's executive and finance committees. Following up, Johnson met with Byrum Makokha, Kenyan national church leader, in Los Angeles in April. Then he returned to Kenya in August to introduce a new budget process effective for the 1980–81 budget year. At that time, missionary George Buck would become an administrative assistant to the secretaries of the Kenyan General Assembly, with responsibilities relating directly to the financial administration of the Assembly.

Unfortunately, these Board actions were not well received by some in the national church. In fact, not all missionaries were completely satisfied with Johnson's response either, leading the executive to note, "There are still rumblings of discontent on the part of the mission staff in Kenya."[43]

MP&R: Ministry Planning and Review

The Missionary Board responded to the milieu of crises and the calls for greater effectiveness in mission activity by seeking outside help. Early in the decade, it brought in Paul Dietterich as a consultant from Parish Development in Naperville, Illinois. "I complained to Paul that I had no time for creative thinking and that I went from one fire to another," Johnson recalls. "Paul challenged me to change my thinking and not to view crises as intrusions upon my time, but rather as a legitimate part of how I was to use my time as the mission executive."

Dietterick retreated with the full Missionary Board to prepare the Board of Directors to become Johnson's supervisor. He also trained the executive secretary-treasurer to supervise Board staff through what was commonly called MP&R—Ministry Planning and Review. By the first half of 1982, MP&R was in operation on a staff level.

Next, from January 1983 through that fall, MP&R training of career and short-term missionaries occurred in six locations (Costa Rica; Curitiba, Brazil; Cairo, Egypt; Anderson, Indiana; Bangkok, Thailand; and Manila, Philippines). Johnson served as the lead trainer in each session, requiring him to be out of the country more than one hundred days that year. After these sessions, area liaison staff persons were to assume supervision of missionaries, helping them be more productive in their ministries and responsibilities.

"The significant time, energy, and money put into this design for staff and missionary personnel was a bold effort to bring coordination into ministry planning around the world," Johnson declares. "The bifocal nature of the missionary's relationship to the Missionary Board and to the national church was the focus of this planning process. It is a disappointment to me that MP&R was later curtailed."

The Missionary Board Celebrates Seventy-five Years

Even as the Board attempted to help missionaries achieve positive forward momentum through MP&R, a past-tense focus also defined some activities in 1983 as it approached its seventy-fifth anniversary in 1984. Ann Smith, coordinator of missionary personnel, explained initial planning for the celebration during the April and May 1983 Board of Directors meetings. With "Global Partnership" as its theme, the commemoration was being designed as something to "help educate and challenge the church at the grass roots level to be more concerned and involved in missions. The goal of the [celebration] committee is to initiate a process that will continue long beyond 1984 and that will make a difference in awareness and involvement on the part of individuals and congregations."[44]

Among other things, a special joint issue of *Vital Christianity* and *Church of God Missions* was in the works. It was published on June 10, 1984, and featured a likeness of Adam W. Miller on the front cover. The elder church statesman was also interviewed within the magazine to speak about his tenure as the fifth executive secretary-treasurer of the Board (1933–46), his missionary service in Japan (1922–27), and his concerns for the Church of God at this critical juncture in its history.

Miller admitted that in retirement he no longer moved around the national church as he did when he was a pastor, college and seminary professor, and Missionary Board executive. Nevertheless, he asserted his sense that enthusiasm for missions in the Church of God was fading. "Fifty years ago, missions was very central to the church," he declared, calling on the church to remember the purpose of global partnership. It was not just for partnership's sake, but for the sake of world evangelism—one of the reasons Miller felt that the anniversary theme did not go far enough to educate and encourage the church towards even greater mission activity in the future.[45]

Donald D. Johnson enlarged upon the theme in an article in *Church of God Missions*.[46] "Global Partnership is much more than a working model for world evangelization. It is a frame of reference, an international perspective, a call for learning in community, a biblical base for discipling the nations," he explained, noting that the concept must be learned because it was not always the way missions had been attempted in the past.

"Partnership learning is a process in which the People of God discover that God in Christ has given us not a first, a second, a third, or a two-thirds world, but *one* world," the Missionary Board executive secretary-treasurer declared. At the same time, he acknowledged that practicing "biblically inspired local expressions of the People of God" would require great time, patience, and long-term commitment.

As had become his oft-quoted theme, Johnson concluded his treatise by calling on North America to remember that the concept of global partnership "does not place more importance on any one part of the body…" Rather, it recognized the necessity of all bodies of the Church of God internationally, working together interdependently if the world would hear the good news of Jesus Christ through its efforts.

A Statistical Study

Despite the Great Commission to go and make disciples of all nations, the world had always been too big for the Church of God (or any church) to accomplish this alone. Twenty years after the beginning of the reformation movement, the population of the world stood at 1.6 billion people in 1900. Eighty years later, the world was home to 4.5 billion people. Even if global partnership wasn't biblically mandated, it was certainly the necessary practical way for the Missionary Board to approach its assignment. After all, what 123 North American missionaries deployed internationally could accomplish in 1984 (the Board's seventy-fifth anniversary) was not even a drop in the bucket of what needed to be happening in the world.

Thankfully, national churches around the globe were proving themselves to be active partners in evangelism. Statistics in the 1984 and 1985 volumes of the *Yearbook of the Church of God* illustrate this and commemorate an historic milestone: The church outside North America eclipsed the membership within the United States and Canada sometime between the two years.

Congregations	1984	1985
In the United States	2,286	2,271
In Canada	54	53
Total in North America	2,340	2,324
Outside North America	1,749	1,904
Membership		
In the United States	182,190	182,481
In Canada	2,947	2,923
Total in North America	185,137	185,404
Outside North America	183,989	197,629

Not only do the comparative statistics indicate a jump of more than 13,600 members outside North America in this one-year period, but they also show a very small growth in membership in the United States and Canada—merely 267 people. Additionally, there was a loss of sixteen congregations in North America while one hundred fifty-five new Churches of God were planted in other countries during the same period. Without a voice of their own, statistics were, nevertheless, boldly trumpeting the call for even greater partnership in missions around the world.

Voices of Dissatisfaction

In addition to the appeal for expanded partnership in mission, there were other calls being sounded during the 1980s. Among them, the Missionary Board was hearing the exasperated voices of missionaries struggling to define and successfully carry out their responsibilities to both supporting and receiving churches. One result of this was the implementation of Missionary Planning and Review (MP&R).

In fact, MP&R was designed to answer another voice of dissatisfaction. The Missionary Board's executive secretary-treasurer, Donald D. Johnson, had acknowledged, "One of the harder tasks for me has been to admit that I cannot do everything related to my own position assignment."[47] Some of his awareness had come after a difficult trip to Kenya during which missionaries confronted him about what they believed was his less-than-prompt attention to their concerns.

One year later, in his 1980 annual report, Johnson wrote that the law of diminishing returns would soon take effect if his overworked Anderson staff did not get help. As a result, regional personnel were trained through MP&R to assume greater oversight of missionaries. This would relieve the Anderson staff of supervising the growing overseas team—by then seventy-eight missionaries—especially since the home office staff also was frequently out of the office visiting churches in North America and the world. In fact, Johnson wrote in a 1980 letter, "The Missionary Board has operated with fewer staff persons in relationship to the responsibility we carry than any other national corporation of the Church of God."[48] It was an increasingly heavy load, and everyone was feeling the weight.

Responding affirmatively, the Board of Directors voted to increase the Anderson staff.[49] By 1985, Johnson's team was comprised of Gary Nicholson, assistant treasurer-controller; Maurice Caldwell, associate secretary with field supervision of Latin America; Donald Williams, associate secretary with field supervision of Africa; David Reames, coordinator of Living Link and promotional services; Ann Smith, coordinator of missionary personnel; Gwen Massey, refugee program coordinator; and office support staff. By this time, however, there were eighty-four missionaries on the field and another thirteen individuals in Grand Cayman, Greece, Jordan, the Dominican Republic, and Guam related administratively to the Missionary Board. Consequently, even with an expanded staff, responsibilities assigned to each person continued to expand.

Nevertheless, the cry for help from missionaries and staff was not the major challenge with which Johnson was struggling. What he felt most deeply was the charge of racism being leveled at the Missionary Board by some African-American church leaders. This stemmed from the April 1979 resignation of Thomas Sawyer, a Missionary Board associate secretary since 1976. Terming this the most significant and difficult administrative situation he had encountered during his seventeen years with the Board, Johnson reported on the sensitive issue in his 1980 annual report.[50]

Saddened by the furor and disharmony that had resulted from Sawyer's resignation, the executive outlined his responses to inquiries and charges, including accepting the request that the National Association of the Church of God be asked to suggest candidates for the position that remained unfilled. Additionally, the Association's chairman was invited to be a consultant at the May 1980 annual Missionary Board meeting. Whatever steps had been taken in responding to the voices of dissatisfaction, however, Johnson admitted that he had failed in carrying out one of his stated responsibilities—keeping missions and the work of the Missionary Board "constantly before the [whole] church in such a way that it will merit and receive favorable response" by the whole church.[51]

A Debt Retirement Strategy

Another critical challenge confronted Johnson, ever aware that urgent needs were always greater than funds received from World Service to meet them. Entering the 1980s, he referred to Missionary Board matters of budget and finances as "a gloomy picture" and presented the predictions of Denton F. Fair, outgoing assistant treasurer-controller, and Gary Nicholson, his successor, that the 1979–80 budget year would end in deficit. The executive secretary-treasurer explained the unhappy situation in his 1980 annual report, lamenting the necessity of significant "painful pruning" of an already slim budget.[52]

In the same document, Johnson also called for creative thinking to augment World Service income so that the Missionary Board could enter open doors. Yet he also spoke about necessary project curtailment to come because Million for Missions was not on track to bring in the million dollars that had been anticipated.

In fact, the situation only got worse. Three years later, the Board executive agonized further while slashing the 1982–83 operating budget to the approved figure of $1,950,000. Some cuts came through savings on salaries with the resignation of David Shultz, who had served since 1978 as minister to the church on mission. His responsibilities would be shuffled to other Anderson staff and he would not be replaced. Even so, by 1984 the Board was operating with a budgetary deficit of nearly $350,000.

How had the Missionary Board come to such a critical financial state? Johnson explains, "There were years when interest was high. As the Board received money from World Service and Women of the Church of God, we could invest and save it for the lean months, usually July to December. During those months, our expenditures were always greater than our income. Our World Service money never came in twelve equal portions over a year, so there were times we had more and times we had less."

But the world financial market began changing in the late 1970s. The 13 percent inflation rate in the United States in 1979 was even worse overseas. Combined with dollar devaluation, the average worldwide inflation rate was 27 percent. According to the April 1979 issue of *The Church Around the World*, mission dollars overseas had 128 percent less buying power than a decade earlier.

"As the interest situation began changing, the Board's financial position was affected too," the retired executive continues. "We began borrowing money from ourselves that had been designated for other uses but hadn't been spent yet and got advances from the expected WCG Christ's Birthday Offering. When cash flow was inadequate, we had a $75,000 credit line from Anderson Banking Company and also could borrow from the Board of Church Extension and Home Missions when necessary. We paid these back during the first half of the year when our World Service income was greater than during the lean last half of the year."

Needless to say, this pattern could not continue indefinitely. Johnson knew this better than anyone. By 1984, he and assistant treasurer Gary Nicholson had collaborated to create what they titled "The Financial Strategy Proposal." Accepted during the Board's May meeting, the plan outlined a sixteen-year strategy (1984–2000) to retire the debt, balance income and expenditures, and reduce the near total reliance on World Service dollars. If successful, the strategy would find the Board in 2000 funded only 80 percent by World Service, with the remaining 20 percent coming from outside sources, including an endowment reserve fund of a million dollars. Another important component was budgeting expenses at 5 to 7 percent below expected income. This was an entirely new practice for the Board, which had always planned operations on the assumption that it would receive 100 percent of its World Service approved budget. Other steps called for soliciting major donors and encouraging fund-raising for missions through the World Concern Fellowship ($50,000 in the first year and increasing to $100,000 by 2000).

By the end of the first year after implementing the new strategy, the Missionary Board's financial situation was somewhat improved. According to Nicholson's 1985 annual report, the deficit in 1985 was $65,277 less than one year earlier.[53]

Changing of the Guard

While 1984 was a year of celebrating seventy-five years of organized Church of God missions, it was also a year of significant changes for the Missionary Board that would lead to a new executive secretary-treasurer. In 1968, Donald D. Johnson had accepted a call from Lester Crose to become his associate secretary at the Missionary Board. With Crose's retirement in 1975, Johnson had become the Board's eighth executive secretary-treasurer. But on October 2, 1984, he faced an especially difficult task. In his 117th monthly letter to missionary colleagues, written that day, he announced that his name was being presented for vote in two days as the next senior pastor of Park Place Church of God in Anderson.

Outlining the struggle in which he had been engaged for six months since being approached by the church's search committee, Johnson wrote of being "hounded by the Spirit of the Lord." But he had finally concluded: "The work of this Board will continue without me. I am not indispensable to either the work or our dreams for partnership and interdependence. The future is safe in a good staff and in all of you [missionary colleagues]. We have a dedicated board and God's man as president of this Board [Gene W. Newberry] for hours like this. My greatest struggle was to be willing to lay it down and see others at the finish line celebrating our greatest day in global partnership."[54]

Subsequently, in April 1985, Johnson began his thirtieth year in Church of God ministry as senior pastor of Park Place Church. He was succeeded by Tom F. Pickens, who had been chosen by the Missionary Board on December 13, 1984, subject to ratification by the General Assembly in June 1985.

A former missionary in Jamaica (1961–67) and London, England (1967–72), the ninth executive secretary-treasurer returned to the Missionary Board after thirteen years of pastoring, editing adult curriculum at Warner Press, and serving as state minister in Western Pennsylvania and Michigan. In his letter announcing the appointment, the Missionary Board president, Gene W. Newberry, wrote that the search committee had met four times to consider thirty-eight names before settling on Pickens.

In addition to the changing of the guard in Anderson, there were also some significant changes on the field as household names in Church of God missions were retiring. Among these, Arthur and Norma Eikamp had served in Japan since 1949. "We went to survey the [post World War II] situation and to report it to the Missionary Board," Eikamp explains, chuckling that their assessment turned into thirty-five years in Japan before their retirement in 1984.[55]

That year also marked the retirement of Homer and Elvira Firestone. Prior to affiliating with the Church of God ten years earlier, the Firestones had given over twenty years as independent missionaries with the Aymara and Quechua Indians in Bolivia. By the time they departed Bolivia in 1984, the Church of God in that South American nation had grown to ninety-eight congregations and a constituency of eight thousand people.

The Financial Crisis Deepens

With the imminent change of Missionary Board leadership, 1985 began with a three-month transitional period between Johnson and Pickens. The new executive secretary-treasurer soon discovered that all he had learned during the changeover had only begun to prepare him for the significant responsibilities he had assumed. Among the challenges he faced, finances were an immediate concern.

During the May and June Board meetings, Pickens heard Gary Nicholson, his assistant treasurer, describe measured successes that had been achieved in the first year of the Missionary Board's new financial strategy, launched on July 1, 1984. "As we look at the specific financial information this year, I do see a trend which would indicate that we are headed in the right direction," Nicholson had reported.[56]

Backing his claim, he quoted financial statements for the seven-month period ending February 28 showing that the deficit was $41,191 less than a year earlier.[57] He also reported that budgetary income for the same period was up by 2.13 percent, even though it was short $145,105 of what had been expected from World Service. At the same time, budgetary expenditures were down by 0.95 percent at the seven-month mark. Nicholson asserted that the key to even more improvement and eventual good financial health was to continue following the new strategy. Consequently, a Finance and Development Committee was created to oversee the one-year-old financial strategy.[58]

Perhaps Pickens's confidence began to be shaken gradually as he gained his footing in leading the organization. But by the January 9, 1986, meeting of the Board of Directors less than seven months later, he had determined that he could no longer support the strategy. Speaking to the Board in executive session, he "shared his discomfort with the present financial situation and his feeling that some serious and immediate steps are needed to correct the situation."[59] Nicholson was then invited in to present the latest financial documentation available (November 1985) and answer questions before being dismissed from the meeting.

When the meeting reconvened that evening, Pickens outlined his understanding of the Board's financial position. There was long-term debt of $39,000 owed to the Board of Church Extension, which was to be repaid in two yearly installments, plus interest. Another $250,000 had been borrowed to cover operational and field expenses. This was to be paid back by the close of the fiscal year on June 30. The Board also had borrowed $253,000 from its own designated funds. To Pickens's understanding, this internal debt was increasing since the Board now owed itself $36,000 more than in February 1985. Although it was unlikely that all designated funds would be called for at once, Pickens determined that it was important to hold 75 percent of this money in a special reserve account.

Board of Directors minutes report "considerable, serious, tearful, and prayerful discussion" concerning Pickens's presentation. Subsequently, the Board voted to abandon the sixteen-year financial strategy and agreed upon seven austerity measures to be taken as soon as possible. These included opening a second bank account for designated funds, cutting all administrative salaries by 5 percent, and reducing both Anderson and field staffs.[60] All told, the cuts would trim expenditures by as much as $145,000 annually, bringing Missionary Board finances into line by 1990 rather than 2000.

"If these seem like sweeping changes, it is only an indication of how seriously the Directors viewed the situation…In the meantime, remember the words of Jesus who said, 'Be of good cheer. I have overcome the world,'" Pickens commented in a letter to the missionary community that was quoted in the *Asian Church of God Magazine*.[61] The cutbacks were also announced in other Church of God publications both in the United States and abroad. What had been seen as a difficult, yet reversible financial situation seemed to be worsening.

A Sense of Alarm

The abrupt departure from the financial strategy inaugurated in 1984 and the significant cuts instituted sent shock waves around the world. Almost immediately, missionary recruitment and deployment came to a standstill. Would the Missionary Board declare bankruptcy and call all personnel home from the field? Even this drastic scenario now seemed possible to worried missionaries. It was a difficult time perhaps best characterized by the word *alarm*.

Eventually concluding that he could not remain as executive secretary-treasurer, Pickens yet asserted that the Board was in serious difficulty financially. He urged the Missionary Board to reconsider its relationship with World Service, asking, "How can we affirm the present system, while at the same time begin to develop a plan that will assist people in giving to the causes that are dear to their hearts? This problem must be addressed in the near future to give the Board a more favorable opportunity to receive donations."[62]

In his final report to the Missionary Board, Pickens stated, "Many of the problems started in January 1986 when we took a good, long look at the financial situation [and saw a corporation] that was in serious trouble… We took steps to make some budget adjustments which involved cutting back on expenditures…I was convinced then [and now] that they were necessary. The question is whether we went far enough. I believe we made some gains in restoring some of the deficits of the Board, but we were only beginning to solve the problem."[63]

Pickens ended his tenure with the Board on May 19, 1987, leaving for an interim pastoral assignment in London, England, where he had earlier served as a missionary.

Interim Leaders Provide Guidance

Not only was Tom Pickens concerned about Missionary Board finances, but he also counseled a lengthier selection process for the next executive. Perhaps recognizing the validity of this criticism, the Board took the unusual step of choosing an interim leader to follow Pickens. Ann Smith, a former missionary to Japan and Korea, had filled several roles in the Anderson home office, including director of personnel and liaison for Asia.

With Pickens' departure, she was asked to assume her most challenging role ever—leadership of the Missionary Board. However, Smith had just become director of church relations for Anderson University. Demonstrating a spirit of partnership, the university not only released Smith temporarily but also paid her salary while she returned to the Board as its interim leader for three months. Smith was the first woman to serve as the executive officer in the history of the Missionary Board.

But she would not be the last. She was soon followed by Doris Dale, who was asked to take a one-year leave from her work as executive secretary-treasurer of Women of the Church of God. During Dale's absence, Nellie Snowden, her predecessor, returned to assume responsibility for the office and financial matters. At the same time, Laura Withrow, WCG national president, took on correspondence and program matters. The second woman to lead the Missionary Board served in that capacity through June 1988.

"Both the Missionary Board and the missionary community needed reassurance and affirmation of their purpose," Dale says, reflecting on that year. "There had been a period of uncertainty and a time of interim leadership, and there was a need to reaffirm the purpose of the missionary thrust. The challenge was to bring continuity and encouragement both to the office staff and the missionary community at large."[64]

Leadership Changes Foreshadow Structural Changes

Change was in the air. Not only had new leaders come to the Missionary Board, even if only for interim periods, but there also was talk of how changes in the home office and its structure of operations locally, nationally, and internationally might help build a bridge to a healthier organization. Some of this discussion was happening in May 1987 at the annual Board retreat, led by Robert Nicholson, president of Anderson University.

In preparation, Ann Smith wrote a memo announcing the upcoming seventy-eighth annual Missionary Board meeting. It would be immediately preceded by the retreat on May 11–12, with Nicholson leading discussions related to the work of the Missionary Board and its governance. The twenty Board and five executive staff members were asked to read the Missionary Board bylaws and policy manual and to bring these with them to the retreat.[65]

Two agreements with international significance came from the 1987 meetings. One was made with the Caribbean–Atlantic Assembly that the next individual chosen to be field administrator would be a national from that very region. (This resulted in the 1991 invitation to Victor Babb, executive director of the Caribbean–Atlantic Assembly, to become regional director.) The second was between the Canadian Board of Missions, the Church of God in Western Canada, and the Missionary Board to bring all Canadian missionaries under the auspices of the Missionary Board. For its part, the Canadian Board agreed to provide a percentage of the missionary's salary, a percentage of other associated costs, and pension.

Recognizing that there was much more to accomplish than could possibly take place during a once-a-year annual meeting, Missionary Board members also determined to add a second mid-year gathering. Also during this important 1987 meeting, Norman Patton was elected as Board president for a three-year term.

The Eighth World Conference, Seoul, Korea

Even as leadership changes and the significant financial challenges that faced the Missionary Board demanded major inward focus in 1987, there was also another spotlight that year: the eighth World Conference and third World Forum in Seoul, Korea. This was the first time these meetings would be convened in Asia, underscoring the special decade-long emphasis on that region of the world.

The Forum deliberated on July 28 and 29, followed by the Conference, July 29–31. Participants from fifty-two nations—including seven hundred from the United States and three hundred registered delegates from other nations—were challenged to greater evangelistic outreach by the Conference theme, "Arise My People," from Isaiah 60:1. "Unity with Diversity" was the adjacent theme that guided the two-day Forum.[66] The strength of the Korean church, with thirty-seven congregations and ten thousand members, swelled participation to as many as two thousand people at each mass rally.

Especially noteworthy was the significant increase in the number of nations represented in Seoul over previous World Conferences. This was due largely to a strategic decision by the Executive Council to reach out more intentionally to all nations in order to promote greater interdependence and cooperation in evangelism and missions. Consequently, funds were appropriated and every assembly in every nation where the Church of God was resident was invited to send at least one delegate, with subsidy provided for travel, food, and lodging if necessary. As a result, participation at Seoul jumped to 73 percent of the seventy-five countries where the Church of God was active.

Planners of the event were as international as the gathering itself. Under Chairman Victor Babb, of Barbados, the steering committee included: Hong Mook Yoo and Kim Dong Sup, Korea; Neville Tan, Singapore; Ramona Mdobi, Tanzania; and Paul Tanner, Edward Foggs, and David Lawson, representing the Executive Council. Together they designed a convention to celebrate what was being accomplished by the Church of God around the world. It also would challenge the church to attempt even more through greater unified efforts born out of relationships forged during the four days in Seoul.

Storytelling became a hallmark of the Seoul experience, with mealtimes utilized as a venue for some of the sharing. A delegate from Ghana explained that his church included practical education on such topics as mosquito control and how to build latrines as part of their Christian witness. Adel Masri noted that the Church of God in Lebanon was continuing to construct new churches despite civil war. Tabitha Gunawan reported how the Church of God had been planted in Indonesia through first reaching out to children. Amos Moore shared how he baptized new believers in rivers under cover of darkness in the Hindu kingdom of Nepal, where prison sentences awaited those who dared to evangelize and anyone who might accept their message.

Especially meaningful was the Lord's Supper observance during the final worship service of the World Conference before delegates, lifting their candles high, pledged their determination to return home and become more effective witnesses of the gospel. Indeed, God's people had answered his call to arise.

A New Leader for the Missionary Board

Back in the United States, the next leader of the Missionary Board was in a kind of apprenticeship. As pastor of First Church of God, Goshen, Indiana, Norman Patton had begun serving as a General Assembly-elected member of the Missionary Board during Tom Pickens's tenure as executive secretary-treasurer. In 1987, he was elected president of the twenty-member body that gave oversight to the vision and resulting activities of the Missionary Board.

The decade of the 1980s had been a tumultuous time for the Missionary Board as it presided over the departure of two executives, the service of two interim executives, and a general feeling of uncertainty among missionaries and in the church. Learning about missions on a worldwide scale in this milieu was an immediate apprenticeship for the Goshen pastor and Missionary Board member. Little did Patton know that it was preparing him for Missionary Board leadership following the temporary terms of Smith and Dale.

Nevertheless, during a special called meeting of the Missionary Board on May 2, 1988, Lester Crose presented Patton's name as the search committee's recommendation to become the Board's president and chief executive officer. This significant change in nomenclature for the Missionary Board executive was a result of governance discussions undertaken during the retreat and annual Board meeting one year earlier. The recommendation was accepted, secret ballots were cast, and Patton was elected to the position, subject to ratification by the General Assembly during their upcoming annual meeting in June. Subsequently, John Campbell of Canada was elected as the first chairman of the Missionary Board, reflecting another change in terminology and understanding of structure as a result of discussions initiated in 1987.

A Fresh Vision for Expansion

Coming from the pastorate to lead the Missionary Board, Norman Patton had much to learn about worldwide missions. He became an eager student who often sought the advice of seasoned missionaries and home staff, Board members, and even his predecessors. Perhaps it was this hunger to learn about missions that prompted Patton to encourage the founding of an annual educational event for the whole church. Billed as the first annual School of Missions, the two-day Board-sponsored program featured Dr. Ted Engstrom, president of World Vision, as its premier speaker during the 1989 International Convention in Anderson.

But the lessons the Missionary Board president had learned during thirty years in six associate and senior pastorates in California, Washington, and Indiana were not lost on his new assignment. This was particularly true of the skills he had honed in sermon preparation and preaching. Patton was soon preaching in pulpits across the United States and around the world, and his messages were also challenging and inspiring the Missionary Board family.

One such occasion was the Missionary Board staff retreat at the Church of God campgrounds in Leesburg, Florida, November 13–16, 1989. There Patton shared devotional thoughts from the book of Nehemiah, challenging those in attendance: "Just as Israel reminded God of his promises to them, the Missionary Board can remind [God] of his promises. Repentance has happened, there has been a turnaround, and the walls can be rebuilt. The responsibility of the Board now is to let the church know where we've been, but more importantly, that we are ready to rebuild the walls."[67]

How did he propose to clear away the rubble from the recent period of uncertainty and retreat, rebuild the walls, and help the Missionary Board advance once again? Patton's answer was explained in nine goals for a new missions thrust into the cities and to unreached peoples. Significantly, it would require enhanced partnership with Church of God sending agencies in such countries as Germany, Brazil, Lebanon, Kenya, India, Argentina, and Canada, and regional associations around the world. The new effort would focus on evangelism, discipleship, leadership training, church planting, health care and community development, and relief work.

Among the goals, the new executive proposed to plant Church of God congregations in thirteen major cities of the world during the following five years—five African cities (Dar es Salaam, Tanzania; Lagos, Nigeria; Kigali, Rwanda; Douala, Cameroon; and Blantyre, Malawi), three Asian locations (Dhaka, Bangladesh; Mandalay, Myanmar; and Auckland, New Zealand), one in the Middle East (Damascus, Syria), one in Europe (Paris), and three cities in Latin America (Buenos Aires, Argentina; Brasilia or Belem, Brazil; and Santiago, Chile). He also earmarked Portugal as a nation into which the Church of God would expand as well as two villages on the Caribbean islands of Dominica and Montserrat. Patton spelled out details, including specific national leaders with whom to work, budgets necessary to achieve the goals, and launch dates.

The results were encouraging. While all the goals were not met within the proposed five-year period (and some not at all), nine of thirteen targeted cities had Church of God congregations by the end of the 1990s (Dar es Salaam, Kigali, Blantyre, Dhaka, Mandalay, Auckland, Paris, Buenos Aires, Brasilia/Belem, and Santiago). Most of these were partnership efforts involving missionaries, national leaders, and national churches.

The New Zealand launch was an especially unique partnership. The Church of God in Australia and its Missionary Board–sent Canadian missionaries, Ben and Marjorie Chandler, commissioned one of its pastors, David Ravell, and his wife Jeanine to plant the church in Auckland after the terminal illness of Jeanine's mother required them to return to her homeland. The couple and their one-year-old daughter were introduced at the 1995 tenth World Conference in Sydney, Australia, where a special offering of more than $13,000 was taken to help launch the new work. A decade later, when the Ravells returned to Australia, the international congregation they had founded called a special assignment missionary from the United States, Chad Davenport, and his wife Diane, from Singapore, as its second pastor. It seemed that the unique partnership nature of the church was a part of its DNA.

The 1989 vision of the Missionary Board's new president also included strengthening existing congregations in major cities of the world by cooperating in leadership training efforts, working more closely with other Church of God sending agencies and regional conferences, and beginning an evangelism ministry among one unreached people group by 1995, a target realized in reaching out to the Maasai tribe in Tanzania.

Financing the Expansion

It goes without saying that any goals for expansion would require money. Having served as an elected member of the Missionary Board, the new executive was well aware of the Board's financial status. He knew that it would be impossible to fund current ministry and take advantage of new outreach opportunities without first addressing these fiscal problems and seeking new means of support.

This is exactly what office manager Darrell Smith said during the 1989 mid-year Missionary Board meeting. He reported, "World Service has stated that they can do no more than what they are presently doing. Therefore, if the Board is going to grow, that growth will have to be done outside World Service,"[68] noting that the Board was borrowing about $300,000 annually to fund cash-flow needs.

Consequently, several financial goals were among those Patton outlined. These included developing an endowment plan to provide a stable long-range financial base for Board operations as well as equity for short-term cash-flow needs. Eventually called the Missionary Endowment Foundation (MEF), this plan included a charitable life insurance program that gifted the premiums and death benefits to the Missionary Board and a real estates gift program that would profit the Board in the long term.

Patton also challenged the Board to develop a new fundraising program to target individual donors and revitalize the Living Link missionary support program in churches so that all missionaries already on the field would be funded at least 75 percent by December 1990. Eventually, a Global Missions Network of representatives around North America became a vital link between the Missionary Board, churches, and individuals. They helped address the Board's financial problems at the end of the decade, allowing attention to turn towards new opportunities in the 1990s, especially in Africa and Russia.

International Speakers Program

Another program—this one initiated outside the Missionary Board—would also prove to be a vital (although temporary) link in educating and exciting the church about greater involvement in and support for missions around the world.

In 1987, Howard Baker was considering new avenues of church service following his retirement from pastoral ministry. From personal experience, especially preaching trips in India, he knew how exposure to the world could light a fire for missions in individuals and churches. In fact, the congregation he pastored in Walla Walla, Washington, had become among the strongest missions supporting churches in the United States.

But not everyone could go abroad for missions trips, so Baker envisioned bringing internationals to visit churches at home. During a Missionary Board meeting in 1988, he proposed an International Speakers Program that was designed "to help extend the kingdom of God around the world; to build bridges of understanding between all peoples of the world; to communicate with the churches in the United States a better understanding of the needs in other countries; to bring about a better understanding of different cultures; to challenge the church in the United States to share in a monetary way; to assist congregations in the United States with their missions programs; and to pray for the work, needs, and ministry of other Christians around the world."[69]

Recognizing the benefits of such a program, the Missionary Board voted to affirm Baker's proposal and sponsor the program. During the following four years, the International Speakers Program helped many churches reach the world from their own localities. At the height of the program, ten speakers from Uganda, Nepal, Thailand, Egypt, Myanmar, Barbados, Ghana, Trinidad, and Argentina were brought to the United States during a one-year period to share exciting testimonies and challenge congregations to greater missions involvement.

The program's success was illustrated when most participating pastors and churches were enthusiastic and wanted to continue taking part. Nevertheless, some concerns had emerged. These included language barrier problems, the worry that too many visitors might cause overexposure and actually hurt the missions cause, and "difficulties with churches sending gifts to international speakers which have caused problems in those countries."[70] Therefore, the International Speakers Program was terminated when Baker retired as its coordinator at the end of December 1992.

The Missionary Board Staff Expands

Even with a detailed expansion strategy and hopes for additional income to fund it, Norman Patton still faced at least two challenges. One of these was helping to define the roles and relationships of the Missionary Board staff and the elected Missionary Board. During the transitional periods of the decade, the Board of Directors had met more often than usual. As a result, lines of responsibility had become blurred by this necessary and increased involvement in day-to-day administration. This presented a challenge to the new executive as he took up the reins of leadership.

Patton recalls, "It took a few meetings for us to get back into the proper role of the staff and the Board. The Board's role was to set policy that the administrative staff would carry forth and also to keep oversight that we were on track financially with the budget. Often we would ask the question during a Board meeting, 'Is this a Board matter or is it an administrative issue?' It helped to keep us on task."[71]

However, Patton's most significant challenge was trying to administer a growing organization without additional staff. When he assumed Board leadership in 1988, there were only office support staff and two additional staff members with specific regional assignments—Sidney Johnson and Maurice Caldwell, representing Asia and Latin America respectively.

It wasn't the first time a Missionary Board executive had needed help. During Lester Crose's administration (1954–74), as his responsibilities grew, the General Assembly–elected Missionary Board had insisted that he share responsibilities with Donald Johnson. As an associate secretary, Johnson became the Board's point person in Latin America. Later, during Johnson's executive tenure (1975–84), he shared administration of Latin America with Maurice Caldwell. In Asia, he had also utilized the expertise of Sidney Johnson and Ann Smith to liaise with national leaders and missionaries. This was especially important for the expansion taking place as a result of the "Asia in the '80s" decade of special emphasis.

But it was not until Patton's administration that a specific job description was created for personnel whose primary responsibility was to represent the Missionary Board in each of the four regions of the world (Latin America, Asia, Africa, and the Middle East–Europe). To be called regional directors (RDs), these individuals would be missionaries who would carry out regional assignments from stateside locations.

"The staff pondered two basic questions," Patton explains. "Can the work of the RDs be as effective if they were stationed in the States, and would this be more economically feasible? We came to the conclusion that they could work as effectively from the States as from a country in their region. We referred back to Sidney [Johnson] and Maurice [Caldwell] being in the States, and this had seemed to work for them. We would have the benefit of RD input in our staff meetings. Also, it would be far cheaper, we thought, to have them living in [the United States]. Budgets were tight, so the decision was made to bring them home."[72]

With Maurice Caldwell nearing retirement in 1990, Willi and Esther Kant were called in 1989 to become the first RDs for Latin America. Their home base would be Florida, as close as possible to the region, but still in the United States. With the upcoming 1991 retirement of Sidney Johnson, plans were in place to name Michael and Debra Kinner, missionaries to

Hong Kong since 1981, as the first RDs for the Asian region (expanded in 1996 to become the Asia–Pacific region). With nearly twenty years of missionary experience in Africa, Robert and Janet Edwards were logical choices for the Africa RD position, although they declined to move back to the United States and remained in Nairobi.

But calling an RD for the Middle East-Europe region was more challenging. Although James and Betty Albrecht had been missionaries in Egypt since 1978 and could represent the Missionary Board well, the concept of a regional director raised red flags in some European countries. What designs did the Missionary Board have on Europe?

"After explaining to the European leadership that we were not trying to cut in on their action but that we just wanted to work in better cooperation with them, the RD position was accepted," Patton shares. "I think that having an RD actually helped develop a better relationship between them and the Missionary Board, and especially with the German church."

At the time, Victor Babb of Barbados was the executive director of the Caribbean–Atlantic Assembly. His election to that position had come from within the region and was entirely independent of Missionary Board action. Rather than duplicate that regional position, the Missionary Board in 1991 invited Babb to represent the Caribbean–Atlantic to them.

"We invited Victor to our meetings and he usually came. We considered him one of us," Patton declares, wondering in retirement about whether the Missionary Board should have looked more closely at pursuing other national leaders to become regional directors because of the success in working with Babb and the Caribbean-Atlantic Assembly.

Looking back, the former Board executive is grateful for the role regional directors played in his administration. "The RDs were invaluable to me, for these were people with expertise in their regions of the world," he says. "I depended on their input for decision making in their areas of the world."

Theological Education by Extension

By the late 1980s, theological training was taking place in a number of institutions around the world, including Boa Terra Bible School in Brazil, Fritzlar Bible College in Germany, Kima Theological College in Kenya (now Kima International School of Theology), Mediterranean Bible

College in Lebanon, and West Indies Theological College in Trinidad. Other Church of God training schools were operating in Mexico, India, and the Philippines.

Regardless of the quality of these programs, they could not meet the needs of everyone. Many pastors and lay leaders had little formal education of any kind and some were even illiterate. Others faced financial challenges and could not leave their families to enroll in residential programs. Additionally, the Church of God school might be so far away from home that it was an impractical choice, especially for older married pastors.

The answer to these challenges was theological education by extension (TEE). According to missionary Larry Sellers, TEE was "a flexible, practical, and inexpensive approach to leadership training." In 1985, he and his wife LeAnn went to Haiti to establish a TEE program for pastors and lay leaders of the island's thirty-three congregations. It was launched with four extension centers, one in each region. Two-day monthly meetings at each center gave students opportunity to correct and discuss the lessons they had prepared at home. Passing bimonthly tests allowed them to progress through three levels of ten courses each and to earn a diploma in theology after completing the entire seven-year program.

Although the Missionary Board provided a yearly stipend to cover half the expenses for materials and meals, participants were required to pay the other half, in addition to their travel expenses. Local churches provided the classroom venue, lodging for students, and help with cooking during the two-day program. It was an effective partnership. By 1990, when the couple left Haiti to become the first French-speaking missionaries deployed by the Missionary Board to Africa, Sellers had trained four regional leaders from among the most promising TEE students and had prepared Jean-Robert Maitre, a Haitian, to administer the program. By 1992, the Haitian church numbered more than a hundred congregations, another testament to capable national leadership and an effective training program.

Some missionaries were experiencing success with other TEE models. Among these were Stanley and Marion Hoffman in Uganda. The Canadian couple could hardly have been prepared for the rapid church growth they would encounter when they arrived in war-torn Uganda in 1983. "No war could stop the movement of the Holy Spirit," Hoffman reported of the miraculous rebirth of the Ugandan church from 2 congregations in 1980 to 321 by October 1989.[73]

But the miracle was also a tremendous challenge, as Hoffman explained: "We soon realized that we had a problem. We lacked enough capable leaders to assist us. New congregations had to have pastors. Where were we to get them? Believers who are not properly taught are a bigger threat to Christianity than paganism. All kinds of false cults and heresies have had their beginnings in this manner."[74]

As in Haiti, TEE was the answer. It would not only train Ugandan pastors and leaders who could bring stability to the rapidly growing church, but it would also ensure that church growth would not be just a passing phase in the reemergence of the church in Uganda. While not a Church of God creation—the theological training program had been used by a number of church groups in Africa since 1970—TEE later would also prove successful in helping the Hoffmans plant the Church of God in four other African nations. In fact, TEE continues to be one of the major methods of church planting and leadership training across Africa even today.

Ephraim Tumusiime, former legal representative of the Church of God in East Africa (Uganda), gratefully recalls the early days of the training program in his country: "At the end of the first term in December 1983, twenty-four students took exams and all passed...By December 1984, the number of students had increased so much that the missionary's garage [in Kampala] could no longer accommodate us. The plan was to travel to where the TEE students live. Thank God for the missionary's vehicle that could carry the missionaries, passengers, and TEE books."[75]

A Different Model of Leadership Training

As successful as they were, extension programs like TEE and residential theological training centers were not the only models of leadership training being employed in the Church of God around the world at this time. In Bolivia, leaders were being developed through an apprenticeship program that identified gifted persons within local congregations and then prepared them for service through hands-on experience.

According to missionary David Miller, local congregations in Bolivia elected seven deacons annually, five men and two women, who were given pastoral responsibilities of preaching, directing worship and leading singing, handling finances and administration, maintaining the building, overseeing the church kitchen, and carrying out compassionate ministries, including visitation work. Although deacons were elected, pastoral roles were not to be handled by only a few "chosen" people. Instead, each member of every local congregation was expected to take his or her turn as a deacon.

"How do they learn what they do? First, by observing the ministry of more experienced leaders. Then, by taking on ministry tasks from time to time themselves, as the congregation appoints them. And finally, by asking questions," Miller explained, noting that the church's apprenticeship model was developed by Homer Firestone, founding missionary of the Bolivian Church of God, and was based upon the biblical model of discipleship training.[76]

In 1989, five years after Firestone and his wife Elvira retired from a lifelong missions career, Bolivia launched an additional leadership training program to prepare urban youth who were more accustomed to formal classroom education than many leaders from the nation's rural areas. Called the Rotating Bible Institute, the once-a-year program soon was attracting as many as sixty students from the 115 congregations in all three regions of the nation.

Milestones of the 1980s

With the exception of a short period midway through the decade when finances—especially shortages—took precedence over most other considerations, expanding the partnership in missions was a theme at the forefront of Missionary Board thinking and planning throughout the 1980s. This is illustrated by the list of nations entered during the decade: Singapore (1980), Indonesia (1981), Spain (1982), Uganda (1983), Zaire (1984), Myanmar and Rwanda (1985), Zambia (1986), and Malaysia (1988).

But missionaries were not sent and funded exclusively by the Missionary Board. In 1983, the Inter-American Conference launched the Church of God in the Dominican Republic, and the church in Meghalaya, India, sent missionaries to begin the work in Nepal. Later, in 1986, Narcisco Zamora, a missionary from Peru, began the work in Ecuador.

Other mission partnerships were launched independently of the Board and were to have an impact upon Church of God missions around the world. One example is Sahakarini, a not-for-profit organization founded in 1979 by Gordon and Wilhemina Schieck, retired missionaries to India (1955–67) from Alberta, Canada. Under the Schiecks' leadership, Sahakarini—the Hindi word for *self-help*—was established to send support to the mission field for development work. It took advantage of offers by the Canadian government to match funds for overseas projects on a scale of four for one. (For every one dollar given, four dollars would be sent overseas.) By February 1990, a partial list of projects supported by Sahakarini included a primary school, twenty-eight tailoring centers, four typewriting institutes, a weaving center, and an institute dedicated to printing technology. Plans also were focusing on a newly dedicated College of Technology in South India.

With the church entering its second hundred years at the beginning of the 1980s, some early leaders in the missions enterprise concluded their earthly tasks during the decade. Among these, Daisy Maiden Boone, a pioneer missionary to China, died February 13, 1986, at nearly 103 years of age. Born in 1883, only three years after D. S. Warner helped pioneer the Church of God reformation movement, Maiden gained early missionary training while witnessing to prisoners at Walla Walla State Penitentiary after her conversion in 1906. Eight years later, she moved from Washington to Indiana to join the Gospel Trumpet Family, her prelude to becoming a missionary to China in 1916. Focusing on the training of national leaders, Maiden remained in her adopted land until the Communist takeover in 1949 resulted in the expulsion of all missionaries. She later married Samuel Boone.

The year 1986 also saw the homegoing of two other long-term missionaries: Mona Moors Tasker, a missionary to India from 1922 to 1955, who died on September 6 at ninety-one years of age, and Paul Edgar Williams, who completed his journey only two weeks later at seventy-eight years old after having served on three mission fields (China, 1947–49; Jamaica, 1953–58; Kenya, 1966–70) and on the elected Missionary Board (1951–54; 1959–66).

L. Y. Janes entered his reward late in the decade at nearly 103 years old. Born on February 21, 1887, Janes gave his heart to the Lord as a five-year-old child and experienced a call to the ministry when he was nineteen. As with Maiden, the Missouri native worked for the Gospel Trumpet Company before marrying Una Daley and going as missionaries first to Jamaica and then to Panama (1911–13). Later, feeling called to gospel publishing, the couple moved to Oklahoma City and later to Corpus Christi, Texas, where they would be closer to Latin America and the Spanish-speaking peoples for whom their hearts were burdened. Before his death on December 19, 1989, Janes had given almost his entire life to sharing the gospel, especially through the printed word in Spanish, Portuguese, and English. He was also active in training young people for ministry through Spanish-language Bible correspondence courses.

Turning toward Africa

In the waning months of the 1980s, eyes were shifting from Asia to the next decade-long missions focus, Africa. Norman Patton's 1989 vision for expansion had included thirteen urban areas around the world where new congregations of the Church of God would be planted. Of these, five were located in Africa (Tanzania, Nigeria, Rwanda, Cameroon, and Malawi). The Missionary Board executive also envisioned beginning a new evangelistic outreach among an unreached people group in Tanzania.

Already the Church of God had entered four new African nations during the decade. In August 1989, Stan and Marion Hoffman relocated from Uganda to Zambia's capital city, Lusaka. It was the first time that a Church of God missionary couple was located on the continent outside East Africa. Sharing borders with Malawi, Mozambique, Zimbabwe, Botswana, Namibia, Angola, Zaire, and Tanzania, Zambia seemed a strategic location for missions outreach into several neighboring nations, some of which represented opportunities for the Church of God to enter for the first time.

Actually, contacts already had been made with Christians in Malawi by the mid-1980s. Some of these were through the efforts of a lay leader in the three-year-old Church of God in Zambia. A Malawi national, he planted three small congregations during a visit in his home country before returning to Zambia. Those three groups soon doubled to six and were calling for the layperson to come home permanently, along with a missionary, to assist the young and growing church. Other Malawis had been reached through Lawrence Chestnut of the Capital Hill Church of God in Oklahoma City after Enos Didimu began reading doctrinal literature written by Chestnut.

For the first time, French-speaking West Africa also seemed a bright prospect for outreach. Ilene Bertschman, a layperson of Church at the

Crossing, Indianapolis, Indiana, had been in correspondence for a few years with Pastor Augustine Meta, leader of a loose alliance of rural churches in Cameroon. At the dawn of the 1990s, this nation also seemed ripe for affiliation with the Church of God.

With this background, "Africa for the '90s" was selected as the theme for the upcoming decade during the 1989 mid-year Missionary Board meetings. At this same gathering, the Board voted to work cooperatively with Living Bibles International to make 150,000 copies of the Bible in four different translations available for distribution in Africa. As the decade-long thrust began, this special program, called Bibles for Africa, would give the Church of God greater exposure in the continent with the inclusion of a personalized message from the church in each Bible. It was also hoped that the campaign would put Bibles into the hands of African laity since most Bibles were owned by pastors.

It is significant that a decade spent expanding missions partnerships was concluding with another new partnership—this one with congregations across the United States providing Bibles for the African continent in cooperation with Living Bibles International. In the most difficult days of the 1980s, some people had questioned the survival and future of Church of God missions. But now, as the decade of "Asia in the '80s" gave way to "Africa in the '90s," the mood was hopeful and forward looking. Surely even greater expansion could be expected in the coming decade.

CHAPTER 9
THE DECADE OF CHANGE
(1990–1999)

At the start of the final decade of the twentieth century, the earth was home to 5.3 billion people (up from 4.5 billion a decade earlier). Of this growing population, the United Nations reported that 823 million, or 16 percent, were fighting for their lives with chronic hunger in 1990.[1] The dismal circumstances being faced by impoverished peoples of the world only looked to get worse with a rapid increase in the incidence of AIDS that would scar many African nations even further during the upcoming decade. Change that would spell hope was needed desperately.

Some nations were attempting to bring change through political strategies. Iraq, for example, invaded Kuwait only eight months into the new decade. Shortly thereafter, East and West Germany were reunited on October 3, 1990. At the same time, although unknown to the world, seeds were being planted for the breakup of the Soviet Union in December 1991.

Change was evident in the Church of God as well. From the North American perspective, the missions focus was changing from Asia to Africa. But no outreach strategy had anticipated the collapse of the Soviet Union and the end of the cold war that suddenly threw open the doors to a new missions frontier in Russia. Such an unforeseen development could be explained only by the working of the Holy Spirit in answer to the unceasing prayers of Soviet Christians who had remained faithful, despite cruel persecution from the Lenin-Stalin eras onwards. That American Christians were actually being invited to Russia to teach ethics and morality in the public schools seemed almost too good to be true. But it wasn't, and the Church of God across North America experienced a collective shiver of excitement as it eagerly anticipated evangelistic opportunities in what had so recently been an impossible mission field.

Yet it had become apparent through the expanding partnerships of the 1980s that the Church of God could no longer define itself primarily through North American eyes. This was true if for no other reason than the fact that church membership outside North America had eclipsed that within North America by the mid-1980s.[2] And the trend was to continue. According to the 1990 *Yearbook of the Church of God*, there were 65,336 more members outside North America than within at the start of the new decade. At the same time, the number of congregations internationally had surpassed those within the borders of the United States and Canada. In 1990, these numbered 2,838 as compared to 2,389 in North America. In fact, the decade of the 1990s was going to see such explosive growth outside North America as well as significant transformations within the Church of God in North America that the time period can best be termed the decade of change.

Launch of "Africa in the '90s"

At the start of the decade, Kenya was the second largest Church of God nation in the world, both in numbers of people and of congregations.[3] Yet despite this successful outreach that had begun nearly ninety years before, Kenya and Africa as a whole represented some of the most significant challenges and needs in the church anywhere in the world. Thus, after a decade of special emphasis on Latin America (the 1970s) and another on Asia (the 1980s), it was strategic action long in coming that the Missionary Board should now turn to Africa.

Although there are fifty-three nations in Africa, it is probable that the Church of God in North America was familiar with few of these at the dawn of the decade. Specifically, Kenya, Tanzania, and Uganda were well known because Missionary Board personnel and finances had been focused primarily on these three East African nations. But, in fact, in 1990 much more than the traditional outreaches of church planting, education, and medicine was happening in East Africa. The Church of God was at work through 1,480 congregations of 151,200 believers located in twelve different African nations.[4] These nations could be divided into two categories: countries where missionary personnel resided (Egypt, Kenya, Tanzania, Uganda, and Zambia) and those where the Board had influence (Rwanda, Malawi, Cameroon, Nigeria, South Africa, Ghana, and Zaire).

Kenya had made the greatest strides in independence from the Missionary Board by 1990. This was evident in its annual operating budget of $90,000, less than 10 percent of it contributed by the Board. Additionally, even though the Kenyan church had received more missionaries from North America in the 1960s than any other church, by 1990, it was home to only two resident missionaries, Caroline Ackerman and Cornelia Kerich, both involved in medical work. Plans were also in the making for Jim and Dorothy Sharp to relocate from Tanzania to Kenya, where they would begin Swahili literature work at the invitation of the Kenyan church. Early projects included a pastor's manual and a Church of God doctrinal overview, both designed to help pastors with backgrounds in other church groups to understand and fit into the Church of God.

Perhaps most significant at this time, Kenya was now a missionary-sending church itself. Its Missionary Outreach Council had been launched during the annual national convention at Kima in 1989 when three Kenyans were commissioned as missionaries to Tanzania and Zambia.

But there was excitement in other African nations as well. Tanzania, under the leadership of Eliazer Mdobi, was anticipating a new thrust at the thirty-year-old Babati Bible School and the arrival of Don and Caroline Armstrong to help develop the school. It was excitement well founded, for during the Armstrongs' sixteen-year tenure, the school graduated over 120 students and the national church grew from seventy-nine congregations to more than three hundred. In 1988, the couple also helped launch Aldersgate Secondary School, also in Babati. By the end of 2007, more than 830 students were enrolled and receiving a top quality education at Aldersgate, which had, by this time, expanded to include a primary school and a high school (in the British system, equivalent to junior college level).[5]

With much of its focus rural, Tanzania was taking a new look at the nation's urban areas. Sherman and Kay Critser had moved to the capital city of Dodoma to help start a congregation there, and a small group was meeting weekly in the northern city of Arusha, praying for success in that church plant. (Those prayers were answered on October 13, 1991, with the dedication of an Arusha church building, a testimony to twenty years of perseverance against many difficulties, including a lack of facilities, which necessitated meeting in homes and classrooms.)

At the same time, the Church of God in Uganda was well acquainted with difficulties, especially trying to reestablish itself after the horrific Idi

Amin regime of 1971–79. Only two struggling congregations existed in 1983. By 1990, however, there were 320 congregations under the leadership of Ephraim Tumusiime, and new missionaries Tim and Colleen Stevenson were working with church leaders to help local congregations become self-sufficient. Colleen also had started a child sponsorship program for Church of God orphans. Other plans called for Magaline Hoops, veteran missionary to Kenya and Tanzania, to help develop a national health care program for the Ugandan church.

By this time, Stan and Marion Hoffman had relocated from Uganda to the central African nation of Zambia. Sharing common borders with eight nations, Zambia was a tactical move for the Hoffmans, whose vision was for the Church of God to extend out of East Africa and into the central and western parts of the continent. Their plan was to reach out into as many surrounding areas as they could from their new headquarters in Zambia's capital, Lusaka, primarily through encouraging, mentoring, and teaching Africans who would carry the church into new regions and countries.

Although missionaries were not resident in either Zaire (now the Democratic Republic of Congo) or Rwanda in 1990, Larry and LeAnn Sellers were planning to move to Goma, Zaire, on the border with Rwanda. This would make it possible for them to work in both nations with national leaders Mianitse Kyambali, of Zaire, and Esron Twagiramungu, of Rwanda. (Unfortunately, strikes, riots, tribal warfare, and civil war in Zaire soon required the Sellers family to move across the border and settle in Gisenyi, Rwanda.)

One way in which the Missionary Board was discovering open doors in Africa was through contacts established by North American congregations. Among these, Samuel Hines and Third Street Church in Washington, DC, had been working in South Africa for more than a decade despite nearly fifty years of government-sponsored and -enforced apartheid (1948–94). Through this, forty-five hundred believers in the country were members of the Church of God at the start of the decade. An elected Missionary Board member, Hines invited Raymond Chin, vice president for church relations, to accompany him to South Africa in 1990. Afterwards, he urged the Board to take over administration of the three-pronged work there—among blacks in Cape Town and with Indians and Zulus in Durban—and to take advantage of a "golden opportunity," a call for fellowship that was even more desperate than the need for funding. Subsequently, Chin was given administrative responsibility since Robert Edwards, regional director for Africa, was unable to travel to South Africa because of restrictions related to apartheid and the disassociation of the rest of Black Africa from its neighbor in the south.[6]

Other national churches whose relationships had been launched outside the Missionary Board included Malawi, Cameroon, and Ghana, thanks to the outreach of Marcus Morgan and the Emerald Avenue Church, Chicago, which also had some of the first contacts with Peter Coetzee in South Africa.[7]

Congregations Support Outreach in Burma

Africa was not the only place where individual congregations were becoming more involved. In 1986, Ann Smith, Missionary Board liaison for Asia, was speaking at a "Mobilizing for Missions" gathering in St. Louis. Endeavoring to garner increased support for the church in Asia, Ann boldly issued a challenge: "Is there anyone who wants the Church of God to evangelize Burma?"[8]

Actually, the work had already begun there. Area missionary Sidney Johnson and Borman Roy Sohkhia of Meghalaya, India, had visited a group of Christian workers in that Southeast Asian nation. Their four days together were so encouraging that Matthew Hla Win, the Burma group's leader, asked Johnson and Sohkhia to pray and commend them to begin the Church of God there. The historic date was October 14, 1985.

Not only was there enthusiasm about the entrance of the Church of God into yet another Asian nation, but there was also excitement about a piece of property for sale in the capital city of Yangon. Already housing a large building that could become headquarters and training facilities, the acreage also had space for constructing a church building. Even more exciting, Hla Win and his co-workers had a vision to evangelize Burma by establishing Church of God congregations throughout the nation. Never mind that 85 percent of the population was staunchly Buddhist and that it had taken Adoniram Judson, first Christian missionary to Burma, seven years of painstaking efforts to baptize his first convert in 1819. Christian evangelism was still a daunting task 165 years later, but the team had no doubts that God still accomplished the impossible.

But where was the money for such a vision? The necessary finances must have been on Smith's mind when she asked the question about evangelizing Burma at the St. Louis conclave only four months after Johnson and Sohkhia's visit. Stirred by the call, Cliff Tierney, executive director for the Churches of God in Southern California, determined to lead his association in accepting the challenge. The result was "Shares for Missions," a three-year project at a cost of $2,700 a month. Congregations, individuals, Sunday school classes, Women of the Church of God units, prayer groups, and even vacation Bible schools throughout Southern California purchased $100 shares to support Burma.

Needless to say, there was rejoicing both in heaven and in California when exciting results began to be reported. Among these, Hla Win baptized thirteen people during the first baptismal service in March 1986. In December that year, another twenty-four people were baptized. Of these, eighteen had been converted from Buddhism, animism, and Islam. Then, only one month later, two more Burmese nationals were baptized, the result of the unexpected hospitalization of Dorothy Colney, general secretary of the church. Although she was so weak she could hardly speak, Colney had managed to witness from her hospital bed! The pattern of congregations partnering in missions outreach was producing good fruit.

All Africa Leaders Consultation

With roots reaching back to 1905, the Church of God in Africa already had a long history at the start of the final decade of the century. Leaders of the twelve African nations where the Church of God was at work were dedicated and eager to see further development. While they appreciated the efforts of the Missionary Board to focus on their continent during the 1990s, they were rightfully determined to be involved in deciding the road map for promoting the decade of special emphasis.

Consequently, December 9–15, 1990, leaders of each national church met in Nairobi with the missionary staff and representatives of the Missionary Board and Women of the Church of God to discuss the future expansion of the church in Africa. Nations attending included Kenya, Tanzania, Uganda, Zaire, Rwanda, Malawi, Zambia, Cameroon, Nigeria, Ghana, Egypt, and South Africa, represented by Peter Coetzee and Jesse Govender, a significant first since, because of apartheid, individuals from South Africa had not previously been able to travel into Black Africa.

In addition to being the first time African leaders all had gathered together, the venue also provided a forum to discuss evangelism, leadership training methods, health care, and development, and to fellowship and worship together. Named the All Africa Leaders Consultation (AALC), the historic gathering agreed upon several goals, including entering new countries on the continent. However, less than a year later, the Missionary Board—while admitting that its mission is to evangelize the world—cautioned, "Before new countries and regions are entered, they must be considered in light of the focus of the Missionary Board and if funds [are] available for such ministry."[9]

The AALC also dreamed about developing an accredited leadership training school and discussed how to deal with congregations and groups wishing to affiliate with the Church of God. Assuring theological unity, accountability, and allegiance to only one church body were challenging issues for which there were no easy answers. One solution was to divide Africa into geographical zones for better administration and oversight. Additionally, the AALC steering committee, headed by Edward Nkansah of Ghana, was charged with becoming the monitoring body for churches seeking affiliation.

Another noteworthy outcome was the launch of a Swahili-language Christian Brotherhood Hour radio broadcast on June 6, 1992. Called *Robo Saa na CBH* (A Quarter of an Hour with CBH), it was directed by an international executive committee of twelve members from Kenya, Tanzania, and Uganda, and Robert Edwards, regional director. Kenyan pastor Obed Ochwanyi became the program's first speaker. He was later succeeded by Daniel Mdobi.

Plans by the AALC steering committee were to have a second conference of all key leaders in December 1992. Although expenses were reduced by almost half from the first one, it would still cost an estimated $25,000 to convene the entire body. As a result, it was reported in the President's Annual Report (1992–93) that the conference was in danger of being cancelled.

"For Africa, the issue has always seemed to be finances," says Edwards today, looking back upon the high hopes for the continent at the start of the 1990s. "We just did not have funds to bring these African leaders together after that first AALC meeting. Eventually, we agreed to divide into three zones, hoping to finance area-wide meetings. That also didn't work out, but it is happening today with regard to KIST (Kima International School of Theology), where East Africa is the major player. Also, the southern countries of Zambia, Malawi, and Mozambique have met together yearly in a sort of union, but not with the authority that we had wished for in an AALC."[10]

When Politics Affects Missions

At the start of the decade, the Church of God was active in less than a quarter of the African nations. It is little wonder that expansion was a major concern of those who met in Nairobi for the first All Africa Leaders Consultation. High expectations for what could be accomplished during "Africa in the '90s" were the heady perfume that enlivened the five-day conference. This was illustrated by the words of the conclave's theme song: "If you believe and I believe and we together pray; the Holy Spirit will come down, and Africa will be saved, and Africa will be saved. The Holy Spirit will come down, and Africa will be saved."[11]

But politics has a way of interrupting even the best of plans. Having already served one term in Haiti, Larry and LeAnn Sellers were to begin their Africa missionary experience in 1991 in Goma, Zaire, now Congo. But only hours before the flight was to leave Nairobi to take the family to their new assignment, there was an attempted coup in Zaire. With ensuing rioting by soldiers, the looting of businesses and private homes, and Tutsi warriors across the border in neighboring Uganda threatening Rwanda's peace, Goma seemed an ill-advised location. Consequently, the couple and their two children spent the next three years living just across the Zaire–Rwanda border in Gisenyi, Rwanda.

With a job description covering assistance to the churches in both nations, Larry and LeAnn planned to cross over to Zaire in the daytime and to return to Rwanda at night. This plan often was modified depending on which country was experiencing unrest at any particular time. While they lived on the Rwanda side, much of their ministry took place in Zaire and they visited churches in both countries on alternating weekends.

Whatever the precautions and flexibility of planning, it was a difficult assignment. The Sellers discovered that many Church of God Christians were among the casualties in Zaire's ongoing ethnic violence. On top of this, the unrest was spreading. Within their first year in Gisenyi, Rwanda's generally well-mannered soldiers had rioted there.

At the time, Zaire was the African nation where the Church of God was growing the fastest. Only two years earlier, there were 313 congregations and 10,841 Christians. However, under the visionary direction of national leader Mianitse Kyambali, there were now 427 congregations and 14,421 Christians. It was a similar story in Rwanda. In 1991, it registered 192 congregations and 7,022 members, including a new outreach to an unreached people group, the pygmies living in the mountainous northern region.[12] Politics had changed the original plans to be sure, but it appeared that the ministry in Zaire and Rwanda was on solid ground nevertheless.

Different Geography, Same Climate

Increasingly, politics was playing a role in the life of the church. Frequently the effects were negative. During the Missionary Board's November 1991 annual meetings, a fax from missionaries Tim and Colleen Stevenson announced the disappointing news that the Ugandan government had just denied registration to the Church of God.

Sometimes there was good news. Despite the setback, the Ugandan church persevered and eventually won registration on July 3, 1992. This positive turn of events was thanks, in large part, to the untiring efforts of the Stevensons and church leaders who, through the reapplication process, formed a strong bond with Samson Kisekka, Uganda's vice president. As a result, Kisekka, during an official visit to Washington, DC, accepted an invitation to visit Anderson on July 11–12, 1992. The result was a very positive meeting hosted by the Board for area church and civic leaders.

Only months earlier, the fledgling Church of God in Malawi had also faced its own politically charged trials. Enos Didimu, national leader, was arrested and detained in February 1992, charged with bringing unauthorized foreigners into the country and operating the Church of God without legal registration. It appeared the Malawi government was targeting the Christian church in general and accusing it—the Church of God included—of fueling calls for democratic reforms in the nation. Although some arrested church leaders were never seen again, Didimu was freed in July.

Africa was not the only place where politics affected the life and mission of the church. In Sri Lanka, where the church registered with the government in 1990 as Church of God Ministries Sri Lanka, civil war had been ongoing since 1983. According to Michael Kinner, Asia-Pacific regional director, the Sri Lankan church had six congregations or fellowships by 1992. One of these was located in the restricted, war-torn area of the Jaffna Peninsula. Although contact with this group was limited, evangelist Kingsley Ebenezar reported working with seventeen families at the time, and as many as twelve converts from Buddhism or Hinduism were waiting for baptism.[13] As the political situation worsened, this congregation was forced to move to a refugee center south of the peninsula. However, Ebenezar and his wife Lalitha, helped in part by relief funds sent by the Missionary Board, continued reaching out to people displaced in two refugee camps.

Elsewhere in Asia, Indian church leaders Asim Das and P. K. Das (no relation) were speakers of an Oriya-language Christian Brotherhood Hour program called *Satya Jyoti* (Light of Truth). Seekers conferences were conducted periodically for listeners wishing to learn more about faith in Christ. In May 1992, of forty people who were invited to attend, twenty-three made commitments to Christ and seven were baptized before returning home. Frequently, conference attendees not only became Christians but also church planters throughout Orissa state.[14]

But evangelism in India, particularly in Orissa, is not easy and does not come without high cost for new converts, usually from Hinduism. The subsequent seekers conference, scheduled for December, was cancelled because of political and religious disturbances around the nation. (Only a few years later, the gruesome murder of Australian missionary Graham Staines and his two young sons while they slept in their station wagon on January 22, 1999, during a ministry trip in Orissa, underlined the difficult state of affairs in this part of India.)[15]

Indonesia, the world's most populated Muslim nation, presented its own challenges. Back in 1981, missionary Sidney Johnson and Neville Tan, leader of the Singapore Church of God, traveled to Indonesia to visit Tabitha Gunawan, Tan's Bible school classmate. That contact led to the establishment of the Church of God in Indonesia and Gunawan's 1986 ordination by the church in Singapore. By 1991, there were two congregations in Indonesia, but the newer group was being persecuted. It had become necessary to gather less frequently and to move from location to location because of harassment, including the stoning of the house where they had been meeting. Despite being legally registered, the group had been denied the right to erect a church sign and, after seven years, was still waiting for its telephone application to be granted.

Half a world away, politics also touched the church in another Muslim nation. Although roots for a Church of God witness in Egypt were planted as early as 1904, the first Church of God congregation was launched after American missionaries moved there in 1923. Seventy years later, in 1994, there were thirteen congregations, although only three had government permits to exist; the other ten were all illegal. One had applied for a license in 1959 and was still awaiting a decision. Nevertheless, against all hope, one congregation in Cairo received permission to worship in 1983 after only three years of waiting for its application to be processed. Three years later, they received a permit to operate a day-care center. In 1993, they celebrated again when authorization came to construct a five-story building. The red tape that bound each step was considerable, but God continued proving himself and strengthening the church at the same time.[16]

Locations in the Western hemisphere had their own tales of how politics affected the church and its ministry. Missionaries Keith and Gloria Plank had relocated to Venezuela in 1991 after eleven years in Costa Rica. Soon they discovered that Venezuela was caught in an especially volatile period characterized by riots, murders, and extreme political tension. Although they obtained one-year visas to work with two congregations, it seemed likely that their second applications would be denied since, according to the government, cults and religious sects were proliferating. All Protestant missionary work in the Amazon region had been banned, and Venezuela was dragging its feet on issuing visas for all religious workers. In answer to many prayers, however, the couple received visas in May 1993, allowing them to remain in Venezuela for one more year.

Different countries, different pastors, different missionaries notwithstanding, politics that touched the church and its ministries could be found the world over. Called apartheid, embargo, guerrilla and tribal warfare, and other names, these situations seemed to make their way into Missionary Board reports and discussions with increasing frequency as the decade advanced. Perhaps one result was a new policy regarding emergency evacuation voted upon in the October 1993 annual Board meetings. Missionaries facing political crises would be "free to evacuate in light of the local situation" and assured of Board support "in any emergency action they may be compelled to take." The policy also stated that the Missionary Board could direct a missionary to evacuate a field in the event of life-threatening danger or liability factors.

Christ's Birthday Offering

Whether it would be on the African continent or elsewhere, funding the expansion of missions outreach in eighty-two nations around the world was a full-time concern of the Missionary Board in 1990. Darrell Smith, vice president for finance and development, was charged with finding new resources to augment the dollars contributed by World Service—never adequate for day-to-day operations, even without any hoped-for increases in mission activities. Raising missionary support levels through creation of a new staff position, Living Link coordinator, became a top priority. Additionally, Missionary Board staff members began traveling more frequently to churches and regional association meetings, illustrated by President Patton's travel schedule for the 1991–92 fiscal year. In addition to his usual Monday to Friday assignments, he spent thirty-one weekends that year on Missionary Board assignments. It was hoped that personal contact would result in greater financial support.

Fortunately, there were others also concerned with the dollar short-falls. Back in 1932, this very issue prompted Nora Hunter to form the Woman's Home and Foreign Missionary Society, the predecessor of today's Women of the Church of God (WCG). The organization's objectives included "[cooperating] with all recognized agencies of the Church of God in promoting missionary work at home and abroad; [making] the cause of missions a heart interest rather than a passing fancy."[17]

Significant in WCG's missions-supporting history, the Christ's Birthday Offering (later expanded to become the Christ's Birthday Observance) was launched in 1950 and raised $41,204 that first year. Another $1,216,404 was given to the annual December offering through the rest of the decade. By the end of the 1960s, cumulative receipts for the Christ's Birthday Offering had almost tripled. Giving doubled again during the next decade, for a cumulative total of $6,986,462. Then, during the 1980s, the year-end offering surged past the ten million dollar mark, bringing in $12,585,192 for Church of God missions during that ten-year period. This included $1,436,816 in 1989 alone. Inspired to do even more, WCG set its 1990 offering goal at $1.5 million.

Birth of the Asian Women's Conference

In addition to promoting the annual missions offering, WCG was active in other ways. Among these, the organization gave seed money for the first Asian Women's Conference, November 28–30, 1990, in Singapore. Conducted in conjunction with the Fifth Asian Church of God Conference, the historic meeting brought together some fifty women from thirteen different Asian nations and the United States, including Doris Dale, representing WCG. Although women had been welcome in the general Asian Conference since its start eight years earlier, this was the first time they had been granted their own venue. Representing Singapore, Nepal, Philippines, India, and Myanmar, speakers explored the theme "The Changing Role of Women in Asia and the Role of Asian Christian Women in This Context."[18]

The women also elected Ng Ngoing Keng, of Singapore, as president and missionary Jean Johnson as advisor. A subsequent women's conference was conducted in Thailand in 1992 and thereafter biennially through 1998, always meeting during hours the general conference was not in session. However, aware of the limited time this allowed them, the women asked to separate from the general conference during the ninth Asia-Pacific Conference in Cochin, India, in 1998. They conducted their first completely independent meeting during their sixth such gathering in Bangkok in 2000. Since that time, the group has continued to meet biennially, although the general conference has convened only once every four years since 1998. At this writing, preparations are underway for the tenth Asia-Pacific Women's Conference, to meet in Bangkok, November 17–21, 2008.

Three World Conferences

While representatives of the Canadian and American churches gathered in Toronto in September 1990 to promote Christian unity, and other segments of the church met in Africa and Asia later that year, 1991 provided an opportunity to invite the entire Church of God to assemble for the ninth World Conference, July 19–21, in Wiesbaden, Germany. A record-breaking sixty-eight of eighty-two nations where the Church of God was resident were represented among the two thousand delegates (although more than three quarters of these were from North America or Germany). Noteworthy is the fact that this 1991 representation of nations is a record that still stands today.[19]

Conference planners, including representatives of Brazil, Germany, Kenya, Italy, and the United States, were chaired by Leaderwell Pohsngap, of India, and chose "Mission in a Changing World" as the theme. Sessions during the three-day event considered such themes as "A Clear Vision for Mission," "A Fresh Anointing for Mission," and "A Joyful Fulfillment of Mission." Immediately preceding the conference was the two-day World Forum, the fourth gathering of this invitation-only assembly of international church leaders.

At least two other strategic meetings were added into the busy schedule: a doctrinal dialogue for key world leaders sponsored by the School of Theology and a gathering convened by the Missionary Board for representatives of missionary-sending or -funding countries. A five-person committee (Eckhard Bewernick, Germany; Borman Roy Sohkhia, India; Arturo Schultz, Argentina; John Campbell, Canada; and Norman Patton, United States) was chosen at this initial get-together to plan a follow-up meeting in 1992. Patton explains, "My idea was that we could work together in sending, funding, and monitoring mission work around the world. We had some good meetings and a cooperative spirit."[20]

Concluding with a Rhine cruise, the five-day Wiesbaden experience garnered some criticism that the primary reason for the World Conference—gathering the international church for meaningful fellowship and dialogue—was being challenged by tour packages designed for North Americans. Robert Edwards, Africa regional director, spoke for many missionaries when he expressed concerns during the annual Board meeting three months later. There he questioned whether World Conference participation might have been a "detriment" to third-world leaders rather than the hoped for encouragement. "We preach austerity and also ask them to cut items from an already 'bare bones' budget, and yet put them up in plush settings [at the World Conference]. This is a contradiction to them," Edwards asserted.[21]

Perhaps in response to this criticism, housing at the tenth World Conference and fifth World Forum in Sydney, Australia, July 18–23, 1995, was quite different. Many third-world delegates stayed at Camp Berachah, the national church's campgrounds outside Sydney, and were bused back and forth to the convention venue at Sydney Harbor. But voices also spoke against this solution, saying that now third-world delegates were being discriminated against because those who could afford it had the option of much better accommodations.

Germany's Willi Krenz chaired the planning committee for the Sydney experience, built around two themes: "Celebrate God's Activity" (World Conference) and "Learning to Celebrate" (World Forum). The overall program drew an attendance of around one thousand, more than two-thirds of whom were from the United States, with one hundred delegates at the Forum. Reflective of the great distance to Australia, attendance was down, with only forty-eight countries represented. As a result, Great Britain was selected as a more central location for the next event in 1999. Victor Babb, of Barbados, and Asim Das, of India, were named to co-chair the planning committee.

Subsequently, the city of Birmingham was selected for the sixth World Forum, July 22–23, 1999, followed immediately by the eleventh World Conference, July 23–25. Both meetings considered the theme "Jesus Is Lord," from Philippians 2:9–11. Unfortunately, although the total number of delegates had increased by five hundred people, there were eight fewer nations represented than in Australia (only forty of eighty-five countries where the Church of God was at work). Once again, the great majority of participants were from North America—eleven hundred of fifteen hundred—in part reflecting the difficulty some nations had in securing visas. Among these, only one member of Kenya's delegation of sixty people was allowed to enter Great Britain.

Missions by Cooperation

Among the most significant results of the Wiesbaden World Conference was the birth of an international missions committee on September 12, 1992. Following up on the discussions of missionary-sending nations during the World Conference, five individuals—Victor Ruzak, Argentina; Borman Roy Sohkhia, India; Norman Patton, United States; John Campbell,

Canada; and Eckhard Bewernick, Germany—met in Fritzlar, Germany, during the 1992 Church of God European Conference to continue the work begun one year earlier. Calling itself the Global Missions Committee of the Church of God, the group hammered out goals, strategies, and a mission purpose statement. They also decided to house administration of the committee's work in Anderson, Indiana, and chose Norman Patton to be chairperson. Not a new agency to duplicate what already was being done by individual nations, the committee banded together to network and coordinate activities. Its next meeting was set for the 1993 International Convention in Anderson.

Subsequently, the smaller planning delegation convened a full meeting sandwiched between the Australia World Forum and World Conference meetings in Sydney in July 1995. Twenty-four participants, including representatives of the major sending nations—the United States, Canada, Germany, India, and Argentina—agreed to the following purpose and mission statement: "The Global Mission Committee of the Church of God is an intentional, cooperative, and coordinated effort of mission sending countries and organizations to work in partnership with each other in mission ministries around the world."[22] They also approved guidelines that respected the sovereignty of each country, promised to partner together in sending personnel and funding projects whenever possible, and pledged to avoid unilateral, competitive, or duplicate missions activities. The committee had high hopes that frequent consultations would result in harmonious goals and effective strategic planning for the future.

"The meeting in Sydney was informative as reports were given by each country [about their] involvement in missions…A feeling of overall support for the Church of God world mission was felt. The Missionary Board is not the only agency in the Church of God doing mission. There must continue to be a cooperative effort with all of these countries," declared Patton after the consultation.[23]

Admitting that he dreamed of a world missions board or committee, the retired missions executive speaks with disappointment that the promising cooperative venture did not survive the 1990s. "There were changes in [national church] leadership in the United States, my leaving, and also leadership changes in Germany. I suppose those may have been the major causes. But I believe [this committee] was a very good thing."[24]

A decade later, Robert Edwards, Global Missions coordinator, Patton's successor, voices the same sentiment about greater missions outreach through better international cooperation. "The desire and the dream still exist," he declares, "but lack of finances and venue that assists in bringing leaders together—such as provided by World Conferences—has kept this from happening."[25]

Missions on Our Doorstep

It didn't take a trip abroad to become involved in the church's cross-cultural missions enterprise. While studying at the School of World Missions at Fuller Theological Seminary in California in the late 1980s, Paul and Nova Hutchins, former Church of God missionaries to Bangladesh and Africa, had learned that half a million international students were enrolled in schools across the United States. Even more exciting, at least fifty thousand were their next-door neighbors in Southern California. Working through a large Protestant church of forty-five hundred members, the Hutchinses realized they were missionaries on their own doorstep.

"Coming from more than 175 different nations, one-third of which are closed to traditional missions, these students arrive in America highly motivated to study so that they can return to their homelands as leaders in business, education, and government," Paul declared of the unique mission field.[26]

Paul and Nova longed to help the Church of God realize this exciting mission field, so they asked the Missionary Board during its 1990 annual meeting to sponsor a new international students outreach. This was approved, leading to their 1991 appointment as special assignment missionaries to direct ARMS Reaching (Americans Reaching Out to Multinational Students).

Following eight years in Southern California, the couple relocated to Indianapolis, Indiana, where they served for ten more years as missionaries to internationals through the Church at the Crossing. One month before retiring in 2005, an Indianapolis university invited them to help some international students. "Sadly, we had to decline the invitation," Nova explained, noting there was no one to assume the reins of ARMS Reaching. "It is our constant prayer that someone will respond to the call of God to carry on this strategic ministry."[27]

Living Link Gets New Life

Shortly after becoming Missionary Board president in 1988, Norman Patton had presented a new vision for expansion into thirteen major cities
around the world. Hand in hand with this vision was a financial strategy to
reduce indebtedness and near complete reliance on World Service dollars.
Among the steps towards financial wholeness, Patton had issued the challenge of increasing missionary support levels to at least 75 percent by December 1990. This was to be achieved through renewed attention to Living
Link, a program launched in the early 1960s by J. Edgar Smith.

The program had originally gotten off to a good start when eighty
congregations signed up immediately to become Living Link partners.
One, First Church of God, Racine, Wisconsin, linked up with Sidney and
Jean Johnson. In fact, the Wisconsin congregation supported the Johnsons
throughout their thirty-seven years of missionary service. It was honored
by the Missionary Board in June 1992 for having the longest continuing
Living Link relationship in the program's history. At the time, more than
four hundred churches across the United States and Canada were involved
in Living Link.

Two other noteworthy early Living Link participants were West Court
Street Church, Flint, Michigan, underwriting the work in Thailand for several years, and the state of Ohio, under leadership of Leonard (Bucky) Snyder as state executive. The Ohio organization fully supported at least three
missionary positions in what Patton says was a first for a state ministry.

However, the picture had not always been so bright. By the time Patton determined to give Living Link renewed attention, only 20 percent of
North American churches—342 congregations—were attempting to fund
all sixty-five career missionaries.[28] In 1991, the Board shifted Eileen Clay
from other responsibilities to become the first full-time Living Link coordinator. It also restructured the program. Originally, Living Link had
provided only basic missionary support, but it soon became responsible for
helping missionaries raise their total budgets even before departing for the
field. Changes also allowed small congregations to join for as little as one
share of support. (Support was figured individually according to the cost of
living on a particular field. This figure was then divided by one hundred to
determine the cost of one share.)

Successes were being reported as early as September 30, when it was noted that Living Link income in the first three months of the 1991–92 fiscal year had increased by $21,000 over the previous year.[29] By the end of June 1992, supporters included three churches in foreign countries and 421 churches in North America—two of these with Sunday morning attendances of only ten—in addition to fifty-three individuals, two state WCG organizations, and four state general assemblies. Subsequently, in his July 1991–June 1992 annual report, Patton announced the good news that collective support had risen from 71 percent in January 1992 to 80 percent by the end of June. This represented nearly $150,000 in commitments that had been secured in the previous six months, thanks to the hard work of Clay; David Reames, vice president of personnel; and Jerry Brandon, teaming up to lend World Service assistance.

Indeed, the news continued to be positive, despite increasing costs as new items beyond basic salary were added to Living Link budgets. These included funds for day-to-day ministry, missionary children's education, medical care, and insurance. Patton explained this conscious decision as "moving from a generic cost of a missionary to actual cost for each field."[30] By May 1993, 90 percent of the overall Living Link budget had been committed, with approximately 70 percent of those funds actually being received. Four years later, Sharon Skaggs, human resources director, reported in the 1996–97 President's Annual Report that "pledges for 103 percent of support needed toward a goal of 100 percent" had been secured.[31]

Educating the Church for Missions

"Living Link was first and foremost a promotional concept. It promoted shared information. It inspired missionary zeal and fostered an understanding of timely trends in mission. Living Link helped the church in the West understand the diversity within Christianity. It promoted cross-cultural understanding and brought into focus the interrelationship so necessary for the church globally. Dollars were incidental to this more inclusive understanding of being linked together in vital concern."[32]

In other words, according to Donald Johnson, by then serving the Board in recruitment, more than anything else, Living Link was created to educate and involve the church in missions. Certainly an important offshoot was financing missionaries, but education was both vital and of principal importance.

This was the philosophy that prompted the Missionary Board in the early 1990s to become more intentional about missions education. As part of his assignment as vice president for personnel, David Reames and Cheryl Barton, a missionary in Japan, developed a series of personnel brochures to help the church know its missionaries better. The two also teamed up to launch *Care Chronicle*, a biannual newspaper, in 1991. Although the Board produced this for the sixty missionary children living at home, an additional benefit came when churches used it as a tool for education and prayer.

Barton was also tagged to work with Raymond Chin in his church relations assignment. Among other things, they produced a series of quarterly bulletin inserts. The first one, in 1992, called for "Prayer for Difficult Places" and highlighted Haiti, Uganda, Colombia, and Nepal. Approximately forty-five thousand inserts were offered to the church for free but with donations requested for postage. Chin also continued the World Calendar of Prayer, with the 1992 calendar focusing on the Maasai tribe of Africa. The calendar was replaced in 2000 with a two-page insert in *Missions* magazine: Global Prayer Concerns.

Another new series of publications was launched in 1993 with *New Every Morning*. This series of booklets of international testimonies compiled and edited by Cheryl Barton is still being produced, although it is now published by Warner Press. Many new brochures also were published, and there was a concerted effort to supply news stories, feature articles, and missions related information to as many Church of God national and regional publications as possible. By the end of the first year of this calculated promotional increase, Norman Patton was congratulating his staff for their work in "revitalizing the church's interest in missions."[33]

My Name Is S.A.M.

That Patton's enthusiasm was justified and that the church's interest in missions was growing could be seen in the special assignment missionary program. Eventually called by its acronym, SAM, the program was targeted for increased staff attention and greater promotional efforts from early in the decade through the efforts of David Reames, vice president for personnel, and his administrative assistant, Jane Thor.

Educating the church about how to become involved in short-term missions and about the wide range of service opportunities available was a top priority. Once again, the written word was utilized in a brochure titled "My Name Is S.A.M." The efforts of Reames and Thor found significant returns. From 1990, when there were seven SAMs, the program grew to place twenty-seven individuals the next year. By June 1992, there were forty SAMs, including sixteen commissioned at the International Convention for Spain, Kazakhstan, Kenya, Grand Cayman, Dominican Republic, Costa Rica, Bolivia, Mexico, Japan, Hungary, and among international students in the United States. By June 1996, there were sixty-five. At the end of the decade, almost half of all missionaries sent by the Board were SAMs (sixty-five careers and fifty-eight SAMs).[34]

A New Regional Director for Asia

Nevertheless, longevity in missions was still the primary hinge on which the Missionary Board door depended. Africa was a major example of where long missionary tenures were the norm. In 1992, seven individuals had given a collective 110 years of missionary service on that continent: Robert and Janet Edwards, twenty-two years; Magaline Hoops Heusel, thirty; Stanley and Marion Hoffman, twenty-seven; and Jim and Dorothy Sharp, thirty-one. In addition, Kenneth and Sue Jo Good had been Church of God missionaries for twenty-nine years, although they had been in Africa for only the most recent ten of those. It was an impressive display of longevity, and all were still going strong.

Asia, too, was known for career missionaries who served both long and well. Interestingly, two couples in Asia at the start of the decade were both commissioned during the 1955 Anderson Camp Meeting. Philip and Phyllis Kinley had gone to Japan, where they continued serving in 1992, while Sidney and Jean Johnson had begun their missions career in India. Not surprisingly, it was a noteworthy day when the Johnsons retired on January 1, 1992, after thirty-six years. Their tenure included seventeen years in India and nineteen in Thailand, from which they served the entire region.

With their retirement, Michael and Debra Kinner became the first regional directors (RDs) for Asia. (Even though Sidney served in an area-wide role, he had resisted the title of regional director because he feared that it would cause misunderstanding among national leaders.) While new to the assignment, the Kinners were not new to Asia. After a special assignment in Japan, they had been career missionaries for eight years in Hong Kong. Their new work began while on home assignment in 1991, overlapping with Johnson for the last six months of the year for an easier transition into the expanded assignment.

Children of Promise

Sidney and Jean Johnson's love for children blossomed between 1955 and 1972, the years they were missionaries in India and lived at The Shelter, the oldest Church of God orphanage in the world. But it wasn't until twenty years later that fruit from the blossoms was harvested and named Children of Promise.

Remembering the events leading up to the launching of the child sponsorship program in 1992, Jean shares, "On our last administrative trip to Asia, we visited with the church in Singapore. During the farewell service, we were standing in a circle as Sister Ng prayed, 'O God, give Sidney and Jean an even wider ministry than they have ever had.' I questioned her if she realized what she had prayed. She said yes and that she believed God wasn't through with [our service] yet."[35]

In fact, the couple had been asking regional leaders how they could continue to serve even in retirement. Again and again, they heard the same reply, "Help our children." Sister Ng's prayer and the needs of children in Asia and around the world were soon answered when the Missionary Board and Women of the Church of God jointly launched Children of Promise and appointed Sidney and Jean as coordinators.

Initially, Children of Promise began by raising support for 174 children in four already existing national programs, including the Grace Family Helper Project in Manila, Philippines. By 2007, that program alone was nurturing more than seven hundred Filipino children. Directed by Ophelia Viray, the Philippine arm of Children of Promise also provides spiritual, nutritional, and educational guidance to the parents of sponsored children who continue to live with their families, thanks to help received from Grace Family Helper Project. Under the Johnsons' leadership, Children of Promise had expanded into fourteen countries by January 1, 2004, the date of their second retirement.

After more than fifteen years as special assignment missionaries in Grand Cayman and Costa Rica, Paul and Brenda Maxfield became Children of Promise coordinators-elect in 2003. (They assumed full responsibility on January 1, 2004.) Three years later, Brenda returned to teaching and Paul was appointed executive director to oversee the organization's work in twenty-two countries. With the addition of Ghana and Zambia in 2006 and Russia in the fall of 2007, Children of Promise had grown to sponsor 3,149 children in twenty-three nations. Tanzania's was the largest program, with 788 children.

Medical Missions Task Force

In addition to supporting Children of Promise in its holistic approach to ministering to children, the Missionary Board also sought similar opportunities in general missions work around the world. Sometimes this support came through missionaries with primary assignments in medicine, including Cornelia Kerich in Kenya and John Ackerman in Haiti. However, not every dentist, doctor, or nurse with a heart for missions could close up shop in North America and move to the mission field. So how could their medical expertise and concern for missions be tapped?

The Medical Missions Task Force (MMTF) was the answer. Launched under Missionary Board sponsorship in 1990, it was the brainchild of two medical doctors, Bill Webb, a general practitioner in Huntington, Indiana, and William Anderson, a medical missionary in Kenya in the late 1960s who now had a family practice in Anderson. They were joined shortly by two others in Anderson—Mark Fulton, a dentist, and Scott Green, a family practitioner—to provide short-term service opportunities around the world for Church of God medical recruits. The group also focused on networking to assist medical missionaries through providing encouragement, support, and funding for projects, equipment, and supplies.

By the mid-1990s, eight MMTF teams had conducted clinics in conjunction with Phyllis Newby and the Church of God in Haiti; in Tanzania, working with Caroline Ackerman and Laura Coe among the Maasai; with Magaline Heusel in Uganda; and more. In 1993, a team visited Church of God dispensaries in Uganda and Kenya and met with church, government, and NGO (non-government service organization) medical officers to evaluate the situation in East Africa and make recommendations for how the church could better help meet medical needs.

In cooperation with Caring Partners International (CPI) in Middletown, Ohio, a MMTF group also helped conduct a chaplaincy training program in hospitals in Sumy, Ukraine. Later cooperative efforts with Caring Partners International included two medical teams that traveled to Ecuador and another group to Nairobi, where they treated nearly one thousand people during the day. In the evening, the team participated in an evangelistic crusade where some two hundred people came to Christ.

Despite the significant ministries of the task force, it dissolved shortly after 1996 when Ray Chin, the Board's liaison with the medical group, took a pastorate in Chicago. Most of the original MMTF members have continued to use their medical expertise in missions work around the world since that time but not under Missionary Board sponsorship.

Groping in the Dark

"The continent of Africa continues to reel from civil wars, military intervention, ethnic cleansing, hyper-inflation, devastated economies, failed starts at multi-party politics, corruption, high-level greed, deception on all levels, an AIDS epidemic that is wreaking havoc to the very roots of the African cultural foundations (the family), [and] the resurgence of yellow fever, malaria, hepatitis, and in some areas, even the plague. It is as if someone has turned the lights off continentally and we are all groping in the dark for a small fire to give us a sense of grounding, location, and perhaps direction."[36]

Despite high hopes engendered by work camps, child sponsorships, special offerings for missions, work in new countries, and even "Africa in the '90s," Robert Edwards wrote these sobering words in 1993 from his vantage point as Africa regional director. Among the challenges he faced was the refugee dilemma, a mushrooming problem especially in Africa. "Africa Refugee Day" had been commemorated internationally every June 20 since 1969. But in December 2000, it was renamed "World Refugee Day" by the United Nations General Assembly, acknowledging that the plight of refugees was a global rather than an Africa-only concern. Nevertheless, Africa was one of the most affected regions.

Edwards described the difficult refugee situation in his 1992–93 annual commentary. Quoting the U.S. Embassy in Kigali, Rwanda, he noted that over one hundred thousand refugees had fled ethnic fighting in neighboring Zaire (now Democratic Republic of Congo). In response, Mianitse Kyambali, national leader of the Church of God in Zaire, was ministering to more than eight hundred refugees living in and around his church in the city of Sake. By then, eight Churches of God had been destroyed in related fighting and more than two thousand Church of God Christians had fled their homes, becoming refugees. With ethnic fighting spreading, the Church of God was also being affected in Rwanda, Kenya, and Mozambique.

Two years later, the situation was even worse. In eastern and southern Africa alone, nearly four million individuals had refugee status (Zaire, 1.8 million; Tanzania, 630,000; Sudan, 660,000; Ethiopia, 360,000; Uganda, 330,000; and Kenya, 195,000).[37] Compounding the problem, by the mid-1990s many NGOs had abandoned their efforts for the safety of volunteers and other reasons. Indeed, considering the worsening state of affairs and news that American citizens had been targeted for execution in Rwanda, the Missionary Board reassigned Sherman and Kay Critser and Larry and LeAnn Sellers. By July 1997, more than 550 Churches of God had been destroyed in Zaire and over 18,000 Church of God people had died.[38] In neighboring Rwanda, when accounting after the genocide was completed in 1996, 151 churches and 7,595 Christians had been lost, although not all deaths occurred during the war and subsequent two years of Hutu exile in Zaire.[39]

Where Did It All Begin and End?

On April 6, 1994, a jet carrying the presidents of Rwanda and Burundi was shot down near Kigali International Airport, killing both men, the chief of staff of Rwandan military forces, and others. Although it was not clear who engineered the assassination, there was no doubt that the Rwandan president had been murdered. Some say it was this incident that ignited the fires of ethnic fighting that quickly escalated into genocide as Hutu death squads determined to rid Rwanda of the minority Tutsis. But racial animosity, seething for a lifetime, was ripe for explosion. When it did erupt, no country in eastern Africa was exempt, although Rwanda and Zaire bore the brunt of the crisis.

At the time of the crash, Sherman and Kay Critser were resident in Goma, Zaire. Noting that the Church of God in the Kivu District of eastern Zaire was being affected most by ethnic fighting in Rwanda, they reported that within a month of the incident some five thousand refugees had fled into the area, with more arriving daily. Among these were Esron Twagiramungu, legal representative of the Church of God in Rwanda, his family, and other Rwandan pastors. Twagiramungu and forty refugees soon found safety in a home in Goma with rent provided by Church of God Hunger and Relief funds.

Eighteen miles west of Goma, the national church headquarters in Sake was also providing food, clothing, and medical help for refugees, while congregations in two other nearby locations cared for yet more exiled Rwandans. Responding to the escalating crisis, the Missionary Board and the Hunger and Relief Committee eventually sent more than $97,000. With this the church in Zaire purchased "123 tons of beans, corn, and other food items; 1,400 beds, 3,600 cups, 3,630 cooking pots, 587 blankets, 243 tarps," and more. As Critser pointed out, "The list of needs is long when over a million people lost everything they had."[40] Suddenly refugees, the Rwandans were housed in tent-to-tent, overcrowded camps lacking basic toilet facilities and water. How could the church bring hope into such desperate situations?

Critser further explained, "We distributed [food and relief supplies] only in our churches and at pre-selected sites outside the camps (for crowd control reasons), and we kept ledgers of those receiving aid…We were able to help between ten and eleven thousand of our people and others who happened to express their needs well enough, through eight distribution centers (churches). Many, many more received help on a need-to-need basis."[41]

Other funds were used to spread fourteen tarpaulin roofs over camp church sites, where preaching and teaching took place. (Kay taught refugee women about women in the Bible while Sherman instructed pastors and evangelists about the Church of God.) Four hundred Bibles in the Kinyarwanda language were purchased and distributed in refugee camps. Looking back on the church's response to those anxious days, Critser wrote:

> I can say without a doubt that the aid given saved the Rwanda Church…[and] prevented the Church in Zaire from being over-whelmed…Seeing the outpouring of support by the church in America did more to solidify the faith of these believers in the unity

of the church than any other act could have. I believe God placed us there for this purpose…We were thanked profusely and repeatedly for the help…

We were not able to function as [before]…We did not always feel we could leave our homes for extended times because of the dangers present, but the overwhelming pain and misery the refugees and the Church in Zaire suffered in this war have brought a far greater sensitivity to God's Word than there has ever been. When people have lost all they own and [their country], then they are a people who are desperately searching for peace and hope.[42]

By late 1998, four years after the gruesome events, the effects of genocide, tribal warfare, and the refugee crisis that developed were still acute in both Rwanda and Congo (DR) (formerly Zaire). It was finally safe enough for Sherman to travel to the border of Congo (DR) and Rwanda in late 1998 in his role of field secretary for the two nations. The news he received from national church leaders was both good and bad.

According to Vatiri Diogratias, the Rwandan church was remaining true to its mission despite great suffering. Between April and September, 134 people had come to Christ. Unfortunately, there was no cumulative growth because of the rate at which others were dying in lingering conflicts. Since 1996, thirteen Church of God pastors and nearly fifteen hundred Church of God believers in Rwanda had lost their lives. Mianitse Kyambali also shared that three Church of God pastors in Congo had been killed recently and many others were without homes.

"One of the greatest problems in Rwanda is being able to find food at a decent price," Critser commented. "Because of insecurity in the hills around Gisenyi, people cannot plant or harvest. So food is brought from the Congo side, but it is very expensive. Too many refugees crowd both sides of the border. When will it all end? When hatred dies, I believe. Until it does, true peace will never come…Only through Christ will real peace ever exist, and the work we have is not going to be easy or short term…"[43]

To Russia with God's Love

It wasn't like Pentecost when three thousand people were added to the church in one day. But there was no mistaking the fact that the Holy Spirit visited Chelyabinsk, Russia, during ten days in the spring of 1992. That God would choose to work through a team of eighteen high school students and fourteen adults from Florida was more of the thrilling story that set the stage for planting the Church of God in that eastern Siberian city of nearly a million and a half people where only six churches yet existed out of two hundred that had been in Chelyabinsk before communism.

Officially, the team and its leader, Mark Shaner, youth pastor in Vero Beach, Florida, had been invited for cultural exchange at Chelyabinsk's Lyceum (school) #31. Unofficially, the delegation was eager to see the Church of God begin a work in the formerly off-limits city where the first atomic bomb was developed and exploded in 1945 and where a third of all Russian tanks used in World War II were manufactured. The city's military enterprises had cloaked Chelyabinsk in secrecy, and it had only opened to the outside in 1991. Bathing their preparations in prayer and fasting, and supported by a host of prayer partners, the delegation saw God accomplish even more than their original objectives.

Wearing matching shirts proclaiming in the Russian language, "To Russia with God's Love," team members saw God working almost immediately. Fascinated by the shirts, Russians bombarded the group with questions, opening the door for witnessing, an activity that continued in a variety of settings throughout the Chelyabinsk experience. Alexander Popov, headmaster of Lyceum #31, announced that what the Russians wanted was not money or food, but help in educating their children. "I am not a Christian, but I feel that God may be coming to us through you," he declared, surprising everyone.[44]

Easter Sunday was the climax of the groundbreaking missions trip. Thirty-three people publicly committed their lives to Christ, and nineteen of them were baptized in a *banya* (bath house) that evening following an afternoon class for new believers. Amazingly, before the group left, Popov—the non-Christian—proposed establishing a fund for the church that was launched as a Sunday school in the classroom of a teacher at Lyceum #31. She had been one of the Easter Sunday converts.

Sensing that something remarkable had taken place in Chelyabinsk, Norman Patton, Missionary Board president; James Albrecht, regional director; and several others traveled to Chelyabinsk in September to follow up. Then, in January 1993, South Lake Wales Church, Lake Wales, Florida, released its pastor, Edward Nelson, for a three-month special assignment to disciple new believers, begin a Bible-training program for teachers, and continue building on the foundation laid by Shaner's team. Having started with twenty people, Nelson left a group of nearly one hundred gathering regularly for worship.

The CoMission Challenge

It was obvious that Russians were not the only people being stirred by the Spirit of God. After Board President Patton visited Chelyabinsk in September 1992, nothing was ever the same again, either in the Missionary Board or in the church at large. Fifteen years later, Patton says leading the Board to involvement in Russia was one of the best calls he ever made as president. Actually, it was less a visionary call than a simple matter of obedience.

"I was invited to attend a conference in Phoenix, Arizona, in January 1993," Patton wrote of his first experience with CoMission, an organization formed by eighty-seven mission agencies that joined forces to evangelize the former Soviet Union. "Along with several hundred other missions leaders and pastors, I was moved by what God could do through us if we were obedient to him."[45]

Patton declares, "It was a risky adventure. The Missionary Board had no money and we were actually in deficit spending. Intellectually, I knew we could not get involved for lack of funds. However, I felt strongly that God was telling me that we should be a part of this great opportunity. After arguing with God as to why we could not be a part, I finally gave in and signed for the Church of God Missionary Board to send thirty special assignment missionaries (SAMs) for a one-year assignment. Later, I signed up for twenty more, making a total of fifty. I had no idea at the time how this would happen."[46]

But God knew. Even though Patton was given only fifteen minutes in the next General Assembly meeting to present the idea, "God's idea caught on, and over the next five years we sent forty-eight SAMs and two full-time career missionaries to Chelyabinsk. We were one of the few organizations of CoMission that established a church, and it is doing well today under Russian leadership."[47]

Celebrating "one of the most successful mission ventures ever launched by the Missionary Board," James Albrecht, then interim regional director for Europe/C.I.S., reported amazing results achieved by CoMission: more than two thousand Americans were deployed in the period from 1993 to 1998; 136 educational convocations for forty-two thousand public school teachers in almost all major cities of the Commonwealth of Independent States; an ethics and morality curriculum based upon the Ten Commandments and Jesus' teachings shared with more than ten million students; and thousands of decisions for Christ.[48]

For the Church of God specifically, working in Chelyabinsk and Meoss, a mining city of two hundred thousand people some sixty miles away, the investment of three-quarters of a million dollars before its final CoMission team was deployed in July 1996 was a significant affirmation that God accomplishes what is humanly impossible when his servants are obedient. Moreover, the new congregation in Chelyabinsk had moved to three different locations by 1996, each time because it had outgrown its previous quarters. Missionaries Kelley and Rhonda Philips were mentoring two pastors in training and other lay leaders who were directing a large children's ministry, small groups and discipleship, music, an orphanage outreach, and all other church ministries. These would be able to continue leading the church in the future, no matter what might happen.

Indeed, some dark clouds were appearing on the horizon. Orlo Kretlow, team leader of the 1995–96 CoMission SAM delegation, reported, "We are told that the Communist party is gaining strength, especially among the elderly who vote. They are promising to take the country back ten years to the 'good old days.' Nationalists are gaining strength and promise a return to the days of the Czars. The Orthodox Church is growing in power and putting pressure on Parliament to expel all parachurch groups (including evangelicals). CoMissioners are told to be prepared to leave…"[49]

But God was not finished with the Chelyabinsk miracle. In December 1995, the church was granted official government registration. At the same time, Albrecht and Philips met with Slava Tarasov, Chelyabinsk's mayor, and Vadim Kespikov, director of education, and signed a new ten-year Protocol Agreement that would permit the Church of God to continue and even to expand its ministries in the city. "You Americans have brought a spirit of hope to our people. Thank you for coming," Mayor Tarasova commended the Missionary Board representatives at the protocol signing.[50]

Patton, however, was thanking God: "God has helped me to understand, 'When I give you a vision of what I want done, trust me to bring it to completion.' He has done it in an amazing way, and so many persons have been obedient to him to bring about this ministry. Thank you, Lord, for stretching my faith and vision in Phoenix."[51]

Lessons from Russia

What resulted from the open doors in Russia and what lessons could the Church of God learn for future mission involvement? James Albrecht shares his observations while declaring that the Russia miracle was the most challenging and energizing project in his nineteen-year mission career.

> God opened the door in Russia after seventy years of near closure to Western influence and Christianity. This began fermenting some years before, but exploded in November 1989. It was almost an avalanche of openness to the world never seen before in Russia. There was a great hunger in the Russian soul for freedom of expression, freedom of religion, and freedom to know foreigners, especially Americans.
>
> The [North American] church was mentally and spiritually ready for this open door. Prayers for the people of Russia had been offered for all the years of Communistic domination. We were ready to share the Good News at this strategic time. At the same time, there was a newfound excitement at the possibilities…of sharing the gospel with a spiritually starved nation. There was also a realization that this was a window of time with perhaps a five-year span of opportunity. It was act now while the door is open.
>
> There was a bold new plan and strategy that was interdenominational and international. The leaders of the CoMission were all full-time directors of some of the largest Christian ministries in the world.[52] They gave freely of their time and energy to see this project succeed. As a representative of the Missionary Board, I had the privilege to join CoMission Executive Committee meetings… There was a deep spiritual tone to all of these meetings. There was a sense of awe that God was working far beyond what we could ask

or think. As a result, the Church of God was mobilized to action as never before in our history.

It is a God-gift that when the CoMission effort ended after five years of Missionary Board involvement, every bill was paid, every missionary had been supported and returned home safely (with the exception of the Philips family who remained to continue nurturing the new church), and the finance department reported to me that there was a surplus of some $10,000 in the Board treasury, funds that had been raised to support CoMission teams.

All of this says to me that when God is in our plans, we need to make them big. The lasting success of the CoMission project is not due to any one individual or group of individuals. For the Church of God, it started with Mark Shaner in leading the first delegations to Chelyabinsk and eventually included the support of the total church. The German Church of God also had a role. With the enthusiastic assistance of Walentin Schüle, the work was given a substantial push as the German Church constructed a building in the Omsk region of Russia (at the fringe of the Artic Circle) and has cooperated well with our own mission. This was a providential moment in time when God lit a fire that is still burning.[53]

At the Halfway Mark

That the opening up of Russia to the teaching of Christian morality and ethics in the public schools had captured the excitement and enthusiasm of the church is evident by the funding and sending of forty-eight special assignment missionaries (SAMs) during a five-year period—a significant display of support by the Church of God in North America. While this was celebrated, some voices expressed dismay that this unexpected missions opportunity might pull the church away from its special emphasis for the decade, "Africa in the '90s."

Nevertheless, at the halfway mark in the decade, the Missionary Board had good news to report of advances in Africa. The launching of the All Africa Leaders Consultation (AALC) had resulted in increased cooperation among African leaders, and four new countries had been entered: Malawi, 1992; Côte d'Ivoire, 1992 (but officially registered in 1997); Zimbabwe, 1992; and Mozambique, 1994. The church in Uganda also had moved across the border into Southern Sudan, where it had planted Church of God congregations, while South Africa and Zambia had begun reaching out into Namibia, a new nation that gained independence from South Africa in 1990.

Other positive markers included the Bibles for Africa campaign through which the church gave nearly $250,000 to purchase Bibles for both Africa and Russia. When the campaign concluded in November 1992, approximately eighty thousand Bibles had been purchased for Africa, including fifteen thousand in Arabic for the Egyptian church to distribute. Another eighty thousand New Testaments were given away in Russia by CoMission teams.

Midway through the decade, Robert Edwards, regional director, reported "tremendous pockets of growth." These were evident in Zaire (ninety-three new congregations), Zambia (sixty congregations and 4,820 new Christians), and Zimbabwe (thirty-nine congregations and 1,980 believers added, a near doubling of the Zimbabwean church in 1994–95 alone). Additionally, more than a thousand believers had been added in Rwanda despite the horrific genocide that had divided the church between those who fled to neighboring Zaire and those who later returned to their homes.

Commenting on the positive church growth, Edwards also noted that the sizeable increase in Zambia and Zimbabwe "is attributed directly to the efforts and relationships of Stan and Marion Hoffman and the national leaders they have raised up." He also commended Mianitse Kyambali, national leader in Zaire, for the growth in that nation despite "extremely difficult conditions."[54] At mid-decade, Kenya continued as the largest Church of God on the continent with more than half the total number of Christians continentally. However, Zaire had overtaken Kenya in numbers of congregations—655 to 531.

At the same time, the new urban emphasis that Missionary Board President Norman Patton had outlined in 1989 was also being realized. Since the 1990s decade thrust had begun, Church of God congregations had been planted in six major urban areas in Africa.[55] "This is a shift for Church of God missions," Patton admitted, pointing out that the Missionary Board must reach into exploding urban centers to have any transforming effect on the rapidly changing world. "In years past, we've been primarily a ministry to the rural segments of the world."[56]

Nevertheless, Patton also took pains to underline that the Board was not forsaking its more traditional rural outreaches. "We're not going to do one at the expense of the other; we're going to do both at the same time," he declared as he outlined a plan to target an unreached peoples group.[57] By 1995, this work was underway with the Maasai tribe in rural Tanzania. Other encouraging reports were coming from Kima International School of Theology (KIST), located in rural Kenya. These two emphases—primary evangelism and leadership training—were so successful that they will be discussed individually.

A New Evangelistic Thrust: the Maasai

Living up to his promise not to abandon rural areas for the world's rapidly increasing urban populations, the Missionary Board president had an exciting plan for a new evangelistic thrust to the Maasai in Kenya and Tanzania. Spearheading this focus to the largely pastoral and animistic tribe would be Donald and Paula Riley, new missionaries who moved to Kenya in July 1993. Soon they began learning the language and culture of the Maasai, not from a classroom, but while living among the people themselves—an innovative approach that the Missionary Board was employing for the first time. Before they completed their year of language and cultural acquisition in Kenya in August 1994, Don traveled twice with Eliazer Mdobi, Tanzanian national leader, and Robert Edwards, regional director, to survey areas of possible ministry. Eventually, they settled on a locale in north central Tanzania so remote that Don joked that they "were not called to the road less traveled, but to the road never traveled."[58]

A year later, the Rileys were living in the remote village of Gelai Meru-Goi in a house built by a work camp from South Meridian Church, Anderson. Excitement was growing, thanks to the responsiveness of villagers to a showing of the *Jesus* film in the Maa language and because Aaron and Cindy Sprunger and their three daughters had been commissioned in June 1995 as the second family for the Maasai Ministry Team. Moving to Tanzania in February 1996, the Sprungers were joined by Chuck and Lisa Dodd in May 1997, seconded as special assignment missionaries (SAMs) from Christian Veterinary Mission. Chuck, a veterinarian, taught animal health care and land management practices while Lisa discipled women and taught literacy to children.

But for all the excitement, life was not easy in this isolated district, especially for Christian missionaries wanting to evangelize in an area relatively untouched by the gospel. Battle lines were being drawn, and the Rileys began experiencing spiritual warfare in many forms, including the following:

> An exciting season of prayer occurred when we consecrated the hillside upon which we reside as a sanctuary—a place where our family is spiritually protected from attack and where all who enter will sense the very presence of God.
>
> It was but a short time later that the enemy began to fight back. The battle was waged physically in the form of pain in Don's chest. Uncertain what was happening, Don lay down, but when the pain continued to increase, he called for help. God revealed to us all what was occurring. Everyone joined in the battle, praying until 1:00 AM when the pain abruptly left. The sweet peace which accompanies the presence of the Holy Spirit was all that remained.
>
> The next day, Don remarked that his chest felt wounded, as if pierced by a knife. With time, this pain disappeared, but we were left with an understanding of the reality of spiritual warfare."[59]

Despite great challenges, God was faithful and stories began to be told of conversions, baptisms, and changed lives—in addition to trials also faced by new Christians. The testimony of one of the earliest new believers, Menya Tatiya, follows:

> Early one Sunday morning we visited Menya Tatiya's village. There we saw two of his cattle literally starving. His sheep and goats were also gaunt and lean. He had asked the visiting veterinarian what was wrong with them. It was hard to tell him medicine wouldn't help. There is no water anywhere for it is the dry season.
>
> In past dry seasons, Menya Tatiya, like all Maasai, moved his family and cattle to a place of water. This year he remained in this "dry and thirsty land" so that his family might hear and know the Word of God. Among his animals, there is not one healthy enough to be an acceptable sacrifice to God. Yet this man truly understands what it means to worship God, and his scrawny animals are a beautiful and pleasing sacrifice.

Last week Menya Tatiya was confronted by a small group of unbelievers who chastised him for giving away Maasai land to the "white men" who are using the land from which to teach about the Christian God. Before these community leaders, he stood firm, sharing his love for God and his commitment to serving him. He then turned his back on his accusers and told them to strike him down if they must, for he knew he would go to heaven to be with his Father. Shamed, his tormenters withdrew their threats and assured him of their support.

Menya Tatiya is not a hero. He is just a man who loves Jesus Christ with all his heart. He is a Maasai who has taught me about sacrifice and about standing firm upon the Rock, no matter what the cost.[60]

Without doubt, the novelty of such cutting edge ministry captured the imagination and support of the church in North America. This was seen through eager participation in work camps and increased support of designated projects, sometimes beyond the upper limit caps determined by World Service. This would prove to be an increasingly sensitive and difficult topic for missionaries and churches that wished to support their ministries throughout the remainder of the decade and into the 2000s.

Although no missionaries were resident among the Maasai after 2006, the work continues. It includes two healthy churches (one located in Gelai village, pastored by two Maasai graduates of Babati Bible School, and the other led by an evangelist studying in the TEE program); a literacy program for children launched and led by two other Maasai who studied in Babati for two years; and sponsorships through Children of Promise. The former missionary house in Gelai is being maintained to allow Tanzania national church leaders, Children of Promise and TEE staff, and others to make occasional visits to encourage and fellowship with the Maasai in that remote region.

Kima International School of Theology

Among the goals articulated at the 1990 All Africa Leaders Consultation was developing a top quality theological school on the continent. Kima Theological College, in western Kenya, had been educating Church of God pastors since 1962.[61] But all was not as well as a forty-year history would appear. Facilities on the campus were rundown, finances were in disarray, and the need for a more qualified faculty that could attract a higher caliber and greater number of students caused some to wonder whether the school had any hope for the future.

The situation began to change during an October 1993 Africa visit by Norman Patton when the Missionary Board president issued a challenge: "Join forces together to create a fully accredited theological school. This school should serve the church's need for leadership throughout English-speaking Africa."[62]

African leaders were keen to accept the challenge. As a result, the Task Force for Theological Education in Africa (TFTEA) was created. The multinational group began its assignment that same year, putting together "a plan for an international school with a distinct African flavor."[63] With the Kima Theological College campus donated by the Kenyan church and financial commitments made by the Missionary Board and church leaders from Kenya, Tanzania, and Uganda, the future of the new school was hopeful indeed. Unique to the school's setup was its administration by a joint Board of Governors consisting of leaders from the three East African churches, the Missionary Board president, the regional director, and representatives of several other Church of God bodies (Anderson University; Fritzlar Bible College, Germany; Gardner College, Canada; and Women of the Church of God). This Board of Governors rather than a single church would own the institution, adding to the optimism about the future of Kima International School of Theology (KIST), as it was renamed on March 25, 1995.

Serving as a transition team, missionaries Jim and Mary Ann Hawkins and Jim and Dorothy Sharp were on campus by April 1995. In August, they welcomed Steve and Diane Rennick when Steve became the new institution's first principal. When the school opened its doors on September 4, 1995, five African nations were represented in the student body. During the first year of operation—which ended in the black financially—three work camps from the United States prepared the campus for its opening, developed a functioning water system for the dormitory and dining hall, and revitalized two faculty houses, enabling them to be utilized starting in September 1996.

Shortly into his tenure as principal, Rennick unveiled an ambitious ten-year plan to continue the school's development. Called the "KIST

Initiative," the proposal included developing both an endowment ($5,000 annually for the next decade) and campus facilities, one of which was a forty-by-seventy-foot library. A generous bequest from Auglaize Chapel Church of God, Oakwood, Ohio, helped expand its holdings to ten thousand volumes. Work camps would also be utilized to create a computer lab, build a woman's dormitory, and construct two apartment buildings for married students.

Another area of development was beginning some self-help projects, one prerequisite for accreditation by ACTEA (Accrediting Council for Theological Education Africa) to make the school 51 percent financially self-reliant. This condition was met through a poultry project to supply meat and eggs, a bakery, and dairy farming, with all profits becoming sustainable support for the school. "Our leadership and theological training school at Kima is succeeding beyond our expectations," reported Bob Edwards, regional director, in his 1996–97 annual report.[64]

Looking back on their years at KIST, Rennick declares,

> The early days were very lean with only twenty-eight students and four teachers. But the student body posted record enrollment each year for the next seven years. The curriculum grew from offering [only] an advanced diploma to include a bachelor of arts in Bible/Theology. Faculty were developed from within the school as well as recruited from around the Church of God in East Africa. Some twenty-four work camps with more than 300 people came from the United States, and the entire campus of eleven dilapidated buildings was renovated and fourteen new buildings were built. A scholarship endowment of $100,000 was established to subsidize tuition.
>
> When we departed in 2002, KIST was debt-free; had a nice campus; was recognized by other church groups who utilized the school for their future pastors, including the Free Methodist and Quaker churches; and had graduated more than 100 men and women into various forms of ministry. We had set an initial ten-year plan that was accomplished in the first four years. So we set another ten-year plan that was realized in the next three years. The school had been in a sprint, and it was time for fresh leadership. Don and Chris Smith answered the call and we willingly and excitedly embraced them."[65]

The good news continues. During commencement exercises on July 29, 2007, thirty-four students received diplomas, making a total of 273 KIST graduates in twelve years who are now carrying out assignments in pastoring, teaching, school administration, chaplaincy, church planting, and national church leadership. A continuing healthy student body of 114 individuals from four nations testifies that opportunity for a premier theological education in Africa emerged as one of the most far-reaching results of the decade of special emphasis on Africa.

Opening Doors for Reconciliation and Partnership

Perhaps one of the most surprising outcomes of "Africa in the '90s" did not occur on the continent at all. Criticisms of the program had been voiced as early as the 1991 annual Missionary Board meetings when Board member Samuel Hines probed, "Have we really done what we need to do in Africa?" Responding, the Board directed President Patton "to develop specific initiates during the next twelve months designed to expand the ethnic and cultural diversity of the Missionary Board employees and ministry appeal."[66]

Consequently, the Board began taking intentional steps to draw the National Association of the Church of God into the "Africa in the '90s" promotional effort. The president also began taking his staff of vice presidents to West Middlesex, Pennsylvania, to meet with the National Association governing board, participate in the National Association annual summer convention, and promote racial reconciliation. "The National Association leadership appreciated it and said it was the first time Anderson came to them and they did not have to go to Anderson," Patton asserts.[67]

At the same time, the Missionary Board made more concerted efforts to recruit African-American special assignment missionaries (SAMs). Success was evidenced when three minority SAMs were commissioned for service in Ghana, Kenya, and Jamaica during the June 1993 International Convention in Anderson.

As word spread of the Board's desire for greater partnership with the National Association, work camps in South Africa, Tanzania, Kenya, and Uganda attracted several African-American congregations in the United States and Bermuda. The first work camp to South Africa in 1991, for example, planted seeds for a continuing sister relationship between Langley

Avenue Church of God, Chicago, its pastors, Noah and Carolyn Reid, and the churches in Cape Town, South Africa, and their leader, Peter Coetzee.

Another constructive outcome came later in the decade in a February 18–21, 1996, meeting at the Buru Buru Church of God, Nairobi, Kenya, between leaders of the National Association, the Missionary Board, members of the African Executive Council, and other African leaders.[68] "The purpose of this long overdue meeting was to form a clear line of communication between the African American Church in the United States and the church in Africa, with reference to the Missionary Board," explained Robert Edwards, regional director, noting that the gathering closed on a high note of reconciliation and partnership with the sharing of Communion and the signing of a tripartite Covenant of Cooperation.

Recalling the impact of the four days of conversations on cooperation, Patton declares,

> We wanted to expose the National Association leadership to the idea that they might partner together [with the Missionary Board] in missions. It was the first time, to my knowledge, that National Association leadership, Missionary Board personnel, and African leaders had been together for such discussions. As a result, some [National Association] churches made one-time contributions to the Kenyan church (for example, to purchase bicycles). The National Association also hosted some African leaders to their convention at West Middlesex (Edward Nkansah, Ghana, and Obed Ochwanyi, Kenya), and Byrum Makokha, from Kenya, later made some connections with National Association pastors. We might have hoped for more, but some good things did happen as a result of the trip. Among these, my relationship with those men was deepened.[69]

Other Examples of Reconciliation and Partnership

According to the Chinese writing of the word *crisis*, crisis is found at the crossroads of danger and opportunity. Surely the same can be said for change. In this "Decade of Change," those instances of change resulting in reconciliation and greater partnership are a beautiful testimony to seizing opportunities rather than to succumbing to dangers. Some of this was accomplished in North America, in improved relationships between the Missionary Board and the National Association, but there are other notable examples.

One such case is the Caribbean island nation of Haiti. Church of God work began there in the late 1960s after Jean Surin trained at Jamaica School of Theology and returned home to plant the church. In 1972, Jamaica sent its first missionary, Phyllis Newby, to the same island. She discovered that Surin had launched an independent work called the Church of God of the United Brethren. It was receiving Missionary Board assistance although it had never actually partnered with the Church of God. Consequently, as Newby's work developed, a rift grew not only between what eventually became three different groups on the island, all claiming to be the Church of God, but also between Newby and the Missionary Board.

Finally, positive changes began when Newby was interviewed during the October 1992 annual Missionary Board meeting. When Samuel Hines asked what she thought could be done to encourage reconciliation and unity among all parties, Newby suggested a meeting between Missionary Board representatives and leaders of the various factions. In fact, President Norman Patton had tried to arrange just such a meeting while in Haiti two months earlier. A reconciliation meeting was convened in Haiti in February 1993, leading Regional Director Victor Babb to conclude, "It would appear that relationships between Sister Newby, the Haitian church, and the Missionary Board are on the mend, and we thank God for this."[70]

Germany was another land ripe for reconciliation. While this had occurred politically when East and West Germany reunited on October 3, 1990, reconciliation was still needed in the church. Despite two world wars, there had been cordial relationships between the Church of God in the United States and Germany going back to 1894 when American missionaries of German backgrounds planted the church in northern Germany. But there was sometimes friction between Germany's Missionswerk and the Missionary Board when their mission activities overlapped. This was especially so in South America and Eastern Europe as countries began opening to the West after the cold war era.

One answer was to promote as many cooperative ventures between the two missionary boards as possible. Patton cited Bulgaria and a much-needed new church building there as one example. Although Klaus Kroeger, national leader of the German Church, described "taking care of the smaller churches throughout Europe, including Denmark, Spain, Holland, Hungary, Bulgaria, England, Switzerland, Ukraine, Italy, and Russia" as part of the mandate of Missionswerk,[71] the Missionary Board also was raising money for projects in Europe through World Concern Fellowship. In the case of Bulgaria, funds generated in North America had been turned over to Missionswerk.

"We're not going to jump in and take the money to Bulgaria ourselves," Patton declared. "We're going to give it to the German Board to help with the development of the church in Bulgaria where they've had an interest for a long time. This is a far better type of cooperation than for those of us in the United States to try to do what needs to be done all on our own."[72]

Approaching his retirement in June 1996, James Albrecht commented on the future of effective mission partnerships: "A key ingredient will be a realization that the Missionary Board is no longer the only or principal player in missions, in this region. A large number of highly qualified national leaders are in the forefront of the work. We must work in close consultation with them. We may have more money, but not necessarily more wisdom, for the task in [this] region of the world."[73]

Illustrative of this desire for a close partnership with Germany, Albrecht met regularly with Missionswerk for planning and strategizing in Europe during his nine years as regional director (including two as interim after his retirement). Among other things, this cooperation resulted in the Missionary Board partnering with Missionswerk to build or buy three church facilities in Bulgaria and to assist the church in Hungary and Spain.

From Kroeger's perspective, the cause of reconciliation and partnership were strengthened when Robert and Janet Edwards moved to Germany in September 1998 as the new regional directors for the Europe–Middle East region. Subsequently, Edwards wrote an agreement that he presented to Missionswerk. It was not their suggestion, nor did the Germans reciprocate with a similar agreement, but Edwards did begin receiving reports from Missionswerk meetings. In the agreement, the new regional director pledged full cooperation in working with the German church where neither party is over nor under the other, to report in writing to Kroeger about all his travels, and that he would not visit any country "in which they have strong missions connections without first contacting them."[74]

As a result, the regional director was pleased to report, "Relations have been very good with the leaders and pastors, and we are learning to work together, especially in Bulgaria and Russia."[75] A tangible sign of the new cooperative spirit was the joint agreement made by the two sending agencies in April 1999 to support a new outreach in Moscow. Later, in 2007, the next regional coordinators for Europe and the Middle East, Kelley and Rhonda Philips moved to Berlin at the invitation of the German church to help launch an international Church of God congregation there. Additionally, another cooperative partnership forged in 2007 sent German missionary Manuel Killisch to Argentina. Reconciliation was reaping the bountiful fruit of partnership.

How the Church Grew

Fruitful partnerships were among the means by which God was growing his church. The Missionary Board long had emphasized training leaders and supporting them to carry out the work in their own countries. In 1994, the Board was underwriting the ministry of 450 pastors and national leaders around the world in amounts ranging from five dollars a month to full support. One of these individuals was India's Borman Roy Sohkhia, who was helping the churches in Bangladesh and Sri Lanka through a partnership with the church in Meghalaya, India, and the Missionary Board.[76]

Other partnerships included those with the Inter-American Conference, chaired by Victor Ruzak of Argentina. The Conference commissioned Narciso Zamora and his family as missionaries to Chile in 1993 in a cooperative effort with the Missionary Board. By 1994, six couples from Latin America were serving in countries other than their country of origin in the growing partnership effort.

The church in the Caribbean–Atlantic was also an increasingly active partner. In 1994, the North Shore Church in Bermuda helped support five churches in Africa, missionaries in Panama and Haiti, and the Caribbean–Atlantic Assembly, giving well over $50,000 to missions that year—"a record giving amount to missions approaching our goal of 10 percent of our income to be tithed to home and foreign missions," according to missionary pastor Vernon Lambe.[77] Even tiny Curaçao sent checks in 1995 to Haiti, West Indies Theological College, and the Missionary Board for its work among the Maasai, a ministry also supported by Barbados in 1996. Indeed, such partnerships in many parts of the world were helping the church grow.

But God specialized in growing his church in many ways. His methodology was as different as the geographic locations in which he worked. Some examples follow.

In 1993, Stanley and Marion Hoffman relocated to Zambia after twenty-seven years in East Africa. As in Tanzania and Uganda before, the veteran missionaries trained leaders through theological education by extension (TEE). They also intentionally located churches on national borders in order to enter neighboring countries. But in Zambia they discovered a new key: a ministry of deliverance.

"Although they did not train for this…or desire it, Stan and Marion encounter demon possession in almost every service they hold," explained Robert Edwards, Africa regional director. "Whereas [others] shy away from this spiritual power encounter, Stan has taken the promises of Christ as true and valid…He commands demons to leave and they flee. The positive result has been a legitimacy of the Christian message and openness to the church. Word of what the Lord is doing precedes [their] visits throughout the nation, and the possessed are brought for miles so that the Hoffmans can pray for their deliverance. And so the church grows."[78]

Illustrating the expansion, Edwards noted 135 Zambian congregations and 11,475 members on May 31, 1992. By May 1994, there were 263 congregations and 21,989 constituents. Statistics in 1996 showed even more growth: 47,484 believers and 442 congregations. At the end of the decade, Donald and Paula Riley, new regional directors, reported that Zambia, Mozambique, Zimbabwe, and Angola "all have active, growing church populations due to the efforts of Stan and Marion Hoffman,"[79] who had pioneered the Church of God in each of those nations while working hand-in-hand with African leaders, including Zambia's Afeck Lungu.

In South America, Venezuela was experiencing growth too—despite prophecies of doom. Soon after Lorenzo and Margaretha Mondragon arrived in 1994, the pastors of two of the three Churches of God resigned. Suddenly, the missionaries were responsible for those two congregations and an English-speaking church in Puerto Ordaz. "Soon people from other church groups were predicting that attendance at La Esperanza Church would decline and that the congregation would eventually die," Lorenzo recalled. "These prophecies focused on church growth by human effort alone and on the resignation of a pastor rather than upon God who was still in control."[80]

Stepping in, the Mondragons quickly organized a leadership team for La Esperanza: a woman to pastor the women's group, a youth to lead the young people, and Lorenzo as senior pastor. Shortly thereafter, the church was experiencing revival, beginning with the youth who launched a children's program, choir, and theater ministry. Likewise, the women displayed a passion for evangelism in an active visitation program. Within a year, La Esperanza Church grew to more than two hundred people, the church at El Tigre purchased land, and a work had begun at Puerto La Cruz. During the following year (1996–97), more than sixty new Christians were baptized and the two-year leadership training program launched by the Mondragons enrolled more than thirty students. Soon new work was started among the Guajibo Indian tribe in southern Venezuela.

But the revival-fueled growth was also feeding something else: spiritual warfare. "Just as we were making spiritual progress among the Guajibo…we suffered a car wreck that suspended our Indian ministry for almost a year…Upon our return to Venezuela, our first priority was to reactivate the Indian ministry. It eventually grew from that first tribal congregation to eight village churches, each with its own native pastor and worship tabernacle," Lorenzo shared.[81]

But more difficulty was ahead. Armed men robbed the Mondragons and the San Felix Church twice. Lorenzo also narrowly escaped being kidnapped by three gunmen in front of his house when he jumped on a bus that was passing at just that moment. Despite such trials, there were eighteen Venezuelan Churches of God and more than thirteen hundred believers by 2006, testifying to God's power to expand his church despite all obstacles.

Directly south of Venezuela, across western Brazil, the largest national church in Latin America was growing yet larger. Although the Bolivian Church was generally made up of poor, oppressed Amyara- and Quechua-speaking Andean Indians, church growth was spectacular. Founded in 1963, the church had more than 180 congregations and twelve thousand constituents thirty years later. According to missionary David Miller, this significant growth could be attributed to two fundamental Church of God teachings: holiness and the priesthood of all believers. In the Bolivian church, this translated into congregations led by deacons and elders who also were active in church planting around the country.[82]

Excited about being part of a "people movement" church, Miller shared the story of how one congregation was planted when a peasant farmer walked three days from his village to a market in Huallata, where he could trade seed potatoes for corn.

> A local villager [in Huallata] had suffered from a stomach ailment for two years. Neither the local…folk doctors nor physicians in faraway Cochabamba could relieve the disorder, and the young man was dying. Then Francisco Flores came and told them about Jesus' power to heal. He prayed for the man, and he miraculously recovered.
>
> The villagers wanted to hear more about Jesus, so they prevailed upon Francisco to stay and teach them the gospel. His message struck a chord, and Huallata residents began to accept Christ as their Savior. Francisco and I baptized eleven of them during my visit.[83]

Radio and television also were growing the church. Although Yemen is an Islamic nation where evangelism is prohibited, radio was achieving what missionaries could not. Fouad Melki, Lebanese church leader, testified about the conversion of a young Yemeni Muslim who listened to the Arabic–language program of the Christian Brotherhood Hour (CBH) in 1994. Later, in 1995, a new evangelical congregation in Ukraine, led by Pastor Anatolij Derkatsch, affiliated with the German Church of God through hearing the Russian-language broadcast and speaker Walentin Schüle.

In 1984, an Indian Hindu temple caretaker named Subodh Rana chanced upon the Oriya-language CBH program. Captivated, he asked for a New Testament, participated with his wife in a seeker's conference offered to radio listeners, and accepted Christ despite severe persecution. Between 1988 and 1995, Rana planted six churches whose members were, as he had been, converted from Hinduism.[84]

By the end of the decade, CBH was a part of the Outreach Ministries Team of Church of God Ministries, along with Global Missions (formerly the Missionary Board). The international church was growing through weekly broadcasts in eight languages: English, Spanish, Portuguese, Oriya,

Swahili, Russian, Arabic, and Mandarin Chinese. "The radio ministry is a great tool for missions and church planting," asserted Asim Das, Oriya-language speaker. "Reaching remote parts, it is doing its work. It is not returning void."[85]

Broadcasting was a tool also employed in Bermuda, where Vernon and Ruth Ann Lambe had been missionaries since 1975. Together they led the North Shore congregation in such significant church growth that by 1997, it was one of the largest congregations on the island and was constructing a new one-thousand-seat sanctuary. The church utilized a variety of outreach methods, including a weekly prime-time television program with Vernon as speaker and a model preschool program directed by Ruth Ann.

Education also was an outreach tool in nearby Haiti. There the church was growing at the fastest rate in the entire Caribbean–Atlantic region according to Victor Babb, regional director. By 1994, there were fifteen thousand Christians in Haiti's 122 Churches of God, all of which had schools that were educating more than fourteen thousand island children. By the end of the decade, 160 churches were teaching thirty thousand children, and Haitians were coming to the Lord even daily. These included four practitioners of voodoo who, along with other family members, were converted in the village church in St. Ard. There twenty-seven people were added to the church in only one month.[86]

Some Challenges of the 1990s

Everyone loves stories of victory. Especially for missionaries raising personal support and field budgets, reports highlighting good news were vital. But the church does not always grow, and its ministry is not always validated by happily-ever-after endings. If the truth were known, some of the challenges faced by missionaries and their Board during the 1990s verged on overwhelming.

There were health issues. Among these was Russ Skaggs's four-year battle with cancer. A second-generation missionary to Egypt (his parents, Wilbur and Evelyn, served there from 1945–58), Russ and his wife Sharon had followed their footsteps in that nation from 1981 until his death on April 27, 1993. Elsewhere, Karvin and Sandra Adams submitted their resignation from Ecuador in 1996, primarily because of Sandra's poor health.

Likewise, Ben and Marge Chandler faced health crises beginning in 1996 when Marge was diagnosed with a brain tumor during their home assignment from Australia. In 1997, cancer was discovered. Although she recovered from both, these health considerations ended their missionary tenure in 1998.

There were leadership issues. Hong Kong seemed to have had its share of such challenges ever since the church was first organized in 1979. Two years later, Michael and Debra Kinner were deployed to help the fledgling group. They recruited K. K. and Angela Mak as the first national pastors. But plans changed with the Mak family's emigration to the United States in 1993, two years after the Kinners had left to become regional directors for Asia. Subsequently, Alan Reed was chosen by the church's board of directors to fill Mak's position, and the leadership search continued. Johnny Yui, the next Chinese pastor, began his ministry in September 1995 but resigned in May 1997. Then, the Reed family did not return following their 1995–96 home assignment.

Not until July 1999 was the challenging leadership issue finally resolved with the installation of Edmund Leung, a young man saved and nurtured in the Hong Kong church. One year later, career missionaries Patrick and Jamie Nachtigall joined the growing ministry team, helping bring stability to the congregation that, by age, seemed more like a youth group.[87] Soon an innovative pastors-in-training program was experiencing success. By 2005, there were fourteen cell groups and a membership nearing 150 people. The congregation had long since outgrown its site and was in a building fund campaign that culminated with a January 6, 2008, victory worship service in a new facility still being renovated.

Although the Church of God preaches unity, the issue of practicing what it preaches challenged many countries, including India. Not only had the church's national assembly disbanded years earlier, but there were regional conflicts as well. Problems in South India, for example, prompted Norman Patton and Kinner to travel there in January 1992 to facilitate reconciliation between the larger group, led by George Tharakan, and a smaller, breakaway group. Unfortunately, little headway was made, although the situation looked more positive by the end of the decade with the scheduling of an All-India Assembly meeting in Cuttack in November 1999.

In addition to India and Haiti, mentioned earlier in this chapter, the Philippines also struggled with unity issues. Tension between two factions, led by Eddie Viray and Rolando Bacani, escalated during 1993–94. With both groups in contact with congregations in the United States, there was confusion over which was the real Church of God in the Philippines. By 1998, the Philippine general assembly had disbanded. Both factions were conducting their own meetings and ministries, and there was little communication between the two. The situation was a difficult one for Kinner, dialoguing with both men and trying hard to restore unity in the Philippines.

Panama had its own unity problems. When Fransico Pitty retired in 1992, Nicolas Alvarado was elected as national coordinator. However, the transition was rocky and conflicts emerged. In addition to this, missionary Amanda Ricketts and Alvarado were dating and eventually married, after which Ricketts resigned from the Missionary Board. Even after a new national coordinator was elected in 1994, problems continued. In 1997, Johnny Snyder, Latin America regional director, finally sent a letter to Panama discontinuing contact between the Board and Alvarado.

Sometimes challenges resulted in decisions to part ways rather than to unify. As early as 1989, when Patton and Robert Edwards, Africa regional director, first visited Cameroon, there were questions about the authenticity of the Church of God there. By 1994–95, the Board determined to disassociate itself with that country. At the same time, it separated from the work in Malawi after Edwards traveled there in May 1995 to investigate charges against the national leader, Enos Didimu. When the allegations proved generally true, the regional director recommended disassociation. During 1997–98, Nigeria also was dropped from the Missionary Board's listing of nations where the Church of God was working after repeated unsuccessful attempts to correspond with the church's leadership.

In other instances, relationships with the Church of God were broken by nationals themselves, as in Nepal. Kinner, in his 1992–93 regional director report, shared the discouraging news that one of the eight congregations there had chosen to affiliate with another group. Nevertheless, thirty-six people were baptized in 1991, with another fifty-three the following year, despite the difficulty of evangelizing in the Hindu kingdom.

Another thorny situation faced the Board in Uruguay. Although the Church of God had been planted there in 1970, Nehiel and Joanna Rojas were the first resident missionaries deployed by the Board in 1983. Helping three small and geographically distant congregations in the strongly atheistic nation was no easy task for them, and 1991 was an especially difficult year. Threats on Nehiel's life by a disgruntled employee of Christ Church in Montevideo had led to his resignation as pastor. Their teenage son Johnny was abducted in May and held at knife point for several hours. (Thankfully, he was released without injury.) Eventually, personal safety issues, liability, and other considerations led the Missionary Board to decide in its June 1992 meeting to recall the family. Regional Director Willi Kant and David Reames, vice president for personnel, were dispatched to convey the decision and the Rojas family returned to the United States in July.

But all was not well. The Rojases did not agree with the decision and felt that it had been made with little input from them. Subsequent Missionary Board discussions centered upon whether the recall had set a dangerous precedent for contradicting policy, which stated that missionaries were free to determine how they would respond to crisis situations. (As an example, John and Jodie Ackerman had elected not to evacuate Haiti in 1991 along with other missionaries.) The matter was finally resolved in the October 1993 annual meetings when the Board went on record to declare that it did have the power to override a missionary's decision and to order a missionary to evacuate.[88]

Additional challenges faced the church in Latin America, where the Church of God was working in twenty countries by 1992–93. Among these, Peru, Colombia, and Venezuela had become centers of intense terrorist activity. By the mid-2000s, the conflicts in Colombia, now in their fourth decade, were claiming thousands of lives annually, including Church of God pastors and members. David Miller, regional coordinator, described the troubled Putumayo region where the church was primarily located as "a problematic battleground between leftist guerrillas, paramilitary groups, and the nation's armed forces."[89] On top of this, national leader Angel Pinto had been detained by guerrillas and threatened with death.

Finances were another test. The economic situations in some Latin American countries were taxing the church to the brink. In Brazil, for example, inflation reached 1,500 percent during 1992–93. And in the economically-depressed Caribbean–Atlantic region, unemployment was at record highs—on many islands reaching 35 to 50 percent.[90]

Of course, finances were not a new challenge for the Missionary Board. Raising funds and helping North America to be enthusiastic about supporting outreach in locations where the church was small or not growing was a difficult proposition. Donald Johnson, serving in retirement as interim Middle East regional director, elaborated:

> We have perhaps the best opportunity we have had in three decades to focus strongly on the Middle East. For years, we have had to combat the "souls for dollar" issue where North American mission boards were challenged to put their dollars into those areas where the greatest response was anticipated. As a result, today, across those same boards' budgets, [only] point six percent of the dollars spent are spent in the [world's] least evangelized, resistant fields.
>
> Missiologists have begun to emphasize the "whole world" understanding of the biblical mandate of missions, and enormous energy is going into efforts to recognize the 10/40 Window (10 degrees north to 40 degrees north of the Equator, West Africa east to and including Japan) as a focus. Unreached people are a priority, and the Missionary Board has taken the challenge and has identified both the Maasai and the Nubian people groups [Tanzania and Egypt, respectively] as target populations...
>
> The work will be slow, and here is where considerable education must be done in the North American church. We have the opportunity to help our people recognize that we are about God's mission and we leave the mathematics to him. We are to be obedient to the biblical mandate and faithful in our response to it.[91]

Financial Strategies

Although Donald Johnson called for thinking "collaterally in a new paradigm" with regard to supporting missions, finances had always been a major concern. Explaining the dilemma, Norman Patton declared, "I am torn between entering more countries and doing a better job where we are presently ministering. At the present financial level, when another country is entered, the pie of finance is merely sliced thinner. Yet, there are projections by countries to push forward in church planting endeavors across borders. We thank the Lord for what is happening, but the financial pressure continues to be felt by requests for needed ministry funds."[92]

Increasingly, Darrell Smith was looking for new sources of income in his role as vice president for finance and development. One of the first avenues he created was the Missionary Endowment Foundation (MEF) in 1993. Participation was offered through cash gifts to develop MEF, a charitable life insurance program, with gifting of the premium to the Missionary Board, and a real estate gifts plan. In 1994, with formal requests for new missionaries from twenty countries but without funds to send them, the Board resolved that endowment monies must be used exclusively for putting new career missionaries on the field. Anticipation was high as retired missionaries Nathan and Ann Smith were tapped as MEF coordinators. Unfortunately, the program did not achieve its intended results.

Another development program was called Preparers of the Path. Established in December 1993, this new group of supporters was dedicated to donating $100 a year to ensure that missionaries were fully funded and able to continue their overseas ministries. With a goal of recruiting more than six thousand supporters, there was excitement when, after only two months of enlistment efforts, individuals in 220 congregations had already given more than $52,000. By June 1996, there were 1,107 Preparers of the Path, who had given $74,465 during the 1995–96 fiscal year.

Next was the creation of the Global Missions Network on October 6, 1994. Designed to liaise between the Missionary Board, local congregations, and individuals, the network utilized Global Missions representatives, located in all states and/or regions, to help educate the church about overseas missionary activity and needs, with more regular and special giving the expected outcome. Russell and Ethel Noss, retired pastors and former special assignment missionaries in Latin America, became the first two of thirty-two Global Missions representatives spread across the United States and Canada by June 1996.

Smith also envisioned a group of supporting congregations, each called a Global Missions Church, to partner with specific national ministries in covenants of prayer and financial support. This program, which encouraged supporters to make eyewitness visits to their international partner churches, was a forerunner of Project Link, the project support program first explained to the church during the 2005 North American Convention.

Technology Touches the Missions Enterprise

As Darrell Smith often stressed in his development work, nurturing personal relationships was a key to effective fundraising, and timely communications were at the heart of relationship building. Hand-written letters carried around the world by ship or across the United States by rail had given way to letters typed on manual machines. Later, electric typewriters created letters delivered by airplane or facsimile machine.

As technology developed more rapidly, there were many plusses for missions. In his 1991–92 President's Annual Report, Norman Patton shared excitedly that a laser printer and the WordPerfect word-processing program had been installed in the offices. After two days of computer training for everyone, greater office productivity was anticipated. One year later, a new financial software system was assisting with the increased workload, but this was already operating at nearly 98 percent capacity by the 1993–94 report.

Technology also was having an increased impact on the sometimes overwhelming task of communicating with the church at home and internationally. "Communication will never be perfect because people are imperfect, but we must keep trying to do our best," Patton instructed, noting in his 1994–95 annual report that the Missionary Board now had e-mail.

After one year of e-mail, Robert Edwards, Africa regional director, pointed out some of the positive results, including more, better, and faster communications with the world. When supporters could be apprised quickly of needs and victories, vital relationships deepened. However, there was also the down side, he cautioned. These included the absence of a paper trail, decisions and responses expected quickly without adequate time to consider both the tone and consequences of the communication, and actually moving farther away from people while spending more time at a desk.[93]

Sharon Skaggs also voiced some concerns about the negative impact of e-mail on itinerating missionaries. As director of human resources, she noted that home assignment can be very stressful. Not only must missionaries fulfill obligations to families and supporting churches while in North America—in addition to squeezing in medical check-ups—but "e-mail communications make it possible…to manage work on the field while in the States; thus they do not get a break…from their field ministry."[94]

But there was no turning back. During the 1996–97 fiscal year, the Missionary Board became part of the new Church of God Web site. CBH *ViewPoint*, by now a part of Outreach Ministries (along with Global

Missions), went on the Internet in August 1999. The radio broadcast also employed a telephone service operating twenty-four hours a day, seven days a week. Staff members alternated carrying a beeper, enabling them to respond to a call at any time from anywhere in the world. Global Missions soon followed suit. For good and for bad, technology was changing the face of missions.

Structural Change a Critical Reality

In 1909, by action of the General Assembly, the Missionary Board was formed as the second Church of God national agency. For the next ninety years, until 1999, this Board functioned as the governing body for international missions efforts. Although there were changes over the years in both the number of board members and in the titles of appointed and elected officers, the stability and effectiveness of this governing body is well documented.

As the church grew, so did the number of its national agencies and their incorporated boards. In 1987, the General Assembly established a Task Force on Governance and Polity. Its purpose was to analyze the structures by which the Church of God functioned and to make recommendations for change to enhance ministry and mission. By 1988, the Assembly and its Task Force called upon the Executive Council and other units of the church, including the Missionary Board, to address a number of significant concerns. Among these were "a greater sense of partnership and interdependence in our mutual mission and ministry…"[95] The beginnings of structural change for the Church of God had been launched.

The planning for this effort would continue for five years, with a final proposal not being issued until 1992. However, there were some important checkpoints along the way.

Church of God missionaries and missions supporters wanted to be sure that the movement's commitment to worldwide outreach would not be diminished by the restructuring efforts. Therefore, they read carefully a June 1988 statement from the Committee on Long-Range Planning, endorsed by the Executive Council, which attempted to articulate the "Mission of the Church of God." The preamble and focus statement of this document declared:

The mission of the Church of God is to be a caring community of God's covenant people under the Lordship of Jesus Christ and the leadership of the Holy Spirit;

- To proclaim the love of God, through Jesus Christ to all persons;
- To enable persons throughout the world to experience redemptive love in its fullest meaning through the sanctifying power of the Gospel and know Jesus Christ as Savior, Master, and Lord;
- To call persons to holiness and discipleship;
- To equip persons to be servants of Christ in the world;
- To live as citizens of the kingdom of God here and now, work for justice, mercy and peace, and abide in the Christian hope;
- To build up the whole body of Christ in unity.

Although this was intended to speak to the church's mission in its entirety, the only references to the international mission obligation of the Church of God in this statement are found in the use of the words "throughout the world" and "in the world." Several missionary leaders felt the statement implied an international mission for the church, but did not clearly articulate one.

In 1995, Leith Anderson was hired as a consultant by the General Assembly's Leadership Council to bring clarity to the work of the Committee on Governance and Polity. Anderson's recommendations were adopted in concept by the General Assembly in its June 1996 meeting. Subsequent to this, an Implementation Task Force began the work of developing a strategy to realize the changes that had been proposed. The General Assembly then approved the recommendations of the Task Force in June 1997, and that Task Force then became an Implementation Transition Team whose task it was to facilitate the approved strategy.

The General Assembly called for discussion of this strategy in several committee meetings and area assemblies throughout the country, and it became clear that ministers and lay leaders wanted to move forward as quickly as possible to develop a new national structure for the Church of God. On December 31, 1998, the following ministry functions merged into a new entity called Church of God Ministries: the Board of Christian Education, the Mass Communications Board, the Missionary Board, the Home

Missions and Church Growth units of the Board of Church Extension, Vision 2 Grow, and the circulation and publishing work of Warner Press.[96]

As the end of the decade approached, these ministries and those retained under the Ministries Council (formerly the Executive Council) were being organized into three ministry teams: Congregational Ministries, Resource and Linking Ministries, and Outreach Ministries. These teams were structured to function under the supervision of the Ministries Council and its general director, Robert W. Pearson.

That titling this chapter "The Decade of Change" is an accurate summation of the events of 1990–99 is substantiated nowhere more than with the restructuring of the Missionary Board. What had been an incorporated and freestanding board with twenty members and an executive committee, charged by the Church of God to recruit, send, support, and administer missionary personnel around the world, was now Global Missions, a unit within the Outreach Ministries Team, whose director functioned under the Ministries Council of Church of God Ministries and a general director. These were extraordinary changes in terms of the governance of the church's missionary program, and in spite of General Assembly approval, they were not well understood by those who supported missions.

Two critical issues faced the church's international missions staff, missionary personnel, and missions advocates during the restructuring: how financial support for overseas programs might be affected by the merger and the complications of decision making in the absence of an executive committee and a board primarily and specifically concerned with the cross-cultural missionary mandate of the church. These two concerns were continually the focus of field correspondence and contacts from the church in North America. The home office staff found themselves in the difficult position of wanting to be supportive of change and yet having to deal with the concerns and criticisms of a wary public. Because Church of God Ministries leaders were preoccupied with the restructuring, one could argue that missions suffered in the late 1990s. Certainly, the Missionary Board and (subsequently) Global Missions were hard-pressed to maintain the momentum that had been acquired over the previous nine decades.

While there would be further mid-course corrections and fine-tuning of the structure in the upcoming decade of the 2000s—as is always the case in any major restructuring—the learning curve for international missions under a merged corporate structure would continue to be a steep one.

Leadership Changes Follow

Even as technology, politics, and critical social challenges were changing the way the Church of God "did" missions around the world, undoubtedly the most drastic changes were the result of the unification of the various national agencies of the Church of God. Whether this change would be for the better or would reduce the Missionary Board to committee status is a discussion recorded in the Board meeting minutes of October 1992 when President Norman Patton expressed his reservations about the "super board" concept. "If the Missionary Board takes five days and can hardly cover business, how much more effective is one large board for all agencies going to be?" he had mused.[97]

Nevertheless, the June 1997 General Assembly voted to restructure the national church. Reflecting on those days of change, the last Missionary Board president shares:

> I had mixed emotions about restructuring. I could see some real benefits as well as some pitfalls. My greatest fear was how will missions in the Church of God fare in the end? Would missions be a priority in the new system or would it be just another program of the church without much visibility? How could we keep missions on the cutting edge of the church's ministries in the new structure? Would the director of missions have the same ability to make things happen like CoMission in Russia or KIST in Africa? A lot of questions ran through my mind.
>
> I also had questions because the [agency] executives were not actively involved in the [restructuring] process. On occasions, we were brought together for updates and some input. At one point, the staffs of each agency were interviewed by Leith Anderson, the consultant. I remember him saying that any structure will work, [depending] on the leadership. I expressed several times to the Restructuring Committee that we would cooperate fully in the process and, if they felt it necessary, that I would step down from leadership in the new structure. They did not feel that was necessary.
>
> I was not convinced that the old system was as bad as it was made out to be. There were some incorrect perceptions in the church

about how the agencies and leaders got along. I always felt support from my other colleagues. Agencies cooperated, and some worked closely together. I cannot speak for the new structure since I have not been a part of it. There are pros and cons to both structures.[98]

Almost as soon as the restructuring decision was made, questions began to ripple around the world that indicated anxiety on the part of the church at large and significant apprehension within the missionary community about the ramifications of the vote. Indeed, Patton admitted that he was asked if the work of missions would come to an end because of the merger, to which he responded:

> The Board, as we have known it, will no longer exist…[But] please note: Church of God missionary work will continue around the world and will be as effective, and even more so, as in the past. The church is mandated by Jesus to fulfill the Great Commission. The new structure is to facilitate mission and ministry in the local church, and I believe the local church will always demand that evangelism and mission work are part of our assignment. So mission work will not die, and it is not even sick, but HOW we do mission is certainly changing.
>
> As we look to the future, the needs are great and the opportunities unlimited…The future is bright for outreach. Our goal is to partner with the local church, national leaders, and missionaries to evangelize the world for Christ. What a history we have had, BUT, oh what a future is ahead of us![99]

For all his enthusiasm, however, Patton believed it would take new leadership to successfully merge the Missionary Board into Global Missions, Outreach Ministries, and Church of God Ministries, and then to help move the restructured national organization into the future. As a result, he resigned as Missionary Board president and reentered the pastoral ministry at North Webster, Indiana.

On November 1, 1998, Doris Dale became interim Global Missions coordinator in her second stint at leading the missions organization. Recalling her thoughts as she began the assignment, she says, "I knew of the tremendous need for a strong missionary presence in the body through my work at the women's desk, interacting often with the missionary community. I was also sensing very strongly the need for affirming and encouraging all of the national entities, especially the Missionary Board. The time of restructuring was one of the biggest challenges ever faced by our national ministries."[100]

Also new to the team was Michael Curry, who assumed the role of Outreach Ministries team director in February 1999, even while continuing his pastoral work at First Church of God, Evanston, Illinois. At the same time, with the merging of both home and foreign missions agencies in December 1999 under Global Missions, Gilbert Davila was named North America regional director, joining the team of other regional directors: Donald and Paula Riley, Africa; Michael and Debra Kinner, Asia–Pacific; Victor Babb, Caribbean–Atlantic; Robert and Janet Edwards, Europe –Middle East; and Johnny and Paula Snyder, Latin America.

Milestones of the 1990s

Statistics do not tell the whole story, but they can give perspective. As the Church of God entered the "Decade of Change" in 1990, there were a total of 2,389 congregations in North America as compared with 2,838 in the rest of the world. Membership in the United States and Canada was listed as 203,148 people, while 268,484 believers outside North America called the Church of God home.

Significantly, while the Church of God in North America suffered a net loss of 103 congregations and gained only 3,830 believers during the decade, it is astounding to see what happened around the world. Outside North America, there was a substantial 52 percent gain of congregations to a total of 4,320, as well as a 66 percent growth in membership to 445,890 people.[101]

One of the factors for this noteworthy growth was the number of new countries entered. These included Sri Lanka (legally registered in 1990); Côte d'Ivoire (entered in 1992, but work registered in 1997); Malawi and Zimbabwe (both entered in 1992); Chile (1993); Mozambique (1994); Serbia (first Church of God worship service, 1994); New Zealand (1995); and Angola and Cambodia (1998). Whereas the Church of God was at work in seventy-four countries in 1990, it was ministering in eighty-five countries a decade later.[102]

Certainly another factor was the meritorious service of a sizeable group of career missionaries who had committed for the long haul. Several of these retired during the decade, including Sidney and Jean Johnson, 1992 (36 years in Asia); Kenneth and Sue Jo Good, 1994 (30 years in Korea, Jamaica, Australia, and Tanzania); Magaline Hoops Heusel, 1994 (completing 35 years in Africa); James and Betty Albrecht, 1996 (19 years in the Middle East and Europe, plus two more in an after-retirement interim assignment); Orlo and Carol Kretlow, 1996 (32 years, Japan and Russia); Jim and Dorothy Sharp, 1997 (35 years in Africa, plus two special assignment missionary postings after retirement); Ethel Willard, 1997 (28 years, Hong Kong and the finance department of the home office); and Phil and Phyllis Kinley, 1998 (43 years, Japan).

During the decade, other long-term missionaries were called home—not to North America, but to heaven. These included Emilia Fleenor (October 18, 1990); Rose Zazanis (March 5, 1991); P. K. Jenkins (September 19, 1991); Ruthe Crose (December 2, 1993); and Adam W. Miller (December 22, 1993). Additionally, some national leaders finished their earthly ministries, including P. V. Jacob of South India (June 10, 1991); Eric Gajewski, Germany (1991); Mendoza Taylor, Colombia (1995); Robin Das, Bangladesh (July 26, 1996); and Fouad Melki, Lebanon (July 1997).

CHAPTER 10
A NEW CENTURY
(2000–2009)

In the same way that an artisan weaver has endless possibilities to design a masterpiece from variously colored and textured skeins of thread, so too at the turn of a new century was the Church of God in North America poised at a critical threshold of opportunity. With the recently adopted new national structure still in flux, relationships within North America and around the world were being redefined perhaps as never before. The prospects were unlimited, but the challenge to birth a new work of art from the 120-year-old reformation movement was formidable indeed.

It is also a challenge to describe a tapestry before it is completed. This is the task at hand in composing this book's final chapter in preparation for celebrating one hundred years of organized Church of God missions activity in 2009. At this writing, two years remain in the decade. Nevertheless, some colors and patterns are apparent as the design takes shape, and these will be reported.

This chapter is followed by an essay of observations about the state of the Church of God at this juncture in its history. These are coupled with questions for thought as the missions enterprise enters its second hundred years of ministry. In short, the Church of God in North America in the year 2000 faced a new century, a new structure for missions, and a new challenge to make it work.

At a New Millennium

It was a new century, but even more noteworthy, it was a new millennium. In preparation for the historic dawning, social scientists were busy analyzing data and publishing prognoses for the future. Among these, John Naisbitt and Patricia Aburdene authored a book about ten megatrends they predicted would characterize the final decade of the first millennium. These included a booming global economy, the emergence of free-market socialism, and the rise of the Pacific Rim.[1]

At the same time, Douglas Welch was analyzing the Church of God. A former missionary to Kenya and then associate professor of Christian mission at Anderson University School of Theology, Welch offered some sobering thoughts as the new millennium approached:

> I wonder what we in the Church of God will need to do to meet the challenges of the new millennium. Surely we cannot continue to foster the view that our greatest achievements have been in the past and it is to those "golden days" that we must return. It may be that we have not yet accomplished anything of significance. Perhaps the new millennium will be our opportunity to do so—if it does not find us unprepared.
>
> And what of our missionary outreach? Is it possible that our imperial age structures and systems sentence us to irrelevance? The new millennium is not likely either to praise us or blame us, but to ignore us. And that, as it has been said, is a fate worse than death.[2]

Likewise, Merle Strege, Church of God historian, raised important questions for consideration. Likening the Church of God movement to a patchwork quilt of many practices, representing various theological and social locations and traditions, the Anderson University professor wrote about the challenge of unity among the diversity of quilt patches:

> The challenge may be best expressed in terms of what organizational and structural developments will provide the backing to which the patches are attached. One temptation is to borrow yet another practice, this one from twentieth century American businesses that thought bureaucratic managers are the unifying agent in any corporation. This backing may make us think more like a business or a corporation than a church; it might produce a greater uniformity, driven by management practices, but it may not result in unity which, of course, is a very different reality than uniformity. Here a historian of the church must ask for the assistance of

theologians who will insist that the church's unity rests on the activity of the Holy Spirit rather than administrative technique.[3]

Whether in answer or not to the musings of Welch and Strege, *Church of God Missions* published "Church of God around the World: Still Making a Difference," a listing of eighty-nine countries where the church was ministering in 2000. The international inventory was presented regionally, giving statistics for Africa (13 countries; 2,366 churches; 273,010 believers), Asia–Pacific (21 countries; 1,072 churches; 115,690 believers), Caribbean–Atlantic (14 countries; 334 churches; 41,770 believers), Europe–Middle East (20 countries; 93 churches; 8,233 believers), and Latin America (19 countries; 610 churches; 39,893 believers). Additionally, North America was listed as Canada and the United States, with 2,353 churches and 234,311 believers. Combining statistics from all nations, the Church of God at the millennium was at work through 712,907 believers in 6,828 churches in 89 countries.

At the time, Global Missions had just moved down the street into the new Church of God Ministry Center. Formerly housing the Gospel Trumpet Company and then Warner Press publishing house, the building represented a kind of homecoming for the national church. "We go, in one sense, back to where it all started; back to our beginnings," declared Arthur Kelly, of the Resource and Linking Ministries team.[4] As a part of the newly organized Outreach Ministries team, Global Missions would share the building with Congregational Ministries, Outreach Ministries, Resource and Linking Ministries, Warner Press, and Women of the Church of God.

At the start of a new century and new millennium, the work of Global Missions was being carried out by eighty career missionaries, sixty special assignment missionaries, eleven regional directors, and an Anderson staff of six individuals and support people.[5]

A Regional View: Africa

Although Church of God missionary endeavors in Africa reached back to 1905, there was much forward thinking about the continent at the turn of the twenty-first century. No one was more enthusiastic about the future than regional directors Don and Paula Riley. Among the ministries they highlighted in a January 2000 report was the work in Babati, Tanzania. Only a short time earlier, the rural, north central market town had been home to a small, struggling Bible school that depended upon outside finances, mostly from North America. Now however, through the efforts of Don and Caroline Armstrong, the school was much more self-supporting as students and teachers alike worked side by side to raise much of the necessary food for the growing campus. Along with special assignment missionary Rebekah Good, the Armstrongs also had launched Aldersgate Secondary School in 1998. Within two years, it was running above capacity and had a large facility and land to accommodate future buildings.

In neighboring Uganda, Tim and Colleen Stevenson were involved in a wide variety of ministries. Among other things, Colleen administered several child care programs in Uganda and Zaire, serving more than three thousand children as a representative for Children of Promise, Compassion International, and Kinderhilfswerk of Germany. At the same time, Tim was the Global Missions representative for Uganda, Rwanda, and Congo (DR), and the official representative of Kinderhilfswerk in those nations, as well as in Ethiopia, where the Church of God was attempting to register.

Southwestern Angola also was an open door at the new decade. A man named Jim Doty had been posted to Angola in 1989 by Cabinda Gulf Oil Company. There he met Dulci Fialho de Silva, a missionary from Brazil working with the Igreja Evangelica em Angola. Married in 1997, they learned that the Church of God wanted to launch into Angola and were led to Stan and Marion Hoffman in Zambia. Having already worked tirelessly for nearly a decade to encourage leaders, teach children, build churches, and even preach, the Dotys were eager to help the Church of God, Jim's roots in Texas. "As long as we are here, you will have someone working to build the Church of God in Angola," they eagerly promised.[6]

Côte d'Ivoire also held great promise. As a hub of the continent's twenty-two French-speaking nations, it was a strategic placement for Larry and LeAnn Sellers in 1996. Their work in the former French colony—including LeAnn's ministry to women and children in Abidjan—helped the Church of God grow to nine congregations and some four hundred members within three years.

With 70 percent of Côte d'Ivoire Muslim or tied to traditional tribal religions, the challenge to grow the church there was significant, even without a vision of expanding into neighboring Burkina Faso, Mali, and

Liberia. It was far more than could be done by one couple. So after more than two decades in East Africa, Sherman and Kay Critser were preparing in 2000 to move to Côte d'Ivoire. Seven years later, they helped launch West Africa Bible Institute in 2007. Its first class of fourteen students was being trained to further the expansion efforts in Côte d'Ivoire and in all of French-speaking Africa.

Reporting from Asia–Pacific

There was also considerable excitement at the start of the new century in Asia-Pacific, the largest geographic region. Especially noteworthy was the work in Southeast Asia by Neville Tan and the Singapore church. As a result of this, the Church of God recently had entered Cambodia, established contacts in Vietnam, and targeted Laos as the next nation for evangelism.

The newest missions frontier, mainland China, also held great promise in 2000. Outreach by the Taiwan church—leadership training and house ministry in the southeast—was bringing results, despite considerable danger. The South Korean church was ministering in China's northeast, especially to Koreans, many escaping economically deprived North Korea. It also was providing financial support for the mainland China ministry of the Taiwan church. At the same time, Hong Kong was poised to join the partnership. In addition to Global Missions personnel stationed in Hong Kong, several individuals working as teachers in China were excited about a "China Team" approach to what had been an almost impossible mission field since the Communist takeover in 1949.

Another stirring opportunity was the outreach to Tibetan Buddhists, a vision of Amos and Semper Moore, missionaries from Meghalaya, India, to Nepal. One of the world's least evangelized people groups, Tibetan Buddhists were found in significant populations in India and Nepal. While targeting them, the Moores also were eager to disciple the Tamang tribal people in an area of central Nepal so remote it could be accessed only on foot. That work had grown to four congregations and 479 believers by 2000. The first Tamang Church of God pastor, a former witch doctor, led "one of the fastest-growing congregations in the country," Moore reported, nothing that thirty neighboring villages had been evangelized in a prelude to church planting efforts.[7]

There was also new life in long-established ministries. In India, partnerships among the Florida Churches of God, the Church of God of Meghalaya and Assam, and congregations in eastern and northern India were growing the church. Examples were along the Bhutan border, where the number of churches had increased from four to seven, and in Sikkim state, where two congregations had expanded to seventeen in only two years. The North India Assembly, directed by Susanta Patra, had also seen expansion in its region from two to seventy churches in less than five years. Even in Orissa state, where fundamental Hindus actively opposed Christian work, some growth was being realized through the Oriya-language Christian Brotherhood Hour radio broadcast and the Evangel Printing Press, cooperating to lead seekers to Christ and then train them to conduct home Bible studies.

But there also were major challenges in the region. A super cyclone that pounded Orissa in October 1999 left some fifty thousand people dead and displaced millions. (An accurate casualty count was never attained.) Church of God Ministries immediately sent $10,000 for initial relief and made plans to later send another $25,000.

Elsewhere in Asia–Pacific, governments were a greater challenge than natural catastrophes. This was particularly true in Myanmar, although a deadly cyclone in 2008 would leave the nation devastated. Without funds to complete building projects, even before the cyclone, much work was carried on in homes. Unfortunately, government restrictions imposed at the end of 1999 and early 2000 closed many of these house churches and caused the suspension of leadership training classes at the Church of God School of Evangelism in Yangon.

In Sri Lanka, ongoing civil war now enveloped the entire nation. A new suicide bomber strategy had upped the tension level in the capital of Colombo, where the Church of God was headquartered. Additionally, communication with our churches in the northern, more volatile region was almost entirely nonexistent because of the escalation in violence.

A Beacon in the Caribbean–Atlantic

"There is no doubt that we live in an exciting age…It also is an age of unparalleled pain and suffering, where many have lost the moral and spiritual certitude that once served to hold our societies together. We who are members of Christ's church, however, cannot sit back in fear and trepidation, wringing our hands in despair at the chaos around us, afraid to take action and looking upward to heaven for our deliverance."[8]

Such was the challenge issued at the start of the new millennium by Victor Babb, Caribbean–Atlantic regional director. Representing a diverse population of 12.3 million people, including "55 percent who are barely existing, many of them living below the poverty line," Babb noted the difficult task facing the 345 Church of God congregations in fourteen different nations and their forty-five thousand believers.[9] Nevertheless, his prayer was that "the Church of God…will continue to strive to be not just a light, but a beacon showing forth the glory and salvation of God."

The planners of regional meetings for 2000 had the same prayer. Three groups—the regional assembly, women, and youth organizations—convened their annual meetings at the same time and place, July 16–21, 2000, in Grand Cayman. The first ever unified gatherings also emphasized the same theme: "Year 2000—Dawn of a Renewed Reformation Movement."

In his 2000 annual report, Babb highlighted the work of several national churches, including Curaçao, where special assignment missionaries Frank and Gemma Drakes had encouraged the small church to become involved in missions. By 2000, they were sending regular funding to Haiti, St. Thomas, and the U.S. Virgin Islands, and supporting outreach to the Maasai of Tanzania through Global Missions, leadership training at West Indies Theological College in Trinidad, and the regional assembly.

In Jamaica, with only thirty-five ordained pastors, lay leaders carried major loads in the 107 congregations. Yet churches were growing as they pursued a national theme, "Reach 2000 by Year 2000." The Montego Bay congregation had built a new sanctuary to seat one thousand worshipers, to be dedicated on March 27, and the national church had constructed a home for widows. Now work was underway to open another facility for homeless girls. This 1971 vision of Claire Gayle and Women of the Church of God in Jamaica would be fulfilled on May 20, 2001, in the dedication of a two-story building for twenty girls and their housemother.

Nevis was another bright light. There the church grew from one hundred to more than five hundred people between 1995 and 2000. So rapid was the growth that Christmas services in 1999 were forced into the recently constructed basement of a new church facility yet to be built. Nearly four hundred people celebrated there, and more than five hundred were present for the first Sunday of 2000. Surely greater growth lay ahead.

West Indies Theological College (WITC) was another regional beacon as it celebrated fifty years of ministry in 2000. With a student body from Haiti, Jamaica, Barbados, St. Vincent, Grenada, Trinidad, and Tobago, WITC was looking ahead to full accreditation by October 2001. Finances from both North America and regional churches also assisted the school, as did the Church of God in London, England. That congregation sent Rev. and Mrs. Everard Harvey in 1999 for a two-year-plus special assignment at WITC.

But there were problems as well. Specifically, churches in Guyana were estranged from each other and from Global Missions. One group related to the Caribbean–Atlantic Assembly; the other acted independently. According to Babb, attempts to resolve the problems had failed, and the case of which group was the real Church of God was to be heard in a Guyana court in February.

Haiti was also a long-term challenge if only because it was home to half the region's people. It was also the hemisphere's poorest country. Nevertheless, the church was making inroads through orphanages, including the House of Blessings Orphanage supervised by missionaries Phil and Lonnie Murphy, and through education and medical missions, supported in part by missionaries John and Jodie Ackerman. Social services provided by the church also opened evangelistic doors. National leader Phyllis Newby, a missionary from Jamaica, shared the exciting testimony of one of the eighty-seven people who had recently come to Christ through St. Ard Church of God:

> I was in the home of one of the most feared mambos (lady witch doctors) and listened as she exhorted a male friend to accept the Lord. I was taken aback. She was only converted about two weeks before. Her son, who was also only recently converted and was instrumental in her conversion, had died the night before. By Haitian standards, she should not even be able to do anything but weep! God is working![10]

The View from Europe and the Middle East

After nearly thirty years in Africa, Robert and Jan Edwards became regional directors for Europe and the Middle East in 1998. One year into this assignment, they reflected upon life and work in a new region in their annual report to the January 2000 staff planning meetings. In a word, partnership was on their minds.

Among others, partnership with the German church was critically important because, like North America, it too was active outside its own borders. Edwards' modus operandi was to build relationships with national leaders, particularly with Klaus Kroeger of Germany. Edwards also worked closely with Walentin Schüle, the German church's overseer for Ukraine and Russia, and his brother Paul, responsible for Bulgaria. One especially positive result of the deepening relationship was a partnership in Moscow, where a new work with Sergei and Natasha Tarasenkov was being sponsored and supervised jointly by the German church and Global Missions.

The German church was also keen for expanded partnerships with Global Missions, according to Andreas Burgin, editor of *Perspektiven*, the German church's quarterly magazine, who wrote enthusiastically about opportunities in Bulgaria: "The door to Bulgaria is still open and the German church alone cannot take advantage of all the opportunities available in this country."[11] (This growing partnership would lead Global Missions to send David and Kathy Simpson as missionaries to Bulgaria in 2005.)

Edwards also built relationships by participating in regional meetings, including the nineteenth European Pastors' Conference on the campus of Fritzlar Bible College in Germany in September 2000. With delegates from twelve different nations, the regional director had opportunity to hear many perspectives. Johnny and Paula Snyder, Latin America regional directors, also attended from Ecuador. They were eager to help strengthen ties between Latin America and Germany, founder of numerous congregations in their region. In fact, Germany's Bible school had trained a number of pastors then serving in Latin America.

Although the future of his work seemed positive, Edwards was learning that the region afforded many difficulties, including a very small church—only ninety-three congregations—stretched thinly over twenty countries. The religious mix was also challenging: nominal (at best) Christians of Europe; Orthodox Christians in such nations as Cyprus, Greece,

Russia, and Serbia; and the predominant Muslim population in the Middle East. Three earthquakes that hit Turkey and Greece in 1999 compounded the challenges. The first and most devastating left seventeen thousand people dead in northeastern Turkey. "Although our [work]…was not affected by the [August 17] earthquake, we still have done some relief work in the nearby city of Izmit through the Protestant Church there. [This]…has highlighted the difficulty of [Christians] attempting to assist in the relief of a predominantly Islamic community. Much misunderstanding has taken place," the new regional director declared.[12]

Nevertheless, there was promise in Turkey through the work of a Christian bookstore and café. It drew in about three hundred people monthly, including an Alcoholics Anonymous group that met there regularly. Describing other activities, our partner in Turkey wrote:

> Another dozen women come twice a week and use the basement facilities for…fellowship and prayer. They are Turkish citizens of Armenian origin, women who have been…brought up in the Orthodox Church and who, along the way, accepted Jesus into their hearts and now desire to live a Christlike life. Some…are not allowed to pray in the name of Christ in their homes or teach the children about Jesus. Fellowship meetings in their homes are not possible. The store is a place of refuge…for them. Some of [them] travel by public transportation and on foot up to one and a half hours each way. Sometimes we suffer an electric cut which may last a few hours. These women remain in the dark, having fellowship by candlelight.[13]

Regional evangelist Franco Santonocito joined Edwards in expressing hope at the turn of the new century and millennium. "True, the church in the Mediterranean area is rather small and weak," he admitted, "but it is very determined to reclaim for Christ the cradle of Christianity. In order to do this, there must be willingness, vision, help, serious prayers, and resources of the whole church. The task is truly awesome, but with God it is possible…The work in Islamic countries needs to be strengthened so that they can reach other Islamic countries. There is no limit to what can be achieved if the whole church is revived and seriously involved in reaching the whole world!"[14]

Life in Latin America

In Latin America, Johnny and Paula Snyder faced a daunting task as regional directors in 2000. Not only were they responsible to liaise between their region and North America, but they also were overseeing fourteen career and eleven special assignment missionaries deployed by Global Missions to six different countries.[15] No doubt this was a major motivation for advocating changes three years into the decade when they wrote:

> We celebrate the expansion of the Church of God around the world. We are also challenged by the task before us to effectively minister to and to administer the efforts by Global Missions. It is our perspective that the current size of the region is too large and the number of persons to fill the regional responsibilities is too small. We support responsible changes that might include, for instance, adding regional office personnel, redrawing the regional boundaries for Global Missions purposes, and/or adding missionary assignments on sub-regional levels. The level of hands-on experience, the need for personal presence, the avalanche of communication expectations, the desire to share the stories of the church, and the need to procure greater levels of funding seem to us to merit such changes.[16]

Despite the sometimes overwhelming assignment, the Snyders happily related regional bright spots during the January 2000 staff planning meetings. Among these, they highlighted Honduras, with five congregations and approximately six hundred believers. Under the leadership of Donny Allen, Honduras had recently established a new congregation in El Pino while also sending monthly donations for ministry in Cuba. Locally, they operated an AIDS clinic and a food bank while also providing community health training.

Nearby, the nation of Nicaragua seemed ripe for the beginnings of the Church of God. In 1998, the church in Panama had sent the Hodgson family on an evangelistic mission to the city of Bluefields, on Nicaragua's east coast. Costa Rica, to the north, was also eyeing ministry in Nicaragua. This was to develop into a partnership between the Costa Rican church, missionaries Wayne and Kathi Sellers, and Global Missions to send

Guillermo and Juanita Herrera to launch a new work in Villa Madre in January 2003.[17]

There was also excitement about church growth further south in Ecuador, where the church was having an influence, especially among young people ages fifteen to twenty-five. Additionally, a new work in the Roldos suburb of Quito had just affiliated with the Church of God and was showing great promise. This new hope was being echoed in the Quito area congregations of Santa Clara de Pomasqui, Zabala, and 24 de Julio.

But the Ecuadorian church also faced challenges from neighboring Colombia. There the effects of escalating terrorism and a profitable illicit drug trade were spilling over into Ecuador. Half the members of the ten Churches of God in Colombia lived in the southern state of Putumayo, where thousands were dying annually in the continent's longest running guerrilla war. In August 2002, casualties included two Church of God lay leaders. By 2005, a Church of God congregation had been forced to close and national leader Angel Pinto had been targeted repeatedly. Pastor of the Puerto Asis congregation, Pinto had been abducted five times and threatened with death.[18] Despite the dangers, he was continuing to lead the Colombian church towards a hopeful future.

Other parts of the region were hopeful too, especially with the twelfth World Conference and seventh World Forum slated for July 2003 in South America, a first time location. Robert Pearson, Church of God Ministries general director, Johnny Snyder, and others had visited potential venues in October 1999 and discussed church planting opportunities with church leaders as they considered launching a Church of God Ministries emphasis on Latin America during 2000–2005. Much enthusiasm was in the air, especially after the intersection of Brazil, Paraguay, and Argentina—Foz de Iguazu—was chosen as the Conference site. Planning committee members[19] were eager that conference-related projects would raise $175,000 for ministries in South America's Southern Cone.

Everything was to change after September 11, 2001, when terrorists commandeered airplanes and crashed them into the Twin Towers of New York City, the Pentagon, and the Pennsylvania countryside. Subsequently, during a May 3, 2002, conference call, planners voted to cancel the 2003 World Conference and to organize a World Forum substitute event at the 2003 North American Convention in Anderson. Although it was not known at the time, this was, in effect, the end of the World Conferences tradition that had begun in Fritzlar, Germany, in 1955. Well before the end of the decade, however, many church leaders around the world were calling for the important international gathering to be revived in some new form.

The North American Missions Picture

The Board of Church Extension and Home Missions was created as the third agency of the Church of God in 1920. Among responsibilities assigned by the General Assembly, the organization was charged with encouraging ministry, evangelism, and church planting in ethnic communities within the United States. This it did for the next seventy-eight years until December 1999, when fifteen North American missionaries gathered in Anderson to witness the historic merging of home and overseas missions activities under Outreach Ministries of Church of God Ministries.

Actually, it was not the first time the two ministries had been unified. In the early years of nationally organized Church of God work, in 1917, the Board of Home and Foreign Missions of the Church of God had been established. As overseas work expanded, however, the Board requested a division of responsibilities, which was granted one year later. Another two years would pass before any agency was charged with home missions responsibilities. But now, in 1999, the two boards were being reunited once again.

At the time, home missions was represented by eleven missionaries working among Native Americans in Alaska, Washington, Arizona, Nebraska, and South Dakota, as well as by four others in the economically depressed Appalachian region. Gilbert and Melba Davila were called as regional directors to represent them and their concerns at the biannual regional director meetings. Six months into their assignment, they admitted they had much to learn as they focused on building relationships and on growing into the new paradigm that had again combined national and international mission's activities.

Reporting on their transition, Gilbert shared about his September 1999 visit to Rapid City and Wounded Knee, South Dakota, and Alliance, Nebraska. He had traveled with Alaska home missionary Simeon Arnakin and had been introduced to American Indian Council leaders and their work, including Smoke Signal Ministries, a new outreach in Rapid City. While looking forward to the next Council meeting in July in Allen, South Dakota, the new regional director was concerned that Native American ministries become better known throughout the church and wondered how to help these sparsely scattered groups communicate better among themselves.

Hispanic himself and long involved in Spanish-speaking ministry, Davila had a natural link to the Hispanic Council, a freestanding national organization of Spanish-speaking churches. This was to prove advantageous in helping Outreach Ministries and the Concilio come to an agreement about partnering together more effectively in home missions work. Particularly exciting were reports of Hispanic church planting efforts in the Northeast and, most recently, in Atlanta, Georgia, in September 1999.

Davila was also learning about the work in Appalachia. Pine Crest Appalachian Ministries had a long history dating back to 1948 and the efforts of Naomi Randall, whose heart ached for disadvantaged children in that area. As of December 1999, Garland and Sue Lacy were supervising the care of 135 sponsored children. That Christmas, they had organized presents for 339 families, who received 763 sweat shirts, 614 pens, pencils, and notebooks, and 994 pairs of socks.[20]

In 2001, the Davilas returned to the pastorate and were not replaced as regional coordinators. Subsequently, in 2003, responsibility for the North American region was transferred to the department of Compassionate Ministries and Homeland Ministry, with North American missionaries renamed homeland missionaries. While this was also a department of the Outreach Ministries Team, the move away from specific Global Missions involvement raised questions in some quarters about the future of North American missions. Indeed, by 2008, the work of only one couple—Ronald and Effie Woodman of Klagetoh, Arizona—was still being supported by the national church. In addition, Obadiah Smith, coordinator of Compassionate Ministries and Homeland Ministry, was laid off at the end of November 2008 due to critical budget shortfall. Plans for this ministry function were not resolved at the time of this writing.[21]

From Regional Directors to Regional Coordinators

Despite being able to educate the North American church for missions and help raise financial and prayer support for their specific regions, regional directors were dismayed to find that their position was often misunderstood by the church around the world. This caused both heartaches and headaches at home and abroad.

As interim regional director for Europe and the Commonwealth of Independent States, James Albrecht had described the position well:

> The office of regional director is not a mechanical…position of simply making the parts work, keeping grease on the wheels, and trying to stretch dollars to meet demands. The real work is visionary and spiritual in nature…There are times when the regional director will make decisions (or not make decisions) that are demanded of him by missionaries or nationals. This office must not be seen as a popularity position. The regional director must be able to stand far enough away to view enough of the whole picture to see God's direction in the process. He must also have the humility to realize that not much credit for successes will be ascribed to him.[22]

But surely regional directors would be assigned blame when something went wrong, especially when funds were not forthcoming for missionaries, national leaders, or projects. One of the heartaches that went with the territory, it seemed to become even more troubling as financial structures were altered under Church of God Ministries, necessitating the creation of Project Link midway through the decade.

Donald Johnson, acting in an interim capacity in Asia–Pacific, helped explain the sensitivity surrounding the position, whose name had been changed to regional coordinator (RC) in 2001. "Whether we like it or not, we as regional coordinators are not always considered necessary within our regions," he declared. "This not-too-unsettling awareness goes with the position. When the term *director* was used, the questions centered around, 'What [or whom] do you direct?'" He further urged regional coordinators "to unapologetically live out the need for a Global Missions liaison by the way we relate to national structures."[23]

In order for RCs to do so, they would need to operate on the basis of several assumptions. The most important of these was that they were partners in mission. Johnson explained:

> There is no intention on the part of Global Missions to imply that our appointment as regional coordinators is in any way to be understood as persons chosen to direct or coordinate the work of a region, area, or country. Global Missions has no power to appoint

such persons. Coordination carries the sense of being a liaison between Global Missions and the region. We are "resident partners"
to help facilitate and interpret for the North American church the
resources needed to help carry out mission strategy in interdependent ways. We are also responsible to interpret for the national
church the limitations when resources are less than [needed]...We
are, in a very real way, a Global Missions presence.[24]

In fact, although Johnson's statements dealt specifically with defining the person and role of the regional coordinator, they were compatible with—perhaps even an outgrowth of—a statement accepted in
June 2001 by the RCs. Titled "Missiological Principles That Form the
Foundation of Our Cross-Cultural Ministry," the treatise noted that all
Global Missions work must be biblically based, Christ-centered, and
Great Commission–driven. The coordinators agreed that evangelism and
discipleship are the two essential thrusts. As such, "theological education
and leadership development are indispensable elements of our ministry
globally" and these "should be meaningful and appropriate to the indigenous culture."[25]

Summing up their understanding of their regional assignments, they
concluded, "We continue to realize the value of global involvement in our
entire mission venture. We have much to learn from our brothers and sisters in the Lord Jesus. We recognize and seek to display the truth of interdependence in mission."

Funding Changes Birth Project Link

Practically speaking, just what did healthy partnership and interdependence in missions look like at this juncture? In much of the history of
the Missionary Board, missionaries and money were elevated as the most
important resources. While not depreciating either, the model interdependent context desired by regional coordinators and Global Missions was one
in which each person and each contribution was seen as part of the mix
from which all resources were drawn and where equal value was assessed to
each piece of input.

At the same time, an unfortunate history of great ideas and hopeful
starts that sometimes died in infancy for lack of funding necessitated the

question: If money is such a crucial ingredient to turn a vision into reality, can partnership be constructed to take this into account?

"Maybe this is North America's share of the partnership," Donald Johnson mused in his role as Global Missions consultant. "Instead of saying 'how sad' that something good did not survive, maybe we had better plan differently in the future." However, with the restructuring of the national church organization late in the 1990s, the funding model for Global Missions was radically changed. Consequently, both visioning for the future and partnerships related to finances became even more difficult than ever.

It is often true of major organizational restructuring that some very important operational patterns can morph into something new without specific planning, communication, or follow-through. It just happens. The financing of Global Missions was one of the more difficult changes that occurred in just such a fashion during restructuring. Under the former agency structure, the Missionary Board, after meeting annually with the National Budget Committee of the Executive Council, was allotted an average of 30 to 33 percent of undesignated dollars given to support the basic budget. World Service disbursed these dollars, providing not only for the Missionary Board's in-house operating budget, including home office personnel, but also a major portion of field operations. Missionary personnel and their operational budgets were supported separately through Living Link.

For the first four years after restructuring (2000–2004), Global Missions continued to create its budget under the same financial concept. There had been no instructions from the Ministries Council that this pattern had changed, except for the fact that there was now no National Budget Committee to consult. But in fact it had changed. The net effect was that although Global Missions continued to budget and send field dollars on the basis of past percentages, these were no longer being made available for this purpose. As a result, Global Missions began accumulating a large deficit during these years.

When Global Missions learned it could no longer budget its ministries by counting on a major portion of basic budget dollars, a way had to be found both to retire the accumulated deficit and to begin distributing to field projects only those dollars that were specifically designated for them. After some difficult negotiations between Global Missions, Outreach Ministries, and Church of God Ministries, June 30, 2005, was set as the final cutoff date for supporting undesignated projects around the world.

By this time, however, a concentrated effort was already underway in Global Missions to create a program that would address the continuing commitment to the international church, including educational institutions and national leader support. This gave birth to the Project Link program, which commenced operations on July 1, 2005. Shortly thereafter, it was put under the leadership of Ed Hyatt, coming to Global Missions after nearly thirty years in the pastorate. His immediate concern was to help raise a total of $531,709 to support eighty projects in the five regions overseas.[26]

To cushion the blow to international ministries dependent upon receiving a designated monthly allotment and to allow time for Project Link to get up and running, projects continued to receive at least half support through the end of 2005. Then, from January 1, 2006, only those funds that were received were routed on to their designated recipients.

According to the 2005 major promotional piece, "Project Link gives Global Missions the flexibility to grow and expand to support more projects as approved. Project Link is a self-funding program with all essential support services included. Normally this is less than 8 percent. Funds will only be disbursed to projects as funds are received."

Looking back over these difficult few years, it is important to note, in all fairness, that Church of God Ministries must live within its income in order to continue as a viable organization. However, Global Missions was discovering that it must do more—perhaps than ever before—to ensure that the mandate to go into all the world would continue as an integral part of the mission and ministry of the North American church. Clear and intentional communication of this vital lifeblood is imperative for smooth operation of all units within Church of God Ministries as the structure continues to be adjusted and corrected for more effective ministry in its second hundred years.

Project Link Testimonies

Although the negotiations from which Project Link emerged were long and sometimes difficult, the end result found increasing involvement by the North American church in supporting international projects, many of which they had not even known about before.

Called Essential Ministry Opportunities (EMO), these projects[27] were sometimes referred to as the "bread and butter" of missions—foundational projects "because they provide training for leadership development, equip the church for evangelism, facilitate church planting, and provide national assembly grants and salaries for some national leaders."[28]

Testimonies of what Project Link funded around the world include the following examples:

In January 2005, a married couple, Antonio and Lilian, were attending Boa Terra Norte in Itaituba, Brazil. As a part of their seminary training, they were required to complete an internship that would take them out of the classroom and put them into the church. They did so in the city of Sinop, where some Church of God families dreamed of planting a church. With Project Link funding to support their training, Antonio and Lilian helped make this dream a reality.

Another training facility was located in La Pastora, Trinidad. By 2007, West Indies Theological College (WITC) had graduated 218 students since its founding in 1950. One graduate, Kelvin Harrinarine, first attended Sunday school under a mango tree as a young boy. Taught there by WITC students, Harrinarine eventually came to Christ—the first member of his family, of East Indian descent, ever to do so. Later, he graduated from the college and became a pastor. In 2008, the little boy who first heard about Jesus under a tree was serving as executive secretary of the General Assembly of the Church of God in Trinidad and Tobago and expressing his thanks for Project Link funds that were supporting leadership training for the Caribbean–Atlantic region.[29]

The church in Niš, Serbia, is representative of projects assisting in evangelism and national leader support. On March 18, 2004, the storefront building housing the Church of God was firebombed, forcing the congregation to begin meeting in the home of its pastors, Obrad and Slavica Nikolić. Despite continued religious persecution, high national unemployment, and a low standard of living in Serbia, support for church development there allowed the Church of God to continue. In fact, over three hundred students from Serbia, Montenegro, Bosnia, and Macedonia were taking a free gospel correspondence course taught by Obrad, with others enrolled via e-mail.[30]

In the same region, Project Link was helping another national church evangelizing amid a different set of difficult circumstances—Islamic fundamentalism. Kelley Philips, regional coordinator, told about a Church of God pastor planning to construct a church building in an area sympathetic to a terrorist-linked Islamic group. When Philips asked about the response of locals, the pastor replied, "They…threatened to kill us," adding, "Of course we don't want to die, but we have no choice. We must proclaim the good news of Jesus no matter what the risk."[31]

Support for national workers was also essential in Bangladesh, one of the world's poorest nations. Over 55 percent of the population lives below the poverty line.[32] "Please don't forget us," Pastor Lawrence Choudhury pleaded with John Johnson, Asia–Pacific regional coordinator, as they spoke about the needs in northeast Bangladesh among Hindu tea garden workers and tribal peoples. Choudhury's passionate appeal was echoed around the world in other locations counting on the North American church to partner through providing funds.[33]

Johnson wrote about the heart-tug of visiting Bangladesh, where six pastors and five evangelists needed to receive forty-three Project Link dollars a month out of which to provide for their families and cover all their travel expenses:

> Religious persecution of Christians in Bangladesh is very real. About four years ago eighteen families accepted Christ in the village of Talpuker. When these Hindu families accepted Christ and were baptized in the pond beside their village, the Muslim landowner decided to deny them sanitation rights…
>
> These villagers are day farmers earning roughly eighty cents per day, but only on days they are hired. Many supplement their income by weaving baskets. To say that they eek out a living is perhaps an overstatement. The truth is that they have close to nothing. Yet, at the close of many impromptu worship services I attended, an offering was taken. I was amazed by the eagerness and joy of these believers. Their faces beamed with delight as they gave back to the One who had given everything to them.[34]

Nearing the end of Project Link's first year, it appeared the church was responding positively to the new initiative. Donors had increased from about 130 to 340 and income from around $155,000 to $430,430. By one year later, support had grown to $465,442—more than 76 percent of the

$635,259 total budget. (Unfortunately, Latin America was receiving only slightly over 43 percent of its budget and the Caribbean-Atlantic region only about 57 percent.)

Recognizing that gathering full support for all projects remained a difficult challenge, Ed Hyatt, Project Link coordinator, declared, "Working with [Project Link] has reaffirmed my belief that the healthiest churches… are Acts 1:8 churches. These are churches actively on mission that understand they are called to minister to the world around the corner from their door and to the world across the oceans. I continue to look for new ways to more effectively raise funds for the projects and involve the local church in ministry on a global scale."

Leadership Changes Define Ministry

Within the nearly 130 years since the founding of the Church of God reformation movement in 1880, the annual General Assembly meetings in June 1996 were among the most historic. Voting to accept in concept recommendations about the church's governance and polity, the General Assembly named an Implementation Task Force, which brought its own proposal a year later about logistics to employ the changes. Subsequently, Robert W. Pearson was ratified in the 1998 General Assembly as the first general director of Church of God Ministries. Previously, he had served as executive director of the Association of the Church of God of Southern California and Southern Nevada.

Leading the demanding restructuring of the entire national organization was not unlike navigating a ship through uncharted waters. It simply had never been done before on such a scale in the Church of God. Nevertheless, by the year 2000, Pearson and the Ministries Council were supervising three teams: Congregational Ministries, led by Jeannette Flynn; Resource and Linking Ministries, directed by James Martin; and Outreach Ministries, under the guidance of Michael Curry, whose assignment gave him oversight of Christians Broadcasting Hope (CBH) and Mass Media, Compassionate Ministries, and Global Missions. Succeeding Norman Patton at the Missionary Board in 1998, Doris Dale was named Global Missions coordinator under Curry, who began his assignment in February 1999.

"The learning curve for Brother Curry [and] the rest of us was very sharp," the retired national coordinator of Women of the Church of God commented in her first annual report as Global Missions coordinator. "But God was faithful and we began to see a fledgling ministry entity known as Outreach Ministries emerge. The days were filled with meetings, dialogue, agreements, and disagreements! But we continued and God honored the efforts. The journey is yet to be completed, but we have made the start and celebrate the infant steps."[35]

Generally speaking, changes do not come quickly or easily, especially when there are different understandings about what the final outcome should be. Agreeing, Dale affirms, "Casting a vision takes much time, struggle, and input from all, and the implementation of the vision takes even longer. [Church of God Ministries] is still revisiting the vision and asking God to grant us wisdom and direction."[36]

Perhaps this was one of the reasons Pearson submitted his resignation as general director. Trying to implement and give order to a new structure for Church of God Ministries, helping refinance Warner Press debt, and moving the national organization into the remodeled Warner Press location were especially difficult tasks Pearson faced during his tenure, which ended on October 1, 2000. He was succeeded by Forrest Robinson, former president of Mid-America Christian University in Oklahoma. Robinson served as interim general director from October 26, 2000, to December 31, 2001. Subsequently, Ronald V. Duncan assumed leadership of Church of God Ministries on January 1, 2002, concluding his work on the Ministries Council and as pastor of Parkgate Community Church, Pasadena, Texas.

Adding to the climate of change were other leadership adjustments during 2002. These included the resignation of Michael Curry as Outreach Ministries team director early that year. Later, on August 15, Dale concluded her assignment and was followed by Robert Edwards, assuming the Global Missions leadership position after more than thirty years of field work, most recently as regional coordinator for Europe and the Middle East.

One year later, during the February 7, 2003, meeting of the Ministries Council in Oklahoma City, Oklahoma, Albert Grant was presented as the new Outreach Ministries team leader-designate. He was ratified by the General Assembly in a mail-in ballot and began his ministry in the national offices on March 31. His short tenure ended with his resignation on October 30, 2005.

Eventually, there was an internal reorganization of Church of God Ministries in 2006. First, Outreach Ministries and Congregational

Ministries were merged on a trial basis that January. With this arrangement proving workable, the umbrella name of Kingdom Ministry Team was used for the first time in November, and the united concept was approved as a permanent change by the Ministries Council in 2007. In another significant decision that year, the General Assembly gave the general director the ability to develop structure as needed. From that time, the appointment of team directors no longer needed General Assembly ratification.

With these changes, Jeannette Flynn became responsible for administering eleven different major departments and programs.[37] If a cursory look at the new structure could paint an accurate picture, the North American church appeared to be turning its attention inward and focusing on national concerns. Perhaps this was necessary as the organization continued developing its structure, but the ever present danger was that international commitments so prominent throughout the movement's history might be minimized.

Likewise on the Field

It was not only in Anderson that significant personnel transitions were taking place during the decade. Robert Edwards's appointment as Global Missions coordinator opened up the regional coordinator position for Europe and the Middle East. This was filled in 2003, with Kelley and Rhonda Philips changing from church planting and leadership development work in Russia to liaise with the entire region from their base in Hungary. Later, at the invitation of the German church, they would reach into the region from the city of Berlin.

Along with the Philips family's move, John and Gwen Johnson also transitioned in 2003 from Lebanon and leadership of Mediterranean Bible College to become RCs for Asia–Pacific. The next year, Johnny and Paula Snyder completed fourteen years of missionary service, six in Mexico and nine as RCs for Latin America. They were followed by David and Barbara Miller, who chose Bolivia as their base. Then, with the resignation of Don and Paula Riley in 2005, Sherman and Kay Critser were named RCs for Africa. Subsequently, in 2006, the Johnsons ended their twenty-five-year missionary career, moving from Asia–Pacific to Warner Pacific College, Portland, Oregon.

The decade also saw the retirement of at least six missionary couples with lengthy field tenures. These included Stan and Marion Hoffman, who, in 2002, completed thirty-seven years of ministry in Africa. (Interestingly, the lure of the continent was so strong that they returned to Angola as special assignment missionaries in 2007. However, visa problems prohibited them from remaining and they relocated to Zambia within a year.)

Next to retire among especially long-term missionaries were Paul and Nova Hutchins in 2005. They had served in East Pakistan (now Bangladesh) and in Kenya, during which time Paul was the Missionary Board's liaision to Africa in a kind of pre–regional coordinator position. Then, from 1991–2005, the couple ministered to international students in the United States as special assignment missionaries, for a total of thirty-three years of missionary service.

There were more transitions in 2006. Paul and Kathy Bentley retired after nearly twenty years as home missionaries to the Sioux in Rapid City, South Dakota. Tom and Jean McCracken, whose assignments had taken them to Trinidad and Brazil, and Jim and Dorothy Sharp, serving in Kenya and Tanzania, all retired in 2006. Nevertheless, both couples remained active in missions. By 2007, the McCrackens were raising ministry funds for Brazil from their Ohio home, and the Sharps had accepted an eight-month special assignment in Uganda. They also returned to the continent in 2008 for a teaching assignment at West Africa Bible Institute in Côte d'Ivoire.

Next, in 2007, Africa bid farewell to three long-term servants. First, on June 30, Caroline Ackerman completed thirty-two years of medical missions work in Kenya and Tanzania. Then it was Joel and Cornelia Kerich's turn. Joel, a Kenyan by birth, was one of Cornelia Barnette's students during her first medical missionary term there. After their marriage, they had served ten years in Kenya. Later, after Neelie taught in the nursing department of Anderson University, the couple relocated to Uganda in 2001. Neelie reentered medical missions and Joel was involved in leadership training among pastors until their retirement at the end of 2007. Altogether, Neelie had served twenty-three years in Africa.

Global Dialogue Convenes in Anderson

Even before Project Link was created in 2005 as a means for the North American church to continue to be faithful to international partnerships, a Global Dialogue in Anderson, June 19–21, 2003, was conducted as a forum where those partnerships could be discussed. Bringing together thirty-two official international delegates, a discussion panel of fourteen people representing eleven nations,[38] and some forty observers, the Dialogue had an agenda of three goals: "list priority concerns globally, talk about leadership development, and address the needed communication of the church's leaders around the world."[39]

Before conversations could begin, however, Ronald Duncan, Church of God Ministries general director, addressed the gathering about the dilemma facing Church of God Ministries in considering the future of World Conferences and World Forums. With increasing worldwide security issues, and especially thinking about finances, "the old paradigm of the World Forums is no longer workable," he asserted. The practice of financing these international conventions, at least in part through large tour groups of North Americans, was an especially questionable practice, he stated.

At the end of the first day, Duncan summed up seven consensus points that had emerged during the discussions, moderated by Robert Edwards, Global Missions coordinator. Chief among these was the "strong feeling that there is clear need for the continuance of an international mechanism(s) that facilitates the necessary global exchange of ideas, cross fertilization, fellowship, and cooperative strategies of mission and specific ministries." It was also observed that ways must be found to make it possible for those who need to attend future international meetings to do so, perhaps through sharing expenses and working toward reducing costs. Additionally, while the Dialogue focused more on how-to questions, delegates agreed that such a future international event "will have theological content, address leadership issues, learn distinctives from the host country, and have impact on the host country for the sake of Christ."

Leadership development was another pressing issue of the Dialogue. Specific concerns included the lack of access to distinctively Church of God schools and materials, the dearth of pastors, and the decreasing number of young people feeling the call to ministry. These concerns and possible answers were addressed in presentations from several Church of God colleges and educators.[40]

In fact, this was not the first time Global Missions had been instrumental in drawing educators together. The first annual meeting of the Church of God Educators and Administrators Conference had been conducted two years earlier, in March 2001, in Germany. It had gathered representatives of Anderson University, Warner Pacific College, and Anderson University School of Theology, as well as the heads of Mediterranean Bible College, Lebanon; Kima International School of Theology, Kenya; and Fritzlar Bible College, hosting the event. By its March 2008 meeting, the group had expanded to include Warner Southern College, Florida, and Gardner College, Canada. In other years, representatives from Nichols-Roy Bible College, India, and Boa Terra Bible School, Brazil, had attended.

As the Internet continued shrinking the world, distance and coalition education had become an increasingly viable way for the Church of God to engage in leadership development—one of the primary mandates the Missionary Board had identified in the 1990s as its reason for being.[41] Thus the topic of leadership development was a particularly important component of the three-day Dialogue. Recognizing the concern "to keep the dialogue process going after this session," the World Forum Planning Committee met again during the 2004 International Youth Convention in Nashville. At this writing, a second such dialogue—to be called a Global Conversation—was being planned to convene immediately after the 2009 North American Convention.

"One World, One Mission"

Calls to continue the international dialogue illustrated how vital it was for the Church of God in North America to engage with the Church of God around the world in order to be faithful and obedient partners in the Great Commission. Regional coordinators, meeting in January 2003, also had considered at length ministry goals and strategies to move Global Missions towards living out greater worldwide interdependence, even while affirming that current world realities required new understanding and approaches to missions.

What were some of these new defining realities? Among the most significant was the thrilling growth of the Christian church worldwide, resulting in a shift in the directional flow of missionaries by the end of the twentieth century. Whereas in 1900 there were approximately 10 million Christians in Africa, at the start of the next century there were well over 300 million Christians among 500 million Africans on the continent. In other words, by 2000 the number of Christians in Africa had surpassed the number in North America. Even more stunning, African missionaries from what once was called the "dark continent" were arriving regularly in the United States and Canada to minister in such cities as Chicago and Toronto. With South Korea now the second largest sending nation in the world following the United States, North America was receiving the Asian nation's missionaries too.

This new general reality also defined the Church of God specifically, with statistics showing that congregations "outside North America now [were comprised] of 125 percent more believers and 40 percent more congregations" than were resident in the United States and Canada. [42]

In a milieu of such astonishing change, an especially critical question for the regional coordinators was, "How can we approach the future as 'one' with our colleagues in mission around the world?"[43] Their discussion was based upon Paul's declaration, "There is one body and one Spirit, just as you were called to one hope of your calling, one Lord, one faith, one baptism, one God and Father of all, who is above all and through all and in all."[44] Seven assumptions for defining Global Missions outreach in the twenty-first century emerged: "Evangelism must be a penetrating dynamic of everything we do together; the gospel must take deep root in the culture of every nation in which we work; nothing is more important than training persons for leadership in the church; resources can best be identified and employed in mission when we focus on our task together and share what each is able to contribute; basic to everything we do together is a desire to learn from one another; and, strategies must be broadly cooperative in their approach."[45]

Another outcome of the meetings was the birth of "One World, One Mission" as the compelling Global Missions theme for ministry in the new century. It was to debut during the 2004 North American Convention when Global Missions hosted its first "One World, One Mission" conference, attended by more than 130 people.

Missionary Patrick Nachtigall shared his thinking about the "One World, One Mission" theme. Admonishing the church to "acknowledge that we have many other brothers and sisters around the world [who] are also on the team, who bring their own knowledge, experience, and resources to the missionary enterprise,"[46] he both asked and answered an important question: "Does this mean that North America should stop sending missionaries? Absolutely not! Both Brazil and China, for instance, suffer from growing movements that teach unorthodox theologies. Theo-logical training and discipleship are vital in many of these regions. The world will always need people who will serve others in the name of Jesus. The mission must continue, but we must realize that God's team is getting bigger and bigger."[47]

It was not an easy paradigm shift, however. In fact, one year later in his annual report, Kelley Philips, regional coordinator for Europe and the Middle East, asserted, "'One World, One Mission' is at best idealistic, at worst unattainable." Nevertheless, the RC cautioned Global Missions to stay the course, sharing about a conversation with Klaus Kroeger after the German church leader visited Egypt and wondered out loud why the Ger-mans had never been involved in that country. "I guess it's always belonged to the American church," Kroeger said. In his report, Philips declared, "We must recognize the difference between stewardship and ownership and model this…At least for this region, 'One World, One Mission' is a neces-sity. We must continue to pursue the unattainable!"[48]

Practically Speaking

"There are many calling today for a new sense of international connection in the missionary effort. There are far fewer who actually explain how to do this. It's easy to say we should all be united and that the missionary efforts of our different countries and cultures are part of one big enterprise. It's also easy to castigate the West and accuse it of not making a sincere effort to truly partner with non-Western sending nations. But once again, how would such partnerships actually work?"[49]

Three years after it was adopted, Patrick Nachtigall raised some foun-dational questions about the "One World, One Mission" Global Missions theme. Attempting to answer them, at least from the context of Hong Kong where he served, he wrote of one example: a 2004 link-up between the Churches of God in Hong Kong and New Zealand to cooperate on a missions trip to a third country in the region.

Another example challenged teenagers in North America to become involved in giving to missions to help the church overseas "Spread the Word" (STW), the name of the campaign launched at the 2002 Interna-tional Youth Convention in Denver. Young people at that convention gave over $100,000 in an amazing display of eagerness to help fund Church of God international missions projects supporting evangelism. By the following spring, five states had reported another $8,733 given by teens at state youth conventions for STW projects in Australia, Turkey, Lebanon, and some African nations. Among state organizations that eagerly got involved, West Virginia youth adopted a specific project, the renovation of a youth center in Budapest, Hungary, and gave over $3,200 at their state youth convention, with a goal to complete funding of the $6,000 project by spring 2003.[50] By August 2008, $457,217 had been given to support work in twenty-three countries on six continents.

In 2006, other young people embraced a partnership ministry in Uganda that developed after Scott Schomburg, an Anderson University student, visited Africa and learned about TAPP (Tumaini AIDS Prevention Program). Recalling the unplanned launching of this partnership, Schomburg explained, "It was the fall of 2006. I reunited with missionaries Tim and Colleen Stevenson while they were stateside in Anderson, Indiana… 'Can you help sell some of these beads?' Colleen asked. 'TAPP is growing, and there are no places to sell the beads in our local Ugandan markets.' The next day we introduced the handmade recycled paper beads to a local high school during their lunch hour. The entire supply of more than three hundred necklaces was gone in a matter of hours. That is where it all started."[51]

At this writing, partners of the yet-developing U.S. TAPP International Support Branch included the Tree of Life bookstore at Anderson University, Women of the Church of God, and Park Place Church in Anderson, providing free-of-charge office space for the business that was launched in January 2007. Beads soon were being made in five of twenty-four TAPP branches in Uganda for sale in Canada, Germany, and the United States. But the partnership story was much more thrilling than simply a good business deal, no matter how successful it was.

"It is important to note that the money TAPP members receive from bead sales has never been the source of their joy," Schomburg emphasized, wonderfully illustrating that ideal partnerships are those where give and take comes from all members. "That is where these people teach us so much. God is alive to them in the midst of their suffering, and the hope of Christ is real and is sustaining them beyond human reason or capacity to understand. They constantly help us reshape our worldview and teach us what it means to have 'life to the full.'"[52]

Another example of a "One World, One Mission" partnership was forged in April 1997 between Salem Church of God, Clayton, Ohio, and the congregation in Mercedes, Parana, Brazil. Beginning with a work camp that constructed a church building and conducted a vacation Bible school for three hundred children, the partnership led several future mission teams from Salem to return to Mercedes. They also built a medical clinic so that the Mercedes church could begin outreach into another area of Brazil. According to Johnny Snyder, then Latin America regional coordinator, this was "a beautiful example of blessing begetting blessing [as] the people of Mercedes are partnering with others in Brazil as others from Salem have partnered with them."[53]

Sometimes "One World, One Mission" was lived out when the ministries of non–North American missionaries were supported by the United States and Canada. One especially exciting example was a three-way partnership launched in March 2007 with the sending of German missionary Manuel Killisch to Argentina in ministry funded primarily by North America.[54] Long-standing collaboration between First Church of God, St. Joseph, Michigan, and Fairfax Community Church, Fairfax, Virginia, was helping the Church of God in Hungary awaken from a period of dormancy. At the same time, such partnerships helped support the region-wide ministry of Franco Santonocito, a longtime evangelist and church planter in Italy and Egypt, as well as enabling Neville Tan to preach and plant the Church of God in a number of Southeast Asian nations.

Then there was Pastor Marcellin in Côte d'Ivoire. His story illustrates partnerships that support national pastors to carry out ministries in their own countries. Larry Sellers recalls his early association with Marcellin:

> From our first meeting, it was obvious that Marcellin had gifts in evangelism and pastoral leadership despite little formal training. In his zeal to reach the lost, he had won several people to Christ and brought them together at his house for worship and teaching. This became our first congregation in central Côte d'Ivoire. The group of about twenty-five adult converts, plus children, came from the poorer class in the capital city, Yamoussoukro. Their offerings were barely enough to pay the rent for the pastor's house, which doubled as a place of worship. Marcellin was struggling to fulfill his call to serve the Lord full-time and yet provide for his family. He

obviously needed some help…Thanks to monthly funds sent by Global Missions…we were able to set up a plan of support for his ministry with the goal that the church would grow and take over his support.[55]

Testifying to the success of this partnership, six years after Global Missions began funding Pastor Marcellin, his congregation took a leap of faith and assumed full support of their pastor. Within two years, the Yamoussoukro church had become the largest Church of God congregation in Côte d'Ivoire, with nearly two hundred people present every Sunday. It also had begun several cell groups in the city with an eye towards planting new congregations.

Partnership examples during the decade of the 2000s could fill a book. They showed that "One World, One Mission" was more than a nice-sounding slogan. Certainly many more partnerships were needed, with opportunities far exceeding resources, but the church was attempting to live out the truth that no matter the nationality, language, educational background, or income, every Christian in every corner of the world is called of God to work in the harvest field. But remembering Jesus' admonition, "From everyone who has been given much, much will be required"[56], it could be argued convincingly that the North American church had no small responsibility for proactively living out "One World, One Mission" in the new century.

New Missionary Residences

Anderson, Indiana was the home of a different kind of partnership—a partnership in building two new missionary residences.

From the time the Crose Missionary Residences were completed in 1981 as a part of the Million for Missions campaign, missionaries on home assignment had called the six colonial-style townhouse apartments on East Tenth Street their "home away from home." With all furnishings donated by Church of God businessman O. C. Lewis of Sikeston, Missouri, the land had been purchased and the two buildings of three apartments each had been built with a loan of $150,000 secured from the Board of Church Extension and Home Missions and paid off in one year.

In April 2003, Church of God Ministries approved a proposal to tear down the old Hunter House, next door to the Crose Residences, and to build a third matching building in its place. But there were two stipulations: the money must be raised and construction should never proceed beyond the money in hand. Donald Johnson was named project manager, and with the help of a $5,000 initial contribution from Women of the Church of God (WCG), the project got underway. Hunter House was demolished in the fall of 2003 and groundbreaking ceremonies for the new townhouse followed on March 15, 2004.

Taking the proviso to heart, Johnson oversaw all phases of the project: commissioning the architect, launching a fundraising campaign, demolishing the old house, and even shopping, cleaning, and painting, often by himself. The new facility, dedicated at North American Convention 2004, was valued at $285,000 while costing only $198,000, testifying to success in keeping costs down and engaging partners in the project. These included Allan Barton and his son, Kirk, furniture store owners in Poplar Bluff, Missouri, who outfitted the two apartments as a gift to missionaries. Additionally, WCG gave another $2,500 for kitchen appliances and donated housewares and linens.

The only aspect of the project that didn't include Johnson was the naming of the building. The two apartments it housed were named for Nora Hunter, WCG founder, and Philip and Phyllis Kinley, long-term missionaries to Japan, now retired. Unbeknown to Johnson, the entire new building was to be called the Johnson Missionary Residences, honoring Donald and Betty Jo Johnson and their contributions as missionaries on the field and in the office, where Johnson had served as an associate secretary and as executive secretary-treasurer. Later, after retiring from pastoral ministry, Johnson had returned to the Board in a variety of roles, including recruiter, interim regional coordinator, and consultant, over thirteen years.

Missions in an Age of Terrorism

A vital function of the Anderson residences was to provide a safe haven, a comfortable place of rest, for missionaries on home assignment. This was important for all missionaries, but especially for those whose field term was stressful. Of course, challenges had always been part of missionary life, but the situation intensified after 9/11—the expression coined for the date of the deadly terrorist attack on U.S. soil, September 11, 2001.

Then America invaded Iraq in March 2003. Without doubt, the missionary stress level was spiraling upwards in the new century. Global Missions Coordinator Robert Edwards said as much in an article titled "Ministry in Times of Violence," in which he declared, "The truth is, we live in a very dangerous world today. Because some missionaries work in countries that are politically unstable and increasingly religiously intolerant, we know that some of them will be in harm's way at times…Do we wish for this to happen? Certainly not. Does it happen? Unfortunately, it does. Is the 9/11 event unusual? Not really. In today's world, the potential for such violence is high."[57]

From Lebanon to Côte d'Ivoire to Bolivia, no posting seemed safe in this dangerous new world where, many Americans were surprised to discover, the United States was increasingly viewed as the enemy. Don Deena Johnson, for one, shared poignantly about this with prayer supporters in the tense days leading up to the Iraq invasion when two young boys playing near her home pointed toy guns at her and, even if only silently, wished the American dead. Because of the unpopular war, the safety of Americans in Lebanon was now questioned, so Lebanese colleagues advised Johnson and fellow missionaries John and Gwen Johnson to leave immediately if the threatened invasion occurred. When it did, they evacuated to Germany.

It was not the first time these missionaries had confronted war. In 1999, John and Gwen and their two children spent the night on mattresses in the entryway of their apartment as Israel bombed Beirut, which answered with anti-aircraft fire. The family huddled together in the safest place possible, praying throughout the frightening night for God's protection for themselves and their many friends in the city.

It was not the last time Don Deena would be evacuated, either. Three years after her first experience, she again found herself leaving Lebanon, this time on a U.S. Navy ship. In her office at Mediterranean Bible College shortly before Global Missions instructed her to evacuate, Don Deena reflected upon war, peace, and the age of terrorism:

> There is that most strange belief among many in the developed world that the evil of terrorism can be defeated by military might. How often in history have we become so embroiled in fighting one

evil that we have crossed the line and forgotten who we are and what we supposedly value. When "the end justifies the means" becomes our creed, that "end" we sought no longer exists. Is it even possible to defeat terrorism by the use of force? For a day, perhaps. But only for a day. Where are the courageous [people] with hope enough to imagine fighting the war of terrorism with the weapons of peace?[58]

Larry and LeAnn Sellers and Sherman and Kay Critser had worked in Rwanda and Zaire during the 1990s when civil wars and genocide demanded their reassignments. Both couples eventually ended up in Côte d'Ivoire, on Africa's west coast, not expecting another evacuation. But it happened in November 2004, following escalation of a conflict in which French peacekeeping troops were killed. When the French government retaliated, Caucasians became targets of violence. Larry recounted,

> As a result, Western embassies called for their citizens to evacuate the country and even sent military planes in to fly people away from the escalating violence.
> Though we did not feel personally threatened, our family stayed home for the next four days due to the anti-white sentiment that was causing the violence. Other missions with personnel in our city decided to evacuate from the country, leading to the closing of our children's school. With this, and at the request of our mission's leadership, we agreed to evacuate Côte d'Ivoire for the second time in two years.[59]

Another Church of God missionary in a sensitive nation where both anti-Western and anti-Christian sentiment were on the rise, declared, "During nearly three decades of challenging ministry here, I have found the needed strength and courage in the example of Jesus Christ…In this place where another major earthquake could occur at any time, a bomb go off anywhere, or an arrest be made at any moment, our ministry team trusts in God."[60] While agreeing that emergency backup plans are important, the missionary asserted that she will not "slip away when danger comes [for] it is in crisis that people realize their spiritual need for true hope." Wanting to be available at just such a time, she prayed, "O Sovereign God…help us to be your instruments and serve you in a violent and unsafe world. Help us to be instruments of your peace and compassion each day."[61]

Tim and Colleen Stevenson agree wholeheartedly. The day after they arrived in Uganda in 1985, they experienced their first coup, followed only months later by a military takeover. The stress was as real as the fields strewn with bodies, but it was a time of unprecedented church growth. They recalled, "Throughout this time of turmoil, many people came to Christ and many churches opened their doors. Opportunities were everywhere. Ugandans were ready to receive the message of the gospel and its assurance of a God-given plan for their lives. They were desperate for hope. People were so spiritually thirsty and needy that the churches were filling up. It was absolutely overwhelming."[62]

Nor were Latin American missionaries and their families immune to violence. In January 2006, Carmen Miller was attacked and shot in the leg while sitting on a curbside in Cochabamba, Bolivia. The teenage daughter of David and Barbara Miller, regional coordinators for Latin America, Carmen testified that "a constant flow of love and support from literally every corner of the globe…pointed to one thing: God's protection. My life had been spared and that was cause for celebration."[63]

These stories are but a few that could be told of how terrorism and violence were increasingly affecting missions. Responding, Global Missions added a crash course in missionary preparedness to its annual August personnel meetings and established some new policies for ministry in uncertain times, including a standard operating procedure (SOP) for missionary personnel evacuations. Approved in 2004, it determined that evacuation decisions could be made by the missionary, by the regional coordinator, or in the Anderson offices. Two other policies adopted in 2002 related to procedures to be followed should a missionary die while on the field.

"But in the end, once we have done what is necessary, it is our covering of prayer that is of greatest assistance to missionaries," Edwards declared.[64]

When Nature Threatens

That same covering of prayer would also be the key for missionaries and the international church when natural catastrophes struck. In fact, nature threatened often during the decade of the 2000s and struck with fury through cataclysmic tragedies and serious worldwide health issues, including AIDS and avian flu, about which Robert Edwards wrote in his February 2006 "State of the Mission" report as Global Missions coordinator:

> This past week it was discovered that the avian flu has now entered Nigeria. While there are only three cases there so far, experts fear that once the disease enters the African continent where immunities are low and health services are scant, the mutations that have been feared may finally begin in earnest. Do we cease sending missionaries and bring our people back to the States? Certainly not. But once again, we must be prepared for the eventualities that we face.[65]

While the worst case scenario never materialized, the World Health Organization reported that the two-and-a-half-year crisis had moved the world closer to pandemic than it had been in more than thirty-five years. And in the midst of the avian flu scare came SARS (severe acute respiratory syndrome). Its outbreak in 2003 in southern China spread rapidly, ultimately killing eight hundred people and sickening ten times that many. Aware of the danger, Patrick and Jamie Nachtigall returned to the United States from Hong Kong after their church suspended most gatherings until the period of high contagion had passed.

Recognizing that AIDS was now a worldwide scourge, *Missions* magazine devoted two issues to the topic, in 2005 and in 2008. In the first, missionary nurses Neelie Kerich and Glenna Phippen wrote on the crisis in Uganda, noting that one in five Ugandans was HIV-positive. Although the nurses practiced all standard precautions in giving direct patient care, some voices were suggesting that it might be only a matter of time before a health-care missionary was infected. But not one Church of God medical missionary on any field was considering retreat. Rather, all saw the health disaster as an opportunity, illustrated by Kerich and Phippen's statement:

> Not only does health care include physical care, but it also emphasizes attention to spiritual welfare...People with HIV/AIDS are particularly hungry for encouragement and hope. The stigma of a positive diagnosis of HIV has led to a high level of rejection,

abandonment, and physical abuse by family and village, as well as discrimination by society in general…Unlike North America, in Uganda there is unlimited freedom to speak to patients about their religious beliefs and convictions. Therefore, sharing the hope of Jesus Christ in the clinic or counseling setting comes naturally. We have the opportunity to demonstrate Christ's love and acceptance through our contact with patients, thus setting an example for family members and others in the community.[66]

In addition to health crises, including the most common disease, malaria, which plagued some missionaries often, nature inflicted other violence on the world. This was especially true in the fall of 2004. That September, hurricanes devastated the Caribbean–Atlantic region. Ivan pounded the region first, bringing destruction to Barbados, the Cayman Islands, and Grenada, where the Church of God lost many of its buildings, including the new church at Belle Isle dedicated only a year before. Shortly afterward, Jeanne caused additional damage on several islands, including Haiti, where the death toll hit two thousand and left more than three hundred thousand homeless. As of November 1, North American churches had sent six thousand dollars for relief in the Caribbean-Atlantic, in addition to collecting offerings for congregations in the state of Florida, also affected significantly by the deadly hurricane season.

Less than two months later, the disastrous Asian tsunami hit on December 26, 2004. Termed the ninth deadliest natural disaster in modern history, the tsunami left an incalculable trail of destruction in lands touching the Indian Ocean, especially on the Bay of Bengal. According to the United Nations, 229,866 people were lost, including 186,983 dead and 42,883 missing. Once again, North American churches responded generously and sent more than $500,000 through Compassionate Ministries for tsunami relief.

Despite this tragedy, Asia was not to be relieved. On May 3, deadly Cyclone Nargis struck Myanmar. Accurate casualty figures may never be known, but by late May, the death toll stood at seventy-eight thousand, with another fifty-six thousand officially listed as missing. (Casualties were certain to rise as the ruling military junta continued to deny outside organizations and governments the opportunity to assist in relief efforts.) Little more than one week later, a devastating magnitude 7.9

earthquake hit China's Sichuan Province on May 12. Within ten days, more than fifty thousand people were confirmed dead, more than thirty thousand were still missing, and five million were homeless. Church of God Ministries, Women of the Church of God, and Children of Promise responded by sending more than $100,000 to support Church of God relief work, headed by Dorothy Colney, national leader. Funds also helped repair three Church of God buildings and rebuild 150 homes of children sponsored by Children of Promise.

Taking Precautions

Even the most technologically advanced weather tracking software cannot do anything to prevent natural disasters. They can only warn those in harm's way, although in many cases, the alarm still is not soon enough for victims to avoid the inevitable. The best precautions taken also may not preclude a terrorist attack or problems with governments that oppose Christianity. But contingencies can be planned and circuitous routes taken.

The birth of Global Care, Inc., was one method employed by the Missionary Board in 1998 when it established the nonprofit Indiana corporation. The organization's presenting goal was to facilitate humanitarian relief in cooperation with the Church of God in sensitive regions. The organization was granted tax-exempt status on May 20, 2003, allowing it to accept tax-exempt contributions from individuals.

Despite this important development, however, it seemed that adequate attention could not be given by Global Missions and Church of God Ministries for the organization to meet its objectives. Jim Lyon, chairman of the Global Care Board, suggested in a memo, dated September 24, 2004, to Ronald Duncan, Church of God Ministries general director, that perhaps the challenges of restructuring the larger national agency were responsible for Global Care–related matters having been left unaddressed. As a result, Global Care was officially closed on January 4, 2005, and all funds in its bank account were transferred to projects in Russia and Turkey.

The MAP Program and Missionary Attrition

The Missionary Apprentice Program (MAP) was created in 2005 to respond to another difficult reality of life in the 2000s: the number of missionaries being sent out by the Church of God through Global Missions was decreasing. This troubling situation was being discussed as early as the annual staff planning meetings in January 2003 when Candy Power, Living Link coordinator, presented statistics showing that 134 people, equally divided between careers and special assignment missionaries (SAMs), were on the personnel roster in 1994–95. However, as of that January, there were only 101—sixty-one careers and forty SAMs.

In fact, the numbers were to continue shrinking. By December 31, 2007, personnel included fifty-three careers, thirty-three SAMs, and two MAPs, for a total of eighty-eight missionaries deployed by Global Missions.

Global Missions Coordinator Robert Edwards raised the topic of missionary attrition in the June 2005 staff planning meetings, asking pointedly, "Where does the problem lie? Recruitment, field preparation, member care on the field, or is it wrapped up in the new generation of persons being called to missions who come to the task with different expectations?"

The reality and severity of the problem were at the heart of MAP. Already the home office was attempting to assist new missionaries in adapting to the field through extensive orientation that included psychological testing and courses at Colorado's Missionary Training Institute (MTI). Some personnel also trained at the HEART Missionary Training Institute in Florida. But all of this took place before missionaries departed for the field, sometimes leaving them to face further necessary and often extremely difficult acculturation alone. More than a few missionaries did not survive. This led to the creation of MAP, an entry-level program for everyone wanting a career in missions. MAPs were to be mentored over a two-year period by experienced missionaries. After successfully completing this apprenticeship, they would have the option of moving into career assignments.

By the end of 2007, there had been six MAP missionaries. Two had moved into career positions, two had left Global Missions, and two were halfway through their apprenticeship, prompting Sharon Skaggs, assistant Global Missions coordinator, to say, "We believe there is real merit to the program, although it hasn't yet worked as well as it could have because of better support needed on the field. But we're fine-tuning the program and looking forward to a stronger program in the future."

Underscoring Skaggs' positive assessment about the viability and future of the program, three MAPs were to be commissioned at the 2008

North American Convention for service in Côte d'Ivoire (Kay Watts) and Kenya (Dave and Bonnie Baylor).

Other Trends in Missions

The shrinking number of missionaries was not the only defining trend affecting Global Missions during the 2000s. Another was the decreasing number of congregations supporting the international missions enterprise. As the organized missions effort of the Church of God approached one hundred years, the character of the church behind the organization had changed considerably.

"The donor base in the United States and Canada is rapidly changing," Bob Edwards reported during the January 2008 annual staff planning meetings. Explaining, the Global Missions coordinator pointed out, "The vast majority of congregations are no longer satisfied with just giving funds to remote programs that they have no influence over or input into how [they] operate."

Illustrating his point, Edwards told of a large Ohio church that was considering drastically changing the way it appropriated its discretionary funds. While that congregation continued to desire a vital connection with the Church of God, Anderson, Indiana, there were a growing number of strong voices among its constituency calling for greater say in where funds were allocated and how they were spent. This church also reported a "level of frustration with Global Missions in how long it takes to initiate new projects" and issued a plea for Church of God Ministries to "challenge the church."

If there was a change in the tone of voices closer to Anderson—the geographic area that had a high per capita of missions giving and traditionally the strongest supporters of the national church—how much more were the ties loosening among churches farther away from the national headquarters. (Those in the Pacific Northwest were the exception to this general rule.) Increasingly, Church of God congregations were supporting local, state, national, and international organizations as well as Church of God Ministries, while others were bypassing Global Missions altogether to fund other programs outside the church. By the 2000s, the days of supporting the Church of God simply because it was the Church of God were long gone in most congregations.

Additionally, the legal problems that faced the Board of Church Extension beginning in 2000 and the resulting loss of trust in Anderson across much of the church also exacerbated the negative cycle and resulted in some churches reducing or discontinuing their Living Link support entirely. Illustrative of the downward support trend, there were 654 of 2,287 congregations in the United States and Canada involved in Living Link in 2005. By January 2008, of 2,215 Church of God congregations in the United States, only 574 were Living Link churches.[67] Admittedly, some of the decrease was because there were fewer missionaries to support—eleven career, three SAM, and two MAP missionaries retired, resigned, or completed assignments in 2007, while only four SAMs and two MAPs were deployed that year. But it was a troubling trend, nevertheless.

"The die-hard Church of God baby boomers don't make all the decisions in church now," Candy Power, Living Link administrator, asserted. "We must look at ways to educate Generation X and the youth in our churches on missions and stewardship. Most churches take their giving very seriously. They determine what to fund and want information on how they made a difference. They want to be involved."[68]

In fact, this question of greater accountability was one of the key points around which Project Link was built. At the time it was launched in 2005 as the fundraising arm for international projects (Living Link being the older sister program for raising missionary support), only 27 percent of the 2,287 churches in the United States and Canada were giving in any way to Global Missions.[69] Much work needed to be done to fulfill the stated goal of involving every North American Church of God congregation in Project Link and Living Link. The accountability theme was given high priority in initial promotional pieces, including the following:

> The importance of accountability cannot be overemphasized. Even minor unaccountability left unchecked can intrude on the effectiveness of the ministry and spread mistrust in the program. The public has high expectation of religious organizations such as Church of God Ministries. Daily, Global Missions works tirelessly and selflessly to address spiritual and physical needs worldwide. Donors recognize those insistent needs, and they want desperately to respond positively. But because of abuse of accountability in the past, they have developed mistrust in the system. We believe that

Project Link will help to reestablish this central issue of accountability and thereby restore trust.[70]

Another attempt to answer the accountability question was giving
renewed attention to work camps and other hands-on opportunities to
involve churches at the grassroots level. A new program called Eye on the
World offered its first international trip to Costa Rica in April 2007. In
addition to several work camps in 2008 sponsored by local churches and
Children of Promise "Journeys of the Heart," Global Missions was planning its second Eye on the World mission trip, this one to West Indies
Theological College in Trinidad in October 2008.

Despite attempts to respond to new donor trends in missions, Project Link administrator Ed Hyatt admitted in 2006 that efforts to recruit
people to help solicit wider church participation had not been as successful as he had hoped. He also reported that the 8 percent administrative
fee built into the program had caused some individuals to choose direct
support routes rather than Project Link. Nevertheless, he declared opti-
mistically, "My hope is [still] that five years from now the voices who are
saying we are abandoning missions will be stilled. Moreover, we will have
God-blessed systems, mechanisms, and networks in place to better serve
the church across the world. The situation we are in today is difficult and
painful. Yet I fully believe God is with us, and he will provide the wisdom
and resources we require."[71]

Technology Offers Hope

Technology was providing other avenues to promote missions. The hope
was that greater missions education would result in increased support by
Church of God congregations for Church of God missions. After all, as Ed
Hyatt, Project Link coordinator, pointed out, "In this day of diminishing
brand loyalty and the multiplicity of appeals, it is imperative that we find
effective ways to communicate to our constituency, the Church of God,
that they are our sole means of support for projects. We are not an agency
like World Vision or Samaritan's Purse that has the freedom and capacity
to cross denominational lines."[72]

One means of reaching the church was the new Outreach Ministries Web address that premiered at the 2001 North American Convention

(NAC). Part of the yet expanding Church of God Ministries Web site (www. chog.org), the Outreach Ministries section included Global Missions and provided information and photographs of all Church of God missionaries and country profiles within their regions of service. Additional clicks brought information about missionaries needing support, service opportunities, and educational resources that were available for order.

Just as the structure of Church of God Ministries developed further, unifying the Outreach Team into Kingdom Ministries, so too did the Web site mature. According to Bob Edwards, Global Missions coordinator, this was absolutely essential for the good health of Global Missions as the computer-savvy younger generation became church leaders. "They are demanding that Global Missions be able to deliver to them information and opportunities at the stroke of computer keys," Edwards declared.[73] As a result, a visit to Global Missions on the Internet in 2008 also made it possible to read *Missions* magazine online and learn about "Eye on the World" and other missions trips, missionaries' itineration schedules, and global prayer concerns.

By this time, e-mail had become almost as important as passports in opening doors and enabling missionaries to accomplish their multiple tasks. It was especially essential for regional coordinators, charged with a three-pronged assignment—relating to missionaries, to national leaders, and to supporters in the United States. As an example, David and Barbara Miller in Latin America sent out a regular e-mail communication titled, "What's Going on with the Regional Coordinator?" But actually, no missionary could live without e-mail.

Attempting to help them communicate better and more easily, Church of God Ministries in 2005 began providing a Web-based e-mail service for Global Missions field personnel. Addressing security issues, a domain was purchased using blind registration, meaning that no one would be able to discover the owner or find links to Church of God Ministries. Additionally, missionaries could now have their own Web sites with support provided through the IT department of Church of God Ministries.[74]

In Anderson, e-mail became indispensable almost immediately after Norman Patton announced around 1995 that the Missionary Board home office had an e-mail address. Within a decade, monthly remittances were deposited directly into bank accounts, missionaries received financial reports by e-mail, and instant communication (or nearly so) between the home office and the field was more often by e-mail than anything else. Also *Global UpLink* had premiered as a quarterly e-mail educational piece about Project Link, providing stories and regional project updates. Later, the launching of a members-only secure Web site in March 2008 gave missionaries access to the personnel directory, career and special assignment missionary manuals, Global Missions and Church of God Ministries policies, and other documents that might answer their questions immediately rather than having to wait on replies from the Anderson office.

An especially exciting use of the Web was to broadcast the worship services of the North American Convention (NAC). This had become standard by mid-decade but developed even further through the first-ever global Communion service during NAC 2008. Despite time differences necessitating some people worshiping at unorthodox hours, the service was broadcast live over the Web with the goal of unifying the church around the world in a sacred moment. Participants registered for the unusual Communion service included 195 churches in nineteen different countries where the Church of God was at work.

The China Consultation

Despite the importance of the annual North American Convention in June, many critical happenings in the Church of God occurred not only outside Anderson but also outside the United States and Canada. These included the biennial Inter-American Conferences in Latin America and the annual European Conference at Fritzlar Bible College in Germany. Another was the January 2006 China Consultation in Taipei, Taiwan.

Compelling facts supported the premise that China had become a strategic ministry location. With 1.3 billion people, it was the world's most populated nation. Even with the one-child policy, its population was predicted to reach 1.5 billion by 2010 and 2 billion by 2050. At mid-decade, more than half its people were under the age of thirty and were poised to help China become an international superpower. Already it ranked sixth in the world as an economic power, and the rise had only just begun. That Beijing hosted the 2008 summer Olympics was a sign of China's growing influence in the world.

The potential was also bright for the church, although atheism had been taught and Christians persecuted for more than half a century. In

1949, when the Communist Party assumed control and expelled all foreign missionaries—including ten from the Church of God—there were an estimated eight hundred thousand Christians in China. By 2006, this number had jumped to as many as eighty million. Moreover, the door to religious tolerance appeared to be opening, albeit slowly. While practical application of the law was not always generous, the constitution now granted freedom of religious beliefs. Additionally, it was no longer criminal to host religious activities in private homes or to share one's faith, although evangelizing young people under eighteen was prohibited.

Not only did it appear that the government was relaxing its stance towards the church, but China watchers were reporting an openness towards religious faith among the general population that had not been seen in decades. Christians were interpreting this as a sign of weariness with the emptiness of life without guiding morals. "If there ever is an open door, a 'right time' for China, it is now," declared John and Gwen Johnson, regional coordinators for Asia–Pacific.

Cooperating with the Taiwan Church of God, the coordinators planned the "A Heart for China Consultation" for January 14–22, 2006. Drawing fifty-five delegates from China, India, Hong Kong, Japan, South Korea, and the United States—all Church of God people committed to ministry in mainland China—the gathering was devoted to worshiping, planning, and pledging to carrying out over the next five years specific missions strategies that emerged. These included: "recruiting and sending ten English language and culture teachers to college campuses in mainland China each year; providing scholarships for ministerial students in China as well as logistical support for teachers inside and outside China; promoting and using short-term missions teams; helping train leaders within the house church movement; and working cooperatively in evangelizing and discipling a specific minority group, with the goal of establishing a church among them."[75]

Without doubt, the Consultation ended on a high note for continued cooperation among the Churches of God in Korea, Taiwan, and Hong Kong. With roots of this three-way partnership in mainland China reaching back into the early 1990s, there were now some new strategies in place for expanding the collaboration and involving others in order to take advantage of growing opportunities in China. The future looked hopeful.

Nevertheless, it was disappointing that leaders of the Asia–Pacific Conference were not represented among China Consultation delegates. So keenly felt was this absence that one discussion group devoted its time to talking about the need for reconciliation between Global Missions and the Asia–Pacific Conference. "This group was so convinced of the need for this reconciliation…that they said without it, everything that we plan during the Consultation would be useless," Bob Edwards, Global Missions coordinator, reported after participating in the missions strategizing event.[76]

Five months later, John and Gwen Johnson resigned from Global Missions. Although they helped to carry out a successful "Heart for China" program during NAC 2006, the wider visions engendered during the China Consultation were put on hold within Global Missions following their departure. Tragically, within months cancer struck both Cindy Lwo, wife of Alan Lwo, of Taiwan, and Lisa Leung, whose husband Edmund pastors the Hong Kong Church of God. Alan and Edmund were two Asian leaders chosen by the China Consultation for leadership on an interim steering committee that would help keep the momentum growing. Unfortunately, these health battles not only challenged development of new strategies but also the continuation of some outreach already underway.

Rift in Asia–Pacific

What was the rift in the region that demanded healing and reconciliation? Complaints from leaders of the Asia–Pacific Conference stemmed back at least to November 2000. At that time, Doris Dale, Global Missions coordinator, met in Bangkok, Thailand, with the Conference executive committee and heard members "humbly ask for our acknowledgement of their maturity as a growing, functioning body."[77] Specifically, they called for a new model of Global Missions leadership in their region that would not be built around a regional coordinator, and they believed their position was understood.

However, Donald Johnson was appointed Asia–Pacific interim regional coordinator in 2001 without consulting the Asia–Pacific Conference. Two years later, John and Gwen Johnson were named to the RC position. Once again, consultation did not take place. To make matters worse, although missionaries had been informed already of the upcoming appointment, there was no discussion of the matter in general, or even of John and Gwen in specific, during the 2002 Asia–Pacific Conference in Chiang Mai, Thailand, despite the fact that Global Missions representatives were present. Consequently, the Johnsons struggled to find acceptance in Asia–Pacific throughout their RC tenure.

The call for reconciliation had been sounded prior to the January 2006 China Consultation. Bob Edwards, Global Missions coordinator, had taken the lead in attempting to repair the damage by inviting Asia–Pacific leaders to a Global Missions–sponsored and –funded reconciliation meeting in Bangkok, Thailand, in September 2003. There he apologized for himself and for Global Missions and expressed the desire to work together with the Asia–Pacific Conference in the future. Although his words and the spirit in which they were spoken seemed to be accepted, relationships continued to be icy and unproductive during the next three years.

"We leave this assignment with a sense that we have not completed our task nor have we lived up to our commitments," wrote John Johnson in his final report to Global Missions. "We do feel that as we step aside, this will provide Global Missions the opportunity to demonstrate its commitment to partnership in very real ways. National leaders need to be consulted as to if or how they believe the regional coordinator's role needs to be filled. Nonetheless, it is essential that administrative support be provided for the career and SAM missionaries in the region. In my opinion, we should not hesitate in identifying the person or couple that will assume this responsibility."[78]

Following the Johnsons' departure, Edwards assumed oversight of Asia–Pacific in addition to his responsibilities as Global Missions coordinator. It was not the best of solutions, especially with his already overburdened desk, but considering the difficult relational problems in the region, it may have been the only solution at the time. Over the next two years, he continued to seek reconciliation, accepting a request by Asia–Pacific leaders in their December 2006 meetings that the next regional coordinator would not have had any missionary experience in the region. Continuing dialogue with regional leaders took Edwards back to Thailand in May 2008 to discuss the potential calling of a new regional coordinator couple. Later in November, with the approval of the executive committee of the Asia-Pacific Conference, Don and Caroline Armstrong accepted the call to become the next regional coordinators. Perhaps the Asia–Pacific rift was finally healing.

Memos of Understanding

Reconciliation and greater cooperation in ministry were also being sought elsewhere during the 2000s. On March 26, 2001, Pastor Reinhard Berle, chairman of Der Sozialdienst des Missionwerks der Gemeinde Gottes (SMGG), the social services arm of the Church of God in Germany, had signed a "Memorandum of Understanding" that explained their operations and structure as a legalized NGO (non-governmental organization). The document ended with these words: "These rules have the purpose to avoid misunderstandings and ease the cooperation in the work together, and to fulfill the lawful requirements."

The document did not, however, solve all misunderstandings or help avoid all future conflicts with Global Missions. In Bangladesh, for example, where both Global Missions and Kinderhilfswerk were operating, an uncomfortable feeling of coexistence rather than true partnership hung over the church, making it ripe ground for controversy and competition. This reality led to the creation of "A Document of Agreement Regarding Cooperative Work in Bangladesh." Signed in Fritzlar, Germany, January 8, 2004, by John Johnson, Global Missions regional coordinator for Asia–Pacific, and Reinhard Berle, Hans-Jurgen Pechmann, and Rainer Klinner, all representing SMGG, the memo began with an apology for anything done in the past that created or perpetuated "a spirit of disunity in the Church of God in Bangladesh, in Lalmanirhat, in particular."

The important agreement also stated that Global Missions and Kinderhilfswerk were committed to working together in Bangladesh and, as a practical starting point, promised to copy all correspondence regarding Bangladesh to each other. Further, the memo admitted that the existing bylaws of the Administrative Council of the church in Bangladesh needed to be rewritten and pledged to do this in three-way cooperation between the churches in Bangladesh, Germany, and the United States. A follow-up meeting in Lalmanirhat in November 2004 was proposed and agreed upon. Subsequently, Global Missions and SMGG met for further discussions in May 2008.

It was reported during the February 2006 Regional Coordinators and Staff Planning Meeting that Global Missions hopes to negotiate similar agreements in Uganda and other countries where both mission organizations are heavily involved in ministry.

Nevertheless, there was good news in 2006 about some other Memos of Understanding. This included one with Children of Promise, whose child sponsorship work in more than twenty countries occasionally overlapped with Global Missions activities and influenced its relationships with national churches. At the time, plans were to develop Memos of Understanding between Global Missions and other parachurch organizations operated by Church of God people eager for ministry to assist the Church of God around the world.

Crises in Australia and Cuba

Unfortunately, not every difficult situation could be resolved with a Memo of Understanding or other covenant to preserve relationships, even long-standing ones. Such was the case in 2007 when Church of God Ministries took the unprecedented and extraordinary step of disassociating with a group functioning as the National Ministries of the Church of God in Australia.[79] Dated November 21, 2007, the disassociation letter was signed by Ronald V. Duncan, general director of Church of God Ministries, and sent to all eighty-nine national leaders associated with the Church of God around the world, as well as to all Church of God congregations in North America.

According to the memorandum, Church of God Ministries, Inc., no longer recognized three Australian individuals as Church of God ministers because "they are no longer in fellowship and doctrinal unity with the Church of God in North America that is headquartered in Anderson, Indiana, U.S.A."

Robert Edwards, Global Missions coordinator, wrote an accompanying five-page letter "to recount a disappointing saga" that led Church of God Ministries "to exercise church discipline for the sake of the body." According to the letter, a team of three individuals[80] had traveled to Australia in May 2007 to investigate charges lodged by a group of disenfranchised members of the national Church of God association. The investigating team found major deficiencies in the national church organization and structure and validity in the concerns that had brought them to Australia. These findings resulted in a sixteen-page letter of recommendations to the Australia board of directors and the National Ministries Board.

Although receipt of that letter was never acknowledged, the national organization responded by removing Sandra Spencer, pastor of Shoalhaven Church, and a Shoalhaven layperson from membership on the National Ministries Board. They were charged as being dissidents for calling investigators from the United States. Subsequently, the Shoalhaven property was taken over and sold by the national board, with proceeds placed under control of the directors.

"We cannot be quiet on this matter," Edwards declared in his letter. "There is an evident, worked out abuse of power that appears to be calculated to financially benefit the few members who are now left standing without any dissenting voice to help to correct their refusal to change their ways."

As of January 2008, the recognized Church of God in Australia consisted of Pastor Sandra Spencer and the Shoalhaven Church in New South Wales, now meeting in a school. Additionally, plans were moving forward to launch a second congregation—Journey Church—on the Gold Coast in February 2009. It would be led by Pastor David Ravell and a launch team that met weekly for nearly a year of praying and seeking God's guidance while holding monthly barbecues and other activities through which contacts were being made for the new congregation.

Regrettably, Australia was not the only national church to experience "a hostile takeover of the reins of administration," the words David Miller used in 2005 to describe what he termed his most disappointing failure as Latin America regional director. He recalled the difficult crisis in the life of the Cuban church in his February 2006 report to the Regional Coordinators and Staff Planning Meeting:

> We began 2005 with the Cuba Task Force (a voluntary forum of churches and freestanding organizations in Ohio, Florida, and Washington state and Global Missions) poised to make a significant investment in leader training and church planting in Cuba. Those plans were stymied by a power struggle among the officers of the Cuba General Assembly that resulted in the expulsion of President Carlos Lamelas and the loss of scores of pastors and workers who were, for no apparent reason other than their support of Carlos, placed under discipline or suspended from the ministry…The Task Force commissioned Greg Wiens [Florida state pastor] and

myself to try and make sense of what was happening and encourage a reconciliation. The attempt was unsuccessful…

But the church in Cuba was growing anyway. Miller reported that despite leadership issues, increasing government restrictions, and a shortage of Bibles, membership in the Church of God was increasing through vibrant house churches. By the end of 2005, there were as many as thirty-three hundred people attending Church of God congregations meeting in eleven sanctuaries and eighty-three house churches.

International Faith and Action Forum

Regional Coordinators David and Barbara Miller are quick to share more good news from their region, especially in leadership development. Called the International Faith and Action Forum (IFAF), this initiative for leader training and evangelism was launched in Argentina in November 2005 in response "to the cry of the Latin American churches to define the doctrinal distinctives of the Church of God movement" in order to equip them to respond biblically to "the rampant rise of neo-Pentecostal movements in the continent that range from 'innovations' on the gospel (e.g., extreme prosperity theology) to downright heresy (sub-Trinitarian teachings on spiritualism)."[81] Pastor Alejandro de Francisco, of Cuba, and the Millers taught the first Forum, sharing about Church of God theological distinctives that build healthy congregations with thirty-five leaders from Argentina, Brazil, Paraguay, Bolivia, and Uruguay.

Cooperating with the Inter-American Conference, the coordinators were eager to involve as many church leaders as possible in the training events. Consequently, the second IFAF event occurred in March 2006 in two separate venues, Costa Rica and Venezuela. Forty-five participants from four countries (Panama, Costa Rica, Nicaragua, and Honduras) joined in the Costa Rica event led by Greg Wiens, of Florida; missionaries Wayne and Kathi Sellers; Arminio Kopp, of Brazil; Victor Quispe, of Bolivia; and the Millers. Both events in 2006 considered the life cycle of churches, pastors and their families, and factors that build healthy congregations and leaders.

Another pair of IFAF training events was conducted in 2007 (Honduras in March and Argentina in October) with "Effectively Communicating the Gospel in the 21st Century" as the theme for both venues. At this writing, plans were in progress for two more sessions in 2008 (Brazil and Panama) to study "The Character of the Servant of God."

Describing the response of the national church, David says, "This was a vision that God seemed to give to our Latin leaders and to us missionaries at basically the same time. We operate on the principle that we do not start new programs or initiatives, but facilitate ideas that the people we serve come up with themselves. The Forums fit that ideal. Thus we have responded to felt needs and have enjoyed enthusiastic participation up to now. The Forums have also spun off cooperative programs between neighboring countries to encourage one another and help raise up workers. Forums or similar programs in themselves cannot prepare people for the ministry, but they can do much to sharpen skills, focus gifts, and raise the level of workers' understanding of the Bible, society, and their own role in the Kingdom."[82]

Challenges and a Hopeful Future

There was also good news coming from Europe and the Middle East, although it was wrapped in an unusual package: the growth of Islam and the reality of the small size of the Church of God in most nations of the region. According to Regional Coordinators Kelley and Rhonda Philips, estimates were that as many as fifteen to twenty million Muslims were now living in the European Union (EU) and represented the largest religious minority. At the same time, Islam was the fastest growing religion. With significant Muslim populations already in France, Germany, the United Kingdom, Spain, Italy, the Netherlands, and Belgium, and given continued immigration and high Muslim fertility rates, projections were that Europe's Muslim population would double by 2025.[83]

Rather than seeing this as an insurmountable obstacle, the coordinators issued a challenge to Global Missions that also touched on the increasing tension in the region as Islam rubbed shoulders with other cultures and religions:

> The growth of Islam in Europe is taking place at an unprecedented rate. Unless we take immediate action…we will miss a God-given opportunity to share the real person and message of Jesus Christ with the people of Islam living in Europe. Perhaps the recent

London bombings [July 7, 2005] as well as the current protest over a caricature of Mohammed (which was first printed in a Danish newspaper in September) will serve as a reminder to us all of the changing face of Europe…

We need a strategic plan by which the Church of God in the region will address this opportunity to share Jesus Christ with the diverse cultures represented…Outreach to the Muslim population of Europe needs to become a top priority [and]…a collaborative effort…[84]

Workers in at least one nation in the region were already responding to the challenge of reaching Muslims. In 2006, this church in an Islamic nation was growing after years of stagnation, struggle, and internal conflict. New churches were being planted, new pastors were being trained, and outreach to Muslims was now a goal to be pursued, even if cautiously. Additionally, social work, including literacy projects among women, elementary schools, and clinics, was also opening doors for evangelism and outreach.

There was other good news from the region in 2008—a new cooperative ministry plan between Global Missions and the German Church in Berlin. Although it was still on the drawing board, Kelley excitedly described how "the vision of what we believe God is calling us to come together and create" came to be:

Six years ago [in 2002] in a conversation with Klaus Kroeger, the topic of Berlin came up as being a high potential location for an international church. So for [the next] five years, Rhonda and I dreamed of what that might look like. Two years ago, one of the German leaders, Helmut Link, cast a vision for a Berlin ministry center. Although we had never shared our vision with this pastor, he described at least 90 percent of the things we had been dreaming. It was pretty exciting! After that, the German church invited us to relocate and join them in [carrying out] their vision. We prayed, sought wise counsel, and in August 2007, we made the move.[85]

Describing the Gateway Berlin project, the RC notes the center will be built in a style reminiscent of the missionary homes in the United States in the early days of the reformation movement. The location will house an English-language international church at first, with plans to expand later into other languages represented in Berlin; a hands-on training center for Church of God young people who would give one to two years for ministry; and the base of operations for a regional and multicultural ministry team that would focus on helping churches with spiritual formation, discipleship, and leadership development. The center would also serve as a gathering place where Church of God people could dialogue, dream, and plan for expanding both the Church of God and the kingdom of God in such European hub cities as Amsterdam, Paris, London, Dublin, and Zurich.

"This will be a post-Christian urban ministry center which employs creative, relevant, and innovative means to tell our story and engage the popular culture in a dialogue through which they can be introduced to Jesus," Kelley explained. He also recognized that such an all-encompassing vision of regional cooperation and hope for the future stands in stark contrast to the current picture of the Church of God in Europe and the Middle East: only eighty-four churches, sixty-one hundred Church of God believers, six national assemblies, and ministry taking place in sixteen countries where eight career and two special assignment missionaries were placed in 2008.

"The recent removal of Denmark from the regional stats was a painful reminder of just how much the small single churches in this region are struggling," the RCs declared, noting that the tiny congregation had banded with another church group because of its dwindling size. "The remaining single churches in Spain, Italy, France, Serbia, and Greece are all facing tremendous challenges and will eventually go the same way as the church in Denmark unless necessary changes are made. Those changes would include better connectivity to one another, as well as to churches in the rest of Europe, especially Germany, [to] encourage, strengthen, and provide accountability for these congregations that teeter on the edge of extinction."[86]

In a sentence, the Gateway Berlin project answers current realities with good news and hope for the future in Europe and the Middle East.

Planning for the Centennial

Even as strategizing for the Gateway Berlin project was underway in Europe, so too was planning in progress for the one hundredth anniversary of the organized missions endeavor of the Church of God in North America, to be commemorated at the 2009 North American Convention.

Although the observance would focus on the Church of God around the world, it would not be the first centennial celebration for the church overseas. Already a number of centenaries had been commemorated in other locations, including Kolkata, formerly Calcutta, India (1901); Germany (1901); Meghalaya, India (1902); Egypt and Jamaica (1907); and Japan (1908). In these countries, Church of God ministry predates the establishment of the Missionary Board, although the efforts of North American missionaries figure into the early days of their church histories.

Bob Edwards, Global Missions coordinator, commenting on the April 2007 Jamaica celebration, declared, "I think one thing [this] tells us is that the Church of God has missions firmly written into its DNA… Even before there was a Missionary Board of the Church of God, [along with] the fact of the dislike that our [forefathers] had for organizations, Christians were feeling the internal fire in their lives and were going out to spread the good news. That was just who we were. And that is just who we are."[86]

While the Global Missions staff had been anticipating the centenary throughout the decade, preparations began in earnest in October 2007 with a two-day meeting at Madison Park Church, Anderson. Three missionaries on home assignment (Susan Hardman, Central Asia; Larry Sellers, Côte d'Ivoire; and Tammie Tregellas, Malawi) joined a group of Global Missions and Church of God Ministries personnel and others to formulate a proposal for how the church could mark the historic occasion during its annual convention. Later, Doris Dale was named to chair the planning and implementation committee for the celebration.

Highlighting not only one hundred years of Global Missions as an organization but also celebrating the Church of God internationally, the five-day NAC program was slated to discuss such themes as "Called to Mission," "Authorized for Mission," "Surrendered for Mission," "United in Mission," and "Live the Mission." Amos Moore, missionary to Nepal from India; Mailesi Ndao, national leader of Zambia; and Patrick Nachtigall, missionary to Hong Kong, were among eight individuals scheduled as speakers in the main worship services.

Unfortunately, a worldwide economic downturn that became especially critical during the latter half of 2008 soon began to affect planning for the centennial celebration. By late fall, the financial crisis was of such concern that there was talk of whether or not there would even be a North American Convention in 2009. Eventually, the decision was made to proceed, although activities would be scaled back from the original planning. Nevertheless, the program would continue as scheduled for the full five days (June 27–July 1). Worship services during the day would be in Park Place Church, with evening gatherings at Madison Park Church. Conferences were being scheduled in the Church of God Ministries building, Park Place Church, and on the grounds of Anderson University.

Additionally, plans were going ahead to convene a Global Conversation on July 2 as a follow-up to the 2003 Global Dialogue. Children of Promise and other missions supporters hoped to enable a sizeable representation of international leaders to participate both in the NAC centenary celebration and in the Global Conversation.

Milestones of the 2000s

As is often true of birthday party planning, Global Missions approached its one hundredth celebration with the family in mind—the Church of God family around the world. While the blood relationship of this family of likeminded Christians was through Jesus Christ, it is interesting to note that there were a number of family members actually related physically who served through Global Missions in the decade of the 2000s.

Representative of parent-child combinations were Sherman and Kay Critser, Africa regional coordinators, and their daughter Carrie, Central Asia; Bernard and Cheryl Barton, Japan, and their son-in-law and daughter, Donald and Stephanie Lyngdoh, Central Asia; Sharon Skaggs, Global Missions assistant coordinator, and her son-in-law and daughter, Patrick and Jamie Nachtigall, Hong Kong; and Stan and Marion Hoffman, Zambia, and their son-in-law and daughter, Tim and Colleen Stevenson, Uganda.

Second- and third-generation Church of God missionaries also were included among Global Missions personnel of the 2000s. Third-generation missionaries were Alta Ruthe (Crose) Jack, Kenya; Jamie (Skaggs) Nachtigall, Hong Kong; Sharon (Helsel) Bernhardt, Southeast Asia; and Stephanie (Barton) Lyngdoh, Central Asia. Representing a second generation of Church of God missionaries were Donald Lyngdoh, Central Asia; Joy

Plummer, Tanzania (although it was her grandparents, Herman and Lavira Smith, who had been missionaries); Elaine (Kerich) Collins, Kenya; Rachelle Bargerstock, Japan; and David Simpson, Bulgaria

Brother-sister combinations during the decade included John Ackerman, Haiti, and Caroline Ackerman, Tanzania; Karen Lambert and Greg Robertson, both in Ecuador; and Don Deena Johnson, Lebanon, Cheryl (Johnson) Barton, Japan, and John Johnson, Asia–Pacific regional coordinator until 2006. (The Johnson siblings were also among second-generation missionaries.)

Some "family" members concluded their earthly ministries during the decade. These included Lima Lehmer Williams and Mae Robinson (2000); Lovena "Billie" Jenkins, Frank LaFont, Walter Tiesel, and Kathryn Kerr (2001); Aaron Kerr, Wilbur Skaggs, Ruben Schwieger, and Hazel McDilda Cage (2002); Ellen High, Nathan Smith, Lester Crose, Marjory Williams, and Velma Schneider (2003); Eva Buck and Grace LaFont (2004); Margaret LaFont and Oakley Miller (2005); Clair Shultz (2006); and Wanda Goodrick, Milton Buettner, and Kenneth Good (2008).

Additionally, some international church leaders were "called home" in the 2000s. Included among these were Theodosia Cumberbatch, Trinidad (2001); Cleve Grant, Jamaica (2003); and Daisy Taylor, a missionary from Panama who helped plant the Church of God in Colombia (2005).

Afterword
The Mission Mandate and the Church of God

The Movement's Early Response to the Biblical Mandate

Just twenty-nine years after the beginning of the Church of God reformation movement (1880), the Missionary Board was formed in 1909. George P. Tasker chronicles this event in his diary, dated June 12, 1909:

> On June 12, 1909, after an address on Government in the Church, H. M. Riggle, after presenting our plans for a missionary paper, to be called the *Missionary Herald*, recommended that "certain brethren should be recognized among us, by common consent, as having and exercising in behalf of the Church, the care of the foreign missionary work. They should be capable of advising, instructing, encouraging and restraining." The names here presented and that were acknowledged by the immediate rising to their feet of the entire assembly of ministers were, D. O. Teasly, J. W. Byers, E. E. Byrum, E. A. Reardon, G. P. Tasker, H. A. Brooks and D. F. Oden. Brother Riggle then said, "It is intended that the entire ministry should cooperate with these brethren," to which all said, "Amen."

Lester A. Crose, in his book *Passport for a Reformation*, calls this a "bold step" for a church that did not regard man-made organization highly (pp. 35–37; see pp. 18–20 in this edition). There was, however, a more strategic purpose in this historic move than primarily providing coordination. It was an organized initiative to take seriously and respond intentionally to the biblical mandate to go beyond North American borders.

Missionary activity outside North America was considered, from the beginning of the movement, a nonnegotiable mandate. The young age and small size of the movement provided no excuse for total preoccupation with local and national mission and ministry. It was true, however, that without a strong vital core, expansion internationally could not have occurred. But the reformation's national agenda always put the missionary thrust "into all the world" at the forefront of any planning wherever the church met. This was a central theme! That theme took in the whole world. It carried no local geographical bias.

As the Missionary Board matured and as the church came to provide strong and consistent support for missions, the organization may have been seen by some to be in competition with the development of the church in North America since, for many years, a large percentage of the national church's total budget went to support and administer missions abroad— a reflection of what was felt to be an appropriate response to the biblical mandate.

Global Missions Attempts to Work within the New Structure

The work of international missions was the principal assignment of the Missionary Board until December 31, 1999. With the merger of several national agencies, ninety years of this singular focus ended. Now Global Missions had the task of doing the work of the former Missionary Board, but under a new corporate structure, Church of God Ministries, Inc. The resulting changes that emerged from the incorporation of the international missionary cause into a merged organization are well documented in chapters nine and ten of this book. The final decade of the twentieth century closed with the cooperation and intention of all entities of the church to make the new structure work and, in fact, to make it work more effectively and more efficiently.

In response to the new structure and to its task of focusing on missions outside North America, Global Missions adopted a mission statement with the intent to clarify its assignment in the new structure. That statement read, "Global Missions of Church of God Ministries exists to identify, prepare, and send missionaries, and to partner with Churches of God around the world to fulfill the Great Commission, Matthew 28:18–20. We do so by: evangelizing and discipling; equipping and sustaining leaders for ministry; establishing churches; [and] modeling the compassion of Christ."

Actually, this statement is not too different from the principles the Missionary Board had followed for more than nine decades, an era that included two world wars and the transition from paternal mission strategies to those valuing true partnership. But the world was changing more rapidly than Christian mission could keep pace. Nevertheless, the worldwide mission of the Church of God made remarkable progress during these years in relating to national leaders and national churches as they matured.

The mission statement above, while similar to the ideas that guided the Missionary Board, now must direct the work of Global Missions through the very different governance structure already noted. Under the new structure, Global Missions does not have a singularly focused board. One result is that decision-making became more time consuming and complicated. Global Missions, whether rightly or wrongly, felt disconnected from the Ministries Council of Church of God Ministries as strategic corporate decisions seemed to be made in a vacuum and without specific understanding of the inherent nature of Global Missions. In order to continue dealing appropriately with individuals, structures, and situations outside North America, Global Missions needed more focused support from the newly structured parent body.

But an organizational commitment had been made, and Global Missions was obligated to make the new structure work. Whatever fine-tuning it would take, the mission mandate needed to be addressed with a vital and specific focus. The commitment for Global Missions was to follow and implement the mission statement, whatever the amount of extra effort it would take. As from the beginning, doing missions globally remained a recurrent theme both in mission statement and practice.

Can a Global Mission Focus Be Coordinated and Operative within the New Context?

On May 10, 2001, the Ministries Council adopted a document titled "The Mission, Vision, Values, and Key Results of Church of God Ministries, Inc." A shorter version of this statement was published in a glossy trifold called "Church of God Ministries, Mission—Vision—Values." In speaking about the mission of Church of God Ministries, the general director shortened the mandate to, "The mission of Church of God Ministries is to serve the local church." Quoting from the lengthier document, the mission statement follows:

> Church of God Ministries (North America) is called to serve, resource, and partner with the people of God to achieve the mission

of the Church of God Reformation Movement which is to Worship the Lord, Reach the Lost, Disciple Believers, Equip for Ministry, Celebrate Unity and Live Out the Love of Christ.

From an international perspective, this statement focuses primarily on North America. The work of resourcing and partnering appears to have the North American church as its service object. Reference to North America's responsibility to an international obligation is only by inference. If there is to be unity of vision between the Mission Statement of Global Missions and that of Church of God Ministries, as is imperative in the unified organizational structure, attention must be given to reconciling the two.

The question must be raised: How is it that Global Missions and its work, organized structurally within Church of God Ministries, cannot find itself in the mission and ministry focus of its corporate parent? In the broadest interpretation, Global Missions might be accounted for, but this seems at best to be another instance where fundamental philosophies are disconnected. There is a danger that both Global Missions and other ministries of the Kingdom Ministry Team will be marginalized without future correction and coordination. At some point, it would be wise that midcourse corrections be made in order that Church of God Ministries comes to know itself and its purpose in a more inclusive statement of mission.

The Five Strategic Goals and the Mission Mandate

In the 2006 Strategic Planning Conference in Nashville, Tennessee, five strategic goals were outlined to guide the future of the Church of God reformation movement. They were designed for the church to "transform culture by being the body of Christ." The five goals are:

1. **Ignite!** Revitalizing the Great Commission (Matt 28:18–20) in the life of every individual, church, and agency.
2. **Permeate!** Engaging every individual, church, and agency in the Great Commandments (Matt 22:37–39).
3. **Free!** Committing to stewardship principles (Matt 6:33) leading to a flexible ministry future and the management of debt (debt free the goal) for every individual, church, and agency.

4. **Cultivate!** Nurturing the spiritual gifts (1 Cor 12:1–7) of every individual, church, and agency.
5. **Refresh!** Renewing our efforts toward relational connectivity and identity (John 17:21–22) for every individual, church, and agency of the Church of God.

As with the "Church of God Ministries Mission, Vision, and Values" statement, it is obvious that these five stated goals are primarily for the North American church. Reference to every individual, church, and agency specifically and repeatedly points to North America. This is entirely appropriate since it is not the place of North America to set goals for other churches around the world. But these goals seemed only to assume the international missional obligation of the church in North America.

Addressing this concern, the general director of Church of God Ministries instructed Global Missions to develop a strategic plan by the end of 2008 that would "establish an enabling strategic connection within the Church of God globally." The result document (see appendix 6) flowed out of the Five Strategic Goals of Church of God Ministries and brought about a revised mission statement for Global Missions. The new statement reads: "Committed to world evangelism and discipleship, Global Missions will send missionaries, resource global ministry, and network through interdependent partnerships with the church around the world."

To revitalize the Great Commission is to recognize that it begins with the words, "Go therefore and make disciples of all nations…" Church of God Ministries must fulfill its own goals by structuring itself to promote this vital function in the church. Loving God and neighbor, promoting good stewardship principles, nurturing the spiritual gifts, and promoting unity and connectedness are all values to be nurtured for the good of the church both here and as it carries out the missional mandate to the rest of the world. These goals are poised to be intentionally focused in more specific ways to include a committed church ministering to a needy world.

As we step into the next century of missions, it is important to consider:

1. That the Church of God in North America is only one part of the world mission effort of the Church of God globally;

2. That the Church of God in North America must not forget its Great Commission obligation for cross-cultural mission outreach within its own territory even while it reaches out into all the world;

3. That Global Missions within Church of God Ministries, Inc., is only one of the sending agencies in North America. It also is only one of the international mission boards responding to the Great Commission;

4. That the Church of God in North America is only one partner, and perhaps not even the principal partner, as the Church of God moves toward living out the "One World, One Mission" theme;

5. That communication (connectivity) between ourselves and our mission partners around the world has never been more important than it is now;

6. That whatever resources it may take, regular, planned conversation between international church leaders is vital for the future;

7. That measuring future success or failure must be more than numbers of new believers, new churches, or money in the bank. We are a part of the body of Christ around the world—it is part of our biblical DNA;

8. That not all of the financial support for missions out of North America is distributed through Church of God Ministries and not all financial support originates from North America;

9. That we are not responsible to develop programs that just "serve them." There is no room for superior posturing in Kingdom work;

10. That we need a strategy that calls for as much sacrifice from ourselves as we expect from our partners in mission; and,

11. That dysfunction in any church around the world highlights our own. The shortsightedness and competitiveness "out there" is often born out of our own.

When the Missionary Board was formed in 1909, it recognized both the call and sacrifice of those who preceded it as they seriously followed the command to "go into all the world." In the appendix of this book is a list of more than twelve hundred individuals who have spanned the globe and served with dignity in countries that were not their own. They were committed though not always perfect. They did the best with what they had. They were supported by those who could not go themselves. The church in North America distinguished itself by keeping the biblical mandate for mission central in its ministry. Whether through Penny-a-Day banks distributed by Women of the Church of God, through supporting Living Link missionaries, or, most recently, by providing for international needs through Project Link, the Church of God has always found ways to highlight carrying the gospel into the whole world.

In the end, working within a new structure is not the real issue for the future. Thoughtful, committed leadership will make this happen. The most important questions that confront the Church of God generally and Church of God Ministries specifically are: Will the mission mandate continue to be a central theme? Will our partnership with churches around the world be enhanced whatever the cost in effort and dollars? Will the church in North America continue to see the fields "white and ready for harvest"? Will we continue to send and support missionaries? Will the church continue the good work in "Jerusalem, Judea and Samaria" while at the same time remembering urgently—as we have for more than one hundred years—our obligation to "the uttermost parts of the world" (Acts 1:8b)?

The Lord is calling us into the future. Creatively sharing the gospel, making disciples, planting churches, assisting in the formation of leaders, and touching the needy among the nations—all these things are essential if we, the Church of God, will be judged faithful. It is not enough to "care for our own." The world is on the heart of God. We are called to care for this planet, to be sure. Yet faithfulness requires obedience and obedience requires that we seriously consider and act upon the clear instructions and bold and loving example of Jesus himself. The nations, peoples, language groups, and tribes are waiting for us. If history serves any purpose at all, it is to call us to search for the places where God's story, our story, and the story of the nations have intersected so that in our day, time, and context we might continue our journey to and with the nations.

Appendix 1
Ministry Partner Biographies

Victor & Yvonne Babb

Government civil servant, housing organization CEO, and bank manager are not a cleric's usual jobs. But for the first twenty-plus years of Victor Babb's ministry on the Caribbean island of Barbados, the multivocational pastor was indeed all of the above—and more.

Born on July 8, 1936, the eldest of eight siblings was introduced to the Church of God as a teenager. Winning a scholarship to a secondary school a distance from his home, he moved in with his aunt, who lived nearer the school, and attended the Church of God with her. After committing his life to Christ, Victor became active in the local and national church, where he met and married Yvonne Bovell in 1961.

From 1969 to 1984, Victor pastored Garden's Church of God. He commends his wife for her ministry involvement that allowed him to work bivocationally to augment the church's part-time salary. Through their partnership, the Babbs saw significant growth at Garden's Church during their pastorate, including building a new facility, beginning a child day care center, and launching a national credit union.

These accomplishments did not go unnoticed. The government invited Victor to serve on its national board overseeing all children's facilities on the island. His vision also helped birth the Church of God Caribbean–Atlantic Assembly, which he served as its first director from 1979 until retiring in 2004. Beginning in 1991, he was also the Missionary Board's Caribbean-Atlantic regional director—the first and only person from outside North America ever to hold such a leadership position.

Although of retirement age, both Victor and Yvonne were continuing in ministry in 2008, but with the tables turned. Leaving teaching in 1998, Yvonne began pastoring the Mile and a Quarter Church of God. Today Victor is her helpmate in ministry there.

MAURICE &
DONDEENA CALDWELL

That Maurice and Dondeena Caldwell have
spent a lifetime in Church of God missions
isn't surprising. It's simply in their DNA.

Dondeena was born in 1927 in Anderson, Indiana, while her parents, William
and Vada Fleenor, attended Anderson Bible
Training School. They took her at age three to Syria, and then to Egypt.
Her father eventually spent more than twenty years on the mission field.
Perhaps not unexpectedly, Dondeena felt called to missions in junior high
school.

Maurice was born in 1923 into a pastor's home in Leavenworth, Kansas. His great-aunt, Minnie Criswell, married George Tasker, first secretary
of the Missionary Board. Later, as missionaries to India, the Taskers visited
the Caldwell home, sparking Maurice's lifelong fascination with missions.
This interest later focused on Spanish-language ministries, including pastoring two Hispanic churches and serving the home missions board. Eventually, he worked thirty years in foreign missions, serving with Dondeena
in Mexico, Brazil, and Spain. He also was the Missionary Board's Latin
America coordinator from 1978 to 1990.

Among many accomplishments, Maurice helped organize the Hispanic Council in the United States and the regional Inter-American Conference. The Caldwells assisted with Spanish and Portuguese publications,
and Dondeena directed Missions Education and edited *Church of God
Missions* for fifteen years. However, it was launching two Bible training
schools—La Buena Tierra in Mexico and Boa Terra in Brazil—that was
most fulfilling. In retirement, they discovered more than fifty congregations pastored by the schools' graduates.

The Caldwells have stayed busy in retirement. Maurice taught Spanish at Anderson University for twelve years and has edited the Church of
God Peace Fellowship newsletter since 1995. Dondeena has written books
and articles on missions for several publications. She also is the Spanish
interpreter for a hospital and mental health center in Anderson, where
they have lived since 1978—except for three special assignment missionary
postings. With missions in their DNA, it seems there's really no retiring.

LESTER A. CROSE

He rightly was called Mr. Missions of the Church of God. A missionary kid in Japan and Syria; missionary in Lebanon, Egypt, and the Caribbean; mission administrator; and graduate school missions professor, Lester A. Crose was born July 29, 1912, and gave a lifetime to Church of God missions before his death on August 11, 2003.

Lester's first cross-cultural exposure came when he and his younger brother accompanied their parents, John D. and Pearl Crose, to Japan in 1920. "The events of that February sailing between San Francisco and Yokohama that stood out in my mind as a seven-year-old boy were the ice cream and fresh pineapple in Hawaii and the typhoon we encountered, during which I almost got swept overboard," he recalled in *Passport for a Reformation* (pp. 84–85; see p. 58 in this edition), the significant missions history he wrote, published in 1981.

With the validity of going "into all the world" well established in his heart, Lester was appointed to Lebanon in 1933 when he was only twenty-one. He returned to America to marry Ruthe Hamon in 1934. Among the few Church of God missionaries sent out during the Great Depression era, the newlyweds purchased their tickets to Lebanon with offerings.

They had been missionaries for sixteen years, including three in Barbados and Trinidad, when World War II kept the Croses out of Lebanon. Lester then became Missionary Board executive secretary-treasurer in 1954. During his twenty-one-year tenure, he led an expansion into eleven new countries by the time he retired in 1975.

But retirement wouldn't mean ending his involvement, only changing it. Among other things, he taught at Anderson University School of Theology, launching their missions department. Donald D. Johnson, Lester's successor as Missionary Board executive, declares, "We do not often enough find people who commit their entire lives to missions. I salute and celebrate Lester as my mentor and as one who was dedicated completely to serving God and the church."

CARLTON & THEODOSIA CUMBERBATCH

Persecution of Christians is as old as the church itself. But the abuse that tested Theodosia Francis and Carlton Cumberbatch in the 1940s was inflicted not because they were Christians but because they were in the Church of God. It was a life-long loyalty that Carlton displayed until his death at eighty-eight years of age on April 1, 2009. This devotion also energized Theodosia until her death on July 3, 2001, at seventy-five years old, only two days after preaching in New York.

Carlton's Church of God roots reach back before his birth. A convert of missionary efforts in Trinidad in the early 1900s, his father Edward was the first national pastor ordained there. When Carlton was five, the family moved to Tobago. There his educational path was blocked twice because of their church affiliation. Carlton persevered both in school and in the Church of God, and eventually was appointed to teach at the island's only government school.

Theodosia knew different persecution on St. Kitts. Finishing school, she began learning dress making from a neighbor who attended the Church of God. When Theodosia later accepted Christ and took her stand with the Church of God, her family abused her. She escaped to live with Wilhelmina Fraser, missionary pastor of the Church of God. When her case went to court, the judge chided her family, declaring, "She could be doing something worse than going to the Church of God."

Carlton and Theodosia met in Trinidad as students at West Indies Bible Institute (now West Indies Theological College) and were married in 1958. Sister T, as she was called, became a well-known evangelist in Barbados, Guyana, Trinidad, Tobago, and St. Kitts, where she joyfully saw family who had persecuted her come to Christ. Carlton served as WIBI president from 1959–88. After two pastorates, one shared with Carlton, Theodosia was WIBI president from 1989–99. The Cumberbatches devoted fifty years to Church of God ministry in the Caribbean–Atlantic region.

WILHELMINA FRASER

Perhaps she was making up for lost time. This might explain the fervor that characterized Wilhelmina Fraser's missionary work in the Caribbean–Atlantic region, where she began her formal ministry on the island of St. Kitts in 1941 at the age of thirty-seven. Her tireless efforts for the next twenty-eight years earned her the loving title of Mother Fraser, and even outside the church her influence was recognized in the nickname given the Church of God—"Sister Fraser's church."

Born on the tiny island of Barbuda in 1904, Wilhelmina left home at sixteen for high school in New York, where she discovered the Church of God seven years later. She also discovered a passion for evangelism. When she was denied Bible school entry because of her race, Wilhelmina began studying the saxophone and business. In 1935, during a trip home, she helped the Church of God on nearby Antigua. After returning to New York, her burden for Antigua was so great that her local congregation sent her back as a missionary in 1939. She was soon known for her visitation work (always in a white dress), saxophone playing (used in tandem with preaching), and her efforts to raise funds for a church building.

In 1941, Wilhelmina relocated to St. Kitts. There she created prayer and visitation teams, using every opportunity for evangelism. At the time, there were only a dozen people in the Church of God. By the time of her retirement in 1969, there were five congregations and widespread influence through missionaries, pastors, and lay people Wilhelmina had mentored who were serving in Panama, several Caribbean islands, Canada, and the United States. One also had begun a congregation in England.

While never married, she adopted several daughters, including Theodosia Cumberbatch.

Wilhelmina's far-reaching ministry from a small island was honored at New York's Lafayette Church of God on November 9, 1969. She died two months later on January 11, 1970.

STANLEY & MARION HOFFMAN

In February 1955, while reading in his uncle's study, twenty-two-year old Stanley Hoffman heard a voice that announced, "I want *you* to be a fisher of men!" That fall, the young Canadian enrolled in Alberta Bible Institute, now Gardner College, in Camrose, Alberta, to begin preparing. There he met Marion Schwartz, from British Columbia, whom he married in 1956.

A native of Saskatchewan, Marion had accepted Christ through reading a Bible used for swearing in ceremonies in the municipal office where she worked. She recalls being called to missions the very day she became a Christian. The call was reaffirmed to both of them when the young couple heard missionary Frank LaFont speak about Kenya in February 1958.

From that moment, Africa was to have a profound impact upon the Hoffmans. Likewise, they were to influence the continent during nearly forty years of missionary work, which included three years in Kenya; pioneering the start of the Church of God in Tanzania, Zambia, Zimbabwe, Mozambique, and Angola; and helping establish the church in Uganda, Zaire (now Congo[DR]), Rwanda, and Malawi. In all, their call to Africa was a call to ten of fourteen nations where the Church of God is present today. More than 2,260 congregations were planted in these countries through their ministry.

Although the Hoffmans retired in 2002, they discovered that their calling to Africa remained strong. Four years later, they were commissioned as special assignment missionaries to Angola, and in 2007, were residing and working once again in Zambia.

Looking back, the Hoffmans cite their teamwork as an especially rewarding part of their missionary life. Stanley also speaks of the thrill of witnessing God's power as it was in the book of Acts, with people being saved from witchcraft, demon possession, and physical illnesses. They also delight that their daughter and son-in-law Colleen and Tim Stevenson are serving today as missionaries in Africa.

NORA S. HUNTER

Courtesy of Anderson University & Church of God Archives

Although she was never a missionary herself, Nora Siens Hunter probably did more for the cause of missions than any other woman in Church of God history through the founding of what is now called Women of the Church of God.

Nora was born on August 16, 1873, in Kansas to devout parents who taught her to pray, read the Bible, and go to church. Although the farm family's income was meager, life was good until Nora was nine. That year, her mother, baby sister, and younger brother all died, and Nora and her remaining brother were placed in an orphanage.

Five years later, she moved in with relatives and began attending Sunday school near their home. Eventually, Nora even taught Sunday school, but the more she taught, the more she realized she had no peace herself. This led her to the altar during revival services held by Dr. S. G. Bryant in 1892. Later, Bryant introduced her to the *Gospel Trumpet* and its teachings that all Christians should be united into one church. When her relatives did not agree with this understanding, Nora began living with the Bryant family and soon was helping them lead revivals. After D. S. Warner heard nineteen-year-old Nora preach her first sermon, he invited her to join his evangelistic team, which she did.

Married in 1896, Nora and Clarence Hunter formed a traveling gospel team; she preached and he sang. Nora's concern for helping women's groups and churches respond to the needs of the world led her to form the Woman's Home and Foreign Missionary Society in 1932, an organization whose objectives included "[cooperating] with all recognized agencies of the Church of God in promoting missionary work at home and abroad; [making] the cause of missions a heart interest rather than a passing fancy." Nora served sixteen years as the organization's president, until 1948. She died in 1951.

SIDNEY & JEAN JOHNSON

No one in Cullman County, Alabama, could have predicted that the sixth of nine children born in 1927 to a poor sharecropper family named Johnson would ever impact the world. But from age seventeen, when Sidney M. Johnson committed his life to Christ, God began to move him from his humble roots to Anderson College, Anderson School of Theology, and eventually missionary service in India (1955–73) and Thailand (1973–86), during which he also was the Missionary Board's liaison for Asia (1973–85). Prior to retiring in 1992, Sidney, affectionately called "Mac," also served six years as the Board's Asia administrator.

But even retirement couldn't stop him. In 1992, he and his wife Jean cofounded Children of Promise, an international child sponsorship program, serving together as directors until 2004. Since then, he has tirelessly promoted the Project Link fundraising program of Global Missions, Church of God Ministries, helping support the church in Asia.

Looking back over fifty-plus years of missions work, Sidney says he is happiest knowing that all his efforts were "along with leaders of the church in Asia." He rejoices in this partnership through which the Church of God entered nine new countries—Thailand (1975), Taiwan (1976), Hong Kong (1978), Singapore (1980), Indonesia (1981), Nepal (1983), Myanmar (1985), Malaysia (1988), and Sri Lanka (1990).

Sidney also is outspoken about his ministry partnership with his wife, Jean Ratzlaff Johnson, whom he married in 1951. Together they served the Shelter Children's Home, the world's oldest Church of God orphanage, and in other ministries in the state of Orissa, India, as well as raising their three children. They also cooperated in refugee work in India and Bangladesh and with Cambodians in Thailand. Even today, the Johnsons participate in the Asia–Pacific Church of God Conference, with which Sidney was involved at its birth in 1982. Jean advises the Asia–Pacific Church of God Women's organization, which she helped found in 1990.

A. D. KHAN

Alla-ud-Din (A. D.) Khan was born in 1878 into a strict Muslim family in India. He knew only Islam and the Koran until, as a teenager, he left home for high school in another city and there joined a Bible study. Although warned by Muslim friends to stop reading the Bible, he continued and accepted Christ when he was fifteen.

Knowing he would be persecuted, A. D. attempted at first to keep his faith a secret. But this troubled him, and one year later he was baptized publicly. As expected, his family reacted angrily, kidnapping him and locking him up at home. There they tried many approaches—even poisoning his food—to change his mind. But young A. D. remained steadfast and finally was released after twenty-five days.

While in Bible college in Calcutta, A. D. responded to an advertisement for some Christian publications. Among those he received was a Gospel Trumpet Company catalogue—his introduction to the Church of God. The company sent a shipment of publications and two hand-operated printing presses so that the nineteen-year-old could begin publishing the gospel in India.

A. D. entered full-time ministry in 1898. In addition to his publishing work in English and Bengali, he helped raise money for famine and plague victims in India. His appeals in the *Gospel Trumpet* were critical to the growing missions fervor of the young Church of God movement in the United States. But his primary service was in India where he helped launch the Church of God in Calcutta, South India, and in the northeast. So integral was he to the founding and development of the Indian church that Lester Crose noted, "What D. S. Warner was to the Reformation Movement in Ameica, A. D. Khan was to the Church of God in India…" (p. 40). His death in 1922 at the age of forty-four was mourned in both India and the United States.

ARMINIO &
HELENA KOPP

If partnerships are the key to ministry success, Arminio Kopp has an impressive resume indeed. Even before he was born in 1945, the roots of partnership began when his family emigrated from Germany to Brazil, where they planted the Church of God in 1923. Years later, Arminio himself was forging partnerships.

But it didn't begin easily. Although Arminio rejected God as a teenager, October 10, 1971, found him in church because he had nothing better to do. His heart stirred, he prayed at the altar with missionary Maurice Caldwell, thus beginning a life-changing partnership with the United States. At the time, Caldwell was seeking students for a new Bible school in Curitiba. Interested, but concerned about his elderly parents, Arminio answered the call when a friend offered to live with his parents and work on their coffee farm in his place. In 1974, Arminio Kopp and Helena Stecko were among the school's first graduates, marrying shortly thereafter.

Beginning their husband-wife partnership ministry in western Brazil, the Kopps moved to São Paulo in 1977, eager to help the Church of God expand from the existing single congregation there. Today, through partnerships in the United States, Canada, and Germany, there are six congregations in Greater Saõ Paulo serving eight hundred children five days a week in addition to other outreach ministries.

In addition, Arminio has chaired the Brazilian General Assembly twice, giving critical leadership to help the national church overcome disunity and understand Church of God doctrine and practice. In 2003, he also was elected president of the regional Inter-American Conference. Despite a cancer scare in 2004, Arminio also partners with Global Missions in conducting forums to strengthen Church of God witness and service throughout the region.

Arminio declares, "Our greatest joy has been seeing hundreds of people born into the kingdom and bringing hope to thousands of impoverished children. We praise God for our rewarding ministry."

Fouad Melki

Courtesy of Anderson University & Church of God Archives

"I used to say, 'Pastor, this is enough. Stop, relax, you have done your job. [Now] watch and support...' He used to say back, 'I cannot do that, son. This is not my life. The doctors gave me until eighteen to live. God gave me fifty years on top of that. These extra years are not mine. They are his.'"

One would expect a son to honor his father, as Chadi Melki did in this tribute to Fouad Melki upon his death in 1997. But the conversation he recounted at his father's funeral speaks volumes about how one man could accomplish so much for God in seventy years.

As a young man with heart problems, Fouad promised God that if he spared his life, he would devote it to worshiping and serving God. The first member of his family to become a believer, Fouad never forgot that vow. He survived some twenty operations during his lifetime to become the preeminent leader of the Church of God in Lebanon and the Middle East. His ministry included pastoring, serving as founding president of Mediterranean Bible College and as chairman of the Church of God General Assembly in Lebanon and Syria, and reaching out to Muslims through being a speaker on the Arabic-language *Christian Brotherhood Hour*. He also was well-known throughout Lebanon for working with the Boy Scouts organization.

But his first love was evangelism. Only days before he died, he preached at a small village church. Afterwards, he asked three young men there if they were believers. They were not. Would they like to become Christians? When they answered that someone needed to tell them more, Fouad responded immediately, leading all three to Christ that day.

Fouad met Aida, his wife of thirty-nine years, while both were Bible school students. They had four sons, two of whom continue in Church of God ministry today.

STEVE &
DIANE RENNICK

Almost immediately from her birth
in 1962, Diane Collier attended
Millville Avenue Church of God,
Hamilton, Ohio. Exposed early on
to the fascinating world of missionaries, she enjoyed reading missionary
stories, especially Charles Ludwig's
Mama Was a Missionary, through which she committed herself to missions
and enrolled at Gulf-Coast Bible College. Twelve years later, now married
to Steve and the mother of two infants, she moved to Kenya, finally a missionary herself. The family lived in the Ludwig House, the very home described in the book that had so compelled her years before.

As a teenager, Steve was invited to Grand Avenue Church of God in
Carthage, Missouri, where he was born in 1964. He credits this congregation with loving him into the family of God on his fourteenth birthday. He
preached his first sermon at age fifteen and later entered Gulf-Coast Bible
College, where he met Diane. Their overseas experience in Guatemala as
students was the first of more than twenty missions trips they would take
before becoming career missionaries in 1995.

The Rennicks' Africa service was devoted to helping develop Kima
International School of Theology (KIST). During their seven years, the
student body grew to represent eleven African nations, the curriculum
expanded to the bachelor's degree level, a $100,000 scholarship endow-
ment was created, and the physical plant was expanded. Eleven dilapidated
buildings were renovated, primarily through work camps, and fourteen
new ones constructed. By 2002, KIST was debt-free, had a nice campus,
was being utilized both by the African Church of God and other groups,
and had graduated more than one hundred men and women.

Prior to their missionary tenure, Steve and Diane held ministry positions in Texas, Indiana, and Virginia. Since 2002, Steve has been an ad-
junct faculty member of Germany's Fritzlar Bible College and Anderson
University School of Theology. In 2003, he became senior pastor of the
Church at the Crossing, Indianapolis, Indiana.

FRANCO &
BEA SANTONOCITO

Esteemed Church of God leaders in the Europe–Middle East region, Franco and Bea Santonocito grew up in Italian Catholic homes in Egypt. Although childhood friends, they traveled to adulthood on different routes: Bea was a committed Catholic while Franco rejected the very idea of God.

Franco's direction changed dramatically one day when he was eighteen years old. At the beach, he chanced to meet a former schoolmate whom he had persecuted for being a Christian. The young man challenged him by asking, "Are you happy, Franco?" and then sharing John 3:16. Three days later, Franco accepted Christ. He also accepted the invitation to attend a Church of God fellowship, where he began growing in faith, eventually committing himself to attend Bible school.

But first he had to help Bea with her own commitment. By the time they married in 1958, Bea had made a new peace with God that bound her not only to the Lord but also to a joint ministry with Franco that has spanned five decades, beginning on their honeymoon when they were challenged by a pastor to earnestly seek God's will for their future. This they did by fasting and praying until it was fully evident that God indeed was calling them into ministry.

After training in Lebanon, Franco and Bea began their work in Egypt in 1963. There they served the Church of God during tumultuous years of civil unrest and war that often endangered Franco as he carried out assignments by motorcycle. When the family went to Italy in 1970 so Franco's kidney could be treated, they discovered an opportunity to plant the first Church of God congregation there. Despite his recurrent heart troubles, including a near fatal heart attack, the Santonocitos continue in ministry even today. They returned to Egypt in 2002 to train and equip church leaders there, pastor Cairo Christian Fellowship, and serve in various capacities in the wider region.

WALENTIN SCHÜLE

When Catherine the Great invited Germans into Russia during the 1700s, she got the farmers she wanted. But she also got missionaries, Germans who brought their faith with them and birthed new generations to share the gospel with their Russian neighbors.

Walentin Schüle is among these. Born in 1951 in Kazakhstan, the son of first-generation German Church of God members in the Russian Caucauses, Walentin was led to Christ by his mother as a ten-year-old. Soon he was involved in ministry in the Sunday school and youth department. By the age of fifteen, he was translating sermons into Russian so that the German-speaking congregation could reach out to its neighbors. A side benefit of this first cross-cultural missionary work was that he learned how to preach, a skill that has served him ever since.

Married at twenty, Walentin and his bride Irma immigrated to Germany in 1974. Shortly thereafter, they moved to the city of Pforzheim to begin ministering to other German immigrants. Thirteen successful years there were followed by the planting of a Church of God in the city of Calw in 1988, where they continue pastoring today.

But, Walentin says, Russia was always on his heart. In 1984, he became the speaker of the CBH Russian-language broadcast, *The Voice of the Gospel*. Even before this, he had launched a mission into Russia that included the 1980 publication by Warner Press of a Russian hymnal, which was distributed among the scattered churches in the USSR. With new religious freedom in the early 1990s, Walentin began traveling into Russia and Ukraine, following up on radio contacts. Today, the radio ministry, also shared by Irma, is helping the gospel penetrate five time zones.

"The Lord has opened doors so that we can reach people from Ukraine to all of Russia, as far as Vladivostok," he declares, adding that he cannot imagine ministry without Irma. "She is a precious helper for me."

LARRY & LEANN SELLERS

Of the world's forty French-speaking nations, the Church of God was ministering in only two before 1985 (Haiti and Lebanon). Since then, the church has entered four others, thanks in part to the ministry of Larry and LeAnn Sellers, the first French-speaking missionaries ever deployed by the Church of God in North America.

That Larry has a heart for French-speaking people is not surprising since he spent his early years in France and Algeria. Saved at ten years old in First Church of God, Odessa, Texas, he dedicated himself to ministry while in high school in Alaska, where he was influenced by the work of Fred and Evelyn Mamaloff with Alaskan Native Americans.

Less likely to have moved far from home was LeAnn Rathfelder, born and raised in Sarasota, Florida, until she entered Gulf-Coast Bible College (now Mid-America Christian University), where she met Larry. Although she too accepted Christ at ten, she made a deeper commitment as a teenager attending youth camp. Her love of children was nurtured by a teacher, and she determined to become a teacher herself.

Following college graduation in 1983, Larry entered Anderson School of Theology, and LeAnn taught in a Christian school in Texas. They were married in December 1985 and honeymooned in Haiti, their first missionary assignment (1985–89). While in language school in France (1990–91), they assisted with the first Church of God congregation in Paris. Starting in 1991, the Sellerses served in Rwanda and Congo (DR) until ethnic genocide caused their evacuation to Kenya in 1994, where they taught at Kima International School of Theology (1994–95).

In 1996, they moved to Côte d'Ivoire to plant the Church of God there. With a vision for evangelizing Africa's twenty-two French-speaking nations, they helped establish the Institut Biblique de l'Afrique de l'Ouest (West Africa Bible Institute) in Côte d'Ivoire in 2007 and are now training French-speaking African pastors, evangelists, and missionaries there.

CLAIR &
RETHA SHULTZ

Clair Shultz was born February 27, 1913, near Lima, Ohio, the youngest of eight children. With finances stretched thin in the large family, Clair developed a talent for making things from discards. He and a brother even constructed an electrical system for their home that, until then, had never had electricity.

Such creativity served Clair well in pastoring in St. Paul, Minnesota, where he reached out to young boys through a garage workshop. It was also valuable on the mission fields of Kenya (1962–70, 1985–86), Jamaica (1958–62), and Trinidad (1945–58), where he helped launch West Indies Bible Institute (now West Indies Theological College). Amazingly, while the Missionary Board blessed this vision, it gave no funds immediately. Consequently, Clair established a woodworking shop at the school to help support students.

Of course, nowhere did the missionary and later Missionary Board staff member in Anderson (1970–78) serve alone. In 1935, Clair married Retha Mills, beginning a seventy-one-year-long partnership that would eventually make them household names in Church of God missions. Daughter of a lifelong Gospel Trumpet Company worker, Retha was born April 22, 1914, in Anderson and worked at the publishing house herself after high school. Offered a full time position, she felt led instead to Anderson College, where she met Clair.

"We have worked well together as a team," eighty-nine-year-old Clair declared in his autobiography, noting this was especially important in overcoming challenges, including inadequate finances in their first full-time pastorate and on the mission field, a stillborn baby, Clair's near fatal automobile accident in Kenya, and Retha's deteriorating health that finally confined her to a wheelchair.

"It has been a great life here, but more is still to come," he wrote, looking forward to his homegoing, achieved December 17, 2006. At this writing, ninety-three-year-old Retha resides in a care facility in Anderson, where she is active in prayer and stays in touch with others by computer.

ANITA TAFOLLA

Courtesy of Maurice Caldwell

To study the foundation of Spanish-speaking ministries in the United States of the Church of God is to discover a number of building blocks named Tafolla. Members of the Tafolla family in San Antonio, Texas, were prominent in home missions efforts throughout most of the twentieth century. Mariano Tafolla, the patriarch, was the earliest Church of God Hispanic leader. He lived and pastored in San Antonio but worked on both sides of the border. Among his evangelistic activities, he led an annual camp meeting near Somerset, Texas, for thirty years and assisted in the development of a Spanish-language church in Los Angeles through conducting special services there.

Brother Tafolla's mantle was passed to his daughter Anita, known by everyone as Annie. Leaving Texas, she worked with the Spanish Literature Company in Anderson and also studied at Anderson Bible Training School. Following her graduation in 1928, she began a forty-two-year elementary education teaching career in San Antonio while also serving as a layperson in the Prospect Hill Church of God. She was a mentor to many San Antonio pastors and evangelists, including Keith Plank, who was to become a missionary in Costa Rica and Venezuela. With a lifelong passion for preparing and circulating printed gospel material, Annie served on the Spanish Literature Committee and was the second editor of *La Trompeta*, the Spanish "Gospel Trumpet," from 1950–53.

Ernie Lopez, former Hispanic Council president and a retired pastor of Prospect Hill Church of God, San Antonio, pays tribute to Sister Annie as "the first Hispanic woman to become an international Church of God leader." She was active in the Concilio, annual national conventions in Mexico, and the Inter-American Conference. She and her sister, Sarah Gerodetti, were a popular singing duet in both English and Spanish.

Called home on October 29, 1988, Sister Annie's legacy today includes one hundred and twelve growing Hispanic congregations in the United States and Puerto Rico.

NEVILLE & ANNE TAN

Delinquent, gang member, con-
victed murderer, parolee—not the
accolades one would expect used
to describe a Church of God national leader known throughout
Southeast Asia and the world. But
they accurately portray Neville
Tan in his life before Christ.

Born on April 27, 1940, the
Singaporean was first introduced
to Christianity when his parents
enrolled their six-year-old in a Christian school. There he was branded in-
corrigible. Expelled six years later, young Neville left with a burning hatred
for Christians and a determination to succeed. This he did by becoming
one of Singapore's most notorious gang leaders by age sixteen.

Everything changed in 1969 when, in a maximum security prison, he
met Christ through a series of events leading him to Psalm 23 in a Gideon
New Testament. Now he had a new life goal—sharing Christ with others.
This he has done through prison ministry, founding a drug rehabilitation
center and a halfway house for ex-prisoners and drug addicts, speaking on
school campuses, at prisons, and in churches and conventions around the
world, and through writing two autobiographical books, one of which, *Iron
Man*, has been translated into several languages. He also introduced the
Church of God to Singapore (1980), Indonesia (1981), Malaysia (1988),
Cambodia (1998), and Vietnam (1999).

His ministry gifts are also seen in the more than ten Church of God
congregations he has planted in an area of the world predominantly known
for Buddhism, Islam, and Confucianism. Included among these is a work
in Cambodia that ministers through a church, school, small orphanage,
and farm.

Although Neville has suffered four heart attacks since 2001, he is
determined to continue the work of missionary and evangelist as long as
God gives him breath. He is joined in ministry by his wife, Anne, a fellow
Bible college student, whom he married in 1974. They are the parents of
three adult children.

GEORGE P. TASKER

George P. Tasker was there at the very beginning—that decisive day in June 1909 when the Missionary Board was born by vote of the Church of God ministerial assembly. Tasker served as the board's first executive secretary-treasurer until 1911 when he and his bride Minnie themselves became missionaries. G. P., as he was known affectionately, gave his next thirty-four years to missions in India.

Surely the seeds of Tasker's long missionary tenure were planted on a trip to Egypt, Syria, and India (1907–9) that introduced him to new fields beyond his evangelistic, teaching, and publishing ministries in North America, some with the Gospel Trumpet family. But the Church of God had not always been his spiritual home, nor would it always be his place of service.

George Pease was born in 1872 in Nevada and orphaned as an infant. Adopted by a maternal aunt, he grew up in Quebec, Canada. The Tasker family provided well for him physically and spiritually, training him as a devout Scottish Presbyterian. These religious roots fueled a seven-year spiritual search that eventually led him to Chicago, where he discovered the Church of God and embraced its teachings in 1897. Years later, however, G. P. was to question some of these doctrines, especially "come-outism." He believed all Christians must cooperate to win the world for Christ and advocated self-governance for the Indian national church. These "liberal" ideas were unacceptable to the Missionary Board, which severed its relationship with the Taskers in 1924. Twelve years later, G. P. and Minnie were still in India as independent, self-supporting missionaries when the Missionary Board passed a resolution expressing regret for the earlier rift.

After Minnie's death in 1940, G. P. wed Josephine McCrie. One year after her death in 1954, he married Mona Moors. Both women had been fellow missionaries in India. G. P. was eighty-six years old when he died in 1958 in British Columbia, Canada.

MENDOZA &
DAISY TAYLOR

Mendoza Taylor could have written his own version of "Amazing Grace." Not that he was a slave trader, but after forty years of life on the sea, this descendant of English pirates who himself had engaged in transporting contraband alcohol and illegal immigrants had his own testimony of how a seafarer was changed by grace.

It happened on December 31, 1960. Sitting outside his native Colombian home, Mendoza was waiting with whisky to welcome the new year when, at midnight, an invisible hand pulled him into the yard and showed him the road to hell he was traveling. Horrified, he cried out to God for forgiveness and began the new year as a new man.

Shortly thereafter, Mendoza moved to Panama to become a tour boat captain. Visiting the Rio Abajo Church of God, he had another encounter with God as affirming as the other had been frightening. "Mendoza, you have finally come home," the Holy Spirit declared to his heart.

Daisy was born in Panama in 1924, the daughter of Jamaicans who emigrated to work in the Panama Canal project. They began attending the Church of God in which Daisy was raised and through which she met Mendoza. After marrying, the couple became active in ministry in the Rio Abajo church and at a maximum security prison. Eventually, Mendoza baptized thirty inmates there.

When they married, the Panamanian Church of God had five English-speaking congregations. Subsequently, they began the first Spanish-speaking church, pastoring it for sixteen years. Then, well into their fifties, they accepted a call to help establish the Church of God in Colombia. With support from Panama and the Inter-American Conference, they planted the church in three locations and mentored several future church leaders. Although Mendoza died in 1995, Daisy continued working in Colombia until 1999. At seventy-seven years old, she retired to Panama, where she died in June 2005.

MARJORY WILLIAMS

Unlike many missionaries, Marjory Williams never crossed national borders during her lifetime, except as a young child when her family moved from Saskatchewan, Canada, to Detroit, Michigan. Nevertheless, the woman who gave more than fifty-five years in loving ministry on the Tulalip Native American Reservation in Marysville, Washington, knew much about traversing borders—cultural borders.

Born in 1921, Marjory was introduced to the Church of God as a teenager. When missionaries visited her church, the fifteen-year-old responded by dedicating her life to missions. This led her to Pacific Bible College (now Warner Pacific College), where she met Adam Williams, the first Native American she'd ever known, who was preparing for ministry to his people. When they married in 1943, his people became hers too. In 1947, Adam answered the pastoral call to the Church of God on the Tulalip reservation.

Although Marjory worked at various jobs to supplement the family income, foremost in her heart was joint ministry with Adam, which often took them outside the church. Among other activities, the couple began an Alcoholics Anonymous group in 1958—the first on the reservation. It grew from a handful of participants to as many as one hundred. They also operated a used clothing closet and a food bank at the church, in addition to reaching out to young mothers and comforting the dying and grieving. Marge was especially tender towards children and the underprivileged, prompting her service on several county and state boards.

Upon Adam's death in 1978, the congregation called Marge to be their pastor. She said yes, not a hard decision since it only continued what she already had been doing unofficially for more than thirty years. Marge carried on in ministry on the reservation for another twenty-five years. In 2003, shortly before her death, she was honored as a Church of God National Treasure for faithful service as a home missionary to Native Americans.

APPENDIX 2
MISSIOLOGICAL PRINCIPLES THAT FORM THE FOUNDATION OF OUR CROSS-CULTURAL MINISTRY[1]

Much of what we wish to state when we speak of Missiological Principles usually comes in the form of questions that are begging for answers. But Missiological Principles should be positive statements that will underlie the answers to the significant questions we face in missions. Many of the principles will not speak directly to the questions that are raised, but will inform the answers by basic missiological assumptions and suppositions that will form the basis for the rationale of how we answer those questions. The following are some of the core issues and principles for consideration. We are dividing them into five general areas: The Place of the Bible and Christ in Mission; Culture and Mission; Leadership and Development; Methodology; and Relationships. Because the word culture comes up so frequently it will be good to give a definition of it here at the onset. One possible definition is: *Culture is the integrated system of learned behavior patterns, ideas, and products characteristic of a society. It is a peoples' primary grid in terms of which they perceive reality.*

Biblically Based, Christ-Centered, and Great Commission–Driven

Within missiological thought and practice, the Bible must always be our guide and ultimate measure (Psalm 119:105–106; Hebrews 4:12). The Bible is the Word among words (1 Thessalonians 2:13; 1 Peter 1:23–25). The Lord Jesus and his teachings are central to all we do (Matthew 5–7).

We believe that without Christ, all people are eternally lost (Acts 4:12). We believe that God wishes all people to come to a saving knowledge of Jesus Christ in their lives, and within their culture (John 3:16; 5:24). We believe that the Holy Spirit speaks to and directs Christians in every land and culture as he does ourselves (Acts 10).

As his ambassadors, we must have an unreserved commitment to God, and a deep, abiding dependency upon him (Luke 9:23–26).

We believe that just as Christ personally sent his disciples into the entire world to call men and women, boys and girls to a faith in him; that same passion of calling, he sends us and all those he calls to himself (Matthew 28:18–20; John 20:21).

Culture and Mission

We are always aware of the way in which culture guides and forms a person's thoughts, perceptions, and decisions. Therefore we are continually students of that culture and of the land in which we minister. We recognize that Christ is above all cultures, and at the same time makes himself known through and relevant within each and every culture.

We realize that we, as Christ's ambassadors, carry with us our own cultural understandings and perceptions, and it is through that mental grid that we interpret words, and actions. We realize, only too well, that much of that cultural map has little to do with the core teachings of Christianity, and therefore we are slow and studied in coming to judgments when confronted with cultural issues.

We recognize every individual's eternal worth before God.

We recognize the vast importance of People Groups. We learn from these various groups so that together viable churches may be established.

We highly value the importance of the primary language of the people with whom we minister. We recognize the importance of learning this language well. Therefore we strive to learn, and to minister in that language to the very best of our ability. We know that God wishes to speak his salvation message to people in their primary language.

In various ways we seek to plant congregations within these cultures, in ways that reflect those cultures. We believe that God wishes to reach all persons in terms of their own culture, and that conversion to Christ Jesus should happen within each person's own culture.

Leadership Development

We recognize the importance of the two essential thrusts of evangelism and discipleship. Thus we will call everyone to a salvation experience and then see that they are discipled to maturity in Christ.

One of the main tasks we do is that of the appropriate development of leadership in the Church.

We recognize that theological education and leadership development are indispensable elements of our ministry globally. We desire that education and leadership development should be meaningful and appropriate to the indigenous culture.

Methodology

We recognize and value the importance of research and planning. The cross cultural witness must continually be a student of the context and culture where they live, so that as they minister with the people the message of the gospel will be understandable in their thought patterns, in their lives, and appropriate for living.

We attempt to discover and use methods that are effective, biblically based, indefinitely reproducible and sustainable.

Planning will be done with local leaders as the transitions to maturity of the church develop. The setting and reaching of goals must be contextually relevant to each setting as we enter and exit each group as "outsiders."

We recognize that the way the budgeting process of resources is done speaks volumes to the sending and receiving church. How it is done illustrates priorities in ministry. No people want to be dependent on others for their ability to minister the gospel according to their context and cultural norms. We recognize that together we will establish models for raising and funding ministry that are biblically sound. Integrity and accountability in the stewardship of resources is the goal.

We will, in all the process of living within a people group, use appropriate and sustainable development methods. We will monitor cultural change as well as the use of the funds we appropriate. We recognize that we will, by the very nature of our living among a people group, lift their social status, but we will always attempt to do this without dislodging them from their culture and near neighbors. We realize that development and relief must never supplant evangelism, church planting and discipleship, but shall serve as a Christian vehicle to relieve suffering and promote development. We need to communicate the totality and the fundamental objectives of our mission organization to those we serve.

Our ultimate goal is to have a reproducing church ministering to the surrounding community in ways that are biblically based and culturally relevant. We seek to establish a church that is not dependent on outside nations and personnel for its continued existence and internal growth.

Relationships

As cross-cultural witnesses we will model servant leadership with the people we serve. We will monitor our words and actions with a view to the future.

We seek to live as conveyors of God's good news, recognizing the need for appropriate biblical life styles in relation to the culture where we serve. Our life styles and relationships must not hinder the message of the gospel.

We will follow the incarnational model of Jesus for mission. In order to be effective cross cultural witnesses we must identify ourselves with people within the host culture to love them, to join them, and to be peers with them. We shall not live above the people we serve, but live and serve side by side with men and women God has chosen as his own. Our attitude towards those with whom we serve must be that which Jesus himself displayed (Philippians 2:5–11).

We continue to realize the value of global involvement in our entire mission venture. We have much to learn from our brothers and sisters in the Lord Jesus. We recognize and seek to display the truth of interdependence in mission.

Appendix 3
100-Year Time Line

1881   Birth of the Church of God reformation movement.

1891   Beginning of outside interests: B. F. Elliott goes to Mexico as first missionary.

1892   W. J. Henry and J. H. Rupert preach in England.

1893   Dr. G. R. Achor conducts evangelistic work in England, Ireland, Scotland, and Wales.

1895   Work in Scandinavia begins.

1896   A. D. Khan, a national, begins Saturday p.m. meetings in Calcutta, India.

1897   Gorham Tufts carries famine relief funds to India.

1901   James S. McCreary begins evangelism in Cuba; George Vielguth returns to his native Germany to share Church of God message.

1902   German workers establish a work in Russia.

1904   Gospel Trumpet Company becomes first organized and incorporated institution of the Church of God movement; first missionaries sent to live in India (George and Mary Bailey, Evalyn Nichols).

1905   A "Home and Foreign Missions Fund" is established under care of editor of the *Gospel Trumpet*; also "Missionary Box Fund" is created to assist in raising support funds for missionaries; Edward B. Grant, from Antigua, takes Church of God to Bermuda.

1907   Church of God planted in Jamaica; work begins in Budapest, Hungary, with contacts from Germany; E. A. Reardon departs for Egypt; regularly scheduled church meetings begin in Switzerland.

1908   A. U. Yajima takes Church of God message to his native Japan.

1909   Missionary Board formed with seven members; nineteen missionaries and eight evangelists appointed by the Missionary Board; George P. Tasker named first executive secretary; outdoor meetings conducted in Bahamas; work begins in Scotland and China.

1910   First Church of God witness to Panama; *Missionary Herald* begins publication.

1912   H. C. and Gertrude Kramer pioneer work in Kima, Kenya, established by the South African Compounds and Interior Mission;

Church of God planted in Barbados and Lebanon; F. G. Smith named president of Board of Directors of the Missionary Board; J. W. Phelps serves as secretary-treasurer.

1914 Missionary Board incorporates with eleven members; first congregation established in Denmark.

1915 Church of God established in Guyana (then British Guiana).

1917 Missionary Board gives permission for first missionaries to go to Africa; Church of God established in Sydney, Australia, by Australian E. P. May.

1918 Work begins in Bangladesh (then East Bengal).

1920 Thirty-two missionaries appointed by Missionary Board; Missionary Board opens first independent bank account; work begins in Tobago.

1921 Missionary Board reorganizes with fifteen members; Board of Church Extension and Home Missions formed.

1922 Missionary Board assumes a work in Kima, Kenya.

1923 First missionary manual printed; Church of God planted in Brazil by German immigrants.

1927 Church of God planted in Argentina by German immigrants.

1929 H. M. Riggle becomes executive secretary of Missionary Board.

1930 Forty-two missionaries appointed by Missionary Board; first Church of God worker (independent) goes to Cuba; meetings begin in Holland.

1931 C. E. Brown becomes president of Missionary Board.

1932 National Woman's Home and Foreign Missionary Society formed; work begins in Cayman Islands and St. Kitts.

1933 Adam W. Miller named first executive secretary-treasurer of Missionary Board; C. F. Mattias begins work in the Philippines; John Edmund Thompson, from Trinidad, begins work on Grenada.

1934 Church of God planted in Antigua by Christena Henry and husband Wilfred.

1936 *Friends of Missions* begins publication; Church of God starts in Korea out of the Holiness Church.

1937 Message of Church of God arrives in Curaçao.

1939 Work begins in Costa Rica.

1945 Sixty missionaries appointed by Missionary Board.

1946 National Woman's Home and Foreign Missionary Society becomes National Woman's Missionary Society; work begins in Greece.

1947   C. Lowery Quinn becomes executive secretary-treasurer.

1949   Ten Church of God missionaries forced to abandon work in China with Communist takeover; Missionary Board offices move into Church of God Executive Offices Building on East 5th Street, Anderson, Indiana.

1951   *Church of God Missions* magazine founded.

1953   Seventy-three missionaries appointed by Missionary Board.

1954   Lester Crose becomes executive secretary-treasurer; La Buena Tierra Bible School begins in Saltillo, Mexico; Church of God established in Guatemala.

1955   Church of God planted in Guam by a former U.S. serviceman.

1957   Church of God begins in Nevis.

1958   Work begins in Peru.

1959   Church of God planted in Tanzania.

1960   Church of God missionaries forced to leave Cuba when diplomatic ties severed by United States; work among the Kuna Indians of San Blas Islands off coast of Panama begun by church in Panama.

1962   First Inter-American Conference meeting in Mexico City.

1964   Ninety-six missionaries appointed by Missionary Board.

1966   Contacts made with Nicaragua; missionaries begin work in Puerto Rico.

1967   Integration of Foreign Missionary Board of the National Association with the Missionary Board.

1968   Guatemalan pastor Isai Calderon makes contact with the World Church of God in El Salvador and they affiliate; Church of God planted in Haiti by Jean Surin.

1970   Missionary Board reorganized; Decade of Advance launched in Latin America; work in Uruguay begins; Jamaica sends missionary to Haiti.

1972   Church of God starts in Honduras and El Salvador; Boa Terra Bible School begins in Curitiba, Brazil; all Missionary Board properties in Kenya and India transferred to the national churches.

1974   A disaster fund becomes part of World Service budget, providing funds for suffering resulting from natural disasters and starvation; work in Paraguay begins; work in Bolivia identifies with Church of God.

1975   Donald D. Johnson becomes executive secretary-treasurer; Church of God planted in Thailand.

1976 Church of God planted in Taiwan.

1977 Crose Missionary Residences dedicated in Anderson, Indiana; work in Australia comes under Missionary Board; Million for Missions campaign begins.

1979 Missionaries from Missionary Board arrive in Venezuela to begin cooperative work of Missionary Board (Anderson) with the Commission on World Missions of the Church of God, General Conference (Findlay, Ohio); Church of God begins in Colombia and Singapore; Church of God Hong Kong Ministries organized; Caribbean-Atlantic Assembly forms.

1980 Seventy-eight missionaries under appointment by Missionary Board; Missionary Board enlarges from fifteen to twenty members; "Asia in the '80s" campaign launched.

1982 Formation of the Asian Church of God Conference; church planted in Spain.

1983 Inter-American Conference launches Church of God in Dominican Republic; church in Meghalaya, India, begins work in Nepal.

1984 Church of God begins in Zaire.

1985 Thomas Pickens becomes executive secretary-treasurer; work begins in Rwanda.

1986 Work begins in Zambia; missionary from Peru begins work in Ecuador.

1987 Ann Smith serves three months as interim executive secretary-treasurer; Doris Dale serves one year as interim executive secretary-treasurer and title changes to president.

1988 Norman Patton becomes president.

1990 "Africa in the '90s" campaign launched.

1992 Church of God work begins in Chile and Zimbabwe; missionaries sent to prepare for new work among the Maasai unreached people group in Tanzania.

1994 Special assignment missionaries sent to Russia under CoMission; work begins in Mozambique; Asian Conference becomes Asia–Pacific Conference.

1995 Church of God planted in Malawi and New Zealand.

1997 Church of God officially registed in Côte d'Ivoire; Church of God in eighty-six countries of the world; last official board meeting of the Missionary Board.

1998 Church of God planted in Angola and Cambodia; Missionary Board reorganizes under Outreach Ministries; Doris Dale becomes interim president.

1999 Missionary Board becomes part of Outreach Ministries of Church of God Ministries, Inc.

2000 Church of God at work worldwide through 712,907 believers in 6,828 churches in 89 countries; West Indies Theological College, Trinidad, celebrates 50 years.

2001 Regional directors become regional coordinators; September 11 attack on the Twin Towers in New York City; Germany celebrates 100 years.

2002 Ronald V. Duncan assumes leadership of Church of God Ministries; Spread the Word (STW) launched to encourage teenage involvement in missions.

2003 Global Missions adopts theme, "One World, One Mission"; Albert Grant becomes Outreach Ministries team director; John and Gwen Johnson become Asia–Pacific regional coordinators; Kelley and Rhonda Philips become regional coordinators, Europe–Middle East; Global Dialogue on international partnership convenes June 19–21, Anderson; Church of God begins in Nicaragua.

2004 David and Barbara Miller become Latin America regional coordinators; "One World, One Mission" launched at NAC; new missionary residences dedicated; Bermuda celebrates 100 years; Asian tsunami hits on December 26.

2005 Birth of Project Link; Albert Grant resigns as Outreach Ministries team director; Sherman and Kay Critser become regional coordinators, Africa.

2006 Global Missions becomes part of the Kingdom Ministry Team, Jeannette Flynn, director; China Consultation held in Taipei, Taiwan; Trinidad celebrates 100 years.

2007 Jamaica and Egypt celebrate 100 years.

2008 In Myanmar, Cyclone Nargis hits, May 3; China experiences earthquake in Sichuan Province, May 12; Japan and Panama celebrate 100 years; Don and Caroline Armstrong become regional coordinators for Asia–Pacific.

2009 100 years of organized cross-cultural mission administration in North America.

APPENDIX 4
CHURCH OF GOD
NATIONAL LAUNCH DATES

Some of these launch dates differ from those listed in *Passport for a Reformation*. Some are the date a Church of God missionary first visited, some are when a missionary moved to the country, some are when worship services first began, and others are the date of legal registration of the church. We apologize for any mistakes. Please direct corrections to Global Missions.

Africa

Angola	1998
Congo (DR)	1982[1]
Côte d'Ivoire	1997[2]
Ghana	1980
Kenya	1922
Malawi	1992
Mozambique	1994
Rwanda	1985
South Africa	1983
Sudan	1983
Tanzania	1959
Uganda	1983
Zambia	1986
Zimbabwe	1992

Asia–Pacific

Australia	1958[3]
Bangladesh	1946[4]
Bhutan	1997
Cambodia	1998
China	1909
Guam	1955
Hong Kong	1978

India

Orissa	1906
Meghalaya	1902
Calcutta	1901[5]
Siliguri	1960
South	1917
Indonesia	1981
Japan	1908
Laos	2004
Malaysia	1988
Myanmar	1985
Nepal	1983
New Zealand	1999
Northern Mariana Islands	
Saipan	1994[6]
Yap	2007
Philippines	1933
Singapore	1979
South Korea	1936
Sri Lanka	1990
Taiwan	1976
Thailand	1975
Vietnam	1999

Caribbean–Atlantic

Antigua & Barbuda	1934
Barbados	1909[7]
Bermuda	1905
Cayman Islands	1932
Grenada	1933
Guyana	1915
Haiti	1968
Jamaica	1907
Curaçao	1937
St. Kitts & Nevis	1932[8]
St. Vincent & the Grenadines	1957
Trinidad & Tobago	1906[9]
Virgin Islands	1971

Europe–Middle East

Bulgaria	1922
Denmark	1914[10]
Egypt	1908
Eurasia	1979
France	1989
Germany	1901
Greece	1946
Hungary	1907[11]
Italy	1973
Lebanon	1912
Netherlands	1914
Russia	1902[12]
Scandinavia	1895
Scotland	1909[13]

Serbia	1994
Spain	1982
Switzerland	1907
Ukraine	1993
United Kingdom	1898

Latin America

Argentina	1927
Bolivia	1976[14]
Brazil	1928
Chile	1993
Colombia	1975
Costa Rica	1939
Cuba	1930
Dominican Republic	1984
Ecuador	1986
El Salvador	1972[15]
Guatemala	1954
Honduras	1972
Mexico	1892
Nicaragua	2003[16]
Panama	1908
Paraguay	1974
Peru	1958
Puerto Rico	1966
Uruguay	1970
Venezuela	1979

North America

Canada	1889
United States	1880

APPENDIX 5
MISSIONARY LISTING

This compilation of Church of God missionaries includes former and current (as of December 2008) career missionaries, special assignment missionaries, and short-term missionaries, as well as some independent missionaries. Most of these were appointed by or responsible in some way to the Missionary Board or to Global Missions. Please excuse errors and omissions. Corrections should be directed to Global Missions.

Due to the vagaries of record-keeping, some beginning dates are the dates missionaries were appointed, while other beginning dates are the date of arrival on the field. For women who served under both maiden and married names, dates under the maiden name indicate the years they served under that name, with the remaining dates of service listed under the married name. Maiden and married names are cross-referenced where this occurs. Throughout, the word *née* (born) refers to a married woman's maiden name. Regional coordinators have two sets of codes in parentheses; the second set indicate the region, the base of operation, and the years of service.

The legend of abbreviations can be found at the end of this list, on pages 427–28.

Abernathy, Amos & Edith (IN 1905–10)
Abrams, Alta (KE 1963–65; TT 1990–96)
Achor, G. R. (UK 1893–94)
Ackerman, Caroline (KE 1970–78, 1982–91; TZ 1992–2007)
Ackerman, John & Jodie (HA 1986–)
Ackerman, Thelma (TZ 1997–98)
Adams, Darrell & Sharon (SK 1982–84)
Adams, Karvin & Sandy (EC 1992–96)
Adams, Robert & Nita (JA 1993; EG 1995–96; LE 1998)
Albrecht, James & Betty (EG 1978–89) (RC EM: EG 1989–92; US 1992–98)
Alexander, Larry & Janeen (PE 1981–84)
Alexander, W. G. & Josie (JA 1909–20)

Allan, Adam & Mary (SC 1909–18; IR 1918–46)
Allan, Naomi (IR 1920–56)
Allen, Steve & Jane (SK 1983–85)
Allison, Vernon & Cathy (PA 1978–82)
Anderson, Chris & Gail (UG 1999–2000)
Anderson, Edwin & Carol Ann (CR 1967–70)
Anderson, William & Beatrice (KE 1967–71)
Andrews, Harold & Ann (JM & CA 1924–41)
Appelqvist, Linda (CY 1996–98; CA 1998–2000)
Arbeiter, Karl & Auguste (SW 1912–20)
Armstrong, Don & Caroline (TZ 1989–2005) (RC AP: 2008–)
Arnakin, Simeon & Barbara (US 1984–2003)
Axup, E. J. (UK 1908–10)
Ayala, Alfonso & Elizabeth (HO 1987–88; BE 1989–)
Bailey, George and Mary (IN 1904–5)
Bailey, Homer & Vivian (KE 1937–46)
Bailey, William J. & Lilly (KE 1924–34)
Baker, Darin & Petie (AU 2003–6)
Baker, Mabel (KE 1914–53)
Bales, Wilma Dean (KE 1967–70)
Bannister, Gladys (KE 1965–70)
Barber, Proctor & Virginia (US 1963–67)
Bargerstock, Rachelle (JA 2004–8)
Bargerstock, Randy & Rhonda (AR 1989–2002)
Barkley, Edith (GU 1994–95)
Barkman, William & Glynda (JA 1980–82)
Barnette, Cornelia (KE 1967–73). *See also* Joel and Cornelia Kerich
Barton, Bernard & Cheryl (JA 1976–79, 1982–)
Barwick, Burd (IN 1922–26)
Baylor, David & Bonnie (KE 2008–)
Beach, Glenn & Alice (IN 1960–63)
Beaty, Deloris (KE 1959–68)
Beaty, Esther (KE 1962–66)
Beisley, Douglas & Danette (NZ 2004–)
Bentley, Albert & Irene (ME 1958–59, 1968–73; BR & AR 1973–75; AR 1977–78)
Bentley, Patricia (JA 1969–72)

Bentley, Paul & Kathy (US 1987–2006)
Berg, Mark & Glenda (RU 1994–95)
Bernhardt, Casey & Sharon (SE 1998–2004, 2005–)
Betts, Samuel & Jane (née Ryan, married 1958) (KE 1958–63) *See also*
  Jane Ryan
Billings, J. Lovena (CH 1946–49). *See also* P. K. and J. Lovena Jenkins
Birkholz, Charles & DeVonna (CA 1998–2000)
Bistritan, Gary & Gwen (GU 1985–)
Blanton, Dan (NZ 2007– 8)
Blaskowsky, Emilia (CA 1949–52; BA 1952–54) *See also* William Fleenor
Bleiler, E. L. & Martha (IN 1926–32)
Blevins, Anna (SA 1992)
Blocher, Bert & Jeanne (JA 1977–80, 1983–85; SK 1980–82)
Blocker-Marble, Tina. *See* Stanley & Tina Marble
Blore, F. C. & Eskell (IR 1924–26)
Blumenberg, Richard & Carol (TZ 1976–77)
Bolitho, Axchie (JA 1921–26)
Bollmeyer, Rosa (KE 1957–60)
Borden, Oscar & Norma (KE 1964–1976)
Bowsher, Mariel (US 2000)
Boyle, Mike (JA 1993–94). And Makiko (married 1994) (JA 1994–96,
  1999–)
Brallier, Calvin & Martha (KE 1950–62; UR 1995; RU 1995)
Bransford, Christopher & Rebekah (KE 1995–97; TZ 1997–99)
Brewster, E. G. & Elizabeth (PA 1908–15). Elizabeth (SN 1934–40)
Bridgeman, Bill & Cindy (RU 1994–95)
Brookover, W. L. & Opal (died 1934) (BWI 1916–38)
Brooks, H. A. (IN 1907–08; UK 1919–20)
Broyles, Kathryn (CZ 1994)
Bruce, Roger & Margaret (KE 1969–73)
Bruss, Verna (UR 1995; RU 1995)
Bryant, Leroy (BA 1916–19)
Buck, George & Eva (JM 1967–71; TT 1971–72; KE 1975–82)
Buettner, Milton & Eleanor (CH 1946–50)
Bullock, Patricia (RU 1995–96)
Burns, Glenn & Francine (KE 1973–77)
Busch, Edgar & Inez (CA 1947–48; US 1963)

Butz, Paul & Mary (died 1977) (PE 1958–86)
Byrum, Bessie. *See* Bessie Hittle
Caldwell, Maurice & Dondeena (ME 1954–62, 1966–69; BR 1970–76, 2000–1)
Caldwell, Timothy & Robin (JA 1978–80)
Callos, Connie (RU 1994–95)
Carll, Bill & Bonnie (KE 2004–5)
Carpenter, Ed & Helen (KE 2005–6)
Carver, Earl & Freda (CU 1952–60; PR 1966–79)
Casey, Brice & Nancy (US 1968–72)
Chambers, Zuda Lee (JA 1917–22)
Chandler, Ben & Marjorie (AU 1991–98)
Cheatham, William & Anna (UK 1906–15)
Chin, E. Raymond & Noreen (BM 1970–75)
Christensen, Bob & Barbara (BR 1985–87)
Clark, Kay (RU 1994–95)
Clark, Robert & Frances (PK 1947–1961; BD 1998–99)
Clark, Samantha (RU 1997–99)
Clarke, Gloria (EU 1989–99)
Clawson, Art & Suetta (HA 1986–91)
Clay, Eileen (RU 1994; CA 1995–98)
Clayton, Heather (EC 2000–2001)
Cockerham, Thomas & Jan (UR 1995; RU 1995)
Coe, Laura (HA 1994; UG 1994–2002)
Collins, Ralph & Mary (PA 1945–46)
Collins, Matt & Elaine (KE 2005–7)
Combs, David & Lorine (CA 1996–97)
Conkis, William and Mrs. (EG 1933–36)
Conn, Angela (BO 1996–97, 1998–2000)
Coody, Ronald & Lorna Jean (KZ 1992–99)
Coolidge, Ralph & Ruth (TT 1946–56; GY 1964–70)
Coplin, George & Maude (TT 1911–14; BA 1916–19; PA 1930–33)
Craig, Ross & Delana (JA 1982–89)
Crane, Isham E. (Joe) & Milli (KE 1992–93; AU 1996)
Crew, Karen (JA 1983–87)
Crippen, David & Karen (KE 1967–76)
Critser, Carrie (CE 2006–)

Critser, Sherman & Kay (née Cummins, married 1978) (TZ 1979–92; CO 1993–95; UG 1996–99; CI 1999–2005) (RC AF: CI 2005–). *See also* Kay Cummins

Croall, Alina (JA 2006–8)

Crose, John & Pearl (JA 1920–22; SY 1923–49; SK 1955–56; US 1958–60)

Crose, Kenneth & Mabel (EG 1947–48)

Crose, Lester & Ruthe (LE & SY 1933–41, 1945–50; BA & TT 1941–45; EG 1950–54)

Cummins, Kay (KE 1969–75). *See also* Sherman and Kay Critser

Dallas, Daniel & Aleta (GR 1958–62)

Dallas, George and Mrs. (EG 1933–38)

Daugherty, John (UK 1893–95)

Davenport, Chad (NZ 2001–2005). And Diane (NZ 2005–)

Davila, Gilbert & Melba (RC NA: US 1999–2001)

Davis, Amy (JA 2001–3)

Davis, Doris (CU 1947–48)

Davis, Willa (SN 1948–50)

Dawson, Shelly (JA 2000–2002)

Dazley, Janet (KE 1968–72)

Dean, Alva & Bernadean (JM 1972–75)

Decker, Jenny (JA 1996–2000)

deFelice, Mark & Sherrie (IT 1980–82)

Desjardine, Stanley & Patricia (TZ 1977–86)

Detwiler, Darlene (KE 1960–70, 1973–74, 1976–77)

Dibble, Bart & Leslie (KZ 1994–2004)

Dietz, Margaret (KE 1970–74)

Diezel, Katie (BA & TT 1913–14)

Dodd, Chuck & Lisa (TZ 1997–2001, 2004–6)

Doe, Randee (JA 2004–7)

Doebert, Otto & Gertrude (GE 1907–13; SW, GE, & RU 1914–26)

Donohew, Wick & Grace (GE 1946–51; KE 1951–62)

Dortmund, Janet (JA 1977–79)

Doughty, Richard & Sally (JA 1986)

Downey, Eddie & Wanda (EG 1993–94)

Drake, John & Cathy (KE 1985–87)

Drakes, Frank & Gemma (CÇ 1991–2002)

Dunbar, Jenny (JA 2003–6)

Duncan, Chip & Jenni (HU 2001–8)
Duncan, Noah & Myrtle (TT 1906–8, 1919–20)
Dunham, Barbara (KE 1967–70)
Dunn, Jack & Bonnie (AU 1976–80)
Dunn, Karen (CA 1991–92)
Dyer, Cayla (BR 1995–2000, 2006–8)
Eastman, Michael & Vicki (EG 1982–84)
Ebel, William & Anna (GE & RU 1910–19)
Eckelbarger, John & Deborah (KZ 1994–95)
Edwards, Dontie (GE 2001–3)
Edwards, Robert & Janet (KE 1967–69, 1982–89; TZ 1972–82) (RC AF:
    KE 1989–98; RC EM: GE 1998–2002)
Eikamp, Arthur & Norma (JA 1949–84)
Elliot, B. F. (ME 1891–1910)
Elston, Gerald & Janice (JA 1987)
Engst, Irene (KE 1947–74)
Erickson, Gerald & Helen (CA 1945–47)
Evans, Karen (JA 1965–69)
Fagin, James (KE 1986–87)
Fair, James & Esther (DE 1957–62)
Farag, Nasser & Marilyn (KE 1973–78, 1987–89; ME 1979–82)
Farmer, Ralph & Gertrude (TZ 1959–72)
Farr, Henry & CoCo (EG 1998–2000)
Fatzinger, Steve & Connie (TT 1976–77)
Fehr, Eugene & Margaret (IN 1965–70; TT 1974–78; BA 1978–80)
Fillmore, Dale & Connie (BR 1995–2008)
Firestone, Homer & Elvira (BO 1974–84)
Firestone, Ronald & Violet (BO 1974–78; ME 1986–88)
Fiscus, Olive (KE 1956–58). *See also* Savas & Olive Joannides
Fisher, Ruth (KE 1922–25). *See also* James & Ruth Murray
Fleenor, William. And Vada (died 1950) (SY 1930–32; EG 1932–34,
    1945–46). Single (EG 1951–55). And Emilia (née Blaskowsky,
    married 1955) (EG 1955–56; JM 1956–57; TT 1957–67). *See also*
    Emilia Blaskowsky
Flewellen, Carl & Mayme (BM 1964–70)
Flora, Dean & Nina (PA 1959–75)
Forsberg, Carl & Laura (SD & DE 1914–18; SD 1920–27)

Foster, Robin (JA 1980–84)

Franklin, Douglas & Michelle (US 1990–2002)

Fraser, Wilhelmina (AB 40; SN 1941–69)

Friedrich, Annie (UR 1995; RU 1995)

Froemke, Heidi (KE 1978–83)

Fuller, Doug & Dontie (KE 1972–74)

Gangwer, Christina (EG 1992–93)

Gard, Diana (KE 1969)

Garrett, Edith (CA 1992–98)

Gaulke, David & Elsie (CH 1946–50; KE 1953–58)

Gee, Jerome & Patty (JA 1995–97)

Geitwitz, George & Marie (ME 1969–77)

Glassman, Caroline (CA 1942–51)

Glover, Clarence & Bernice (SN 1979–86)

Goens, Donald & Arlene (JA 1954–63)

Goldman, Dwayne & Kara (RU 1996–97, 2007–)

Gonzales, Luz & Carol (ME 1967–70; CR 1970–74)

Good, Kenneth & Sue Jo (SK 1961–66; JM 1967–70; AU 1972–82; TZ 1983–94)

Good, Tim & Licia (UG 1989–91)

Goodman, Delena (KE 2003)

Goodrick, Lew & Wanda (KE 1957–66)

Goodwin, Eva (IN 1920–26)

Greer, Hester (CU 1934–46)

Gregory, Danny & Natalie (KE 2001–3)

Groeber, Chris & Jeannette (RU 1994)

Habel, Dennis & Elaine (KE 1965–75)

Hale, Alice (IN 1907–12)

Hall, Jewell (KE 1944–72)

Hansen, Hjalmer (DE & NO 1920–23)

Hansen, Lydia (KE 1949–73)

Hardman, Susan (CE 1988–)

Hart, Jon & Mary (UR 1995; RU 1995)

Harting, Clyde & Rowena (KE 1965–69)

Harville, Jenny (GU 1992–97)

Hastings, Raymond & Elna Mae (CA 1951–54; JM 1958–60; GY 1960–62; ME 1962–65)

Hatch, John (JA 1909–16)
Hawkins, Jim & Mary Ann (KE 1990–98)
Hayward, Chad (EC 1993)
Hazel, Bruce & Jenny (TZ 2000–2001)
Hazen, Joyce (RU 1997–2002)
Hedeen, Peter & Janice (EG 1988–89)
Hehr, Elsie (CA 1944–47)
Heinly, Candace (KE 1962–71)
Heinly, Floyd & Maude (IN 1918–49)
Helsel, Marvin & Karen (TH 1977–89)
Henry, W. J. (UK 1892)
Herrmann, Jeremy & Jennifer (HK 2000–2002)
Hetrick, Bessie (CA 1990–94, 1996–97)
Heusel, Lorton & Magaline (UG 1991–94). *See also* Roy & Magaline
    Hoops
High, Ellen (IN 1937–58)
Hill, Max & Neva (CA 1949–50)
Hilt, Kenneth & Dawn (JA 1982–84)
Hines, Sophia (ME 1901–2)
Hinton, Abbie (HA 1994–95)
Hird, Dick & Vila (AU 1996)
Hittle, Bessie (SY 1912–14)
Hoak, Ron & Sheryl (GT 1995–97)
Hoffman, Mark & Amy (ZA 2002–4)
Hoffman, Stan & Marion (TZ 1959–75; KE 1975–77; UG 1983–92;
    ZA 1993–2004; AN 2006–)
Holeton, Al (CA 1995–98)
Hollander, Emil (SY 1923–24)
Hoogeveen, Larry & Verna (KE 1973–75)
Hoops, Roy (died 1980) & Magaline (KE 1959–69; TZ 1971–80).
    Magaline (TZ 1981–83; KE 1984–90). *See also* Lorton & Magaline
    Heusel
Hoskins, Dale & Carole (KE 1995–2008)
Hossler, Elmer & Jeanne (VE 1992–93)
Howland, Ron & Marcia (BA 1967–70)
Huber, Merlene (KE 1955–65)
Huber, Ruth Ann (JA 1986–89). *See also* Dan & Ruth Ann Murrell

Humes, Mary (KE 1967–69)
Humphries, Jerry & Minnie (US 1968)
Hunnex, Charles & Annabel (CH 1910–49)
Hunnex, William & Gloria (CH 1909–21)
Hutchins, Paul & Nova (PK 1958–70; KE 1980–86; US 1991–2005)
Hutchison, Camille (JA 1997–2000)
Hutton, Howard & Mary (KE 1969–71)
Igarta, Robert & Linda (GU 1982–85)
Igarta, Steve & Maxine (GU 1978–81)
Ikast, Jens & Cora (DE 1923–36, 1946–49)
Ingram, Jeff & Nancy (EC 2000–2006; SI 2006–)
Irwin, Randy & Sandra (JA 1978–80)
Isaacs, Mike & Karen (ZA 2003–7)
Isenhart, Mae (IN 1918–21)
Jack, Ron & Alta Ruthe (KE 2006–)
Janes, L. Y. (JM & PA 1911–13)
Jarvis, Marie (IN 1905–6)
Jarvis, Robert. And Laura (died 1908) (IN 1903–8). Single (IN 1908–10).
    And Lottie (née Theobald, married 1910, died 1914) (IN 1910–14).
    Single (IN 1914–16). *See also* Lottie Theobald
Jeffcoat, Ethel (CA 1950–52)
Jenkins, P. K. & J. Lovena (née Billings) (HK 1949–85). *See also* J. Lovena
    Billings
Joannides, Savas & Olive (née Fiscus, married 1958) (GR 1963–68). *See
    also* Olive Fiscus
Johnson, Dewey & Thelma (CA 1963–70, 1976–79)
Johnson, Don Deena (JA 1983–86; LE 1999–2000, 2002–8; UK 2008–)
Johnson, Donald D. (Don) & Betty Jo (GY 1955–56; TT 1956–61)
Johnson, Harold & Barbara (JA 1964–66)
Johnson, Ira & Adeline (AU 1996–97)
Johnson, John & Gwen (SK 1980–83, 1985–91; EG 1992–96; LE 1996–
    2003) (RC AP: GU 2003–6)
Johnson, Morris (DE 1913–15)
Johnson, Sidney & Jean (IN 1955–72; SE 1973–92)
Joiner, Samuel and Mrs. (KE 1922–23)
Jones, Kenneth & Elizabeth (JM 1960, 1962)
Jones, Paul (BO 1996–99). And Kattia (married 1998) (BO 2004–)

Jones, Russ & Marsha (JA 1999–2000)
Jordan, Freda (RU 1996–97)
Kant, Willi & Esther (BR 1977–84) (RC LA: US 1989–94)
Kardatzke, Carl & Eva (KE 1955–56)
Kee, Michael & Wendy (CE 2000–4)
Kelly, Arthur & Judy (GE 2008–)
Kelly, Charlotte (CA 1997–2000)
Kemmer, Rick & Jeri (TZ 2000–2007)
Kerich, Joel & Cornelia (née Barnette, married 1973) (KE 1986–96;
     UG 2001–7). *See also* Cornelia Barnette
Kerr, Aaron & Kathryn (BWI 1949–51; IN 1951–55; GY 1959–61;
     KE 1970–76; GU 1976–78; ME 1979–82)
Kiess, Jim & Ingrid (BE 1993, 1996–97)
Kilmer, C. Jean & Ruth (EG 1954–56, 1957–62, 1987–89; KE 1956–57,
     1984–85)
King, Linda (KE 1968–70)
Kinion, Warren & Devie (ME 1975–78)
Kinley, Philip & Phyllis (JA 1955–99)
Kinnard, Connie (CA 1981–83; KE 1985–87)
Kinner, Michael & Debra (JA 1976–78; HK 1981–91) (RC AP: US
     1991–2000)
Kirk, Heidi (HO 1999–2001)
Kirkpatrick, Paul & Noreda (GY 1970–71; PE 1971–75; KE 1999–
     2000)
Kleinhenn, Lois (JA 1972–75)
Kline, William & Patricia (BR 1980–88)
Kluge, Arthur & Mary (CA 1954–63)
Knowles, Jeannette (GU 1993–96)
Knudsen, J. G. & Anna (DE 1919–25)
Koch, Kevin (BE 1989–92)
Konstantopoulos, Bill & Kay (CR 1976–77; US 1977–78; AR 1978–80)
Kraft, Susie (IN 1903–11)
Kramer, H. C. & Gertrude (KE 1912–27)
Kramer, Norm & Carol (CA 1979–81, 1984–99)
Kretlow, Orlo & Carol (JA 1964–95; RU 1995–96)
Kreutz, Karl & Hazel (CH 1923–27)
Kriebel, James (UK 1893)

Kufeldt, Tim & Beth (JA 1986–88)

Kurrle, Norberto & Julie (PG 2002–)

Lacy, Garland & Sue (US 1983–2002)

LaFoe, Freda (JA 1960–72)

LaFont, Ernest & Grace (PA 1947–51; EG 1952–71; LE 1972–76; JA 1985–86)

LaFont, Frank & Margaret (KE 1946–73)

LaFont, Harold & Donna (KE 1960–65)

Lambe, Vernon & Ruth Ann (BM 1975–2000)

Lambert, Jon & Karon (EC 1997–)

Lamka, Melanie (BE 1996)

Lange, Harold & Pauline (TZ 1988–89)

Latham, E. L. (PA 1915–18)

Laughlin, Nellie (SY 1913–28; EG 1937–42)

Lautaret, Larry & Maxine (US 1963–67; GT 1969, 1971; UY 1974–75; PH 1984)

Lavender, Paul & Cathy (KE 1984–85)

Lehmann, Walter & Margaret (TT 1961–64)

Lehmer, Lima (KE 1937–62). *See also* Edgar Williams

Limbach, Joyce (PE 1970–78)

Linamen, Harold & Maxine (KE 1981–82)

Linamen, Janice (KE 1968–75)

Lindemuth, Robert & Evelyn (KE 1974–76, 1978–79)

Linn, Otto (DE & SD 1923–25)

Little, Ralph & Helen (JM 1960–69)

Livingston, William & Hope (BWI & PA 1946–60)

Livingston, David & Joan (KE 1956–67)

Livingston, Nannie (JM 1909–10)

Ludwig, John & Twyla (KE 1927–49)

Lund, Julie (RU 1994–95). *See also* Joel Workman

Lunn, Lida (DE & SD 1910)

Lyngdoh, Donald & Stephanie (CE 2006–)

Lyngdoh, Rivulet. *See* Leaderwell Pohsngap & Rivulet Lyngdoh

Maiden, Daisy (CH 1916–49)

Maiden, Victor & Florence (IN 1906–8)

Malone, Edith (CA 1946–48)

Manners, Sheryl (CZ 1994–97)

Manners, Tyler (CZ 1994–97)
Marble, Stanley & Tina (née Blocker) (US 1980–2001)
Martin, Raymond & Nina (TZ 1980–82; KE 1982–87)
Martin, George & Mrs. (EN & SC 1898)
Martin, Russell (BE 1995)
Martin, Vera (KE 1954–69)
Marvel, Gerald & Rena (TZ 1999–2000)
Massey, James Earl & Gwendolyn (JM 1964–66)
Matlock, John & Kathe (TZ 2006–)
Matthews, William (CÇ 2000)
Mattox, Joseph & Elva (PR 1978–81; ME 1981–88)
Maurer, Ronald & Jacqueline (JA 1974–83, 1997)
Mauritson-Binkerd, Cindy (UR 1995; RU 1995)
Maxfield, Paul & Brenda (CA 1990–92; CR 1992–2003)
May, Edward & Anna (AU 1917–26)
McCracken, Tom & Jean (TT 1967–74; BR 1974–86, 1990–2006)
McCrie, Josephine (IN 1904–41). *See also* George Tasker
McCurdy, Robert (KE 1968)
McDaniel, Paul & Dayla (JA 1984–86)
McDilda, Hazel (KE 1951–61)
McPherson, Charlotte (EU 1986–)
Meier, David (died 1965) & Lillian (BR 1935–41, 1947–76;
     AR 1941–47)
Michael, Millie (JA 2007–)
Miller, Adam & Grace (JA 1922–27)
Miller, David & Barbara (BO 1980–2002) (RC LA: BO 2004–)
Miller, Dwain & Brenda (CA 1991–92)
Miller, Oakley & Veryl (TT 1952–67)
Miller, Orville & Bernice (TT 1965–2003)
Mitchell, Dennis & Etta Mae (JA 1997)
Mitchell, Keri (JA 1997–2000)
Mitchell, Zonia (JA 1989–)
Mitschelen, David (JA 1972–74)
Mondragon, Lorenzo & Margaretha (VE 1994–2005)
Montague, David & Margaret (KE 1970–78)
Moore, Julie (HK 1994; BE 1994–95)
Moors, Mona (IN 1922–55)

Morgan, Robert & Dorothy (BA 1953–55; TT 1955–56)

Morgan, Clifton M. & Mary (IN 1960–70)

Mottinger, William & Betty (BR 1972–82)

Murphy, Phillip & Lonnie (HA 1991–2007)

Murray, James (KE 1921–25). And Ruth (née Fisher, married 1925) (KE 1925–40). *See also* Ruth Fisher

Murray, Jerry & Sue (née Pruitt) (ZA 1997–98). *See also* Sue Pruitt

Murrell, J. Daniel & Ruth Ann (née Huber) (KE 1998–2001). *See also* Ruth Huber

Muse, Sharon (RU 1993–94)

Nachtigall, Harry & Jene (died 1991) (KE 1964–68; CR 1970–71; PA 1971–72 & CR 1972–78). And Julia Monge Ureña (married 1992) (CR 1998–2004)

Nachtigall, Patrick & Jamie (HK 2000–)

Neff, Thaddeus (IN 1906–11). And Katrina (married 1912) (BWI 12–22; EG 1923–51)

Neils, C. G. (GR 1906)

Nelson, Ed (RU 1993)

Nelson, Loren & Dora (JA 1993)

Nelson, Thomas (DE 1895)

Nevin, Wilford & Vernie (JA 1972–73, 1976–78)

New, Andrew & Rebecca (AU 1977–84)

Newberry, Gene & Agnes (KE 1973–74, 1981–82)

Nichols, Evalyn (IN 1904–8). *See also* J. J. M. & Evalyn Roy

Noss, Russell & Ethel (CR 1989–92; AR 1992–93)

Nulph, Lonnie & Pam (GU 1996–99)

Oldham, Edward & Meriam (GY 1962–65)

Olsen, Lars & Ellen (DE 1927–40, 1949–57; BA 1943–46; SD 1947–49)

Olson, George & Nellie (JM 1907–54)

Olson, Mary (JM 1940–63)

Orr, C. E. (TT & JM 1906–7; UK 1913–14)

Osgood, Dorothy (JA 1980–83)

Otis, Amber (RU 1996–97)

Palmer, Ellsworth & Hilaria (CU 1950–61)

Parnell, Charles (IN 1901–8)

Patterson, D. W. & Mae (ME 1908–10)

Pauley, Jim & Elaine (GU 1992–93)

Pedersen, Jim & Joyce (TZ 2002–4)
Petersen, I. Glenn (TT 1990–92)
Peterson, L. P. & Alexina (SD 1925–30)
Phelps, Vivian (CA 1955–58; KE 1959–68)
Philips, J. Kelley & Rhonda (RU 1993–2002) (RC EM: HU 2002–7; GE 2007–)
Phillips, Bryan & Marjo (JA 1982–84)
Phippen, Glenna (UG 2004–)
Pickens, Thomas & Dorothy (JM 1961–67; UK 1967–72)
Pierce, Rebecca (KE 2000–)
Plank, Keith & Gloria (CR 1958–64, 1980–91; VE 1991–94)
Plank, Wanda (JA 1987–90)
Plummer, Rex & Joy (TZ 1999–2004)
Pohsngap, Leaderwell & Rivulet Lyngdoh (KE 1981–84)
Pomeroy, Jon & Cathy (CY 1990–96)
Porter, Ida (CH 1919–20)
Portice, Elden & Katrina (TT 1994–96)
Pruitt, Helen (TT 1953–54)
Pruitt, Sue (KE 1985–87). *See also* Jerry & Sue Murray
Pye, George and Mrs. (TT 1906–08)
Railey, Robert (KE 1966–69)
Rather, Archie (TT 1911–12). And Rebecca (married 1912) (TT 1912–15; JM 1919–28; BA 1934–37; PA 1937–53)
Ratzlaff, Leslie & Nina (CA 1941–46; JM 1946–56)
Rawlings, Almeda (CA 1946–48)
Reames, J. David & Greta (JA 1974–76, 2002–03; SK 1979–84)
Reardon, E. A. (EG 1907–08)
Reed, Alan & Diane (JA 1980–82; HK 1985–96)
Reedy, Edward and Mrs. (TT 1911–14)
Reinholz, Carlton & Patricia (CA 1958–62)
Renbeck, Mary (DE 1912–15)
Renbeck, Nels & Edel (DE 1909–34)
Rennick, Steve & Diane (KE 1995–2003)
Renz, Russell & Velma (KE 1951–52)
Rhodes, Angie (RU 1996–97)
Rice, Lowell & Linda (KE 1970–72, 1976–79)
Richardson, Harley & Bonnie (KE 1958–60)

Ricketts, Cova Amanda (KE 1980–84; BR 1985–89; PA 1991–95)
Rigel, Jim & Cheryl (JA 1972–74)
Riggle, H. M. & Minnie (SY 1921–23)
Riley, Donald & Paula (TZ 1992–98) (RC AF: KE 1998–2005)
Ring, Otto & Eunice (SD 1937–40)
Roache, Leonard & Sylvia (PA 1984–88)
Roark, Warren & Alvina (BA 1926–28)
Robbins, Dick & Terri (PH 1980–86)
Roberts, Pamela (KE 1969–71, 1972–74)
Roberts, William & Marti (1993–99)
Robertson, Gregory & Linda (EC 2004–5, 2006–)
Robinson, Simon and Almeda Mae (KE 1962–70; TZ 1970–71, 1986–87)
Rodriguez, Joseph & Grace (CU 1943–46)
Rogers, Sidney & Fern (KE 1934–44)
Rojas, Nehiel & Joanna (PE 1979–83; UY 1983–93)
Root, LaVern & Darlene (BA 1964–67)
Ross, Patricia (TZ 2000–2003)
Roy, J. J. M. & Evalyn (née Nichols, married 1908). (IN 1908–1964). *See also* Evalyn Nichols
Royster, James & Elizabeth (IN 1960–62; EG 1962–64; KE 1964–65)
Rupert, John & Mrs. (UK 1892–93)
Russell, Martin (BE 1995)
Ryan, Jane (KE 1952–56). *See also* Samuel & Jane Betts
Ryder, Wilma (CA 1944–45)
Saltzmann, Paul (KE 1966–68)
Sanderson, Ruth (KE 1946–58)
Sandlin, Charles & Bernell (RU 1994)
Schieck, Gordon & Wilhemina (IN 1955–67)
Schneider, Velma (KE 1952–68)
Schwieger, Ruben C. & Nora (KE 1947–67)
Schwieger, Ruben D. & Virginia (KE 1963–68; JA 1985)
Sellers, Larry & LeAnn (HA 1985–90; RW 1991–94; KE 1995–96; CI 1996–)
Sellers, Wayne & Kathi (CR 1991–2008)
Senseman, Melissa (CY 1991–93)
Sewell, Gale (ZB 1998–2000; ZA 2001–3)

Shaffer, Mark & Casandra (CA 1998–2000)
Sharp, James & Dorothy (KE 1961–81, 1990–96; TZ 1982–90; UG 2006; CI 2008)
Shaw, Frank & Susan (BWI 1911–17, 1920–34)
Shell, Debbie (KE 1973–75)
Shiffler, Andrew (IN 1901–26)
Shively, Fred (CR 1990)
Shoffner, Lena (UK 1893–95)
Shotton, Ronald & Ruth (ME 1963–75, 1991–95; PA 1976–79)
Shular, Ben & Kelli (TZ 2004–)
Shultz, Clair & Retha (TT 1945–58; JM 1958–62; KE 1962–70, 1985–86)
Siehl, Summer (TW 1982–89, 1996–97; HK 1997–2001)
Sigl, Jennifer (CI 1998–2000, 2002–5)
Simpson, David & Kathy (BU 2005–)
Simpson, James & Sibyl (EG 1961–64)
Skaggs, Russell & Sharon (EG 1981–93)
Skaggs, Wilbur & Evelyn (EG 1945–58)
Sloan, Rose (KE 1993)
Smith, Dean & Karen (KE 1974–76)
Smith, Don & Chris (KE 2001–)
Smith, Donald & Ruth (UG 1997)
Smith, F. G. & Birdie (SY 1912–14)
Smith, Herman & Lavera (TT 1943–45; KE 1946–50; GY 1951–59)
Smith, John & Margaret (SK 1981)
Smith, Nathan & Ann (JA 1951–77; SK 1978–80)
Smith, Richard & Donna (KE 1957–62)
Smith, Tom & Norma (EG 1996–2003)
Smothers, Deidre (JA 1991–93; HU 1993–94)
Snowden, Christy (JA 1992–97). *See also* Terence & Christy Van Dam
Snyder, Johnny & Paula (ME 1981–86) (RC LA: EC 1995–2004)
Snyder, LeeAnn (EC 1999–2000)
Soetenga, Peter (EG 1992–93)
Sowers, Austin & Nancy (AU 1970–77)
Speer, Abby (JA 2007–8)
Spires, Joseph & Ramona (PK 1961–65)
Springer, Robert & Mrs. (RU & SW 1912–17)
Sprunger, Aaron & Cindy (TZ 1995–2003)

Steers, Bertram & Marian (died 1965) (IN 1965–68)

Stegman, Clara (RU 1908–9)

Steimla, Frank & Jennie (TT 1916–20; JM 1924–43)

Steinke, Gary & Doris (HK 1985–88)

Steinke, Gordon & Betty (LE 1998)

Stephenson, Manasseh & Gretchen (CU 1946–50)

Stevenson, Tim & Colleen (UG 1986–89, 1990–)

Stewart, Faith (IN 1913–26; CU 1930–58)

Strawn, James (IN 1907)

Strenger, Frieda (KE 1935–46)

Struthers, Charles & Florence (JM 1946–58)

Stull, Stephen & Janet (JA 1972–74)

Stull, Stephen (JA 2002–4)

Susag, S. O. (DE & SD 1911–37)

Sweeny, Naomi (KE 1955–60)

Swisher, Rolla & Juanita (VE 1989–90; VI 1993–94)

Tadlock, Heather (HU 1994–95)

Tallen, James & Frances (BA 1914–16)

Tanner, Sam (RU 1993)

Tasker, George. And Minnie (died 1940) (IN 1912–40). And Josephine (née McCrie, married 1941) (IN 1941–46). *See also* Josephine McCrie

Tate, Bob & Jo Ann (PE 1974–84; TT 2007–9)

Taton, Ollie Mae (UR 1995; RU 1995)

Tefft, Ruthann (KE 1969–72, 1974–75; RU 1994–95)

Theobald, Lottie (IN 1907–14). *See also* Robert Jarvis

Thimes, Edna (KE 1960–79)

Tiesel, Walter & Margaret (BA 1947–63; TT 1964–66; CA 1981–85; GY 1990)

Titley, William (UK 1907–08)

Tregellas, Tammie (HU 1992–94; KE 1997–2005; ZA 2005–7; MA 2007–)

Tufts, Gorham (IN 1897, 1905)

Turner, Allen & Clovis (SN 1969–76)

Turner, Arthenia (KE 1961–66, 1968–71)

Ummel, Diane (KE 1986–88; JA 1989–93)

Upchurch, Carolyn (KE 1964–67)

Valdez, Amelia. *See* Amelia Vazquez

Van Alstyne, Eugene & Barbara (KE 1977–81)

Van Dam, Terence & Christy (née Snowden) (JA 2000–2003). *See also* Christy Snowden
Van De Veur, Nick & Nina (US 1960–62)
Van Der Breggan, Aletta (HL 1949–53)
VanDerHeyden, Carol (RU 1994, 2005–6)
Varner, Aaron (GE 2008–)
Vazquez, Amelia (née Valdez; married Samuel Vazquez, 1976) (ME 1971–88)
Vielguth, George (GE, RU, SW 1901–13)
Von Bargen, Daniel (KE 1967–69)
Wagner, Michael (JA 1984–86, 1992– ; TW 1987–90)
Wallace, Mamie (IN 1921–27)
Walls, Thomas & Mary Lou (VE 1978–88)
Wamer, Ron & Karen (VE 1987–90)
Ward, Sheryl (KE 1967–69)
Warman, Dale & Marilyn (JA 1991)
Watson, Annabelle (CH 1916–37)
Watts, Kay (CI 2008–)
Webb, Matt & Eva (HA 2000–01)
Webb, Mike & Heather (SE 2004–06; TZ 2006–)
Weber, Dick & Linda (TZ 2004–5)
Weems, Amanda (EC 2004–6)
Weixel, Elroy & Harriet (RU 1994–95)
Welch, Douglas & Ruth (KE 1960–75)
Wells, Melissa (HU 1991–94)
West, Tim & Cindy (AU 2001–5)
Whitaker, Lynne (1995–97)
Wiebe, Roger & Fern (JA 1979–81)
Willard, Ethel (HK 1969–81)
Williams, Adam (died 1978) & Marjory (US 1947–2004)
Williams, Edgar. And Mildred (died 1965) (CH 1947–49; JM 1953–58). And Lima (née Lehmer, married 1966) (KE 1966–70). *See also* Lima Lehmer
Wilson, Charles & Evelyn (KE 1980–90)
Wilson, Ken & Paula (AU 1998–99)
Winters, Pina (CH 1910–14)
Woodman, Ronald & Effie (US 1973–)

Woodmore, Lori (JM 1993–94)

Woods, Vivian (KE 1970–75)

Woodsome, Richard & Georgia (KE 1962–68)

Workman, Hank (CY 1987–94)

Workman, Joel (UR 1995; RU 1995). And Julie (née Lund, married 1996)
(RU 1996–97). *See also* Julie Lund

Wyant, Don & Doloris (PE 1965–67)

Wyant, Doug & Susan (BR 1989–90)

Yamabe, Richard & Marianna (JA 1997–98)

Yoder, Harold & Velma (PE 1972–73)

Yoder, Lydia (TT 1906–08)

Yohe, Tom & Dena (RU 1998–2004)

Young, Edith (JM 1927–64)

Yutzy, James & Glenna (KE 1952–63)

Zaugg, Ira (IN 1906–12)

Zazanis, Nicholas & Rose (EG 1928–33, 1938–42; GR 1946–58)

Zoretic, Paul & Mickey (PE 1976–79; PR 1979–84)

Key to Codes

AB	Antigua Barbuda	CH	China
AF	Africa	CI	Côte d'Ivoire
AN	Angola	CO	Congo
AP	Asia–Pacific	CR	Costa Rica
AR	Argentina	CU	Cuba
AU	Australia	CY	Cyprus
BA	Barbados	CZ	Czech Republic
BD	Bangladesh	DE	Denmark
BE	Belize	EC	Ecuador
BM	Bermuda	EG	Egypt
BO	Bolivia	EM	Europe–Middle East
BR	Brazil	EU	Eurasia
BU	Bulgaria	GE	Germany
BWI	British West Indies	GR	Greece
CA	Cayman Islands	GT	Guatemala
CÇ	Curaçao	GU	Guam
CE	Central Asia	GY	Guyana

HA	Haiti	RU	Russia
HK	Hong Kong	RW	Rwanda
HL	Holland	SA	South Africa
HO	Honduras	SC	Scotland
HU	Hungary	SD	Sweden
IN	India	SE	Southeast Asia
IR	Ireland	SI	Singapore
IT	Italy	SK	South Korea
JA	Japan	SN	St. Kitts & Nevis
JM	Jamaica	SW	Switzerland
KE	Kenya	SY	Syria
KZ	Kazakhstan	TH	Thailand
LA	Latin America	TT	Trinidad & Tobago
LE	Lebanon	TW	Taiwan
MA	Malawi	TZ	Tanzania
ME	Mexico	UG	Uganda
NO	Norway	UK	United Kingdom
NZ	New Zealand	UR	Ukraine
PA	Panama	US	United States
PE	Peru	UY	Uruguay
PG	Paraguay	VE	Venezuela
PH	Philippines	VI	Virgin Islands
PK	Pakistan	ZA	Zambia
PR	Puerto Rico	ZB	Zimbabwe

Appendix 6
Global Missions Strategic Plan

The following plan flows out of and will be measured against the Five Strategic Goals and the Ends Policies of Church of God Ministries, Inc.

Missiological Underpinning

The ministry work of Global Missions is performed within and to persons of cultures other than our own and, therefore, is built upon a missiological foundation that instructs and informs how we do that ministry.

We believe that God created all humankind equal and valuable in his sight. His Word, understood within each person's culture, is for all people and all generations. His teachings are central to all we do. God wishes all people to come to a saving knowledge of Jesus Christ within their culture. As his ambassadors, we have a deep, abiding commitment and dependency upon him as we proclaim his good news to everyone.

Evangelism and discipleship are done in tandem as we call all to a salvation experience and then disciple them to maturity in Christ. We are committed to leader development. Meaningful and appropriate theological education and leader development are indispensable elements of our ministry. We seek to discover and use methods that are effective, biblically based, indefinitely reproducible, and sustainable.

Our goal is to have reproducing churches ministering to their surrounding communities in ways that are both biblically based and culturally relevant. The church will not be dependent on the outside for its life force and direction as we follow the incarnational model of Jesus for mission. We will love others, join them, and be peers with them, serving side by side with the men and women God has chosen as his own. Our attitude towards those with whom we serve is that which Jesus himself displayed.

Mission Statement of Global Missions

"Committed to world evangelism and discipleship, Global Missions will send missionaries, resource global ministry, and network through interdependent partnerships with the church around the world."

I. Sending of Missionaries

Using the Five Strategic Goals as a measure of what we do, Global Missions will:

1.1 Review and evaluate missionary designations, titles, and roles by April 30, 2009 (i.e., career, special assignment, missionary apprentice, regional coordinator, as well as the actual term *missionary*). These new designations will be implemented by December 31, 2009.

1.2 Review and evaluate our current recruitment processes by September 30, 2009. Determine necessary changes and implement changes by December 2010.

1.3 Develop a strategy for member care that includes missiological education, spiritual formation, and organizational procedures by December 30, 2009.

1.4 Research and identify fraternal and compatible sending agencies with whom we can partner to send missionaries to limited-access countries by September 30, 2009. Establish relationships as necessary and implement appropriate working agreements by March 2010.

II. Resourcing of Global Ministry

Using the Five Strategic Goals as a measure of what we do, Global Missions will:

2.1 Develop criteria to evaluate and approve requests (projects and/or missionaries) for funding through the lens of the five Strategic Goals and Ends Policies by June 2009 to be implemented with the 2010 budget.

2.2 Create strategic agreements (memos of understanding) by the end of 2009 with partners involved in international ministries for the purpose of authentic cooperation in world evangelism and discipleship (e.g., Children of Promise, Caring Partners, NICE, Partners in Missions, and Helping Hands in Motion).

2.3 Participate with the Kingdom Ministry Team in the development of a clear statement of definition, understanding, and strategy for Global Learning Centers by June 30, 2009.

2.4 Participate with Church of God Ministries in the development of a clear statement of understanding and strategy for Eye on the World by June 30, 2009.

2.5 Cross-train Global Missions staff to access and maintain, per approved standard operating procedures, approved Global Missions Web pages and "members only" Web site by February 28, 2009.

2.6 Develop a strategic plan for Missions Education (theological, organizational, and missiological) for the church by September 2009.

III. Networking through Interdependent Partnerships

Using the Five Strategic Goals as a measure of what we do, Global Missions will:

3.1 Increase by 5 percent the number of Church of God congregations in relationship with cross-cultural ministry by the end of 2009: Living Link, Project Link, and Eye on the World. To be reviewed annually.

3.2 Facilitate an annual international forum that may include mission pastors, missionaries, international pastors, paramissions groups, and international partners. The first will take place immediately after the 2009 NAC as a Global Conversation. The next ones will be regional in nature and will be facilitated by Global Missions. This will begin with the Latin America International Forum for Kingdom Workers that will meet in Nicaragua in October 2009.

3.3 Identify and reestablish relationships with the Church of God international missionary-sending countries and organizations (examples:

The Himalayan Regional Missionary Board and the Church of God in Germany) by September 30, 2009, for information sharing, mutual coordination, support, and mutual accountability.

3.4 Establish intentional partnerships with the International Youth Convention (IYC) as well as the colleges, universities, and seminaries of the Church of God to connect students with missionaries and international partners in order to strengthen relational connectivity with Global Missions, the Kingdom Ministry Team, and Church of God Ministries by the end of 2009. Create a culture of mentorship for youth who are called to missions through which they are identified and nurtured.

3.5 Facilitate the relationship of Church of God Ministries leadership, Partners in Ministry, area administrators, college leadership, and pastors with the international church through two annual strategic Eye on the World vision trips. Create a clear statement of expectations for ministry trips by June 2009.

Revised January 2009.

ENDNOTES

Introduction

1. A song on the mission and ministry of the church by Frederick G. Shackleton, *Worship the Lord: Hymnal of the Church of God* (Anderson, IN: Warner Press, 1989).

Chapter 1: Pioneers in Mission (1880–1900)

1. Calcutta is today known as Kolkata.

Chapter 2: Toward a United Outreach (1900–1918)

1. Calcutta is today known as Kolkata.

Chapter 3: Moving Out Between the Wars (1918–1945)

1. Calcutta is today known as Kolkata.

Chapter 4: Regaining Momentum (1945–1955)

1. Calcutta is today known as Kolkata.
2. Peking is known today as Beijing.
3. Burma is today generally known as Myanmar.

Chapter 5: Churches Emerge from Missions (1955–1965)

1. Calcutta is today known as Kolkata.

Chapter 7: Partnership in World Missions (1975–1980)

1. Bombay is known today as Mumbai.
2. Peking is known today as Beijing.

Chapter 8: Expanding the Partnership (1980–1989)

1. *Yearbook of the Church of God*, 1980, 304–5.
2. Published in three parts in *Church of God Missions*: September 1980, 8–9; October 1980, 12–13; November 1980, 12–13.
3. Donald D. Johnson, "International Partnership in Mission: A Missiologist's View, Part III," *Church of God Missions*, November 1980, 12.

4. Oral Withrow, "Cyprus Conference," *Church of God Missions*, March 1981, 6.

5. Underscoring its importance, Withrow listed the Cyprus consultation alongside an Asian conference for missionaries in Tokyo (1978), a tandem Asian conference for Asian leaders in Bangkok (1979), an African planning consultation in Kenya (1979), and a similar one for the Caribbean –Atlantic region on the island of St. Kitts (1979).

6. Withrow, "Cyprus Conference," 7.

7. Fouad Melki, "The Mediterranean Bible College," *Church of God Missions*, July–August 1996, 11.

8. Dondeena Caldwell, "Dreams Come True," *Church of God Missions*, February 1986, 6.

9. From a conversation between James Albrecht and Cheryl Johnson Barton, April 28, 2008.

10. In July 1978, a five-day consultation was conducted in Tokyo for thirty-six current and retired missionaries from the region and staff from the United States who attended on behalf of the Missionary Board and World Service. Seven months later, in February 1979, a three-day meeting in Bangkok brought together six national leaders: Robin Das, Bangladesh; Koesuke Nishitani, Japan; Hong Mook Yoo, Korea; Wichean Watakeecharoen, Thailand; Eduardo Viray, Philippines; and Stanley Nichols-Roy, India. Additionally, Donald Johnson and Oral Withrow represented the Missionary Board and Paul Tanner, the Executive Council.

11. "Guidelines for the Asian Church of God Conference," November 23, 1995, 1.

12. Asim Das, editorial, *Asian Church of God Magazine*, October 1985, 1.

13. Kozo Konno, "The Church of God in Asia," *Asian Church of God Magazine*, October 1985, 3.

14. Sidney and Jean Johnson, "An Ending and a Beginning," *Church of God Missions*, November 1989, 3.

15. Konno, "Church of God in Asia."

16. Norman S. Patton, President's Page, *Church of God Missions*, September–October 1994, 3.

17. Maurice Caldwell, "Report of the Associate Secretary to the Missionary Board," May 14, 1980.

18. David Lawson, "Million for Missions—Year Three!" *Church of God Missions*, September 1979, 2.

19. Survey team members were Donald Johnson and Oral Withrow, representing the Missionary Board; Paul Tanner, Executive Council; David Lawson, World Service; and Marvin Hartman and Tom Smith of the Board of Church Extension and Home Missions.

20. David Lawson, "Demand and Supply," *Church of God Missions*, July 1977, 5.

21. Oral Withrow, "Overseas Missions Projects," *Church of God Missions*, September 1979, 16–17.

22. Cheryl Johnson Barton, "Kenya Welcomes Church of God Seventh World Conference; Korea to Host 1987 Assembly," *Vital Christianity*, October 2, 1983, 24.

23. Million for Missions accomplishments outlined in a World Service report to the 1980 General Assembly.

24. Ibid.

25. Sidney and Jean Johnson, "An Ending and a Beginning," *Church of God Missions*, November 1989, 2.

26. Sidney M. Johnson (unpublished history of the beginnings of the Church of God in Nepal).

27. Nina Martin, "Meet the Pohsngaps," *Church of God Missions*, July 1983, 12.

28. Johnson (unpublished history).

29. Japan's support of one hundred dollars a month was relayed through the Missionary Board.

30. Douglas Welch, "Toward a Biblical Theology of Mission," an unpublished paper, 1982, 2.

31. Maurice Caldwell, "Evangelizing on the Equator," *Church of God Missions,* April 1992, 5.

32. David Miller, "Dreaming Dreams in Latin America," *Church of God Missions*, November–December 1995, 4.

33. From a conversation between Arlo Newell and Cheryl Johnson Barton, December, 2007.

34. According to Maurice and Dondeena Caldwell, the Gospel Trumpet Company, now Warner Press, was involved in such a cooperative effort in the 1920s with "Olaf and Mary Bertelson, home missionaries living in California, who worked with A. T. Maciel in Los Angeles and the Tafollas in San Antonio, Texas, to produce literature for Spanish speakers on both sides of the border."

35. "Nine Decades of Caring, Sharing, and Giving," *Church of God Missions*, May–June 1999, 19.

36. Resolution: Refugee Committee, in the Executive Council report to the 1980 General Assembly, 16.

37. "Report of the Coordinator of the Refugee Program of the Church of God," May 13, 1981, 4–5.

38. 178 individuals were resettled in 1982, 170 in 1983, 125 in 1984, and 85 in 1985.

39. Unless otherwise cited, statistics related to the Seventh World Conference are from Paul A. Tanner and David L. Lawson, "History of the World Conference of the Church of God," private collection.

40. Cheryl Johnson Barton, "Kenya Welcomes Church of God Seventh World Conference; Korea to Host 1987 Assembly," *Vital Christianity*, October 2, 1983, 23.

41. Ibid.

42. Information about the World Forum is excerpted from the official minutes written by Lester A. Crose.

43. Donald D. Johnson, "Report of the Executive Secretary-Treasurer," May 16, 1979, 14.

44. The anniversary commemorative logo showed two hands, one black and one white, clasped together in the center of a circle with the number 75 superimposed upon them. Reversed out of the purple circle were the words, "Missionary Board of the Church of God" and "Global Partnership." Special activities included a spring 1984 continuing education class in "Global Awareness" through Anderson School of Theology; a series of messages on global concerns and awareness by *Christian Brotherhood Hour* speaker David Grubbs; 150 key pastors attending a special breakfast at the 1983 International Convention in Anderson to learn about the celebration and to become more globally aware, with follow-up banquets during the upcoming year at regional ministers' meetings and pastors' fellowships; new Missionary Board publications, including a historical booklet, a book of meditations and prayers on missions (*Lord, It's Late But I Can't Sleep* by Dorothy Nicholson), and promotional materials such as slide sets, bulletin inserts, brochures, and a specially designed world map to identify countries where the Missionary Board was helping through providing either personnel or funds (forty-eight of sixty-two countries where the Church of God was present, not including the United States and Canada), countries

where there were Church of God countries without direct Missionary Board involvement, and nations where there were no known Church of God congregations.

45. Ann Smith and Richard Willowby, "Concern for Evangelism, Missions, and Education: An Interview with Adam W. Miller," *Vital Christianity*, June 10, 1984, 5.

46. Donald D. Johnson, "Global Partnership: Our Theme," *Church of God Missions*, July 1984, 2–3.

47. Donald D. Johnson, "Report of the Executive Secretary-Treasurer," May 16, 1979, 10.

48. In a letter to The Reverend Mr. Lawrence P. Wyatt from Donald D. Johnson, April 8, 1980.

49. This action was in a January 10, 1980, Board of Directors executive session.

50. Johnson wrote, "The Missionary Board continues to be characterized as racist. The Tom Sawyer resignation is cited as an example of unchristian behavior, unfair treatment of a minority employee, and symbolic of the erosion of black administrative leadership in national corporations. Our explanations regarding Mr. Sawyer's termination have not been accepted. This Board was asked for an apology for its behavior. The Board's recruitment and placement of black missionary personnel has been downgraded. Our strategy and implementation of missions is under critical scrutiny. The Board's intention to recruit and hire a black staff person is viewed with suspicion."

51. Ibid.

52. Excerpts from Johnson's report follow: "The average increase in the Basic Budget over the past five years has been 8 percent…Mission Latin America and Million for Missions have provided much needed capital funding during the past ten years. The fact of the matter is, however, our operating budget is severely restricted. Run-away inflation at home and abroad will nullify any increase we can expect for the 1980–81 budget year. The increase in the operating budget which we need to keep pace with inflation and record minimal progress will require a 24 percent increase in Basic Budget. This would amount to $394,250. If we receive the average of 8 percent, we will need to cut our operating budget by $306,250. Impossible! By the time you read this report its sequel will be off the press. We will have presented our 'Asking Budget' to the National Budget Committee

and have received their response. The painful pruning will have been done. You will be asked later in this meeting to approve the skeleton which will be left. This is a pity, when it could be different!"

53. Page 1 of Nicholson's report elaborates: "Each year I have begun my report by using a phrase that best describes the year as it relates to my area of work at the Missionary Board. Last year I used the word 'survival.' The phrase this year would be, 'Not out of the woods, but on the path.' The Missionary Board is not out of the woods financially, but we have definitely found the path that leads out of the woods."

54. From a letter to missionary colleagues by Donald D. Johnson, October 2, 1984.

55. Cheryl Johnson Barton, "Reflections on a Missionary Life: An Interview with Arthur and Norma Eikamp," *Vital Christianity*, June 10, 1984, 22.

56. "Report of the Assistant Treasurer-Controller," 1985, 3.

57. One year before, the deficit had been $347,715. It stood at $306,524 on February 28, 1995.

58. Finance and Development Committee members were Gene Newberry, Board president; Ruben Schwieger, Board member; Nellie Snowden, executive secretary-treasurer of Women of the Church of God; Pickens; and Nicholson.

59. "Minutes of the Executive Session of the Board of Directors of the Missionary Board," January 9, 1986, 1.

60. Specifically, the Missionary Board reduced its personnel by one administrative staff member, an office support person, and one missionary family in Tanzania, and phased out the African liaison position. The Board also determined to seek extra funding for the Refugee Program from the Executive Council. When this did not materialize, it cut the Refugee Program coordinator position from full to half time.

61. "Church of God Missionary Board Major Cutbacks," *Asian Church of God Magazine*, April 1986, 28.

62. Tom Pickens Report to the Missionary Board, May 1987, 3.

63. Ibid, 1.

64. From a conversation between Doris Dale and Cheryl Johnson Barton, December 2007.

65. At the time, executive Board staff members were the executive secretary-treasurer, two associate executive secretaries (Donald Williams, with

major emphasis on Africa, and Maurice Caldwell, assigned to Latin America), a field administrator for Asia (Sidney Johnson), and a coordinator of personnel (J. David Reames).

66. World Forum highlights included a foot-washing service and speakers from twenty-one countries explaining their views on such topics as "United for a Purpose," "Celebrating Our Unity," "Affirming Our Diversity," "Conditions for Unity," and "Toward Greater Unity."

67. Minutes of Staff Retreat, November 13–16, 1989, 1.

68. Minutes of the 80th Annual Missionary Board Meeting, November 7–10, 1989, 15.

69. Minutes, Special Called Missionary Board Meeting, May 2, 1988, 9.

70. Missionary Board Meeting Minutes, October 5–9, 1992, 44.

71. From a conversation between Norman Patton and Cheryl Johnson Barton, January 2008.

72. Ibid.

73. Stanley Hoffman, "Leadership Training in Uganda and Zambia," *Church of God Missions*, October 1992, 5.

74. Ibid.

75. Ephraim Tumusiime, "And So the Church Grows," *Church of God Missions*, May 1990, 7.

76. Dave Miller, "Apprenticeship Training in Bolivia," *Church of God Missions*, October 1992, 2.

Chapter 9: The Decade of Change (1990–1999)

1. C. Ford Runge and Benjamin Senauer, "How Biofuels Could Starve the Poor," Foreign Affairs, May–June 2007. http://www.foreignaffairs.org/20070501faessay86305-p0/c-ford-runge-benjamin-senauer/how-biofuels-could-starve-the-poor.html.

2. While membership in the Church of God has always been problematic to define, the 1984 *Yearbook of the Church of God* reports a North American membership of 185,137 people and a membership outside North America of 183,989. However, the figures one year later are 182,481 in North America and 197,629 members outside.

3. According to the 1991 *Yearbook of the Church of God*, which reported statistics for 1990, Kenya had one hundred thousand members and five hundred churches at the start of the decade.

4. Robert E. Edwards, "1990s: Africa! An Overview of the Church of God in Africa," *Church of God Missions*, March 1990, 2.

5. Most important about this story, according to the Armstrongs, is that "with the establishment of the Aldergate schools, the Church of God in Tanzania is now seeing their youth advance into occupations other than farming or menial labor positions. We have Church of God youth who have gone all the way through the school system and through university and are now lecturing at major universities as professors and working in business as accountants and managers. The school is allowing people in the church a chance at something better for their kids than farming two acres and living in a village in the Tanzanian bush."

6. Minutes of the Annual Meeting of the Missionary Board of the Church of God, November 14–16, 1990, 4–6.

7. The beginnings of Malawi and Cameroon are recounted in Chapter 8.

8. Since 1989, Burma has become better known as Myanmar.

9. Minutes of the Annual Board Meeting, November 12–15, 1991, 18.

10. From a conversation between Robert Edwards and Cheryl Johnson Barton, March 25, 2008.

11. Robert E. Edwards, "All Africa Leaders' Consultation," *Church of God Missions*, July 1991, 6.

12. Norman S. Patton, President's Annual Report: July 1991-June 1992, 17.

13. President's Annual Report, July 1991–June 1992, 35.

14. Read one such story, P. K. Das, "From the Temple of Gods to the Temple of God," in *His Praise Glorious*, ed. Cheryl Johnson Barton, 1–4 (Anderson, IN: Warner Press, 2007).

15. Violence against Christians in Orissa erupted again in August and September 2008. Churches, schools, and homes of Christians were vandalized, with more than forty Christians killed. More than ten thousand had fled into the jungles for cover, their whereabouts and fates unknown at this writing.

16. A Church of God pastor, "The Miracle-Making One," in *At My Right Hand*, ed. Cheryl Johnson Barton, 25–27 (Anderson, IN: Missionary Board of the Church of God, 1994).

17. John W. V. Smith, *The Quest for Unity and Holiness* (Anderson, IN: Warner Press, 1980), 275.

18. Ng Ngoing Keng, "Asian Women Convene in Singapore," *Asian Church of God Magazine*, April 1991, 18–20.

19. Unless otherwise cited, information related to the three World Conferences is from Paul A. Tanner and David L. Lawson, "History of the World Conference of the Church of God," private collection, 7–9.

20. From a conversation between Norman Patton and Cheryl Johnson Barton, March 19, 2008.

21. Minutes of the Annual Board Meeting, Missionary Board of the Church of God, November 12–15, 1991, 6–7.

22. President's Annual Report, Fiscal Year: July 1994–June 1995, 37.

23. That the missionary enterprise headquartered in Anderson, Indiana, "is not the only agency in the Church of God doing mission" and that greater partnership and interdependence in mission are mandates for the North American church is a theme repeated continually by executives, regional coordinators, missionaries, and missiologists, especially from the 1980s onwards. Donald Johnson expands upon this tenet in his essay, "Afterword: The Mission Mandate and the Church of God" (pp. 370–76).

24. From a conversation between Norman Patton and Cheryl Johnson Barton, March 19, 2008.

25. Robert Edwards shared his thoughts with Cheryl Johnson Barton in a conversation on March 25, 2008. In the Afterword to this book, Donald Johnson underlines the necessity of bringing leaders together, declaring, "That whatever resources it may take, regular, planned conversation between international church leaders is vital for the future."

26. Paul C. Hutchins, "A Multitude of Keys," in *Jars of Clay*, ed. Cheryl Johnson Barton, 62 (Anderson, IN: Warner Press, 2006).

27. Cheryl Johnson Barton, "Building Disciples: Celebrating the Ministry of Paul and Nova Hutchins," *Missions*, May–June 2006, 10.

28. The real financial situation of Living Link was worse than even these figures indicate. According to a report given by Eileen Clay to the Mid-Year Missionary Board Meeting (April 23–26, 1991), the 1990 budget was $1,226,540. Of this, $995,582 was committed for support, yet only $600,883 was actually received (49 percent of the total budget). In addition, Living Link had a $625,657 deficit.

29. Minutes of the Annual Board Meeting, Missionary Board of the Church of God, November 12–15, 1991, 11.

30. The actual decision to include ministry funds under Living Link was authorized in the October 1993 Missionary Board meeting.

31. The disparity between pledged support and actual receipts was addressed at least by the 1993–94 fiscal year when the President's Annual Report listed as its number one goal the need "to continue raising Living Link support to a commitment of 110% and 100% actual." In that same report, it was noted that missionaries joining the Maasai Ministry Team would be required to have 110 percent Living Link support pledged and all start-up funds raised before they could leave for the field.

32. Donald D. Johnson, "Living Link: The Vital Connection," *Missions*, May–June 2000, 6.

33. President's Annual Report, Fiscal Year: July 1991–June 1992, 8.

34. SAM statistics were taken from various annual reports of the Missionary Board president, with the final accounting from the Global Missions coordinator's annual report (July 1998–June 1999).

35. Sidney & Jean Johnson, A History of Children of Promise, private collection.

36. President's Annual Report: July 1991–June 1993, 13.

37. President's Annual Report: July 1994–June 1995, 9.

38. Robert Edwards, "News from Zaire/Congo," *Church of God Missions*, July–August 1997, 17.

39. President's Annual Report: July 1996–June 1997, 2–3.

40. Sherman Critser, "Rwanda: The Aftermath," *Church of God Missions*, January–February 1996, 4.

41. Ibid., 5.

42. Ibid.

43. Sherman L. Critser, "When Will the Wind of Peace Come?" *Church of God Missions*, January–February 1999, 8.

44. Mark Shaner, "Taking High Schoolers to Russia," *Church of God Missions*, July 1992, 3.

45. Norman S. Patton, President's Page, *Church of God Missions*, March–April 1996, 3.

46. From a conversation between Norman Patton and Cheryl Johnson Barton, November 28, 2007.

47. Ibid.

48. James A. Albrecht, "Celebration and Commitment: CoMission at the Crossroads," *Church of God Missions*, September–October 1997, 14.

49. James A. Albrecht, "New Agreements in Chelyabinsk!" *Church of God Missions*, January–February 1996, 17.

50. Ibid.

51. President's Page, *Church of God Missions*, March–April, 1996, 3.

52. The CoMission executive committee was chaired by Bruce Wilkinson, president of Walk Through the Bible. Other members included Paul Eishleman, director of the Jesus Film Project; Joseph Stowell, president of Moody Bible Institute; J. B. Crouse, president of OMS International; representatives of Campus Crusade for Christ, who provided the curriculum used; Peter Dyneka, president of Russian Ministries; Wayne Wright, president of Wesleyan World Missions; and Norman Patton, with James Albrecht often sitting in for Patton.

53. James A. Albrecht, "Mission to Chelyabinsk, Russia, 1991–98: A Model for Missions in New Fields," private collection, January 16, 2008.

54. Church growth statistics and comments by Robert Edwards quoted in the Missionary Board President's Annual Report: July 1994–June 1995, 9.

55. The new urban church plants were Goma, Zaire; Blantyre, Malawi; Abijan, Côte d'Ivoire; Harare, Zimbabwe; Lusaka, Zambia; and Johannesburg, South Africa.

56. "Missionary Board Outlines Five Year Vision," *Church of God Missions*, July 1991, 14.

57. Ibid.

58. President's Annual Report: July 1993–June 1994, 3.

59. Don and Paula Riley, "Battling the Enemy," in *Five Loaves and Two Fish*, ed. Cheryl Johnson Barton, 16 (Anderson, IN: Missionary Board of the Church of God, 1996).

60. Aaron Sprunger, "The Fingerprints of God: Tanzania," in *No Other Rock*, ed. Cheryl Johnson Barton, 45–46 (Anderson, IN: Missionary Board of the Church of God, 1998).

61. The school was first launched in the early 1950s as Kima Bible College through the efforts of missionary Wick Donohew. Twelve men completed their studies in 1955 in the first graduating class.

62. Steven L. Rennick, "Kima International School of Theology," *Church of God Missions*, September–October 1996, 18.

63. Ibid.

64. Edwards' comment was included in the President's Annual Report: July 1996–June 1997, 1.

65. From an interview with Steve and Diane Rennick by Cheryl Johnson Barton, September 2007.

66. Missionary Board Meeting Minutes, October 5–9, 1992, 48.

67. From a conversation between Norman S. Patton and Cheryl Johnson Barton, November 29, 2007.

68. Participants from the United States included Timothy Clarke, Michael Curry, Robert McClure, and Ronald Fowler (National Association) and Patton, Raymond Chin, and Robert Edwards (Missionary Board). Particpants from the African Executive Council included Byrum Makokha, Kenya; Edward Nkansah, Ghana; Eliazar Mdobi, Tanzania; Moses Abasoola, Uganda; Afeck Lungu, Zambia; and missionary Stanley Hoffman.

69. From a conversation between Norman Patton and Cheryl Johnson Barton, March 17, 2008.

70. President's Annual Report: July 1992–June 1993, 33.

71. From an interview with Klaus Kroeger by Cheryl Johnson Barton, September 2007.

72. "Missionary Board Outlines Five Year Vision," *Church of God Missions*, July 1991, 14.

73. President's Annual Report, Fiscal Year: July 1995–June 1996, 43.

74. Doris Dale, Global Missions Coordinator's Annual Report, Fiscal Year: July 1998–June 1999, 34.

75. Ibid.

76. Norman S. Patton, "Fruitful Partnerships," *Church of God Missions*, March 1994, 3.

77. President's Annual Report, Fiscal Year: July 1994–June 1995, 22.

78. President's Annual Report, Fiscal Year: July 1991–June 1992, 18.

79. Global Missions Coordinator's Annual Report, Fiscal Year: July 1998–June 1999, 8.

80. Lorenzo Mondragon, "When Prophecies Fail," in *Jars of Clay*, ed. Cheryl Johnson Barton, 55 (Anderson, IN: Warner Press, 2006).

81. Ibid., 57.

82. Paul Jones, "Lessons from Bolivia," in *Like a Blazing Fire*, ed. Cheryl Johnson Barton, 64–66 (Anderson, IN: Warner Press, 2005).

83. David Miller, "Principles of Planting in Bolivia," *Church of God Missions*, May–June 1995, 18.

84. P. K. Das, "From the Temple of Gods to the Temple of God," in *His Praise Glorious*, ed. Cheryl Johnson Barton, 1–4 (Anderson, IN: Warner Press, 2007).

85. Asim Das, "Church Planting Challenges in Orissa," *Church of God Missions*, May–June 1995, 17.

86. Statistics for 1994 from Victor Babb, "Church Proclaims Hope in Caribbean/Atlantic," *Church of God Missions*, September–October 1994, 6. Later statistics and conversion stories were reported in the Global Missions Coordinator's Annual Report, Fiscal Year: July 1998–June 1999.

87. Patrick Nachtigall, "A Teenage Church Grows Up," in *Like a Blazing Fire*, ed. Cheryl Johnson Barton, 30 (Anderson, IN: Warner Press, 2005).

88. Missionary Board meeting minutes for October 5–9, 1992, 3–6, 31–32.

89. Dave Miller, "Caught in the Cross Fire," in *Like a Blazing Fire*, ed. Cheryl Johnson Barton, 56 (Anderson, IN: Church of God Ministries, 2005).

90. These variances were reported in Missionary Board meeting minutes for 1990 and in the President's Annual Report, Fiscal Year: 1991–92.

91. President's Annual Report, Fiscal Year: July 1997–June 1998, 38–39.

92. President's Annual Report, Fiscal Year: July 1994–June 1995, 38.

93. Edwards' reflective essay, "The Internet and Missions," was included in the President's Annual Report, Fiscal Year: July 1995-June 1996, 5.

94. Global Missions Coordinator's Annual Report, Fiscal Year: July 1998-June 1999, 3.

95. Edward L. Foggs, 1988 Annual Report to the General Assembly by the Associate Executive Secretary of the Leadership Council, 64–65.

96. Barry L. Callen, *Following the Light* (Anderson, IN: Warner Press, 2000), 381.

97. Missionary Board meeting minutes, October 5–9, 1992, 44.

98. From a conversation between Norman Patton and Cheryl Johnson Barton, February 15, 2007.

99. Norman Patton, President's Page, *Church of God Missions*, July–August 1998, 3.

100. From a conversation between Doris Dale and Cheryl Johnson Barton, December 2007

101. Statistics are from the 1991 and 2001 volumes of the *Yearbook of the Church of God.*

102. There is a discrepancy between statistics in the 2001 *Yearbook of the Church of God* and the September–October 2000 issue of *Church of God Missions,* which reported that the Church of God was at work in eighty-nine countries, inclusive of the United States and Canada, and 6,828 churches, and had total worldwide membership of 712,907 people.

Chapter 10: A New Century (2000–2009)

1. John Naisbitt and Patricia Aburdene, *Megatrends 2000: Ten New Directions for the 1990s* (New York: Morrow, 1990).

2. Douglas E. Welch, "On Megatrends 2000," *Church of God Missions,* September 1990, 9.

3. Merle D. Strege, "The Church of God at 119 Years," *Yearbook of the Church of God* (Anderson, IN: Church of God Ministres, 2000), 4.

4. "How Can We Serve You?" *Missions,* September–October 2000, 19.

5. Regional directors: Victor Babb, Caribbean–Atlantic; Gilbert and Melba Davila, North America; Robert and Jan Edwards, Europe-Middle East; Michael and Debra Kinner, Asia-Pacific; Don and Paula Riley, Africa; and Johnny and Paula Snyder, Latin America. Anderson staff: Doris Dale, Global Missions coordinator; Sharon Skaggs, assistant coordinator; Sandy Hall, itineration coordinator; Judy Hughes, missions education specialist; Donald Johnson, recruitment specialist; and Candy Power, Living Link coordinator.

6. Don and Paula Riley, January 2000 Africa Regional Report, Part 3, 2.

7. Amos Moore, "Reaching Tribal People of Nepal," *Missions,* July–August 2000, 7.

8. Victor F. Babb, Caribbean-Atlantic Assembly Report to Staff Planning Meeting, January 2000, 1.

9. Babb's statistics differ slightly from those in the September–October 2000 issue of *Missions* quoted earlier in this chapter (334 churches and 41,790 believers).

10. Victor F. Babb, Caribbean-Atlantic Assembly Report to Staff Planning Meeting, January 2000, 4.

11. Andreas Burgin, "Church of God in Germany," *Missions,* September–October 2000, 16.

12. Robert E. Edwards, Yearly Report 1999 to the Staff Planning Meeting, 4.

13. "The Greenhouse," *Missions*, September–October 2000, 6–7.

14. Franco Santonocito, "Reclaiming the Cradle of Christianity," *Missions*, September–October 2000, 14–15.

15. Argentina, Belize, Bolivia, Brazil, Costa Rica, Ecuador, and Honduras.

16. January 2004 Field Report for Latin America, 3.

17. Kathi Sellers, "God Calling," in *His Praise Glorious*, ed. Cheryl Johnson Barton, 76–79 (Anderson, IN: Warner Press, 2007).

18. For a more complete story of the complex civil war in Colombia, see David Miller, "Caught in the Cross Fire," in *His Praise Glorious*, ed. Cheryl Johnson Barton, 57–59 (Anderson, IN: Warner Press, 2007).

19. Tabitha Kurrle, Paraguay; Helmut Krenz, Switzerland; Amos Moore, Nepal; Sheila Proctor, Trinidad; Hardy Steinke, Canada; and Byrum Makokha, Kenya.

20. Gilbert Davila, 2000 North American Regional Report, 2.

21. In fact, a total of eight individuals were laid off by Church of God Ministries in November 2008 because of this budget shortfall. Among these was the editor of *Missions* magazine, the primary mouthpiece of Global Missions for many years. The future of the publication was unknown at press time.

22. Norman S. Patton, President's Annual Report, Fiscal Year: July 1997–June 1998, 25.

23. Donald D. Johnson, Final Report of the Interim Regional Coordinator (Asia/Pacific), June 2003, 3.

24. Ibid., 3–4.

25. Read the full text of "Missiological Principles That Form the Foundation of Our Cross-Cultural Ministry" in the appendix on pages 398–401.

26. Africa, 16 projects ($67,920); Asia–Pacific, 13 ($76,100); Caribbean–Atlantic, 8 ($120,889); Europe–Middle East, 13 ($148,800); and Latin America, 30 projects ($118,000)

27. Under World Service, they had been tagged as 30,000 accounts.

28. Logan E. Ritchhart, "Urgency," *Missions*, May–June 2005, 6.

29. Kelvin Harrinarine, "Under a Mango Tree," in *Yet I Will Rejoice*, ed. Cheryl Johnson Barton, 37–38 (Anderson, IN: Warner Press, 2008).

30. The moving story of the Serbian church surviving and growing in the face of trials is told in Obrad Nikolić, "Nevertheless," in *Jars of Clay*, ed. Cheryl Johnson Barton, 39–41 (Anderson, IN: Warner Press, 2006).

31. Kelley Philips, "Project Oasis," *Missions*, May–June 2005, 11.

32. Patrick Johnstone and Jason Mandryk, *Operation World*, 21st Century Edition, (Waynesboro, GA: Paternoster, 2001), 94.

33. "Partnership with Promise," the 2007 Gift-Giving Guide of Church of God Ministries, 19.

34. John Johnson, "Essential Ministry in Bangladesh," *Missions*, May–June 2005, 14.

35. Doris Dale, Global Missions Coordinator's Annual Report, Fiscal Year: July 1998–June 1999, 1.

36. From a conversation between Doris Dale and Cheryl Johnson Barton, December 2007.

37. Church Multiplication/Health and Growth; credentialing; SHAPE (a pastoral health ministry initiative); Christian Education and Congregational Life; Christian Education, Youth and Family; Leadership Development; National Prayer Ministry/Pastoral Health and Growth; Chaplain Ministries; CBH; Compassionate Ministries and Homeland Ministry; and Global Missions.

38. Australia, Canada, Ecuador, Germany, Hungary, Japan, Kenya, Nepal, Paraguay, Switzerland, and the United States.

39. Most information in this section is gleaned from the "Official Report of the Proceedings, Global Dialogue of the Church of God," written by Barry L. Callen, Dialogue recording secretary.

40. John Fozard, Mid-America Christian University, Oklahoma; John Johnson, Mediterranean Bible College, Lebanon; John Howard, Gardner College, Canada; James Edwards, Anderson University, Indiana; and Sherman Critser, representing theological education by extension (TEE).

41. The others were evangelism, discipleship, church planting, health care and community development, and relief work.

42. Donald D. Johnson, "Looking Back to Go Forward," *Missions*, January–February 2004, 8.

43. Donald D. Johnson, "One World, One Mission," *Missions*, July–August 2003, 7.

44. Ephesians 4:4–6 (NRSV)

45. Johnson, "One World, One Mission," 7.

46. Patrick Nachtigall, "The Gravitational Shift," *Missions*, January–February 2004, 7.

47. Ibid.

48. Kelley and Rhonda Philips, 2005 RC Report for Europe–Middle East, 6.

49. Patrick Nachtigall, "Thoughts on 'One World, One Mission,'" Global Snapshots, *Missions*, March–April 2007, 13.

50. Spread the Word updates appeared in *Missions*, March–April 2003 (p. 12) and May–June 2003 (p. 12).

51. Scott Schomburg, "TAPP Necklaces: Much More Than a Business," *Missions*, March–April 2008, 3.

52. Ibid., 5.

53. Johnny Snyder, "Mercedes and Salem Church of God, Partners in Mission," *Missions*, January–February 2000, 8.

54. Manuel Killisch, "South America on My Heart," in *Yet I Will Rejoice*, ed. Cheryl Johnson Barton, 60–62 (Anderson, IN: Warner Press, 2008).

55. Larry M. Sellers, "Growing the Church in Number, in Spirit, and in Financial Strength," *Missions*, March–April 2006, 4.

56. Luke 12:48 (NASB)

57. Bob Edwards, "Ministry in Times of Violence," *Missions*, January–February 2008, 1.

58. Don Deena Johnson, "Reflections Under Siege," an e-mail column sent to prayer supporters, July 20, 2006.

59. Larry Sellers, "Peace in Unlikely Places," in *Like a Blazing Fire*, ed. Cheryl Johnson Barton, 14–15 (Anderson, IN: Warner Press, 2005).

60. A missionary to Eurasia, "Mission Possible!" *Missions*, September–October 2006, 8.

61. Ibid., 9.

62. Tim and Colleen Stevenson, "A Message of Hope," *Missions*, January–February 2008, 11.

63. Carmen Miller, "My Shield and Protector," *Missions*, September–October 2006, 2.

64. Edwards, "Ministry in Times of Violence."

65. During its December 2003–July 2005 reign of terror, avian flu viruses had infected nine countries in Asia. Church of God missionaries were serving in three of these.

66. Neelie Kerich and Glenna Phippen, "Perspectives from Uganda," *Missions*, March–April 2005, 6.

67. Candy Power, Living Link Comparison Giving Report to Regional Coordinators, January 2008.

68. Candy Power, Living Link Report to Regional Coordinators, June 12, 2006, 2.

69. Project Link Ministry Plan 2005–2008, 10.

70. Ibid., 2.

71. Ed Hyatt, Project Link Report to the Regional Coordinators' Meeting, June 12–16, 2006, 5.

72. Ibid., 2.

73. Robert Edwards, Global Missions Coordinator Report to the RC/Staff Planning Meetings, June 13–17, 2005, 3.

74. This Web-based e-mail service for missionaries was discontinued in 2008.

75. "Missions Consultation: Fifty-five Hearts Contemplate Missions Strategies for China," BODYnews, *ONEvoice!*, April–May 2006, 29.

76. Bob Edwards, Global Missions Coordinator Report on the State of the Mission, February 2006, 5.

77. Doris Dale, "Future Ministry in the Asia/Pacific Region," *Missions*, March–April 2001, 13.

78. John M. Johnson, Regional Coordinator's Report, Asia–Pacific, February 13–18, 2006, 2.

79. In the past, some relationships with national churches had been severed by the Missionary Board or Global Missions. But this time, it was the national church in the United States that had cut ties.

80. Robert Edwards; John Walters, CBH coordinator; and Jim Lyon, CBH speaker and pastor of Madison Park Church of God, Anderson.

81. David and Barbara Miller, Annual Report to the Regional Coordinators and Staff Planning Meeting, February 2006, 2.

82. From a conversation between David Miller and Cheryl Johnson Barton, April 20, 2008.

82. Kelley and Rhonda Philips, Regional Coordinators' Report to Global Missions, Winter 2006. Statistics quoted from "Muslims in Europe: Integration Policies in Selected Countries," CRS Report for Congress, November 18, 2005, http://www.fas.org/sgp/crs/row/RL33166.pdf.

84. Kelley and Rhonda Philips, Regional Coordinator Report to Global Missions, Winter 2006, 2–3.

85. From a conversation between Kelley Philips and Cheryl Johnson Barton, April 29, 2008.

86. Kelley and Rhonda Philips, Regional Coordinators' Report to Global Missions, Summer 2006, 2.

87. Quoted from the April 11, 2007 edition of "Bob's Desk," a weekly e-mail letter from Robert Edwards, Global Missions coordinator, written as he was preparing to travel to Jamaica to join in the church's centennial celebration.

Appendix 2: Missiological Principles
That Form the Foundation of our Cross-Cultural Ministry

1. Written January 3, 2001, by the regional coordinators; last revision, February 26, 2001.

Appendix 4: Church of God National Launch Dates

1. *Passport for a Reformation* lists 1984.

2. *Passport for a Reformation* lists 1992, when contacts were first made in Cote d'Ivoire.

3. *Passport for a Reformation* lists 1917.

4. *Passport for a Reformation* lists 1918.

5. *Passport for a Reformation* lists 1896, the date A. D. Khan began his ministry there.

6. The Church of God in South Korea and in Australia independently launched works in 1994, in February and September respectively. There is no longer any Church of God work on the island.

7. *Passport for a Reformation* lists 1912.

8. *Passport for a Reformation* lists St. Kitts, 1932, and Nevis, 1957.

9. *Passport for a Reformation* lists Trinidad, 1906, and Tobago, 1920.

10. There is no longer any Church of God work in this country.

11. Work begun by the Church of God in Germany.

12. Work begun by the Church of God in Germany.

13. There is no longer any Church of God work in this country.

14. *Passport for a Reformation* lists 1974.

15. There is no longer any Church of God work in this country.

16. Work began in the 1970s, but the work today dates to 2003.

INDEX

This index is largely one of proper names. Note that appendices 4, 5, and 6 have not been included in this index. See appendix 5 for missionary names that do not appear in this index.